Crime a*** _
in the Twentieth Century

The South Wales Experience

Crime and Policing
in the Twentieth Century

The South Wales Experience

DAVID J. V. JONES

UNIVERSITY OF WALES PRESS
CARDIFF
1996

British Library Cataloguing-in-Publication Data.
A catalogue record for this book is available from the British Library.

ISBN 0–7083–1366–3

Cover design by Olwen Fowler, The Beacon Studio
Typeset at the University of Wales Press
Printed in Great Britain by Dinefwr Press, Llandybïe

Contents

List of Illustrations   vi

List of Graphs and Charts   vii

List of Tables   viii

Foreword by Ieuan Gwynedd Jones   xi

Preface by David J. V. Jones   xiii

Chronology of the main organizational changes
in South Wales policing   xvii

Map of the South Wales Constabulary 1989   xix

1   Dealing with Crime and Criminals   1

2   Crime: A General Survey   55

3   Crime and Society   112

4   The Police   187

5   The Police, Crime and People   240

Epilogue   282

Note on Graphs   298

Select Bibliography   302

Index   322

Illustrations

Map of the South Wales Constabulary 1989   xix

Unclaimed property in Cardiff in the early 1970s   9

Extracts from Constable Hodge's notebook, Cardiff, 1922   15

A Welsh Office poster of 1973 notifying the public of a
new traffic regulation   44

Letter from the Chief Constable of the South Wales
Constabulary to the Prime Minister, June 1984   135

A policeman on point duty, regulating traffic in Cardiff
in 1938   179

A Glamorgan policewoman on school crossing patrol
in Barry in the late 1940s   214

Extracts from the Hopkinstown Police Journal of
1911 showing notifications of swine fever as part of
the duties of the police   229

An early panda car; the introduction of unit-beat policing
in 1968   256

*All illustrations are copyright of the South Wales Police Museum and are
reproduced by permission of the Chief Constable.*

Graphs

2.1 Indictable offences recorded by the police in Wales
and South Wales, 1900–1989   64

2.2 People prosecuted for non-indictable offences in
Wales, 1900–1989   64

2.3 Indictable offences recorded by the police in the districts of
Dyfed-Powys, Gwent, North Wales and South Wales, 1900–1989   73

2.4 Crime and the economy, 1948–1980   76

2.5 Crime and unemployment, 1924–1932   78

2.6 Adults and juveniles proceeded against for indictable offences
in Glamorgan, 1935–1968, and proceeded against and
cautioned for indictable offences in South Wales, 1969–1989   98

3.1 Violence: indictable offences (excluding sexual assaults)
recorded by the police in South Wales, 1900–1989   115

3.2 Sexual offences recorded by the police in
South Wales, 1900–1989   125

3.3 Burglaries and break-ins recorded by the police
in South Wales, 1900–1989   139

3.4 Offences of theft and handling stolen goods recorded
by the police in South Wales, 1900–1989   139

3.5 Proceedings for drunkenness in South Wales, 1900–1989   173

4.1 Police numbers in Glamorgan and South Wales, 1900–1989   211

5.1 Detection rates, 1938–1989   270

Charts

Chronology of the main organizational changes in South
Wales policing, 1835–1989   xvii

Cardiff City Police organizational chart, 1935   194

South Wales Constabulary organizational chart, 1989   198

Tables

1.1 Comparison of British Crime Survey figures and notifiable
offences recorded by the police, 1991   8
1.2 Subject of telephone messages at Abercwmboi station,
October 1946   16
1.3 Record of offences and prominent occurrences from
Peterston-super-Ely station, 1964–1966   17
1.4 Emergency telephone messages to Swansea Police
Communications Room in 1950   18
1.5 Telephone messages received at the Porth station, 1988 and 1990 19
1.6 Reporters of crime: Cardiff Central 1963 (100 cases),
Bishopston 1967–8 (77 cases) and Tonyrefail 1973 (100 cases)   21
1.7 Persons cautioned in South Wales in 1989 for indictable
and summary offences   35
1.8 Effects of probation, Cardiff magistrates' courts 1919–1923   50
2.1 Welsh population (age and sex, percentage distribution) and
crime, 1901–1989   61
2.2 Indictable offences 1913–1919 in Glamorgan, Cardiff and
Swansea   65
2.3 Recorded indictable crime in South Wales,1939–1945   67
2.4 Indictable offences committed by juveniles, Swansea,
Glamorgan and Cardiff, 1933–1945   68
2.5 Notifiable offences recorded in England and Wales in 1989,
per 100,000 of the population   72
2.6 Seasonality of Merthyr crimes: Merthyr Tydfil Crime
Register, 1924–1932   83
2.7 Seasonality of recorded indictable offences, South Wales,
1981–1989   84
2.8 Swansea divisional returns 1917: persons proceeded against   86
2.9 Areas of Cardiff where juvenile indictable offences were
committed, 1950–1965   87
2.10 Recorded indictable offences per 1,000 of the population:
thirteen police beats in Swansea, 1985   89
2.11 Crime rate per 100,000 of the population, using the average
number of crimes committed in Glamorgan police
subdivisions, 1945–1947   92

2.12 Selected high- and low-risk police sections in 1986   93

2.13 Comparison of numbers of males and females apprehended
and summonsed, Swansea 1912 and Cardiff 1913   96

2.14 Persons charged with indictable offences, Merthyr Tydfil, 1924   97

2.15 Ages of Cardiff defendants, 1989   98

2.16 Samples of the rate of juvenile indictable crime: Glamorgan
1947–1949 and Cardiff 1963   99

2.17 Inmates of Cardiff and Swansea gaols, 1903: birthplace,
occupations and literacy   102

2.18 Average cost of property crime in 1989   107

3.1 Reported indictable offences against the person, and
persons proceeded against for non-indictable assaults,
1900–1989   116

3.2 Recorded indictable crimes, Merthyr Tydfil, 1924–1946   118

3.3 Persons officially cautioned, proceeded against at magistrates'
courts and tried at crown courts in South Wales in 1989   119

3.4 Homicides in South Wales, 1901–1990   122

3.5 Area differences in the rate of recorded crime per 100,000
of the population, 1978   141

3.6 Seven types of theft in South Wales, 1969 and 1989   149

3.7 Types of property stolen in Merthyr in 1944 and 1952   149

3.8 Places of property crime, Cardiff 1934 and Merthyr 1944   154

3.9 Ages of persons cautioned and proceeded against for
property crimes in South Wales, 1989   160

3.10 Prominent victimless crimes in South Wales, a selection,
1900–1975: persons proceeded against at magistrates' courts   164

3.11 Age of persons proceeded against for simple drunkenness,
and for being drunk and disorderly, South Wales, 1989   175

4.1 Academic qualifications of police recruits, 1955–1959   209

4.2 Reasons for resignations from the Glamorgan force, 1946–1948   212

4.3 Geographical and occupational origins of recruits: three
samples of the Glamorgan force (percentages of total)   216

4.4 Deployment of Cardiff force in 1920 (1912 in brackets)   233

4.5 Deployment of South Wales force (percentages) at
31 December 1985   234

4.6 Timing of individual duties in Port Talbot section and
Clifton Street, Cardiff, 1986   236

4.7 Tasks of a divisional detective constable, Skewen, in a typical
month, 1965–1966   237

5.1 Police numbers, recorded crime and incidents in 1986   263

5.2 Notifiable offences recorded by the police: clear-up rate
by offence group for 1989 (percentages)   272

5.3 Rates of detection in 1986: best and worst performances   273

Foreword

by

IEUAN GWYNEDD JONES

It was in the spring of 1990 that Professor David Jones determined to write a history of crime in Wales in the nineteenth and
twentieth centuries. No one was better equipped than he to
accomplish such a demanding project. He had already collected a
huge body of factual material as part of his SSRC project on crime
in Wales from the annual series of Judicial, Criminal and Police
Statistics 1810–1902, and he had worked extensively on the
quarter sessions records for the county of Gwent. At that point in
his research his intention had been to publish a commentary on
the tables and graphs which he had distilled out of that material in
the form of a short monograph of some fifty or a hundred pages.
But, like Topsy, the work grew in stature and weight. It now
included local material collected from every County Record Office
in Wales, and by October 1990 he wrote to say that he had broken
the statistical back of a book on nineteenth-century crime. A year
later, in August 1991, the book was ready for the press, and was
published under the title *Crime in Nineteenth-Century Wales* in April
of the following year.

Meanwhile, and before the book was published, he continued to
work on the second part of the long-term project. But time for
research was at a premium, and he was very gloomy about the
possibilities of completing it. Then came the opening of the South
Wales Police Archives, which is one of the best, and probably the
biggest, collection of police records outside London, thus
presenting a unique opportunity to work on a project which was
complete in itself but which was also complementary to the
history of crime in the twentieth century which still remained his

long-term objective and which he was determined to complete.
The award of a British Academy Senior Research Fellowship in
1992 for the following session enabled him to press ahead without
delay. The completed typescript was due to be handed to the
University of Wales Press in April 1996.

Throughout that sabbatical year he worked unceasingly, and by
early summer he had almost completed what he called a first draft
of the book: he referred to it in conversation as a 'report' rather
than the finished product of his research: and when, in early
autumn, he became aware that he was suffering from cancer, he
arranged for the draft to be sent to the Press in the hope that it
could be published rather than 'be left in a drawer, perhaps for
ever'. Some weeks later, on 30 October 1994, he died.

David Jones was a meticulous craftsman, and his books were as
perfect as he could make them before they were sent out into the
world, but death intervened before he could perfect this most
original of all his books. Yet it is difficult to see how precisely it
could be improved. It conveys something of the excitement of a
pursuit into territory where few scholars had ever been before –
his friend Jane Morgan, whose life was likewise cut tragically
short, was one of those pioneers – and it is full of fresh insights
into the nature of society in the different parts of the region at
different times in their developing histories. The material in it is
entirely new and original. It conveys all the quiet assurance of a
mature scholar who has mastered his subject, a mastery which
remains undiminished by its lack of footnotes. It deals with issues
that always were, as they still are, highly contentious and politically
sensitive, but David Jones brings to them a quality of objectivity
and judiciousness which raises the book above any contemporary
dispute. This is why the conclusions, and the research on which
they are based, are important not only to social historians but also,
perhaps especially, to criminologists and social workers who have
to grapple with problems and issues of seemingly increasing
complexity. So, in the midst of our sorrows, it is a cause for
rejoicing that David Jones in this last book has left such a rich and
useful legacy for this and future generations.

1996

Preface

This book follows another, that on crime in nineteenth-century Wales.* It took a little time to decide whether a sequel was feasible and necessary. There are major problems of sources, which are outlined in the first chapters, and few guidelines along which to work. Although writers such as F. H. McClintock, Nigel Walker, Michael Brogden and Terence Morris have a strong historical perspective in their books, these, and the host of other publications on modern crime in the Select Bibiography, are essentially essays in the social sciences. There is no general historical survey of crime in twentieth-century Britain. In terms of Welsh history little has been done, either on crime or policing, except for Jane Morgan and Barbara Weinberger's volumes, the articles on race and rioting by Neil Evans, Colin Hughes and others, and a small number of important sociological and geographical studies of the contemporary scene.

The need for a general survey is becoming more obvious each year. The present discussions on the problem of crime and the efficiency of the police have been rather circumscribed by the absence of a historical dimension, as well as by political and sociological in-fighting. Since the 1970s the problem of law and order has been an ideological battlefield, and may well become a dominant factor in the next general election. This book sets the current debates in a chronological context, and examines the historical roots of today's fears, myths and prejudices. To that extent, it should be of interest to the general reader.

*D. J. V. Jones, *Crime in Nineteenth-century Wales* (University of Wales Press: Cardiff, 1992).

The other purpose of the book is to provide a basic framework for those students embarking on research in this field of Welsh history. It is essentially a first report, which will give the student a general idea of the modern world of crime and policing, and of the records which can be used to re-create it. If it raises as many questions as answers, it will have served its purpose. Not everything can be covered in such a book. I have, for example, kept the material on disturbances and strikes to a minimum, and have touched only briefly on matters such as crime and gender, and crime and punishment. Unlike the book on nineteenth-century crime, which was a considered reflection on a well-researched subject, this is a pilot study.

One of the surprises of doing this work was the discovery that our knowledge of society in the twentieth century is, in some respects, less good than that of earlier periods, whilst the records themselves are frequently disappointing and inaccessible. Government economies during the century, a contraction in the publication of official papers, problems of storage space, rules of confidentiality and the limited life of computer information have all combined to make life difficult for the historian of twentieth-century crime.

The district covered by this book has been carefully chosen. It will take several years, and a number of researchers, to complete a detailed study of crime in twentieth-century Wales. Even then there will be major gaps in the picture. The destruction of the legal and police records has been extensive. In the North Wales, Dyfed-Powys and Gwent police districts, it will be a major task just to evaluate what has survived and what has been lost. On the other hand, the records of the old county force of Glamorgan have been well preserved. Most of these have been deposited in the Glamorgan Record Office, but some remain in an archive at the South Wales Police Headquarters in Bridgend. The survival of crime and police records for Cardiff, Swansea, Merthyr Tydfil and Neath has been more patchy. During the First World War the chief constable of Cardiff ordered the mulching of the old occurrence and charge books in the city, an example which has since been copied elsewhere, especially at the time of amalgamation of the police forces in 1969. However, enough material is in existence for us to attempt a general study of crime and policing across South Wales.

'South Wales' for the purpose of this book is the present area policed by the South Wales Constabulary, from Pontarddulais in the west to Cardiff in the east. Before 1969, it covered the districts policed by the forces of Glamorgan, Cardiff, Swansea, Merthyr Tydfil and Neath. It is a good region for the historian of crime. Almost half the Welsh population of nearly three million people live within its boundaries, and it contains a rich tapestry of communities. The South Wales police patrol isolated villages and market streets, old and new industrial centres, seaport and seaside towns, and, of course, the two largest cities in Wales. The district has the geography of a county police force, and some of the problems of a metropolitan police area. The population is overwhelmingly Welsh by birth; at only 2 per cent the ethnic minority is well below the British figure. Less than 10 per cent of the people are Welsh-speaking. Of the almost half a million households in 1994, 72 per cent are owner-occupied, and 15 per cent are occupied by lone pensioners.

In recent years South Wales has achieved a little notoriety, for the level of its recorded crime, the scale and dangers of its car thefts, the riots in the Ely district of Cardiff and the violence against its police officers. The district has one of the worst crime rates in Britain, and one significantly higher than that of the other Welsh police-force districts. There have also been a number of much publicized murder cases here, such as the killing of a Swansea sex-shop manageress in 1985, and of a young prostitute in Cardiff three years later. In the same years, South Wales experienced at first hand the last great miners' strike, which itself recalled memories of the ferocious industrial unrest of earlier generations. This was, after all, the home of the Tonypandy riots of 1910, of the angry demonstrations of the unemployed in the 1930s, and of the redoubtable Captain Lionel Lindsay, Glamorgan's chief constable for the first third of the century, whose reputation and influence remained long after his departure. Of course, there were quieter periods in the history of South Wales, but events in this district have often held press and political attention.

The subject of this book is crime and policing. One cannot understand the former without describing the latter, and vice versa. The nature of both has changed considerably in the last hundred years. In 1900 the modern problems of motoring and drug offences, for example, were hardly mentioned, and the character of policing was similar to that of half a century earlier. Yet within a generation the roots of our modern anxieties over crime and policing were already visible. Even so, it was the years of the late 1950s and 1960s that witnessed the major change in criminal activity, and transformed policing and public attitudes. Since the amalgamation of the police forces in 1969 the story has been equally dramatic, and people are now convinced that times have never been worse. The book will chronicle all these developments, and show the role of the public as victims, reporters and criminals. The volume ends in 1989, when Robert Lawrence took charge of the South Wales police force, and set in motion changes in territorial divisions, policy and financial management, which make comparisons with previous years very difficult.

I am grateful to many people for providing me with information about, and access to, the various records on crime and policing. I received assistance from Margaret Ayres of the Research and Statistical Unit of the Home Office, the staff of the Glamorgan Record Office and the Local History Department of the Central Library in Cardiff, and Mary Bodger of the Computer Centre at the University College of Swansea. I am particularly indebted to the British Academy, which gave me a one-year Senior Research Fellowship to study Glamorgan police records, and to Robert Lawrence, chief constable of the South Wales Constabulary, for allowing me to examine material at Bridgend and Cardiff. Above all, I must thank Jeremy Glenn, curator of the Police Museum at the South Wales Police Headquarters, Bridgend. Jeremy generously placed his unrivalled knowledge of police records and personnel at my disposal, and commented on the first draft of this publication. Like several other people who kindly looked at parts of the manuscript, he is not responsible for the views and errors which it contains.

David J. V. Jones
1994

Chronology of the main organizational changes in policing in South Wales 1835–1989

1835	Municipal Corporations Act.	Police forces established by Boroughs of Swansea, Cardiff andNeath
1841	Glamorgan County Constabulary established. Four districts . .	Merthyr Newbridge Ogmore Swansea (excluding the forces of Neath Borough, and Borough of Swansea police)
1880 reorganization	Merthyr District remains unchanged, but now called	Merthyr Division
	Newbridge District lost some of its detachments and became	Pontypridd Division
	Ogmore District lost some detachments, acquired four detachments from the Swansea District and became	Bridgend Division
	Swansea District – Apart from losing some detachments to Bridgend, Swansea District (whose headquarters had long been situated at Neath), remained substantially unaltered and was now known as	Neath Division (excluding the forces of Swansea and Neath Boroughs)
	Out of the detachments removed from the former Newbridge and Ogmore Districts was created	Canton Division
1908	Creation of Merthyr Borough Police necessitated some reorganization of the County Constabulary resulting in the formation of	Treharris Division

Date	Description	Divisional codes
1911 reorganization and redistribution county	Resulted in 8 Divisions plus Headquarters. This provided the framework of police administration in the county until 1947. The practice of assigning a letter to each division had been introduced 1894 to replace the earlier system of numbering each district, and this practice was maintained in the 1911 and subsequent reorganizations.	A – Aberdare B – Pontypridd C – Bridgend D – Neath E – Barry Dock F – Treharris G – Ton Pentre H – Gowerton I – Headquarters
1947	Abolition of Neath Borough Police – some reorganization of County Force again necessary. Parts of the Neath and Bridgend Divisions created a new division . . . . Port Talbot Division while Neath Borough was added to the Neath Division Divisional Organization 1947–1969	Port Talbot Division A – Aberdare B – Pontypridd C – Bridgend D – Port Talbot E – Barry Dock F – Treharris (Ystrad Mynach 1927–) G – Ton Pentre H – Gowerton N – Neath K – Headquarters (moved to Bridgend from Canton 1947)
1 June 1969	Formation of the South Wales Constabulary. Borough police forces of Cardiff, Merthyr and Swansea were amalgamated with the Glamorgan Police Force to form the new force.	South Wales Constabulary A – Merthyr B – Pontypridd C – Cardiff Central D – Cardiff Greater E – Barry F – Bridgend G – Port Talbot H – Swansea J – Swansea (1973–1986) K – Headquarters T – Traffic W – Communications (from 1973)

SOUTH WALES CONSTABULARY

1989

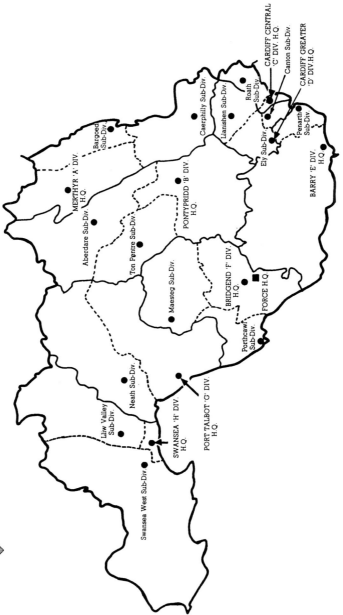

MERKTHYR 'A' DIV. H.Q.

Bargoed Sub-Div.

Aberdare Sub-Div.

Ton Pentre Sub-Div.

Caerphilly Sub-Div.

Llanishen Sub-Div.

Roath Sub-Div.

CARDIFF CENTRAL 'C' DIV. H.Q.

Canton Sub-Div.

CARDIFF GREATER 'D' DIV. H.Q.

Ely Sub-Div.

Penarth Sub-Div.

BARRY 'E' DIV. H.Q.

PONTYPRIDD 'B' DIV. H.Q.

Maesteg Sub-Div.

BRIDGEND 'F' DIV. H.Q.

FORCE H.Q.

Porthcawl Sub-Div.

Neath Sub-Div.

Lliw Valley Sub-Div.

PORT TALBOT 'G' DIV. H.Q.

SWANSEA 'H' DIV. H.Q.

Swansea West Sub-Div.

1

Dealing with Crime and Criminals

The definition of crime has been the subject of much sociological discussion. There are offences created by legislation, and forms of behaviour of which society disapproves. These are not always the same, as we shall see throughout the book. In general, it seems that there is remarkable agreement across communities and classes about what constitutes a serious crime. Few dispute that activities such as murder, wounding, sexual assaults and burglary fall into that category. Other misdemeanours are regarded by the public as 'borderline' or 'technical offences'. Examples of these are stealing at work, shoplifting, some cases of vandalism and disorderly conduct, certain kinds of sexual behaviour, experiments with soft drugs and drunkenness. This chapter will consider the differences in the perception, reporting and recording of illegal behaviour, and will follow the stages by which an action becomes a crime, and a criminal finds himself or herself in court. Without such an analysis, our understanding of the meaning of the crime, detection and prosecution rates is inevitably flawed.

Anxiety and the fear of crime

Concern over crime has always been somewhat different from the experience of delinquency. In the nineteenth century there were a number of collective 'moral panics' over crime, which were linked to fears of political and social upheaval. During the twentieth century there have also been times when society has been unduly sensitive to the dangers of robberies, violence, prostitution, heavy drinking and drug-taking. The first few years of the century were one such period. Against a background of religious revivalism, social reformers in 1901–4 denounced the iniquities of 'Black Glamorgan', and called large assemblies at Cardiff and Swansea to demand action over the 'appalling' level of crime and immorality.

During the First and Second World Wars there were similar gatherings, as we shall see in the next chapter, but this time the fear was of juvenile delinquency, a problem which has returned to haunt each generation since. In the mid-1950s an increasingly prosperous society felt threatened by the Teddy Boys, and ten years later the activities of Mods and Rockers seemed to epitomize the worst aspects of youth culture. During these years national opinion polls consistently indicated that people regarded 'juvenile crime' as the most serious social problem. Women and elderly people across South Wales claimed that they were afraid to leave their homes for fear of young burglars, muggers and drunken hooligans. Nor were they satisfied when chief constables produced statistics to counter these, and other, public perceptions of the dangers to life and property.

Over the last twenty years various surveys and polls have revealed that anxiety over crime has grown. According to the British Crime Surveys of 1982, 1984, 1988 and 1992, about a third of the population now feels 'fairly' or 'very' vulnerable, and the figures are higher for the elderly, females and inhabitants of the inner-city estates. This is a more complex phenomenon than at first appears, for it is related to a wider dissatisfaction with social change, the quality of life, the depth of neighbourhood feeling, and people's control over their environment. Thus, when asked, people living in parts of working-class Cardiff, Swansea and Barry in the 1970s and 1980s complained about many things besides crime, including teenagers, dogs and noise, bad housing, the lack of facilities and poor public transport.

According to the Penlan (Swansea) project report of 1987, burglary, vandalism and 'autocrime' (thefts of and from motor vehicles) were rightly high on the list of people's anxieties, but there was also evidence on this, and the other large council estates of South Wales, of tensions caused by the harsh conditions of life, the state of the labour market, the vulnerability of single women and the problems of old age. The police telephone message books reinforce the point; many of the calls from these places are not about serious crimes but about the annoying habits of children and teenagers, conflicts within families and between neighbours, and harassment, actual and feared. We are told that the closer and more settled the community, the lower the level of such complaints, at least to the authorities.

It has often been said that the fear of crime is as much a problem as crime itself. This was confirmed by M. Albrow's survey of the elderly in Cardiff in 1982, and by press reports of the same year. Peter Underwood, in his newspaper articles on the large Ely and Llanrumney estates in 1982, claimed that the fear manifested itself either in aggression, hostility to strangers and anger with authority, or turned inwards into withdrawal. The most frail inhabitants of these large estates retreated behind locked doors. A report in January 1994 confirmed that such behaviour has become increasingly common, especially after dark, amongst the elderly and the women of South Wales. They stay at home, or avoid certain localities.

In the opinion of some academics and police officers, these levels of anxiety are, in part, the creations of politicians and the media who exaggerate the shifts in the crime rate, select certain offences like mugging for undue attention, and pour invective on the young. The press throughout the twentieth century has retained its fascination with crime, and with the quarterly and annual public utterances of chief constables. Eighty-eight large volumes of local press cuttings, compiled by the Cardiff police between 1889 and 1966, give some idea of the scale of this interest. Murders, robberies, rape and spectacular burglaries were the stuff of life for the *Western Mail*, the *South Wales Daily News*, and the *South Wales Echo* in these years, and so also were stories of drunken prostitutes and sailors, stone-throwing children and violent families.

It is impossible to estimate the effect of such coverage, though David Smith and Jeremy Gray, from their sample of over 2,000 Londoners in the early 1980s, believe that it is significant. Others take the opposite view. Not unnaturally, the press in the 1980s, as in the 1960s, vigorously denied that biased and inaccurate reporting contributed to 'the problem of crime'. When Chief Constable John Woodcock stated in 1982 that the elderly were over-influenced by the violent crimes seen on television, journalist Peter Underwood insisted that the perceptions of the elderly inhabitants of Ely and Llanrumney were not formed by the media.

Many of these old people were either themselves the victims of crime or knew people who were. In the same year an Age Concern poll at Barry found that a third of the respondents had lost property or had been attacked in the previous twelve months.

The main defence of the media has always been that it reflects rather than generates public concern over delinqency. In the early years of the century this concern found expression chiefly in the letters, speeches and meetings of the respectable and the organized. Thus the people from Pontypridd, Abercynon and Mumbles (Swansea) who complained to the police committees at this time about thefts and weekend violence were, typically, tradesmen, professional people, and groups of ratepayers and councillors. Whilst welcoming such interest, the chief constable of Swansea hoped, in the middle of the century, for 'the development of this public-spirited action on the part of a wider circle of citizens . . .' After the Second World War, and more particularly after the late 1950s, the police files and letters to newspapers contained complaints from a broader social spectrum. Council-house tenants, describing repeated break-ins, were amongst the angry band. Although the chief constable of Swansea insisted in 1964 that the public were still 'not crime conscious' because they failed to secure their property, there was growing pressure, from all quarters, for official action to 'stop the rising crime rate'.

In academic circles the evidence of anxiety about crime during this period was largely ignored by those criminologists who followed the agenda set by the new radicals. For a generation, sociological research focused on power in society, definitions of crime, and artificial aspects of the changing crime rate. The emphasis was placed on the offenders rather than the victims, and on the labelling of criminals. Special attention was paid to victimless offences, such as those connected with drugs, prostitution and homosexuality. The point was made that statistical swings in the reports of these crimes were largely the result of political and policing decisions, made at the highest level.

Meanwhile, outside academia, people in the late 1960s and 1970s were expressing growing alarm at the incidence of violence, break-ins, autocrime, hooliganism and vandalism. In South Wales George Thomas MP, promoted to the Home and Welsh Offices, called on his local constituents to turn this concern into a campaign for higher 'moral standards'. Law and order, which had hardly been mentioned in election debates in the 1950s, suddenly became a political issue, and one which, by the mid-1970s, was near the top of the agenda.

Rather slowly, sociologists grasped the depth, context and significance of the popular and political mood. Comparative work in America, detailed national and local crime surveys at home, and the new political climate of the early Thatcher years all helped to change perspectives. Sociological studies were begun on delinquency in London, Nottingham, Liverpool, Glasgow and Sheffield which revealed that the level of public anxiety over crime was not created by governments or the media, but was formed mainly by the actual day-to-day experiences of people. This was true of virtually everyone, whatever their differences in sex, age, race, class and abode.

In South Wales there have been few comparable in-depth sociological surveys, but the researches of Lesley Noaks in Gwent, and other smaller projects, have confirmed that the inhabitants of Swansea, Cardiff, the Rhondda and Newport have equally sound instincts about the extent of crime across their localities. It is a depressing picture. On average the police recorded one crime for every eleven people in South Wales in 1989, and for some of these, break-ins, autocrime and vandalism were not a new experience. In the fairly peaceful community of Bettws, Newport, just outside our region, Lesley Noaks found in 1988 that four out of ten of her respondents admitted that, at some time in the past, they had been victims of crime, the highest rate being amongst females aged 14–60 years. In the most affected parts of Cardiff and Swansea in the same decade the *annual* rates of victimization were as bad as this.

Inevitably, these people became, in a way that they had not been twenty-five years before, 'crime-conscious'. The 'problem of crime' is now the subject of endless public and committee meetings, and crime prevention has reached remarkable proportions. In spite, or perhaps because, of this, local polls in the 1980s and 1990s suggest that the fear behind the action shows little sign of diminishing. At the latest count, between a third and a half of the population in the most populated urban districts of South Wales feel 'unsafe', and a similar proportion express dissatisfaction with local policing.

Although people have, generally, an accurate perception of the crime problem, and of police effectiveness in dealing with it, there has been some exaggeration perhaps of the dangers of serious violence, and certainly of mugging. South Wales does not have the statistics of a particularly violent society. Yet the apprehension of the elderly and of single women, and their retreatist and security-conscious behaviour, are not completely unreasonable. As we shall see in chapter 3, many of the crimes against property and people in the second half of this century were directed at the most open and vulnerable of targets, and the reporting of violence has always been notoriously poor. Intensive studies of female victims in other parts of Britain have revealed much higher levels of threatened and actual assaults than one would have expected from official accounts.

The dark figure

Not all the crime that is experienced by the population, even by an angry one, is reported. The existence of a large dark figure of unrecorded crime has been known to each generation of police officers. In the countryside of South Wales the loss of vegetables, fowls, rabbits and fish was almost certainly much greater than the historical records suggest. According to the St Nicholas station journals, there were some years in the inter-war period when almost no crime was reported, and yet searching for 'lost' animals, fowls, game, corn and tools was a common police activity in that district, and the checking of farms, outbuildings, fences and ricks a daily routine. Similar disparities were apparent in the industrial districts. During the worst economic years of the 1920s and 1930s, when the official crime figures were comparatively low, policemen in the Rhondda informed magistrates of the situation so well described by Lewis Jones in his novels, of great quantities of coal taken and hundreds of sheep and rabbits killed by unemployed miners.

In the same period there were claims that the victims of break-ins did not bother about minor losses, and later, in the 1950s and 1960s, there was growing awareness of the extent of unreported thefts in shops, committed both by customers and employees. 'It is certain', wrote the chief constable of Glamorgan in February 1956, 'that only a small proportion of them is detected or brought to the attention of the Police.' Studies in America and Britain have recently established the truth of this; many of the crimes perpetrated in shops, at work and in school are never discovered, and less than a quarter of known offenders in these cases are prosecuted.

An attempt has been made since the 1960s to estimate the dark figure of unrecorded offences, using self-report and victim surveys. These, together with information from the British Transport Police, insurance companies, government agencies and societies like the NSPCC, provide a valuable commentary on the official crime rate. They indicate that delinquency is extremely common, especially amongst males at a young age, and that no more than about a fifth of committed indictable offences are recorded by the police. Certain crimes, like car thefts and burglary are well reported, whereas sexual crimes, petty theft and criminal damage are not. Of course, crimes such as drug abuse, domestic violence and others committed behind closed doors are impossible to quantify accurately even when using self-report and victim surveys. As we shall see in chapter 3, court cases of domestic violence and the sexual abuse of children were often the final product of years of hidden assaults.

The point is particularly pertinent to Wales, as the small number of interviews conducted here for the British Crime Survey indicates a significant under-reporting of violent offences. In 1983, for instance, the rate of victimization (personal offences) revealed by the Crime Survey was in Wales 29.4 per cent above the British rate, and 6.9 per cent below that for household offences. The former is a considerable surprise, as it is at odds with the police figures. Table 1.1, which is based on information from the latest British Crime Survey, shows how these England and Wales rates compare with the police figures and how, over the past ten years, the increase in the BCS statistics has been more moderate.

The reasons for not reporting crime are legion. The most common excuse given in modern surveys is that people regard many activities as trivial or 'borderline' crimes. This was probably even more true of the past; minor assaults and petty vandalism, for instance, were ignored more by previous generations than they are today. The class, sex and age of the victims of lesser offences are also important determinants. A study of Cardiff in 1973 disclosed that most people, especially if they were male and elderly, believed that children who committed assault and burglary should be reported, but not those who drank under age, travelled without a

Table 1·1: Comparison of British Crime Survey figures and notifiable offences recorded by the police, 1991

Offences	1991 figures in 000s		% reported	% recorded of no. reported	% recorded of all BCS crimes	% change 1981–1991	
	Police	BCS				Police	BCS
Violence	198	809	48	51	24	93	21
Acquisitive crime	2264	6174	60	62	37	95	96
Vandalism	410	2730	27	56	15	105	1
Total	2872	9713	50	60	30	96	49

ticket, and stole at school. The higher the social class, the less the willingness to report the second group of misdemeanours, especially if they were carried out by their own children.

The reaction of victims to property crimes during this century has also been influenced by the effectiveness of police action, and by whether the stolen property was insured or not. The detection rate was, as we shall see in chapter 5, rather lower than is often assumed, not least in relation to thefts of bicycles and articles from vehicles. Many people felt that reporting these offences, and others such as vandalism, was a waste of time. In Cardiff, which had a poor recovery rate, the chief constable was astonished in the inter-war years by the large pile of unclaimed goods, including bicycles, in the police stores, and wondered how working-class families could be so indifferent to their losses. In recent years people have become even better informed about the very low detection rate for such property crimes, but report them for insurance purposes and as their contribution to raising crime awareness in their neighbourhood.

Some victims of crime were reluctant to call the police, because of the embarrassment which accompanied the reporting of offences like harassment, indecent exposure, abuse and assault, or because they did not wish to implicate family, friends and

Unclaimed property in Cardiff in the early 1970s.

neighbours. Police message books provide examples of furious
relatives who ignored the sensitivities of these victims and rang the
authorities. A few violent sons were, in this way, brought to justice,
and thieving neighbours finally trapped. Many, however, remained
undiscovered. The occurrence books for rural districts contain
very few references to family and neighbour troubles. One
suspects that in this, and other areas of village life, country folk
preferred, as one constable remarked in 1920, 'to keep it amongst
themselves'.

Employers, too, were wary of revealing too much about crime at
the workplace. Many of the thieving workmen at the Great
Western collieries in the Rhondda in the inter-war years, and
employees at some of the chain-stores in more recent times, were
cautioned and dealt with internally. William James, manager of the
Great Western and Tymawr collieries, thanked Constable Welsby
for bringing the stealing of coal and vandalism to his attention, but
said that he preferred not to prosecute. Other employers were not
so generous. As one Glamorgan police report stated in 1959,
officers were very dependent, for details of business, factory and

shop crimes, on the zeal and openness of each new manager. J. P. Martin, in his study of Reading, published three years later, found that only a quarter of them were prepared to call in the police when employee pilfering was discovered. Fraud and embezzlement by employees were sometimes kept secret because of embarrassment and other consequences of prosecution. Finally, employers were ignorant of a number of offences committed on their premises, and only became aware of them when confessions were made by people taken into custody for other crimes.

In some areas of South Wales there was a reluctance to call the police, whatever the crimes. 'Many years ago', said the Swansea chief constable during the Second World War, 'it might have been thought alien to British principles to give any helpful information to the Police.' In mining communities like Gilfach Goch during the early years of the century it was said that the police received little information about delinquency, and even less assistance in dealing with it. This was not strictly true. A glance at the station journals of Hopkinstown in Pontypridd shows that people did report a number of assaults, larcenies and other crimes. Although most of these were tradesmen, professional people and publicans, the complainants included colliers and their wives.

The following entry in the journal is one such case:

> At 11 p.m. [16 January 1912] P.C. [Jones] was called to Thorp's house by his wife. P.C. saw Thorp standing on his doorstep with a kettle of hot water in his hand which he threw against the railings. He was shouting at the top of his voice. 'Let the Bloody fucking Police come. I will kick his fucking balls out'. Several females who gathered around could hear the language he used.

John Thorp was forced, with difficulty, back into his house. Ten days later the collier received a summons, and, on 31 January 1912, a fine of 15s. 0d. at the local police court.

Officers in this mining town were subjected to insults and violence, and in major industrial disputes the relationship between them and the public broke down. Constables were then busy protecting the property of coal-owners and blacklegs, and information on crime from colliers and their families dried up. The same scenario was evident during the miners' strike of 1984–5; in the most affected divisions 'hostility', 'distrust' and 'apathy' characterized the relations between miners and the police, and may well, admitted the chief constable, have distorted the statistics of known indictable crime.

The scale of reporting also reflected the public's attitude towards the legislation that had been breached. In Hopkinstown and Cardiff early in the century the police had little popular support in their campaigns against Sunday trading, street betting and soliciting, and had to wear plain clothes to obtain evidence. Similarly, public reporting of offences against the Road Traffic Acts of the 1930s and 1950s was initially disappointing, though later, as the police message books illustrate, people were more willing to inform on those speeding, driving dangerously and, especially, parking badly. In the case of drug offences, publicity over the horrors of heroin and cocaine, and the setting up of free telephone lines, has not changed the public's reluctance to give unsolicited information on the taking of soft drugs.

From time to time, newspaper correspondents wrote about 'the fear of reporting' crimes in South Wales. The term was commonly used in the inter-war years, and again in the 1980s, when it was associated with mining communities and the inner-city poor. In such places, there were people who dreaded physical reprisals, or who disliked the thought of a police visit once they had reported an offence. Information from Penrhys and Ely residents in the 1980s sometimes came with the rider: 'does not wish to get involved'. In 1982 the chief constable of South Wales asked the working-class residents of Ely and Llanrumney to put such anxieties aside and to be more open with the authorities about the incidents and agents of delinquency. The victims of assaults in these areas were sometimes unwilling to concede that a crime had been committed, even when the police had the suspects in the cells. It would be wrong, however, to postulate a simple class model for reporting; research in England and Scotland suggests that people on council estates with high offender rates are often very ready to seek police help over crimes and 'quality-of-life' incidents.

Changes in the reporting of crime

It is important, but extremely difficult, to make judgements about changes in the reporting of crime, and in the way it was recorded by the police. Many of the historical studies of criminal statistics are based on Quetelet's assumption that the ratio of unreported to reported offences remains fairly constant. Yet there can be little doubt that reporting has improved since the nineteenth century. In 1901 Chief Constable Lionel Lindsay

> found that people were getting more particular every year. Small things which were allowed to pass unnoticed years ago were continually being brought to the notice of the police. The formation of the county, urban and parish councils has created in every part of the district bodies whose members brought any case of disorder or breach of the law to the notice of the police.

'Mind', added the Glamorgan chief constable, 'I'm not complaining about this. I think it is a very excellent thing, but it has a tendency to add to the number of convictions.'

During the following decades complaints of public 'apathy' over the reporting of crimes were still fairly common, but, by the 1950s, the overall impression was that 'greater co-operation has become evident'. The chief constables of Swansea and Merthyr Tydfil noted the improvement in 1961, and were grateful to the public for 'communicating suspicious circumstances immediately and in some instances by active participation in the detection and arrest of criminals'. During the 1970s and 1980s it has been possible, using comprehensive surveys, to monitor the change. In some categories, such as burglaries, we know that a higher proportion of offences are now reported to the police than was the case twenty years ago. As we can see from the last table, about half of all the offences discovered in the British Crime Survey of 1992 were so reported, as against about a third ten years previously.

Four main reasons have been given for better reporting: changes in public attitudes, the contribution of the press, the presence of the police, and better communications. It seems that people became less tolerant of some crimes, especially those of a violent nature, after the Second World War, and more willing to approach the police. The chief constable of Swansea believed that the latter trend was the result of closer contacts formed between the public and the police during the war years. He was also impressed by the role of the press in encouraging people to take a responsible attitude to crime reporting. From the early 1960s onwards all the South Wales forces transmitted information on crime to newspaper editors, and to radio and television stations. How much effect this had is open to question, but it seems to have had most impact in new and loosely knit communities where people felt fairly isolated and anonymous.

Twenty years later the common experience of crime, especially break-ins of domestic residences, had reduced people's tolerance of delinquency still further. In addition, the public were bombarded with crime-prevention material, and subjected to pressure from consultative panels, neighbourhood watch schemes and other groups to take crime seriously and to report anything which might be of value to the police. The results have been mixed but generally encouraging. We are assured that the new forms of community policing have produced, in certain areas of South Wales, 'a more accurate picture of the total crime committed', than hitherto.

The physical presence of the police was, for many years, of vital importance in the reporting of offences. In Glamorgan during the first quarter of the century, country people often had to travel long distances to find assistance. Farmers and labourers sometimes waited for days before giving news of a crime or incident to a passing constable. There were industrial communities, too, like Trelewis (population 1,200) in 1900, which had no resident constables. Even in Swansea, inhabitants said in 1929 that they had difficulty in tracking down a police officer. Across South Wales at the beginning of our period there was only one officer for just over a thousand inhabitants; seventy years later there were proportionately twice as many.

The character of these policemen and women was also important. Some were kept at a distance from the people whom they were meant to serve. The Cardiff force appointed large numbers of English recruits at the turn of the century, and in Glamorgan, Chief Constable Lindsay liked to move his men around the county. Public support for these officers was welcomed, but too much casual contact was not encouraged. The chief constable of Merthyr, writing in 1964, adopted a different approach. As many as 83 per cent of his force were natives of the town, and knew the people on their patrols extremely well. This was, he felt, essential for good reporting. The removal, in the late 1950s and 1960s, of some of these policemen for unit-beat work, and the closure of local stations, a feature of the 1970s and 1980s, were both criticized for reducing the dialogue between police and public. The introduction of community constables, of whom 365 were appointed by 1981, was intended to rectify the situation.

Better communications were another response to the difficulties encountered by the victims and witnesses of crime. Swansea was at the forefront of these developments, being the first Welsh force to introduce a police box system (in 1927). This was followed soon afterwards by the creation of an information room, having direct contact with the boxes, patrol cars and the emergency 999 service. By 1950 over a thousand emergency 999 calls were received annually from the public at Swansea headquarters, about a half of which were crime-related, whilst in Cardiff four years later there were 2,306 emergency calls (leading to seventy-five arrests) and 5,572 'normal telephone calls' for police attention (producing sixty-nine arrests).

The chief constables of both places enthused over these figures, which rose sharply during the 1960s. They were convinced that better reporting was one explanation for the soaring crime rate at that time, though they emphasized the need to contact the police 'without delay', a recurring request, especially in connection with vandalism. In recent decades the widespread acquisition of private cars and telephones has given the public instant access to the police, and the setting up, in the 1980s, of Crime Stoppers, and Help and Hot lines for those with information about rape, child abuse and drug offences, has assisted in the process.

The nature of reporting

The scale of public reporting, both of crimes and of occurrences such as domestic disputes, sudden deaths, fires, straying animals and missing persons, has reached exceptional heights in the last twenty-five years. In 1974 the South Wales police recorded 58,636 indictable crimes, 5,088 road accidents and 265,141 occurrences, most of which were brought to their attention. In July 1983 the Incident Resource and System Computer (IRIS) was switched on, and it was estimated that in the next three and a half years public demand for police assistance increased by 44 per cent. It has continued to grow. In 1990 the number of crimes and incidents recorded was twice that of 1974.

The police have always been, in practice if not in theory, a reactive force. It has been estimated that in South Wales, as in many other forces, about 84 per cent of operational police work at the present time takes the form of responding to calls from the public. These

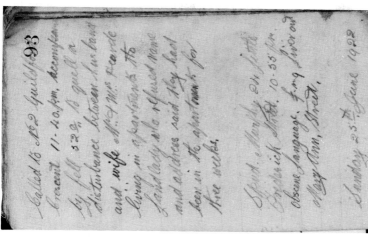

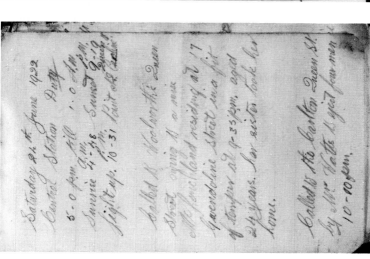

Extracts from Constable Hodge's notebook, Cardiff, 1922.

have been, and are, more varied in character than one might expect. In 1908 the Swansea police received 'numerous complaints' of children annoying people and damaging property, whilst in Neath three years later there were 'constant complaints' about the noise of those who sold papers in the streets. For Cardiff we are fortunate to have the notebooks of Constable Hodge for the years 1921–37; these reveal that people asked him to deal with chimney fires, barking dogs, noise with refuse bins, youthful vandalism, obscene language and behaviour, lost property, missing husbands, accidents, the sale of poor-quality goods and the non-payment of wages.

After the Second World War a greater proportion of complaints and requests to the police arrived via the telephone. At Abercwmboi, just north of industrial Mountain Ash, about 200 messages were received per month in the mid-1940s, and many of these were concerned with the loss of ration books, clothing coupons, bags, cash and keys. The breakdown of calls at the Abercwmboi station over a typical month is given in table 1.2.

Table 1·2: Subject of telephone messages at Abercwmboi station, October 1946

	%
Lost and found property	45·0
Animals strayed, lost and found	9·1
Missing people	7·2
Road accidents	1·9
Stolen vehicles	12·4
Break-ins	7·2
Stealing	6·2
Homicide and assaults	1·4
Sheep-worrying	0·5
Wanted persons	5·3
Persons absconding and escaping	3·8

There is not a comparable set of telephone message books for a rural district, but a station journal of Peterston-super-Ely gives details for the mid-1960s in table 1.3. It is a complete record of the known crimes, and a selection of the more prominent occurrences dealt with. The great majority of both the indictable crimes and the occurrences were reported by the public.

Table 1·3: Record of offences and prominent occurrences from Peterston-super-Ely station, 1964–1966

	No. of incidents
Indictable crimes reported	89
Non-indictable crime reports	56
Road accidents	51
Vehicles badly parked and abandoned	10
Noisy machines and motor cycles	6
Property lost and found	57
Stray animals	33
Missing persons	4
Vandalism	9
Fires	6
Worrying dogs	10
Noisy, and ill, dogs and cats	5
Malicious telephone calls	16
Domestic disputes	8
Sudden deaths	6
Children behaving badly and suspiciously	5
Peeping Tom and prowler	3

To illustrate life at the Peterston-super-Ely station, between 1 January and 16 February 1965 no crime was reported, but the local constable was busy in those weeks responding to news of accidents, flooding, deaths, abandoned vehicles, dangerous dogs, stray animals and vandalism.

The urban police received many more calls, which were rather different in content. Table 1.4 gives a breakdown of the 1,092 '999' calls taken by the Swansea police in 1950.

To bring it up to date, table 1.4 can be compared with the analysis in table 1.5 of a sample of 816 telephone messages received at the Porth police station in 1988 and 1990. Porth, which lies just west of Pontypridd, is one of the oldest of the Rhondda towns, and is surrounded by small industrial communities and poor housing estates.

A few lines are needed by way of explanation. The primary target of the many instances of criminal damage in table 1.5 were cars, followed by houses and shops. Vehicles were also a prominent target

Table 1·4: Emergency telephone messages to Swansea Police Communications Room in 1950

Disturbances (domestic and drunks, etc.)	144
Accidents (street, domestic and industrial)	425
Breaking into premises	57
Other crime	56
Suspected or suspicious persons	54
Missing, lost or insane persons	49
Indecency	8
Common assault	29
Suicides, and attempts at	14
Stolen motor vehicles	21
Private ambulance calls	46
Miscellaneous (complaints of children causing annoyance; petty damage; animal straying, etc.)	153
False calls (malicious)	23
Calls from outside borough	6
Sudden deaths	7
Total	1092

for the arsonist. The thefts in the table were chiefly from shops, houses and building sites, and the break-ins were of houses, shops, schools and offices, with accompanying theft in only about half of the cases. Obtaining goods by false deception was either taking petrol without paying or misusing credit cards. The complaints of badly parked vehicles included protests about the obstruction of entrances, cars mounted on the pavement, and others left in a restricted street overnight. The division between assaults and 'domestics' in the table was sometimes blurred, whilst the complaints against children and youths were mostly over playing games in the street, throwing stones, shooting air-rifles, riding motor-bikes, driving cars, making excessive noise and glue-sniffing.

Contrary to claims in some comparative studies, the reports in the message books for Porth and other stations contain a considerable share of genuine crimes. People were more willing to report thefts from cars, and especially criminal damage, for instance, than is sometimes suggested, though the discovery of the offence was usually too late to make detection feasible. The other main areas of concern, revealed by the message books, were

Table 1·5: Telephone messages received at the Porth station, 1988 and 1990

Criminal damage	89
Fires	18
Rubbish left or dumped	3
Theft from vehicles	79
Theft	72
Burglary, break-ins	95
Vehicles stolen and taken away	56
Abandoned vehicles	31
Obtaining goods by deception	9
Forgery	1
Insecure premises, fences and machines	9
Reports of alarms, and from key-holders	26
Lost and found property	27
Gas leaks	2
Vehicles broken down, obstructing, bad parking	29
Accidents, mainly road	34
Reckless, dangerous and disqualified driving	7
Motor-vehicle and driving licence offences	9
Assaults	30
Domestics, family and neighbour	27
Harassment and threats	18
Child abuse	1
Indecent exposure	2
Sudden deaths	7
Hoax and obscene calls	7
Noisy neighbours and builders	3
People causing a disturbance	6
Persons acting suspiciously	9
Licensing and conduct of hotels, clubs and public houses	7
Drunks, and drunken and disorderly conduct	4
Complaints about children and youths	35
Missing children and older persons	12
Complaints about dogs	11
Injured animals	2
Straying animals	1
Reports of the old, and the mentally and physically ill	8
Notices of weddings, funerals, fêtes, etc.	14
Notices of road, building, and shop developments	9
Reports relating to school and zebra crossings	3
Licensing and holding of firearms	4
Total	816

parking, children and neighbours. It is quite clear that many people, especially of middle and old age, wished to have a controlled and peaceful environment, and anything which disrupted that was liable to be the subject of a telephone call. In a few instances individuals sustained levels of surveillance which, in other circumstances, would have been frowned upon.

As in the nineteenth century, the police station remains the first call for many people, not least those of the working class, when faced with a problem. People in Porth contacted the police when locked out of their homes and cars, when families quarrelled, when children ran away, when a neighbour cut the hedge too much, and when a pet seemed to be maltreated. Many of the offences reported were minor, or even civil, in character, and those responsible for the calls sometimes remained anonymous or, more commonly, did not want the police to contact them. On occasions, often in conflicts within families and between neighbours, one has the impression that the police were being used: to warn someone, to end a confrontation and to provide evidence for a future suit. Only a minority of telephone calls received by the police officers at Porth were about crimes which were likely to lead to a conviction.

The police notebooks and the occurrence and crime complaint books and forms provide further evidence on how the police learnt about offences. Constable Welsby and his colleagues at Hopkinstown in 1911–12 relied on the public, and especially the victims, to bring indictable crimes to their attention. For their part, the Hopkinstown officers were busy catching beggars, drunks, gamblers, Sunday traders and people breaking the highway regulations. In Cardiff during the inter-war years, Constable Hodge also depended on the public to give him news of serious crimes, though he did, on his rounds, come upon stabbings, muggings and break-ins in progress. A few miles to the west, at Peterston-super-Ely, and to the south at Sully, Constables Brooks and Man in the 1930s and 1940s had a more passive role. They discovered very few indictable crimes indeed in these semi-rural localities, but were able, when victims contacted them, to devote much more time than Hodge to the subsequent enquiries.

The evidence which has survived since the 1960s indicates that four-fifths or more of the indictable crimes recorded by the police were brought to their attention by outsiders. The sample in table

1.6 of 277 cases from the crime complaint books underlines the minor role played by the officers themselves:

Table 1·6: Reporters of crime: Cardiff Central 1963 (100 cases), Bishopston 1967–8 (77 cases) and Tonyrefail 1973 (100 cases) (percentages)

Victims	63·2
Friends of victim, family and witnesses	9·0
Company, government and council staff,	
health and social workers	8·3
Store detectives and security officers	2·5
Police	12·6
Company police	1·8
Other people	2·5

As many as two-thirds of those who reported crimes were actually the injured party; a few of them also provided the names of likely offenders, and a larger number badgered the police if there was a delay in following up their information. The smallest proportion of victim-complainants was in the Cardiff Central division (57 per cent). Store detectives, security officers and British Rail policemen reported some 12 per cent of the Cardiff cases, and often boosted the detection rate by adding the names of the persons suspected or held.

Four-fifths of the non-police reporters in the Cardiff–Bishopston–Tonyrefail sample were male, and 52.8 per cent were 31 years or over. Only 1 in 10 were 20 years of age or younger, confirming that people become better crime reporters once they are adults. The spread of occupations amongst the complainants was very wide, with housewives, factory workers, drivers, miners, students and salesmen as prominent as contractors, managers and shop and garage proprietors, except amongst those over fifty years old where the middle class came into its own.

All the extant complaint books in South Wales show that police discovered only a small minority of reported indictable crimes, chiefly ones which were committed outside the home. At Nantgarw in the early 1960s, and at Bishopston ten years later, where the police reported as many as two out of ten cases, it was the result of information received 'during enquiries', usually from people already under arrest, or the reward for speedily attending to alarms and patrolling in known trouble spots. Officers on patrol saw people acting suspiciously and noted unreported vandalism, thefts from vehicles and break-ins. On the Treforest industrial estate and in the vicinity of the Nantgarw coke ovens, the police caught a number of burglars and coal thieves red-handed.

The police were also responsible for reporting public order crimes, some cases of corruption and fraud, most drug offences, and a large number of lesser and technical offences. There is no doubt, for instance, that the police were an important influence on the changing statistics of drunken and disorderly conduct, just as they were the main reporters of offences committed on the highway. In the final pages of Constable Welsby's station journal and Constable Hodge's notebooks are listed the results of local court hearings, and in most of the cases of drunk and disorderly conduct, breaches of the licensing regulations, indecent language, throwing stones on the highway, obstruction by fighting, gaming with cards, having an unlicensed dog, begging alms, driving without lights, and Sunday trading, police officers were the prosecutor and only witness. The response of these people, when being reported by the police, varied from 'You are not going to make a case out of it, are you?' (for having a vehicle with no lights – Cardiff 1922) to 'Go on, you fucking shithouse' (riotous prostitute – Cardiff 1924).

Since the 1920s erring motorists have had good reason to blame the police for their cautions and fines. Individual members of the public complained of bad driving, obstructive parking and other misdemeanours, but the men on point duty, and later the traffic police, picked out most of the motoring offences. The St Nicholas (Mobile) Journal of the 1930s, the earliest of its type, shows how easy it was for the motorized police to find offenders, and to pass them on to Cowbridge police court. 'I did not think that I was doing that speed', 'I did not know that it was out', 'Yes, it's dangerous' and 'Very well' were typical comments in the journal that betray drivers' feelings when they realized, too late, that they had been going over 30 m.p.h. and were without one or more lights. At Nantgarw in the early 1960s the police were the chief witnesses in at least nine out of ten motoring offences. Nantgarw, north of Cardiff, was (and remains) a major traffic centre, and the great majority of the 200–300 non-indictable offences reported annually at that time were those of drivers caught by the police patrolling the Cardiff Road.

The police have also been the main reporters of drug offences. 'There appears to have existed for some time a misapprehension that occurrences of drug offences were confined to the Port areas centred on Cardiff and Swansea as these were the only areas in which such offences came to light,' ran one report of 1973. The explanation was simple; only at Cardiff and Swansea were there small squads of officers 'trained for and employed solely on Drugs work'. The introduction of divisional drug liaison officers at this time doubled the offences recorded elsewhere in South Wales. 'If more police resources were available', said one officer in 1987, 'many more offences would be detected.' The pattern, therefore, is quite distinct: the most serious indictable crimes are discovered by the public, and only in the field of victimless or technical offences can the police be accused of manipulating the criminal figures.

Recording crime

In the next stages of dealing with crime, namely recording, classifying and prosecuting, the police have a greater input, and one which might have distorted the true picture of crime in Britain. It has been suggested by a number of sociologists that as many as a half of the reports of indictable offences which the police receive are not listed as recorded crimes in the returns made to the Home Office. This shortfall was, almost certainly, less in South Wales than in some other districts, though it is difficult to trace the precise number of 'lost crimes'.

One has the strong impression that great discretion was exercised early in the century when 'criming' a report, which helps to explain the low crime and high detection rates. In rural districts weeks, and sometimes months, passed before an indictable crime was formally entered in the lists of reported crime, and yet during that time journals and notebooks reveal that constables were busy making enquiries about lost items that might have been stolen, and checking details of newly born babies found dead in the area. Officers in places like St Nicholas, Peterston-super-Ely and Sully were wary of completing official crime reports until they were certain about them, and, possibly, about likely offenders.

The chief constable of Cardiff implied in his report for 1921 that a recent change had taken place in the way his force compiled their statistics. 'The practice in recording undetected crime varies,' he wrote.

> In some Police Forces a crime is not recorded as such unless there be sufficient evidence available or ascertained to sustain a charge. In other Forces a more elastic rule is applied, it being sufficient that there are circumstances present which make it reasonable to believe that a crime has been committed. The latter policy has now been adopted as presenting a more accurate reflex of the crime in the City.

From at least 1940, if not before, a similar policy was in operation in the Glamorgan force. This was based upon the recommendations of an internal police review in 1938, possibly with Home Office direction. The county police were instructed that 'upon a complaint of crime being received, that is in all cases reported as crime, and all occurrences which reasonably suggest that a crime has been committed', a form must be 'properly completed'. Crime complaint books and crime report forms were distributed to all stations, and entries were checked by senior officers.

Although the evidence is, by its nature, unsatisfactory, it seems probable that since the Second World War there has been less room for discretion in police recording, and this was undoubtedly the case after the mid-1960s, with new Home Office guidelines for the force on such matters and the computerization of information. Over three-quarters of the reported indictable offences documented in the occurrence books for Nantgarw and Tongwynlais in the 1960s were officially returned as crimes, and the same is true of the entries in the latest message and 'work outstanding' books rescued from the dampness of Porth police station. It is possible that some messages were just never written down, but officers knew the dangers of such tactics; as one South Wales police manual states, it is best 'to report too much'.

The reasons for the clerical discrepancy between reporting and recording are countless. Some reports are defined, with the approval of a senior officer, as 'no crimes'; 'stolen' items are mislaid, break-ins and assaults prove to be imaginary, and some complaints are malicious. In Merthyr Tydfil, one in ten reported offences were described as 'no crimes' in 1909, and one in six in

Swansea in 1938 were discounted as 'unreliable'. Messages in telephone books, like those for Abercwmboi in the 1940s, and crime complaint forms, often have large 'CANCELLED' lines across them, usually made by the investigating officer. There was, as the chief constable of Neath noted in his annual statement for 1944, 'a racket' during these years in false claims of stolen and lost coupons. 'Nowadays', he declared, 'most of the suspect crimes relate to clothing or clothing coupon thefts.'

In Cardiff, 2,009 of 13,785 reports in 1966 were said to have been 'unfounded'. An extreme example, and one not included in the indictable crime returns, is that of the reports of bombs and incendiary devices. During the 1960s and 1970s there were hundreds of malicious reports of bombs placed at schools in South Wales, and, in the 1980s, at offices, shops, clubs and other premises. Otherwise, the reporting of offences is reasonably reliable. In 1983, when the Home Office published the statistics of reported and recorded indictable offences, South Wales had the lowest rate of crimes 'written-off'.

The gap between reported and recorded crimes owes something to vagaries of both the public and the police. By no means all of the reports that arrive by telephone, letter and word of mouth can be followed up. Victims occasionally tell the police of offences like assault and indecent and threatening behaviour, and then act as if they had never happened. Many complainants disappear when officers try to contact them, or withdraw their stories when statements and visits to stations are requested. Station journals and diaries of detectives contain innumerable instances where initial reports of assaults and domestic incidents are followed by notes such as: 'Mr and Mrs X refused to make any written statement of complaint', and 'Mrs X just wants Mr Y to be kept away from her home'.

This is one explanation of why only a small proportion of the reports of indecency between males, rape and unlawful sexual intercourse were, and are, ultimately 'crimed'. Records from the 1960s and 1980s reveal that when complaints of sexual assaults on young girls were made to the police, sometimes they went no further than 'initial enquiries' because the stories were malicious and false, or the victims unwilling to co-operate. In 1981 forty-five accusations of rape on women were eventually withdrawn. A police surgeon in South Wales said in 1982 that he saw three or five times more rape complainants than appeared in the official figures. Many of these females refused to go through the court ordeal, or agreed to lesser charges of indecent or common assault.

The view of some social scientists, that the police deliberately ignore or hide information about crime, does less than justice to the problems faced by the police. However, there is evidence that over the years policemen developed a sixth sense about what information was likely to lead to a conviction, and used their discretion over whether to follow it up and file a crime report. This was, as we have seen, true of the early twentieth century, and the evidence of the Cardiff divisional discipline books shows that constables were also reprimanded during the inter-war years for not recording offences like assaults which were reported to them. In the occurrence and message books of South Wales for the 1960s and 1970s, the marginal notes of 'matter not yet crimed' and 'for information at present' suggest that officers were making further enquiries, but not all these cases were transferred to the 'work outstanding' books and the outcome of some of them cannot now be traced.

The police response to reports of offences against property and the person has always been affected by the character of the complainant, the seriousness of the crime, the chances of detection, and the priorities and culture of the officers. Reports of burglary, for example, were unlikely to remain hidden, though they were sometimes changed at the recording stage to thefts from a dwelling house. In the crime complaint books of the 1960s and 1970s, the discovery of a bicycle or vehicle soon after it had been taken often meant the cancellation of a complaint or crime report form. They were then discounted, or included as crimes 'written off' in the annual returns. Reports of small thefts, especially if they were of doubtful character, were occasionally filed away as 'lost property', and, as vandalism was so common and difficult to detect, there was even more temptation to remove these cases from the indictable classification by valuing them at less than £20.

The most controversial aspect of recording has been the police response to reports of violent and sexual offences. Studies by sociologists have revealed that the majority of the original reports are either 'no-crimed' or reduced to a lesser crime. This has good historical precedents. For generations the police in South Wales who visited complainants in assault cases were influenced by the signs of injuries; when these were minimal, a warning was usually given to both parties, or the victim urged to see a doctor and contemplate a court action. Where such violence occurred within families and between neighbours, several options presented themselves. Some offenders were charged with wounding and assault, or arrested under the Domestic Violence and Matrimonial Proceedings Act of 1976, but in many instances the reported offence was reduced to a 'domestic incident'. Police officers tended to regard 'domestics' as an intrusion on 'proper policing', and the withdrawal of about half the complaints only underlined their feelings of exasperation. Information on these incidents was sometimes given to other services, and the victims advised to consider civil proceedings. No crime complaint forms were then completed.

Responding to reports

In the 1960s and 1970s the standing orders for Glamorgan and the new South Wales Police clarified the clerical procedures to be adopted once a convincing report of an indictable offence had been received. The officer concerned had to make out a crime complaint form, and forward copies of it to various departments in the force, notably the CID. Unless detection was synonymous with reporting, the crime was then allocated to an investigating officer and given a number. Supplementary information was added to the complaint and crime report forms as the days passed, and eventually the completed report was given to a senior colleague to be filed away as another undetected offence, or for consideration as a possible prosecution.

The nature of the crime, as well as the changes in the character of the police forces, governed the operational response. At first almost all offences were dealt with by local constables, but during the inter-war years detectives began to take over more serious investigations, even in Sully and Peterston-super-Ely, whilst in murder cases it was common to seek assistance from the Metropolitan police force. In Cardiff, where London's help was kept to a minimum, things were more advanced, and from the first decades their detective officers used the latest fingerprint and photographic equipment. After the Second World War, scene-of-crime people in all the forces were called out to all major offences, and eventually, following the lead of Cardiff's 'flying squad', serious-crime squads were established to co-ordinate proceedings.

The standing orders of the 1960s, subsequently revised, laid down the precise nature of the operational response to reports of ordinary indictable offences. A uniformed officer was expected to visit the victim as soon as possible, make enquiries in the vicinity, and take statements. He or she had to give details of the crime to the local patrolmen and collator, to CID and headquarters, and to the record or intelligence office. Information was then circulated around the force by the collators via daily bulletins and crime information sheets, and, when the networks were established, it was entered on district and national computers. If the crime fell into a particular category, such as child abuse or social-security fraud, contacts were made quickly with other government agencies, and, when the offence seemed to threaten national security, Special Branch was called in.

The speed and effectiveness of the reaction was largely determined by the character of the crime, the nature of the community, and the pressures on the police at the time. In the first third of the century there were many communities where a slow physical response to reported offences was compensated for by the intensity and length of the police investigation. Thus, enquiries into fowl-stealing in Peterston-super-Ely, where there was only a handful of indictable cases a year, sometimes lasted for as long as six months and during that time everybody in the village was questioned.

One case, exceptional in its speed, illustrates the commitment of the Peterston constable. At 12.00 noon on Monday, 17 January 1937, Constable Clark received a report of the theft of a railway signal lamp in a nearby village. He made enquiries until 2.30 p.m., when he interviewed Alfred Wills, a local farm labourer. Wills claimed that he had just borrowed the lamp, and fully intended returning it. After cautioning him, he accompanied Wills to his house and found the lamp. Most of the rest of the day, until 12.00 midnight, was taken up with collecting statements and making the report, and in the afternoon of the following day Clark handed over the crime file to a superior.

In urban communities, where the police had to deal with many more reports and incidents, they gave complainants the benefits of swift attendance at the scene of the crime, and specialized detecting officers. By 1932 Cardiff had a mobile police of thirteen men and six vehicles. Although their main task was to regulate traffic and driving habits, 'a secondary and equally important service is rendered by the patrol to the citizens by their use to deal with urgent calls for police assistance and the expeditious investigation of crime'. 'There have been instances', continued Cardiff's chief constable, 'where the rapid mobility of the police has been the means of arresting offenders, who might have, under former conditions, eluded the Police . . .' By the 1950s the improvement in communications and transport meant that the police in the largest towns of South Wales were able to promise a five-minute response to any emergency call.

Unfortunately, the actual investigation of the crime, and the detection rate, never matched the speed of the police drivers, as we shall see in chapter 5. The CID, which took charge of more and more cases as the years passed, were often blamed for this. The diary of a Skewen detective, which covers the years 1965–8, reveals just how busy and difficult life in the CID had become. On some occasions the detective constable, after a full day's work, attended three scenes of crime (typically house break-ins) between tea and going off duty at midnight. 'Made search of area & made enquiries with neighbours. Made examination (finger-prints and photographs) of the scene – negative' was the usual entry in his diary at such times. Observations, enquiries, interviews and searches followed, and, a few weeks later, an inconclusive crime report, or, less commonly, the recommendation to proceed with a case and a file of supporting evidence.

In recent years the pressure of work, and the number of calls, has meant that certain complainants have to wait more than twenty-four hours for a police visit. The computer terminals continue to issue reminders of the required 'follow-up', and busy officers have to pacify the frustrated caller. In the case of serious offences, speedier action is required, and in 1984 the South Wales force set out three response times: an immediate one for very serious (about one in five) reports of crimes and accidents, a delayed response of one hour, and a scheduled response of more than that to reports of lesser crimes.

Beleaguered Welsh police chiefs have since warned that economies are likely to worsen the times of these graded responses, and make detection more difficult. The overworked CID is obliged to screen out the cases which have little promise, and concentrate on those with a high profile and a good chance of being solved. Although it seems very far removed from the days of early rural constables like Clark of Peterston-super-Ely, one suspects that the old officers would have understood the priorities of the new.

Summonses and arrests

The criminals referred to in this book were apprehended at the time of their offence, or brought to court via a summons or warrant. In Hopkinstown Constable Welsby served summonses on a wide range of people, from those charged with using indecent language to those accused of driving a cart without lights. Amongst those arrested in his district during 1911–12 were serious offenders like Albert Showell who stole 46 lb of lead, Arthur Farrell of no fixed abode (begging alms) who could not be trusted to obey a summons, and Thomas Lewis of Trehafod and other disorderly drunks who ignored Welsby's advice to depart his presence. As the discipline books of these years show, a few individuals were arrested without explanation and without reasonable suspicion.

Typically, at this time, at least a tenth or more of the arrest warrants could not be executed because the accused had vanished or because he or she successfully resisted arrest. 'It has been the invariable custom to resist an arrest by the police . . .' ran one report from 'rough' industrial communities above Abercynon in December 1911. Police officers were advised in the standing orders to seek assistance when going for an arrest, and to use only 'sufficient force' to obtain it, but this was not easy in difficult country. The same report of December 1911 claimed that at Ynysyboeth and Matthewstown in the Cynon Valley it took three policemen to convey prisoners to the cells.

Nevertheless, once in police custody the business of searching, identifying, photographing, fingerprinting and interviewing began. The 'habitual offender' was questioned to see what else he or she would confess to, or inform about. Lesser-known characters were pressed to admit to their offence, and over half of these eventually pleaded guilty. At this point the 'working rules' of the police sometimes clashed with the 'legal rules' described in these paragraphs. Bargains were arrived at, threats were used, and in Cardiff at the beginning of the century prisoners were occasionally beaten up in police cells. The accused had few rights once in custody, though access to solicitor and friends was one of them.

As the years passed, the treatment of people in police custody became more strictly controlled by general and standing orders, but, as we shall see, these were breached in the observance. In the case of female prisoners who were searched and questioned, the presence of police matrons (later policewomen) was an early requirement. Similarly, the experience of those aged under seventeen in custody was improved by the Children and Young Persons Acts of 1933 and 1969. Children had to be examined in the presence of parents or guardians; and social services, probation and education authorities had to be informed of their arrest. Only in exceptional circumstances could these youngsters be placed in police cells, prisons and remand homes. In addition, their cases, unless they were as serious as homicide, had to be heard in the juvenile or magistrates' court within a matter of days.

Adults were given less favourable treatment. Once a charge had been confirmed, prosecution at the magistrates' court usually followed within a week, or the case was held over until the next meeting of the assize and quarter sessions (crown court). In the mean time, some of the accused sought bail from the court, or, for lesser offences, from senior policemen. One of the major conditions of court bail was that the applicant should appear regularly at the police station. If he or she failed to do that, and did not surrender into custody prior to the trial, further police action was necessary. Court bail became easier to obtain in the post-war years, and worried policemen in South Wales cited instances of fortunate applicants adding to their criminal record before the court appearance.

The same grievance was heard again in the 1980s and 1990s, when the efficacy of the new Bail Act was the subject of police and public protests and some dispute at the Home Office. One problem, which it is hoped soon to rectify, has been the lack of secure remand accommodation for juveniles in South Wales. As a result, hundreds each year have been bailed and placed in the care of the local authority, only to abscond and recommit offences before the original case comes to court. One of the persistent complaints of the police in Cardiff, Port Talbot and Swansea in the last few years has been the extra work-load which this has entailed.

Alternatives to prosecution

The number of people prosecuted for indictable crimes was very much smaller than the number of reported offences. This was not due simply to a low detection rate. The decision to prosecute was a sifting process, and at each stage police discretion was very important. Informal police action was widespread at the beginning of this century, and remains so today for 'trivial' offences committed by the young. Drunks in 1900 were frequently sent home with a verbal caution rather than taken to the station, women caught fighting were often just 'warned of their conduct', and children were cuffed with and without the approval of their parents. There was much sense in this. When the police were pressed in 1903 by the Cardiff Temperance Association to execute the new Licensing Act strictly, by taking all drunks to the station, opponents declared that it would mean locking up 'many more of the working class with which they (the police) had good relations', and be a waste of time, space and money.

In most cases of domestic violence at the turn of the century a police officer simply lectured the accused man, wife or son about their future behaviour. Policemen even organized alternatives to legal prosecutions, such as formal apologies and reparation. Sheep-worrying and fowl-killing dogs were put down in the presence of officers, and out-of-court compensation offered to Gower farmers, Cardiff householders and other victims of petty thieving and vandalism. Such a policy had its risks. The chief constable of Neath was accused in 1907 of extortion, when he received 15s. 0d. from a grateful tradesman, after the police had warned the children responsible for damaging his shop signs, and arranged for their parents to pay for replacements.

The chief constable claimed that he was only following the precedent of Hull, where efforts were being made to keep as many children as possible out of court. Formal and informal cautioning of children by the police, as well as by the courts, became especially popular at the time of the First World War. It was said that 'magistrates do not like to convict children of tender age', notably if they were first offenders. In Cardiff, where 467 youngsters under sixteen years of age were prosecuted in 1914, 259 police letters were sent, as a warning, to the parents of others. As in Swansea, these children were cautioned for minor offences like breaking street-trading regulations, playing games in the street, stone-throwing and riding bicycles without lights.

In Merthyr Tydfil and Glamorgan, where there was support for Liverpool's method of dealing with 'young people on the fringes of delinquency', the police began a systematic policy in the 1950s of visiting the homes of 'suitable children' under fifteen years of age, usually first offenders, who admitted minor crimes or who were 'in (moral) danger'. They were given a formal caution by a senior officer, and placed under police supervision. In Cardiff a similar, though less organized, scheme of cautioning juveniles who admitted to indictable offences was introduced early in 1958, and within ten years 917 of them had benefited from it. Of these, 313 subsequently appeared in court for another offence.

In 1964, when the government was concerned about the numbers of people before the courts and in gaols, the cautioning policy was strengthened in Glamorgan by the appointment of policemen as juvenile liaison officers in each subdivision. By the time of amalgamation five years later, 1,937 boys and 299 girls, chiefly thieves and burglars, had passed through their hands, and only 5 per cent of them had, it was claimed, committed a further offence whilst under supervision. The scheme was reinforced by the provisions of the Children and Young Persons Act of 1969, and gradually extended to the whole of the South Wales police district during the 1970s.

Adults also benefited from cautions during the century. Amongst them were parents who neglected their children, people who ill-treated animals, elderly and sick individuals of good character, and regular law-breakers like prostitutes, heavy drinkers and motorists. In Cardiff, and later in the South Wales police district, up to a half of the prostitutes charged with an offence were cautioned by the police. 'The law on the subject is weak and the Police are unable to provide Courts with the evidence they require before they will convict prostitutes for importuning,' admitted James Wilson, Cardiff's chief constable, in 1935. Cautions under the Street Offences Act of 1959 were also a warning to the newest recruits to mend their ways, as were the letters sent by Cardiff's police force to publicans who had placed their licences at risk.

Police discretion was especially important in relation to motoring offences, and not without its critics. In 1939 Swansea's watch committee, mindful of Parliament's wishes, requested their motor patrols to be generous with written and verbal cautions, and to give 'appropriate advice' when breaches of traffic regulations occurred. During the next thirty years the police of the town gave an annual average of 850 official cautions to motorists, more than twice the number of cautions for other crimes, as well as thousands of verbal warnings to drivers.

In Cardiff, James Wilson was less keen to give drivers the benefit of the doubt. In 1928 he refuted 'the prevailing idea that motorists are the special prey of the police'. Five years later he sent 753 letters of caution to motorists, and another 356 to persons guilty of other minor offences, but remained sensitive to the claim that he had, by this procedure, 'usurp(ed) the functions of the Courts of Summary Jurisdiction'. In 1938 he denounced the 'experimental courtesy scheme' for motorists, recommended in Parliament. During the war, hundreds of people in Cardiff were cautioned for infringements of the Lighting (Restrictions) Order and for various driving offences, but the city police were still accused of being tougher on the motorist than their counterparts in other South Wales forces. In 1948 it was suggested that they would be better employed raising their poor crime-prevention and detection rates.

'In the past', declared the chief constable of Merthyr in 1962, 'police action in relation to parked vehicles has been moderate because narrow streets and limited off-street parking create difficulties.' 'Many instances of faulty driving or minor breaches of the law are being dealt with courteously without resort to prosecution,' he admitted five years later. Breaking the speed limit was noted, but reported 'only on rare occasions'. Cautions were thus a useful alternative to prosecution, as well as a way of ushering in new traffic legislation and being a reminder to people of the dangers of 'omission rather than commission'. Even so, there were problems when the law was vague, as it was over the lighting of vehicles in built-up areas. According to the chief constable of Merthyr Tydfil, the police officer on the spot 'is not only enforcing the law, he is in effect making it', and those who were selected for prosecution were doubly annoyed. In Cardiff, as the complaint books show, there were similar problems over the police's interpretation of obstructing the highway.

Statistics of cautions for indictable and non-indictable (other than motoring) offences were regularly published after 1954, and the numbers for Wales almost quadrupled between that year and 1989, the fastest rate of growth being in the decade following the Children and Young Persons Act of 1969. In 1983 two schemes were launched in South Wales to speed up the delays in the treatment of juvenile (and elderly) offenders: an instant caution for first-time offenders, and the promise of a caution or court appearance within four weeks for those with a criminal record. Six years later, at the end of our period, 2,200 juveniles and 580 adults were officially cautioned in lieu of proceedings for serious offences, and 692 juveniles and 6,611 adults for other offences, excluding motoring. As table 1.7 shows, South Wales had one of the lowest caution rates for indictable offences in Britain, especially for those aged seventeen years and over:

Table 1·7: Persons cautioned in South Wales in 1989 for indictable and summary offences

Area	Percentage of persons	Males				Females			
		10–14	14–17	17–21	21+	10–14	14–17	17–21	21+

Persons cautioned for indictable offences, excluding motoring, as a percentage of persons found guilty or cautioned

Area	Percentage of persons	10–14	14–17	17–21	21+	10–14	14–17	17–21	21+
South Wales	22	86	63	5	4	98	83	11	16
Eng. and Wales	29	88	64	17	14	95	82	31	31

Persons cautioned for summary offences, excluding motoring, as a percentage of persons found guilty or cautioned

Area	Percentage of persons	10–14	14–17	17–21	21+	10–14	14–17	17–21	21+
South Wales	10	71	51	9	9	100	84	16	4
Eng. and Wales	18	87	65	17	16	93	78	28	8

Typical of the crimes now considered for caution are theft, common assault, intercourse between consenting but under-age people, criminal damage and minor drug offences. Studies have indicated that the important factors in the decision not to prosecute, besides considerations of age and sex, are the wishes of the victim, the seriousness of the offence, the previous record and attitude of the offender, and the sentencing policy of the local courts. Where, for example, juvenile recidivism is common and courts comparatively lenient in their treatment of it, cautions are often low. If the persons being cautioned are adults, questions of class and locality become more significant, and, in all cases, the character and prejudices of the police officers cannot be discounted.

The senior policemen in South Wales who have administered the caution procedure have, since at least 1931, praised its influence on those affected, on police–public relations, and on the court time saved. Yet some people in the inter-war years were concerned that, because of the procedure, too many youngsters were being placed, for trifling offences, in police hands and police files. According to scholars like Professor Cohen, this 'net widening' has been an integral part of the enveloping process of control and surveillance in modern times. Others, in contrast, wondered aloud about the ultimate value of too many cautions, especially for young people, and shared Chief Constable James Wilson's doubts about the political wisdom of dealing with crime outside the court system. Some of this feeling resurfaced in the 1980s, and greater scrutiny, and possible contraction, of cautioning seems likely in the future.

The decision to prosecute

The nature of prosecution has changed markedly during the century, chiefly in the erosion of individual and local control over it. In 1900 prosecutions were still largely the responsibility of the victims of crime, agencies like the RSPCA, government departments and local councils, and the police who had a special interest in street and public-order offences. Thus, at the Pontypridd police court prior to the First World War, industrial and railway companies brought forward a good proportion of the stealing and vandalism cases, wives and single women instigated a number of assault cases, and Police Superintendents Cole and Williams were responsible for most of the victimless prosecutions. At the assizes and quarter sessions it was, until 1912, a similar mixture.

The urban and rural district councils, together with the Poor Law authorities, were also busy in the courts, collecting rates, establishing maintenance payments, and so on. They worked alongside representatives of the Inland Revenue, Customs and Excise, and charitable organizations. In 1901 the Cardiff, Penarth and Barry branch of the NSPCC reported that it had dealt with 361 cases of neglect and cruelty in that year, and prosecuted sixteen people successfully. Large organizations of this kind were able to handle the cost and inconvenience of legal proceedings, but individual victims of crime found the business ever more daunting, and, after the First World War, the police replaced them everywhere as the main prosecutors. In particular, the police were responsible for the prosecutions that were most rapidly increasing in number, those against drivers of motor vehicles. They were accused, on many occasions, of being altogether too involved in the legal process, both as prosecutors and chief witnesses, but until 1986 this situation did not radically change.

In their capacity as prosecutors, the police were subjected to considerable pressure, not only from central government and police committees, but also, in South Wales, from groups like the temperance societies, the Free Church Council, the Lord's Day Observance Society and branches of the Citizens' Union. In addition, associations of ratepayers and shopkeepers, local councils and Poor Law guardians made their presence felt. These bodies complained that senior police officers did not prosecute a sufficient number of people for speeding, for immoral behaviour, and for breaches of licensing, trading and entertainment regulations.

In Cardiff, during the first quarter of the century, chief constables had to face the combined weight of the Vigilance Association, clamouring for the closure of public houses and brothels, the Early Closing Association, denouncing the number of shops open after hours, and the Society of Retail Fruiterers and Grocers, demanding an end to hucksters selling goods in the city centre. The police replied that they lacked the resources to deal with these and other difficult cases. Besides, they were not always certain of the benefits of the above prosecutions, especially as they tended to penalize only the poorest offenders and their clients.

Even so, the reformers on the police committees persisted, and Neath and Merthyr chief constables in the early 1900s were obliged to prosecute people for, amongst other things, swearing in the street, smoking under age and Sunday trading. Lionel Lindsay in Glamorgan, who shared some of his colleagues' doubts about 'moral policing', stopped prosecutions under the last heading in 1908, but was promptly told to rescind the order by the standing joint police committee. He was unhappy, too, in 1903 about the Nonconformist campaign to bring more publicans before the magistrates' courts, though he was quite content to accede to requests for more prosecutions over sheep-worrying nine years later.

A number of individuals were notorious for their determination to use the law to raise standards. James Wilson in Cardiff, chief constable of Cardiff between 1920 and 1946, was an outspoken opponent of 'joy-riding', careless driving and the commercialization of working-class leisure. In 1922 he said of the 'numerous prosecutions' against negligent and reckless motorists, that 'no laxity has been or can be permitted in this respect'. Eleven years later he stirred up a hornets' nest by prosecuting people responsible for whist drives in the capital, and followed this with denunciations of late drinking on public holidays and the tone of Sunday concerts and variety theatre. Degwel Thomas, Baptist minister of Neath and a prominent member of the county police committee, conducted similar campaigns, and others of a semi-moral character. In 1941, for example, he called for more prosecutions against those who obtained public assistance by false pretences, and against those who profited by ignoring the Food and Drugs Act.

In subsequent years the campaigns for legal action were rather different. Prosecution drives, sometimes involving the combined resources of the police, the Ministry of Transport, Customs and Excise and other departments, were launched against offences such as speeding and dealing in drugs. In 1966 it was decided to enforce the new traffic orders in Swansea by prosecuting 'almost every' transgressor, so that no one could harbour doubts about the importance of the orders. Nineteen years later, in Cardiff, a similar, though rather less rigorous, policy was adopted over dropping litter, and seasonal campaigns against badly lit cars and drink-driving became commonplace in the capital.

Unless the offence was a very serious one, the police had considerable discretion over taking on a prosecution, a situation which allowed scope for abuse and resulted in much criticism. The decision was made by a senior police officer such as a subdivisional commander, acting on behalf of the chief constable. He was guided not only by the circumstances of the case, but also by the common difficulties which all prosecutors faced. If the accused were very young, old or infirm, and the offence rather petty or doubtful, it was decided that 'no useful purpose was served' in going on with the case; about a quarter were jettisoned. In many summary motoring offences, 'N.F.A.' letters were sent out almost as a matter of course.

The social background of the accused and the victim was another consideration, as was the age, status and reliability of the witnesses. The attitude of the victim was especially important, as many of them had doubts about seeing a prosecution through. Sometimes, as in cases of assault and rape, decisions were taken to proceed with the original charge, with the expectation that it would be reduced later to a lesser one. Early in the century, in a tenth or more of the cases at magistrates' courts, victims and witnesses did not have to make an appearance, and many assault, malicious damage and even a number of larceny prosecutions collapsed at the last moment. In prosecutions against motorists, which aroused strong feelings, great care was taken to ensure that the police case was watertight before proceeding to court.

The Cardiff police, in a new departure, appointed their own full-time prosecuting solicitor in 1936, whilst in Glamorgan at this time the police relied heavily on the county solicitors for help in dealing with serious offences. Lindsay's force even considered asking the same solicitors to institute a 'great proportion of (ordinary) road traffic prosecutions'. Many actions against breaches of motoring and licensing regulations were considered by the county police, and then aborted. Together with other doubtful cases, they eventually became part of the statistics of undetected offences.

The rest of the crime files, over which there was greater optimism, were either completed by a formal police caution or were the basis for a court prosecution. Those intended for the assizes, and later the crown courts, were carefully drafted, but in less serious cases, a brief report was quickly passed to the prosecutions department. In the latter instance, the accused frequently appeared before the police court within one or two days of the offence, though in the country the business took longer.

People charged with minor crimes in Hopkinstown in 1911–12 were dealt with by the Pontypridd magistrates within a week or two, whilst Peterston-super-Ely defendants, in 1935–8, usually had to wait two or four weeks for a hearing at the Cowbridge and Cardiff police courts. Prosecutions for motoring offences, being common and simple, were generally dealt with quickly. In some cases, including those related to heavy goods vehicles, the accused appeared in court almost immediately. From the mid-1970s onwards, selected courts along the A48 and M4 motorway were waiting to receive them.

In other more serious and difficult cases, the officer in charge usually submitted his report and the papers on the crime within fourteen days of a person being charged. A senior policeman in the subdivision then made a decision about a prosecution, or passed the responsibility on to his superiors. Their conclusions were influenced by the peculiarities of the case, established practice and rules, and the legal advice which they received from their solicitors, clerks of the peace, and possibly from the Director of Public Prosecutions and the Attorney-General.

From the 1960s onwards the consultation procedure was summarized in the revised standing orders which all members of the force in Glamorgan, and later South Wales, received. These stated, for example, that when proceedings were contemplated against juveniles, the police had to communicate with the social services and the education authority, and even more extensive liason was required in child abuse cases. After discussions between all these parties, an agreement was reached to caution the juveniles and the parents, to seek a care order, or to go ahead with criminal proceedings. In the last instance the police were obliged to act with discretion and speed.

In particularly difficult cases, especially if the defendant had his or her own counsel, the police were warned in standing orders to seek the services of the force's chief prosecuting solicitor. He was regularly consulted over licensing, firearms, and public order prosecutions, and where there was an element of doubt and a possible counter-claim against the force. In other cases the police were required to consult the Director of Public Prosecutions, who, in certain circumstances, took charge of proceedings. This happened over homicides and those prosecutions where the police and magistrates were themselves the defendants.

During the 1970s and 1980s police prosecutions became a matter of political debate and media fascination. The obtaining of evidence, and the presentation of material in court, had occasionally brought the police into disrepute in earlier years. There were complaints, which have survived in the Cardiff and Glamorgan police records for the first half of the century, that officers harassed suspects in their homes, failed to obtain search warrants or to tell people of their legal rights, bullied and subjected defendants to excessively long interviews in police custody, made false statements and failed to disclose vital information. Some of these points were remembered in the drafting of the new standing orders of the 1960s. These orders, which incorporated Judges' Rules, were clear about how the accused should be treated – 'not unfair or oppressive' – in police custody, how identification should be confirmed, how confessions should be secured and recorded, and what material should be disclosed to the defendant's solicitors. In practice, police officers sometimes ignored or bent the rules in their efforts to get a conviction, and this became ever more apparent as one police force after another in the 1970s and 1980s was investigated for various wrongdoings.

A number of the most notorious trials of the 1980s were from South Wales. Controversy surrounded the prosecution at Cardiff in 1983 of eight people, including the secretary of the Welsh Socialist Republican Movement, for causing explosions. Most of the defendants were acquitted, and a self-appointed public enquiry, on behalf of the Welsh Campaign for Civil and Political Liberties, found that the Special Branch, MI5 and the South Wales Constabulary had indulged in dubious 'political policing'. There was, too, anger over the convictions of the Darvell brothers (in 1985) for the Swansea sex-shop murder and the Cardiff Three (in 1988) for the killing of a prostitute, and these were overturned on appeal. In these, and other cases, accusations were made of over-long and aggressive interviewing, and of police evidence being withheld or doctored. As a result, several police officers in the force were investigated, and some of these have been charged and acquitted.

The Police and Criminal Evidence Act of 1984, with its insistence on greater legal rights for prisoners and the taping and transcribing of interviews, was one response to public concern in this field. Another followed two years later when the Crown

Prosecution Service took over executive control of virtually all prosecutions, and increasingly dispensed advice about ongoing police investigations. Neither development has received the wholehearted support of civil liberty groups, the judiciary and the police service. Whilst the last complained of wasted time, duplicated secretarial effort and excessive caution in the prosecution of serious cases, others have argued that the reforms of the mid-1980s have only modified the more dubious police practices of the past.

The burden of prosecution

The burden of prosecutions on the police and the courts during the century is easily documented. In the Glamorgan police district in 1900, 1,698 people were proceeded against for indictable offences, 22,869 for non-indictable, and 4,461 applications were made under quasi-criminal proceedings and 2,454 orders made. The highest rate of prosecutions, serious and otherwise, at this time was in the Pontypridd police division, and the lowest in the Neath division. There were police courts in the former division at Pontypridd and Porth (two courts), and in the latter at Neath and Pontardawe. Altogether, the county was served by assizes, quarter sessions and thirteen police courts in 1900, some of which, like those at Merthyr, Barry Dock and Bridgend, were extremely busy. Within eleven years, eight police courts had been added at Abercynon, Tonpentre and other centres of rising population.

Lindsay claimed in 1911 that the chief clerk at headquarters, and the superintendents in the divisions, who were responsible for many of the court cases, had no time for other work. In fact, the burden had already eased somewhat, and was to be comparatively light during the inter-war years, as the number of prosecutions against drunkenness, and against breaches of the education acts, county by-laws and other legislation fell. In 1935, when Glamorgan had twenty-three magistrates' courts, they dealt with over 15,000 people for indictable and non-indictable offences. Thirty years later the number had increased to almost 26,000, most of whom were charged with motoring offences.

The weight of prosecutions was heaviest in the large towns, and because of this special police departments were created at an early date. These were responsible for consulting with prosecuting solicitors, ensuring that warrants and summonses were executed and served, checking that cases were properly prepared, and informing defendants, prosecutors and witnesses that their presence was required at court on a particular day. In Swansea in 1938 the prosecution department, which comprised an inspector, a constable, a civilian clerk and two warrant officers, served the two magistrates' courts which met daily in the town, and assisted with the cases before the quarter sessions and assizes. In that year 2,611 offences were dealt with at the magistrates' courts, and the length of time spent on each case increased, as a greater proportion of defendants were represented by solicitors and barristers, a trend reinforced some years later with the introduction of legal aid.

The police and magistrates in places like Swansea and Cardiff were already, in 1938, having problems with the number of motoring offences, which had grown astonishingly during that decade, and was threatening to bring the courts to a grinding halt. After the war there were similar anxieties about other prosecutions, and justices, police officers and witnesses complained of spending excessively long hours in court. In South Wales, as elsewhere, reformers advocated the setting up of separate traffic and family courts, and the removal of all remaining quasi-criminal-type duties from the police.

During the mid-century matters came to a head. Accommodation was a growing problem, as rooms had to be found for parallel adult and juvenile courts, as well as offices for probationers, and resting rooms for magistrates and witnesses. In Cathays Park, where the Cardiff police shared space with the law courts, the issue was especially urgent. There were complaints, too, about the costs of cases, the remuneration of clerks, and the expenses paid to the police and witnesses. The police said that they were unable to pay, or pay adequately, the expenses of prosecution witnesses, especially in non-indictable cases, and there were calls, then as now, for additional government money to fund more proceedings.

The expansion of court work in the second half of the twentieth century placed unprecedented demands on the police, the judiciary and the penal system. This was recognized by the Magistrates' Courts Act of 1957 which allowed people to plead guilty to lesser charges by letter. This increased the paperwork, but removed at a

From June 1st the three on the right are breaking the law

From June 1st 1973 all riders–
including pillion riders–of
motorcycles, mopeds and scooters
<u>must</u> wear safety helmets.
If you don't you risk a fine of up
to £50. You also risk your life.
When you buy a new
motorcycle helmet make sure it
bears the British Standards
Institution's Kitemark.

GET YOUR HELMET NOW!

A Welsh Office poster of 1973 notifying the public of a new traffic regulation.

stroke a large percentage of summary offences from the courts. Further relief came with the introduction of the fixed penalty system for parking misdemeanours. In 1986 this system was extended to cover certain traffic offences, with the motorist paying a fine within twenty-eight days instead of appearing before the magistrates. Three years later the number of fixed penalties issued in South Wales was as high as 124,038, and so another large body of people was drawn, however marginally, into the criminal justice system.

For their part, the police have generally welcomed the gradual separation, physical and otherwise, of police and legal institutions. The responsibility for maintaining some of the courts, attached to stations, was transferred from the police in the middle of the century. The building of new magistrates' courts, with an expanded civilian staff, meant a reduced role for the police. In 1972, when the new crown courts were established, small police liaison departments were set up at Cardiff, Swansea and Merthyr. Although the creation of the Crown Prosecution Service thirteen years later took over some of their responsibilities, the police remain a vital component in the prosecution process. They present likely prosecution files to the CPS, and are key witnesses in many cases. The number of court cases has, largely because of the fixed penalty system mentioned above, been curtailed in recent years, but the scale of prosecution is still formidable; in 1989 19,597 persons were proceeded against for indictable offences, and 51,342 for non-indictable.

Sentencing criminals

The criminal courts underwent their greatest change in 1972. In that year a new network of crown courts was introduced to replace the old system of higher courts. Until that time there were county assizes and quarter sessions, as well as Cardiff city sessions, and Swansea and Merthyr borough sessions. The assizes met three times a year, alternating at Cardiff, Swansea and Merthyr, whilst the county sessions met, in adjourned fashion, on ten or twelve occasions by the 1960s. Many of the borough cases were actually sent to the county sessions. The crown courts, which replaced both the assizes and quarter sessions, were held at Cardiff (five courts, meeting continuously), Swansea (two courts) and Merthyr (one court).

At the start of the century only one defendant in a hundred appeared before the higher courts and was tried by a jury. At least four in five of this small number were convicted of a crime. The position has not altered greatly in subsequent years. In 1989 the proportion of defendants at the higher courts had increased slightly, but the conviction rate remained similar. Comparisons of these rates between Wales and England do not reveal major differences, though studies have indicated that the character of punishment varies considerably, even between neighbouring localities. In 1989 the crown court at Swansea, unlike its counterpart in Cardiff, was one of the most generous in the land, with a low rate of prison sentences, and a high rate of probation and community service orders.

At the lower courts in South Wales the conviction rate for non-indictable offences fluctuated between periods and divisions, but it was frequently higher than that for indictable crimes. This is not surprising in view of the many charges of drunkenness, non-payment of rates and licences, and motoring offences, where the evidence left little room for doubt. The impression in this century, which does not always reflect the actual treatment of indictable offenders, is that magistrates are more likely to bring a conviction for a serious crime than one's peers. It is a belief which informs the present debate over a defendant's choice of courts and trial by jury.

The punishment of the guilty changed less during the century than might have been expected, though judges and magistrates in 1989 had a wider range of penalties from which to choose. In the first quarter of the century two-thirds of the people found guilty at the assizes and quarter sessions in South Wales were imprisoned. Thereafter, the relative importance of the prison declined, the above proportion being about a half in the immediate post-war years and a third in the 1960s. The decline is more marked if we examine the sentences of persons convicted of indictable offences at both the higher and lower criminal courts. By 1989 only one in thirteen of these people in South Wales was placed in a gaol, though another tenth received the punishment of either youth custody or a suspended sentence. Research elsewhere in Britain indicates that the highest rate of custodial sentences in that year was in city courts, and the unemployed were given more than their fair share of them.

Although the proportion of defendants incarcerated has fallen since the last world war, the rate of prosecutions for indictable crime and the character of the gaol sentences has placed great pressure on prison accommodation. The prison population at Cardiff and Swansea doubled between 1946 and 1962, and then, after a short decline, remained high for much of the 1970s and early 1980s. This situation has been exacerbated by the tendency of judges in recent years to impose long custodial sentences on half of the adults convicted in their courts.

This in itself represents a significant development. During the century the longest periods in gaol have usually been reserved for people found guilty of murder, manslaughter, and the worst cases of sexual assault, robbery, burglary, white-collar crime and counterfeiting. At the time of the First World War, six to twelve months was the typical punishment for those found guilty of such crimes in South Wales. More common, however, until mid-century, were the sentences of one to three months which were delivered for wounding, indecent assault, repeated stealing and forgeries.

The ending of capital punishment in 1965, widespread concern over the level of serious crime, and a succession of Criminal Justice Acts have done much to change this situation. By 1989 the average gaol sentence for those aged twenty-one years and over at the crown courts of South Wales had increased to nineteen months. Partly for this reason, Britain at present has one of the highest prison populations in the western world and a gaol-building programme that dwarfs its predecessor of the middle of the century. The state of prisons, however, still leaves much to be desired, and riots at Cardiff and other overcrowded institutions at the end of our period were a warning of what may lie ahead.

At the opposite extreme, forms of conditional discharge and probation have always been part of the modern criminal system. The Probation Acts of 1907 and 1925 formalized procedures. In 1920 one in five of those convicted at the assizes and quarter sessions in South Wales was freed on recognizance or probation, and, on the eve of the Second World War, probation orders became even more popular for young thieves, rioters, warring neighbours, fraudsters, abortionists and those who had attempted suicide. For twenty-five years afterwards, probation orders were imposed on about a fifth of those found guilty at assizes and quarter sessions, and on a sixth of those convicted of indictable offences at magistrates' courts. The recipients were usually young, first-time offenders convicted of stealing offences and break-ins, whilst in more recent times probation has also become fairly popular for criminal damage and certain sexual crimes. P. Raynor's work on Wales suggests that some probation schemes, with adult offenders, are quite successful, but there have been tensions in the 1980s and 1990s over whether modern probation has lost some of the reforming zeal of its Liberal creators in 1907.

In 1989 probation was the punishment for only a tenth of those found guilty of indictable offences in South Wales, but the range of possible sentences has expanded. This was the long-term effect of political decisions since the 1960s to divert people away from custody. In particular, conditional discharge has recently become twice as common as probation, and the 1970s and 1980s witnessed new alternatives such as supervision orders for the youngest criminals, overseen by the social service departments, and community service orders. Conditional discharges have been used quite liberally for offences such as shoplifting and assault, whilst the other orders have been directed towards the violent youth, the burglar and the thief. A community service order, which was introduced by the Criminal Justice Act of 1972, consists of several hundred hours' work during a year. It has become a central plank of the Home Office's new policy of 'punishment in the community', and has been denounced by Cohen, Vass and other social-control sociologists as a replacement for *alternatives* to custody, not for custody itself. Its achievements have yet to be established.

The fining of offenders, whatever its limitations, has obvious advantages for the government of the day. It has always been a minor form of punishment at the higher courts, but has become the dominant one for indictable crimes at magistrates' courts. Fines of £2 for an assault, £5 for attacking a policeman, £2 for riotous behaviour, and £1 for coal-stealing were typical of the early decades. For petty and victimless offences, fines were a matter of course. At the Pontypridd police court, which punished the Hopkinstown offenders, 10s. 0d. was the common fine in 1911–12 for being drunk and disorderly, 15s. 0d. for gaming with cards, and 1s. 0d. for throwing stones on the highway, whilst at the Cowbridge court the inhabitants of Peterston-super-Ely in 1935–8

**Table 1·8: Effects of probation, Cardiff magistrates' courts
1919–1923**

Year	Placed on probation		Number on probation who committed another one offence	
	Adults	Juveniles	Adults	Juveniles
1919	22	36	12	14
1920	27	82	13	44
1921	33	36	10	11
1922	25	50	9	13
1923	29	38	5	4

had to hand over 4s. 0d. for ignoring traffic signs or being without a dog licence.

After the war, fining became even more popular, and by the end of our period, 38 per cent of the persons convicted in South Wales of indictable offences at all courts, and 88 per cent of those convicted of non-indictable offences, were fined. Thousands of motorists and heavy drinkers were so punished. One of the complaints, from an early date, was that fining was an arbitrary form of punishment which bore heavily on the poor, and led them, through non-payment, into gaol. This was true, but only partly so, for attempts were made to fine the embezzler and the illegal bookmaker, for example, much more heavily than the shoplifter and drunkard. However, a finely tuned grading system, such as that embodied in the Criminal Justice Act of 1991, has proved to be unworkable.

The Children and Young Persons Acts of 1908, 1933, 1969 and 1989, together with the Criminal Justice Act of 1948, increased the differences in treatment between adults and juveniles. The differences can be summarized thus: special conditions for prosecuting juvenile offenders, a new system of juvenile courts, greater anonymity for defendants, a range of distinct punishments, care and protection orders, and the provision of new remand, attendance and detention centres. It was not, however, a consistent line of development; the move to decriminalize juvenile misdemeanours, and to replace punishment with treatment, was brought to a halt in the 1970s and 1980s, when attitudes towards delinquents hardened, and more youngsters were cautioned and sent to secure and penal institutions.

At the beginning of the century, it was customary to offer the juvenile first offender a second chance, through a caution or probationary order. Cardiff had probation officers at an early date, including the redoubtable Daisy Childs of the Church Army. In the inter-war years a committee of magistrates monitored their effectiveness. The figures in table 1.8, from the Cardiff magistrates' courts for 1919–23, are a comparison of the numbers of juveniles and adults (mainly thieves) placed on probation, and the gradual improvement in its effects.

Praise for these improving statistics was given to religious social workers, and to D. Scourfield, the probation officer who found employment for his clients.

Industrial schools, detention centres, reformatories and approved schools were other early-twentieth-century options for the young recidivist, and borstal training of two or three years for the older ones who had progressed from petty theft to break-ins. Magistrates were reluctant to impose custodial sentences on the young, for South Wales was poorly provided with penal institutions, as it was with detention and remand homes for the young. Between 1939 and 1941 Glamorgan courts ordered 174 boys to be sent to approved schools, including those at Neath and Dinas Powys, but places could not be found for all of them. Nor, in this reformative age, was corporal punishment very popular. A small number of young people were birched each year in South Wales, but gradually one magistrate after another declared himself unwilling to impose this form of punishment, and it would have probably disappeared altogether but for the anxiety over juvenile delinquency during the 1930s and the early years of the Second World War.

The Criminal Justice Act of 1948 ended corporal punishment for juveniles, and sought to reduce the number sent to prison, but this humane legislation also reflected the growing irritation with the behaviour of rebellious children. One result was that during the 1950s over a hundred boys each year were obliged to attend weekend centres at the police headquarters in Cardiff and Swansea. These provided 'a short sharp lesson' in physical education, hygiene and woodwork. Other juveniles were placed under care and supervision orders, and lodged in community homes. Incarceration, however, recovered some of its appeal after the Children and Young Persons Act of 1969; more youngsters were sent, with the government's blessing, to the detention centres and borstals in Monmouthshire and further afield, and, when borstals were replaced in 1982, to the youth custody centres. Most recently, efforts have again been made to divert the young away from custodial punishment, though, at the same time, the government has tightened up provisions for alternative punishment.

The situation at the end of our period illustrates the difference which has now emerged between the treatment of the youngest and oldest juveniles. Most of those under fourteen years of age convicted of indictable offences in South Wales during 1989 were given conditional discharges. Those between fourteen and sixteen years received a more varied mixture of punishments, including conditional discharges, supervision orders, fines and regular visits to the attendance centres at Cardiff and Swansea. Gaol was no longer an option in 1989 for seventeen- to twenty-year-olds convicted of indictable offences, but a larger proportion of this age group (13 per cent) than adults in South Wales experienced the rigours of (youth) custody. Otherwise, apart from a slightly higher proportion of young people sentenced to probation and community service orders, the treatment of those just below and above twenty years of age can hardly be differentiated. The debate over the wisdom of this has been considerable; whilst some argue that young males, who form a large proportion of our convicted criminals, should feel the weight of society's displeasure, others believe that the harshest punishment creates the most recidivists.

Penal policy and its critics

Several modern writers have described the modern criminal process by which so many offenders, not least juveniles and women, are cautioned, discharged and placed on probation, as one which undermines the very purpose of penal policy. This is not a new reaction to the more tolerant sentencing patterns which have, with interruptions, been a feature of the twentieth century. Many people in South Wales have been, at various times, openly angry about the punishment inflicted by judges and magistrates on murderers, robbers, burglars and lesser criminals.

The police, and some of the public and the press, have generally been supportive of tough legislation and punishment. They were delighted, for example, by the action of Judge Lawrence at the

Glamorgan spring assizes in 1908, when he added 'the cat' to gaol sentences for a score of violent robbers. Twenty years later there was a similar police reaction to the stricter sentences imposed on Swansea shoplifters, and, in the early 1950s, to the 'salutary terms' of imprisonment and preventive detention which removed 'very many of our habitual housebreakers' in Cardiff and Glamorgan. In each case a claim was made for beneficial short-term effects on the rates of those crimes. It was not, however, even on these narrow terms, a story of complete success, for other judicial campaigns against, for example, drink-driving in the 1950s had more ambiguous results.

Nowhere was the annoyance of the police, and a good proportion of the public, greater than in the treatment of juvenile delinquency. The anger surfaced at conferences on the subject in South Wales in 1941 and 1951, at meetings of the police committees, and in the letter columns of the local press. In 1951 Elizabeth Andrews, chairwoman of the juvenile court at Ystrad in the Rhondda for twenty-eight years, denounced such 'uninformed' people for their Neanderthal approach to penal policy. One of the latter, minister Degwel Thomas, told the Glamorgan standing joint police committee that corporal punishment had done him no harm as a boy, and it should be extended to more offenders. 'Well-meaning cranks', wrote a sympathizer in 1942, 'have had a long innings . . . Namby-pamby methods are not only useless and expensive in the long run, but pernicious.'

In Swansea, under pressure from the watch committee, a decision was taken in 1944 to reduce the proportion of probationary sentences for juveniles, and for a while people announced themselves satisfied. Sixteen years later, when another crime wave resurrected old anxieties, the conservative lobby was again vociferous. Chief Justice Parker, on a visit to Cardiff, called for a return of corporal punishment for those young men who contributed so much to the crime statistics, whilst others wanted more and longer gaol sentences now that prison accommodation had expanded. The election manifestos of the Conservative Party in the 1970s promised these people a return to 'old-fashioned values'.

The debate over the purpose and effect of punishment, especially of imprisonment, has been refuelled by Home Secretary Michael Howard's declaration in 1993 that incarceration 'works' and will be increased. His remarks were not too surprising, in the context of Tory politics and law-and-order policy since 1979, but they ran counter to widely held beliefs dating back to the later nineteenth century. Until the late 1950s, when the crime rate began its remorseless rise, there was still much confidence inside and outside the Home Office in a rehabilitative penal policy. Llewellyn Williams, MP and recorder of Cardiff, said in 1915 that the low crime figures were the result of the law being administered more sympathetically towards the weak and the wilful. There was a strong conviction then, and in the inter-war years, that incarceration was of limited value, at least as a reforming influence, and should be confined to the worst criminals only.

Every effort was made to keep juveniles away from gaol, and to publicize the success of alternative punishments. At least two-thirds of the juveniles cautioned across South Wales in mid-century did not, it was estimated, commit another offence within two or three years. By contrast, the records of the Swansea juvenile court for the same period reveal that once they appeared before the magistrates a half of the delinquents returned shortly afterwards. Those placed on probation by the same court were, nevertheless, comparatively well behaved; only a fifth of them committed another offence or otherwise broke the conditions of the order. Of all the other punishments, fining seems to have been the most successful in the middle of the century, in terms of reconvictions, as one might have expected. Such results were, in fact, in line with later academic studies, most of which suggested that fines, conditional discharges, probation and community service orders produced less recidivism than borstals; though borstals, as the recorder of Cardiff noted in 1957, had lower reconviction figures than prisons.

Most of the people sentenced to gaol had, almost by definition, bad criminal records, and their return to a life of crime was anticipated. Of the inmates of Cardiff and Swansea gaols in 1900 six out of ten males and eight out of ten females had previous convictions, and a large number, especially of females, had been in trouble with the authorities on more than half a dozen occasions. The proportion of inmates with criminal records had decreased somewhat by mid-century, but today, once again, the situation is close to that of 1900. Currently, about two-thirds or more of those who have been in penal institutions commit offences within a couple of years of being freed. This is disappointing but hardly surprising. Studies of these 'committed criminals' have revealed that their career is probably influenced less by the terrors of incarceration and more by their 'social make-up', employment prospects and age.

There was, so far as this writer can judge, no apparent long-term correlation in South Wales between the shifts in sentencing and the changes in the crime rate. Both are, after all, influenced by many independent factors. The pattern of punishment, for instance, is related to political, economic and ideological developments, of which crime is only a part. Thus the present prison-building programme, like the reforms of the police, is not a simple reaction to the fear and experience of crime. Since the days of Robert Peel, dealing with crime and criminals has been a government priority, but it is not the only one.

2

Crime: A General Survey

Evidence

Despite the intrinsic problems, people have tried for two centuries to discover the scale of delinquency. The most consistent and comprehensive attempt, at least until the 1980s, has been that organized by the central government. Since 1810 the annual parliamentary papers have included official returns to the Home Office, first of cases tried at the higher courts, and then, after 1857, of indictable offences known to the police, and of proceedings at the courts of summary jurisdiction. The first of these tables, now renamed 'notifiable offences recorded by the police', was the summary of first quarterly, and then monthly, statistics compiled in each police force. For the first half of the twentieth century this information appeared annually, except for the years of the First and Second World Wars, and even these gaps can be partly filled by using the local returns which have survived for Glamorgan, Cardiff, Swansea, Neath and Merthyr Tydfil.

Unfortunately, the annual command papers, with their statistics of indictable crime for each police force, were published in shortened form after the Second World War. Only the national picture was given in the parliamentary papers. The historian seeking the returns of recorded indictable offences in South Wales, as well as detail of the proceedings at magistrates' courts, has to seek out the loosely bound booklets of supplementary statistics produced by the Home Office in limited numbers. These were replaced in 1980 by four, and then five, bound volumes of supplementary tables, distributed by HMSO.

It is important to compare the information in these returns with other statistical and literary evidence. We saw, in the last chapter, the value of victim and self-report surveys, and company, tax and insurance records, for the recent past. For earlier decades there is nothing comparable, though there were occasions when the authorities sought and obtained special reports on crimes which were causing concern. Thus the first Cardiff and Swansea chief constables of this century provided interesting accounts of vagrancy, prostitution and licensing offences, stretching back over long periods. Later, there were local enquiries into juvenile delinquency, and into the scale of robberies, burglaries, shoplifting and motoring offences.

Some of this evidence can be found in the chief constables' annual reports, which have survived in reasonable numbers, at least for Glamorgan, Cardiff, Merthyr Tydfil and Swansea. At the beginning of the century these reports had long and valuable appendices, but these soon disappeared. Thereafter, until the improved format of the 1960s, they were short statements, with brief summaries of information on the state of the police, crime and other matters. These documents were carefully prepared, and disguised as much as they revealed, but they are required reading for attitudes, and for material on communications, complaints, crimes and prosecutions. During the 1980s they became lavish productions, of well over a hundred pages and thirty-six tables.

In certain years, such as 1929 (Swansea), 1938 (Glamorgan), 1965 (Cardiff), and 1972, 1979 and 1986 (South Wales), the chief constables' reports were accompanied by major reviews of the police forces. In these reviews, and in the various working-party reports just prior to and following amalgamation in 1969, attention was focused on the problems and requirements of the police. Fortunately for the historian, these reviews were illustrated by valuable tables and graphs on crime and occurrences, often at a divisional and subdivisional level. Such information was supplied to the compilers of the reports, as it has been to a number of modern criminologists and social geographers, by force collators and CID statisticians. During the 1990s the management information unit at Bridgend took over this function, and now produces substantial monthly booklets on a range of statistics.

For further information on offences and offenders, the annual Home Office and police force publications must be supplemented by records of assizes, quarter sessions and petty sessions, some of which are held at the Glamorgan Record Office. Access to the most recent files is restricted. This is less of a problem for the higher courts, as the press coverage of these was good, but evidence is sometimes missing for the cases dealt with summarily and for the quasi-criminal proceedings. These last occupied about a tenth of the time of magistrates' courts in the first half of the century, and included cases of bastardy, the guardianship of children and the maintenance of wives. Statistics on these proceedings were transferred from the criminal tables proper at the turn of the century.

The records of non-indictable proceedings in magistrates' courts present particular difficulties. The national returns in the command papers were reduced in size and quality in the inter-war years, but at least they have survived. Some of the later Welsh material, compiled by the Home Office in extra-parliamentary papers, has disappeared altogether. Sadly, local court and police records do not cover all the gaps that exist after the 1940s, so that we cannot reconstruct the full picture of less serious offences across the century. This is unfortunate, as the non-indictable tables contain statistics of assaults, which were largely dealt with at the magistrates' courts, malicious damage, certain types of stealing, and licensing and motoring offences. In the case of the last two categories, however, separate government returns on these crimes adequately compensate for the missing information.

Material on offenders comes from a variety of sources. The historical records that have survived in Cardiff and Swansea gaols supplement the annual command papers which provide basic information on the numbers and character of prisoners. There are also court calendars, court warrants, registers of prisoners and persons under police supervision, fingerprint and photographic books, charge sheets and police circulars of wanted people. This information found its way onto the card, and later computer, indexes of suspected and actual criminals which were held in each force. Much of this secondary material, including Lionel Lindsay's notorious collection of files on Communists kept at the Glamorgan police headquarters in Canton, Cardiff, has disappointingly vanished.

The police archives at Cardiff and Bridgend offer a variety of other sources on crime and criminals. The police notebooks are of

limited value for this chapter, as are a number of the station
journals, but the police committee minutes are essential reading,
and some of the registers and charge books are useful. To these
can be added the message books, the crime complaint forms, the
daily and monthly summaries of crime, and the crime information
sheets. Ironically, the most recent material has often survived the
worst; forms and computer disks have gradually replaced books
and registers, and the South Wales force has obediently executed
Home Office instructions about the destruction of these files after
short periods of time. Unless a national policy is adopted for
retaining a selection of police records, future historians of crime
and policing will have very little to study.

There are, of course, other kinds of records which offer very
different perspectives from those of the Home Office and the
police. The literary evidence on crime in South Wales in the
twentieth century comprises novels, like Gwyn Thomas's *Sorrow
for the Sons* (1935) and Lewis Jones's *Cwmardy* (1937) and *We Live*
(1939), reminiscences by old criminals, magistrates, policemen
and prison officers, and diaries, letters and speeches by everyone,
from miners' leaders and politicians to landowners and ministers
of religion.

Together with oral, film and television history, these sources
provide us with snapshots of crime at particular moments in time,
and offer an insight into contemporary attitudes towards illegal
activities. They have been drawn upon by Jane Morgan, David
Smith, Hywel Francis and other historians of South Wales, to
illuminate episodes such as the Tonypandy riots of 1910, the 'stay-
down' protests of the 1930s, and the miners' strike of 1984–5, but
they have hardly been used to improve our understanding of
delinquency generally. Finally, there is the evidence provided by
the press, whose abiding interest in crime we discussed at the
beginning of this book.

Statistics and their context

All of the above records have their value, but the basis of this
chapter will be the statistical material. Criminal statistics have,
since their first publication, stimulated interest in delinquency and
influenced popular perceptions of it. By the mid-twentieth century
they were regarded with growing suspicion in academic circles. It

was claimed, rightly, that official statistics were not neutral indices, and could not be used in the old empirical fashion to describe changes in delinquency. In fact, the crime rate was dismissed in some quarters during the 1960s as an artificial construct, a reflection of the authority and wishes of the most powerful members of society. More recently, such fundamentalism has been modified in the light of new crime surveys and the research projects chronicled in chapter 1, but the crime rate still remains a complex phenomenon, the outcome of a variety of attitudes, pressures and processes.

The dangers of relying too much on statistics are well known. In the last chapter we saw that the rate of recorded indictable crime is an incomplete record of both known delinquency and reported offences. It has been, during the century, inconsistent in its relationship to the dark figure of crime, and in its representation of different offences. The reasons for this are many, but, as we have seen, of crucial importance was the prevailing anxiety about crime, the character of reporting decisions made by the public, and the changes in the way the police processed the information which they received.

The evidence points to an improvement in the actual recording of this information during the second half of our period. In the late 1930s and early 1940s, one force after another in Wales moved away from the cautious recording of indictable offences, whereby the police made returns of only those crimes which they had a reasonable chance of detecting. In Neath, where the crime rate more than trebled between 1943 and 1944, the chief constable stated in his annual report for the latter year that 'revised methods of recording and dealing with crime have been introduced. The inelastic methods of reporting prevent other than the true state of crime being recorded.'

Twenty years later, after pressure from the government and inspectors of constabulary, there was greater uniformity in preparing statistics. During the 1960s the Home Office issued instructions to assist in this. Forces came into line, for example, over calculating cases which crossed yearly boundaries and those which had been committed by one person, and greater care was taken over defining break-ins. In the late 1960s the Glamorgan force decided to standardize, centralize and modernize its own recording procedures, but the possibility of extending this to all the South Wales forces at amalgamation was not considered because of the imminent publication of the report of the Home Office Departmental Committee on Criminal Statistics (the Perks Committee).

The recording of crimes was not, as we saw in the last chapter, a simple procedure. Attacks on people, both sexual and others, were sometimes redefined before final entry on the official lists, whilst the classification of property offences was influenced by several considerations. Thus an act of criminal damage might be entered differently, according to the preference of an officer, the chances of detection, and the changing rate of inflation. Similarly, the political and economic climate, especially public concern over crime, had a bearing on whether an offence was returned as a robbery or stealing from the person, and as a break-in or theft from a house. It was, admittedly, not easy to distinguish between such activities. In fact, one of the criticisms of the official classifications has been that they are too rigid, and have failed to keep pace with the changing character of modern crime. Since the 1960s a number of scholars have rearranged the material in the Home Office tables, in an attempt to provide a more worthwhile picture of delinquency. This will be tried, where it seems necessary, in this volume.

The crime rate given in the graphs and text of this book is normally the number of recorded indictable offences per 100,000 of the population. As many offences, like indecency, shoplifting, autocrime, fraud and criminal damage, are carried out by one person in a given year, the rate is only an approximation. The accuracy of the population figure in the crime rate is more certain, as most of the police-force boundary changes in this century took place within South Wales. Since 1969 the only alteration to the South Wales district came with the reorganization of local government in 1974, which added 41,330 people from neighbouring police-force districts.

The population did, however, change in other ways during the century, as in its sex and age structure, but less perhaps than is sometimes imagined. The notion, for example, that the level of delinquency is explicable by fluctuations in the size of the most criminal age groups cannot stand. In 1921, for instance, there were 90,389 more people in Wales aged 15–24 years than in 1971. Table 2.1 compares the number of recorded indictable offences with the proportions of age groups of males under twenty-four during the century.

Table 2·1: Welsh population (age and sex, percentage distribution) and crime, 1901–1989

Year	1901	1911	1921	1931	1951	1961	1971	1981	1989
Males as percentage of population	50	51	50	50	49	49	49	48	49
Ages 0–14	34	33	31	27	23	23	24	21	19
Ages 0–19	44	42	40	35	29	30	31	29	26
Ages 15–24	19	18	18	17	13	13	14	15	15
Indictable offences recorded, per 100,000 of total population	222	279	385	392	979	1720	3395	5057	6818

Nor were other changes to the population, like immigration and urbanization, of such a magnitude as to invalidate the use of a simple crime rate over a long period of time. The rate deserves to be analysed, both for its own sake, and for the evidence which it provides on authority and delinquency generally.

In fact, recent research has confirmed that the crime rate is a fairly accurate index of changes in the incidence of most serious offences. A major sociological study of Sheffield has shown that the official returns of indictable crime and serious offenders complement rather than contradict more detailed crime-survey information, and are even a reasonable guide to differences in the experience of delinquency across communities. Lesley Noaks, in her study of a Gwent suburb, also found that the police account of delinquency was not that different from the one which emerged from her own survey. This provides a little comfort for the historian, who cannot check the accuracy of many of his or her sources, and is obliged to proceed in a cautious and instinctive fashion. In this chapter the official statistics will be used as a starting-point for our enquiry, as the alternatives are even more daunting, if not impossible.

The legal framework

One of the advantages of working outwards from the official records of crime is that they constantly remind us of the legal definitions of delinquency. The crime rate only makes sense when set against the changing legal framework. All police officers in 1900 were provided with summaries of key statutes and by-laws, and since that time senior policemen, detectives, collators, court staff and Home Office compilers have necessarily been aware of the broad outlines of criminal legislation. Some of the important Acts with which they were all familiar, like the vagrancy statutes of 1824 and 1898, remained unchanged for generations. Others were the result of modernization and codification, like the Criminal Damage Act of 1971, which made a wider range of vandalism indictable, and the Misuse of Drugs Act of the same year which addressed the expansion and complexities of drug abuse.

There were also new laws for behaviour which once had needed few or no controlling mechanisms. Thus, in the early decades of the century, hundreds of people were prosecuted each year for offences connected with dogs, or for not sending their children to school, whilst driving and other pleasures were increasingly licensed. Of all the new legislation, the Road Traffic and Safety Acts of 1930, 1956 and 1967 were perhaps the classic crime-making statutes, which brought thousands of people for the first time before the magistrates. There were, as well, temporary wartime legislation and orders such as those restricting aliens, controlling the sale of liquor and food, prohibiting looting and regulating lighting. More recently, laws have outlawed racial and sexual discrimination, and new traffic orders fall on the chief constables' desks every week. All of these innovations have been used, at one time or another, to explain away increases in the annual crime statistics.

The Public Order Acts of 1936, 1963 and 1986, the Criminal Justice Acts of 1948 and 1982, the Prevention of Terrorism Act of 1976, and several other statutes have added considerably to police powers and to the work of the courts. On the other hand, certain Acts have had negative effects on the crime rate. In the 1960s, a decade of great legal changes, attempted suicide, abortion and homosexual acts between consenting adults ceased to be criminal offences. Similarly, the betting and gaming legislation of the 1950s and 1960s, and the drink licensing Acts of 1961 and 1990 brought new freedoms.

It seems probable that much of the above legislation had only a limited impact on the rate of serious indictable crime, but the effect of other statutes is more difficult to estimate. The Children and Young Persons Acts of 1908, 1933, 1963, 1969 and 1989 contained important changes, which undoubtedly affected the reporting and treatment of crime. The age boundary between juveniles and adults was moved from sixteen to seventeen years by the Act of 1933, and thirty years later the age of criminal responsibility was raised from eight years to ten years. This distorted the crime rate, and, so it is assumed, did the the legislation permitting certain offences to be dealt with summarily, and possibly other administrative reforms.

The most direct intervention affecting the scale and character of the published criminal statistics was that ordered by the Home Office. This included new instructions in 1950 on the way indictable offences against the person should be listed, and the three-year experiment from 1972 to 1974 of not including thefts of a low value in the national figures, thus giving the erroneous impression of a sharp fall in the crime rate. A few years before, in 1968, the Theft Act widened the definition of break-ins, and the offence of taking and driving away motor vehicles was added to the indictable tables, as was criminal damage worth under £20 nine years later. Nor was this the end of the changes: in 1977 the Criminal Law Act redefined indictable offences and three years later a new counting procedure was introduced; in 1972, when the fixed penalty system was finally established throughout South Wales, many motoring offences were dropped from the non-indictable prosecutions; and in 1988 the Home Office reclassified a number of offences as summary. In the light of all this, the graphs below should be regarded with the suspicion bestowed on most other types of historical evidence.

Crime: chronology and commentary

This section provides a general commentary on the crime rate; a more detailed analysis of the extent and nature of illegal activities will follow in chapter 3. Graphs 2.1 and 2.2 comprise the rates of indictable offences recorded and of persons prosecuted for non-indictable offences per 100,000 of the population. The rates of indictable offences recorded fall into four distinct periods: 1900–20, 1921–40, 1941–56, and 1957–89. In the first two decades newspapers, judges and chief constables frequently commented on the 'exceptionally good' conduct of the population

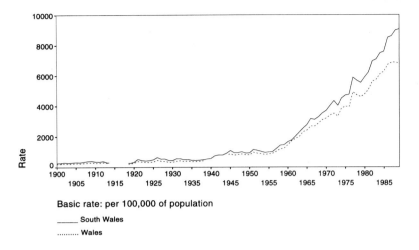

Basic rate: per 100,000 of population

_____ South Wales

.... Wales

**Graph 2.1: Indictable offences recorded by the police in
Wales and South Wales, 1900–1989**

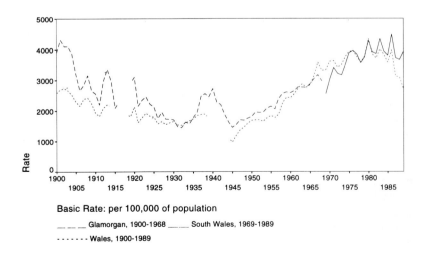

Basic Rate: per 100,000 of population

_ _ _ Glamorgan, 1900-1968 _____ South Wales, 1969-1989

- - - - - - Wales, 1900-1989

**Graph 2.2: People prosecuted for non-indictable offences
in Wales, 1900–1989**

both before and during the war, though there were claims that the war on the home front undermined commercial probity and encouraged juvenile delinquency. The police records and the statistics of indictable crime which have survived for Cardiff and Swansea seem to confirm the optimistic picture (see table 2.2). In Cardiff, where many policemen joined the colours, special constables found that 'there is very little crime' for them to handle.

Table 2·2: Indictable offences 1913–1919 in Glamorgan, Cardiff and Swansea

	Chief constable's return of people prosecuted for indictable offences	Indictable offences known to the police		Juveniles proceeded against for indictable offences
	Glamorgan	Cardiff	Swansea	Swansea
1913	2433	663	709	–
1914	2565	461	848	89
1915	2713	312	635	173
1916	–	298	737	167
1917	2412	371	799	183
1918	2364	370	752	116
1919	2121	399	834	130

Although there were serious industrial troubles in this period, and, as we shall see, a high level of non-indictable offences, people of the city and country were described as increasingly 'well behaved' by 1918, in part because of the decline in heavy drinking, which was encouraged by the war conditions. In some districts, higher rates of pay and better education were said to have brought greater respectability. Llewellyn Williams, as we noted earlier, affirmed in 1915 that changes in penal policy had also helped, though he was doubtful if the 'diminution' of criminal activity would long outlast the war years.

During the next twenty years the rate of recorded indictable crimes moved onto a higher plateau, with peaks in 1921, 1926 and 1931–2. In Merthyr Tydfil, one of the most affected areas, the mid-1920s resounded to loud complaints of coal trucks looted, stores and offices burgled, goods taken illegally from shops, and churches and chapels vandalized. The stealing of coal amounted to a half of recorded indictable crime in the town, and those charged were men and women in their twenties and thirties, and young teenagers. They frequently operated in separate sex groups. In 1924, for example, one of the coal-stealing gangs at work was Elizabeth Keough (32 years of age), her daughter, Elizabeth (15), Mary Hughes (15) and Ivy Cottrell (13); we know their names because they were caught in the act of removing 2 cwt. from colliery screens at Merthyr Vale.

The inspectors of police met in 1930 to express their concern at the increase in crime, and in South Wales the press and the pulpit denounced juvenile delinquency, break-ins by young male adults, and the industrial troubles. An editorial in the *Weekly Mail and Cardiff Times* of 9 May 1931 was entitled 'Epidemic of Juvenile Crime'; it disclosed that in the previous eighteen months some 80 per cent of offenders before the Cardiff magistrates were between fourteen and nineteen years of age. Even in Neath, which had proudly trumpeted its low criminal record since 1924, proceedings against under sixteen-year-olds in 1931 were unusually high, and the interest in the subject was sustained by the debate over the Children and Young Persons Act of 1933 and exaggerated apprehension that, with the heavy migration of workers from South Wales in the 1920s and 1930s, 'it was becoming a land of little children and old people'.

The chief constable of Glamorgan worried about other matters, including the Communists who, he believed, were behind the General Strike and the stay-down demonstrations. Across the county his subdivisional inspectors organized constant checks on people who could be described as 'seditious', and every Friday, at the chief constable's office, a weekly intelligence report was compiled. Lindsay also expressed concern about the burglars who threatened valuable house property in his county, and about the 'perpetrators [of ordinary robberies who] . . . now make so much use of the motor cars, buses, and other transport in order to get to and from the scene of their activities'. In November 1938 his successor, Joseph Jones, argued for a stronger police force, basing his case on the 38-per-cent increase in cases dealt with by Glamorgan's criminal courts over the preceding six years, and the 181-per-cent rise in recorded offences relating to motoring.

It is, for obvious reasons, difficult to establish the crime pattern during the Second World War, but the total number of indictable offences recorded in Glamorgan, Cardiff and Swansea rose by 70 per cent between 1938 and 1941, and once again the crime rate moved onto a much higher plane. In Neath and Merthyr Tydfil, where there was corporate pride over the difference, the process took rather longer. Initially, the threat of a common enemy, and the 'magnificent' manner in which the South Wales population responded to the air raids, raised hopes of 'a truce' between 'the gentlemen of crime' and respectable citizens, but it was not to be. Table 2.3, which illustrates this, combines the figures for the three main categories of crime in Glamorgan and the four towns.

Table 2·3: Recorded indictable crime in South Wales, 1939–1945

Year	Offences against the person (including sexual)	Offences against property with violence	Offences against property without violence (excluding malicious damage, currency offences, etc.)
1939	237	1042	4773
1940	262	1169	5135
1941	316	1521	6779
1942	369	1431	6990
1943	381	1351	6894
1944	455	1801	7770
1945	380	2603	8161

In Cardiff and Swansea the war-damaged buildings and the cover of darkness proved irresistible to the thief, and in the latter town Brinley Evans and Arthur Harris, two labourers, were given six-month sentences in an effort to stop widespread looting after the bombing raids of 1941. In both towns there was some evidence of the professionalism and modernization of crime which, Edward Smithies claims, was a product of the war. At Swansea, where there were several large-scale raids on shops and warehouses, the rewards of property offences rose sharply (£2,329 in 1938, and £16,378 in 1945) and detection and recovery rates fell.

Certain individuals made small fortunes on the black market. In December 1945 the Glamorgan chief constable wrote:

It is regrettable that in this County, in common with other parts of the country, crime has shown a gradual increase since the outbreak of the war . . . The shortage and rationing of goods, the need of coupons to effect purchases, account for a great deal of additional crime; and, furthermore, the extortionate prices which can be obtained for second-hand goods, clothing and jewelry, tempt individuals to resort to crime as a means of getting money.

All kinds of property were, he complained, now targeted, and where the thief failed, the vandal succeeded.

The war and immediate post-war conditions were blamed in particular for a rise in juvenile crime. On this, the official statistics (in table 2.4) were, for once, less startling perhaps than the literary evidence.

Table 2·4: Indictable offences committed by juveniles, Swansea, Glamorgan and Cardiff, 1933–1945

	Juveniles proceeded against		*Juveniles charged*
	Swansea	*Glamorgan*	*Cardiff*
1933	87	–	120
1934	130	–	186
1935	210	699	261
1936	211	605	306
1937	210	639	278
1938	143	632	223
1939	224	644	207
1940	245	978	271
1941	305	1168	434
1942	262	953	320
1943	253	999	306
1944	311	1194	222
1945	311	1163	304

During 1941 the complaints of juvenile behaviour reached a crescendo, with evacuees unfairly blamed. 'Crime among young boys in this valley is something terrible,' said a Rhondda inhabitant in May of that year. In September, at Cardiff, Sir William Jenkins, chairman of the county education and police committees, hosted a conference on the subject of juvenile delinquency. Speakers attacked the widespread truanting, shoplifting and break-ins committed by younger children, and demanded better parenting, more religious education and stricter punishment. A few also voiced common middle-class anxieties about the high wages, freedom and low cultural ambitions of those just starting employment.

After the war the expected return to normality never quite materialized, though the evidence on this varies from district to district. At Swansea the chief constable continued to denounce the 'serious departures from the older and stricter standards of honesty, fair dealing and truthfulness', which lasted as long as shortages and rationing. Elsewhere there was more optimism, and praise for the Criminal Justice Act of 1948. At Cardiff, prominent individuals claimed that the new generation of eleven to thirteen-year-olds was less criminally minded than its predecessor, and a juvenile delinquency committee was appointed in 1950 to encourage this move away from delinquency. In the same year, however, Glamorgan held another conference on the subject, and learnt that as many as four out of ten defendants in indictable court cases were under seventeen years of age, a situation which even the capital city could not match.

The following year was widely regarded as one of the worst on record. The Home Secretary talked of the growth of violence in society, the chief constable of Glamorgan protested about the level of property crimes and sex offences, and committees on juvenile delinquency were formed right across Wales. It was all rather premature, for the next few years were marked by talk of improving 'standards', lower criminal statistics, a greater willingness to use police cautions, and growing confidence 'that the peak of the post-war crime wave has been passed'.

The reality proved to be very different. The years from 1957 until the present day have been rightly regarded as the most astonishing period in the history of modern crime. The initial, and staggering, rise in the rate of recorded indictable crime offences during the late 1950s and the 1960s will be looked at in more detail in the next chapter. The courts were suddenly full of burglars, thieves and motorists, and the process was accompanied by innumerable sermons, reports, and editorials which described the 'negative' and 'debilitating' effects of prosperity, the welfare state and changes in family life. Degwel Thomas warned of the evils of both parents working by day, and enjoying a drink and bingo in the evenings, whilst other observers commented that people experiencing rapid material progress were less willing than previous generations to tolerate relative deprivation.

The first signs of national anxiety over the rise in the criminal statistics can be found in the parliamentary debates, the reports of professionals and the popular press during the 1960s. In Cardiff the authorities warned that burglaries, break-ins and larcenies, together with vandalism, hooliganism and traffic offences, were stretching the forces of law and order to their limit. The chief constable of Glamorgan complained in a similar fashion, but in Swansea and Merthyr Tydfil there was less pessimism. Although the public mood was one of anger over the behaviour of juveniles on council estates, the police chiefs in both towns insisted that 'organized crime' was still comparatively rare. Sensibly, in view of the coming changes, the watch committees in Swansea and Merthyr during the 1960s expressed confidence in the quality of their independent police forces.

The chief political response to the rising crime rate at this time was organizational. Governments were persuaded that the amalgamation of police forces, the creation of inter-force agencies, and the establishment of unit-beat policing would tilt the balance against the criminal. In addition, a long-term Home Office campaign was begun to enlist public support for the police, largely by crime-prevention measures. The amalgamation of the four forces in South Wales in 1969 did not, however, bring the desired results. Apart from two brief interruptions, the crime rate has continued to rise ever since.

In the 1970s the dangers of drug abuse, violence and vandalism featured prominently in newspaper articles and public meetings, and it was estimated that over 60 per cent of these and other crimes in South Wales were committed by under 21-year-olds. Regional committees were formed to deal with these problems, and, to the relief of many chief constables, the election of a Tory government heralded a boost in police pay and morale. These developments, together with the initiatives of neighbourhood watch and community policing in the early 1980s, were widely regarded as essential moves in the fight against crime. In 1983 David East, the new chief constable of South Wales, reflected positively on these changes, and declared that 'at long last the battle appears to be swinging against the criminals'.

It was a brief respite. The many protests and demonstrations of the early 1980s climaxed in the miners' strike, which in turn affected both the incidence of crime and the policing of it. In 1986 it was announced that on average one serious offence was recorded by the police every five minutes somewhere in the South Wales district, and many more went unreported. The publication of victim, self-report and insurance surveys in these years confirmed that this shortfall was, in Wales even more than in England, especially true of crimes of violence.

By 1989, as we shall see in the next chapter, people's experience of crime had probably never been greater, but there was also an element of hysteria and self-interest in the fascination with the crime rate. Newspapers like the *Western Mail*, the *South Wales Echo* and the *Glamorgan Gazette* became obsessed with the crime problem in the 1980s and 1990s, and editorials regularly returned to it. Consultative committees across South Wales, and groups of residents, businessmen and councillors called for more constables on the beat and the reopening of police stations, and local Labour politicians in 1986 began their long campaign to steal the law-and-order mantle from the Tory Party.

The late 1980s and early 1990s have seen South Wales near the top of the British crime table, with a reputation for high levels of drunken hooliganism, violence against the police, criminal damage, break-ins and car thefts. In the local press, the drugs problem, domestic violence and child abuse have been other recurring themes of the past decade. For a while in 1989, South Wales made the national headlines, with the Ely riots, joy-riding, and attacks on police officers, but the most disturbing feature of modern crime has been its frequency and the impact of that on both the public and the police. People are now 'crime-conscious' to a remarkable, and sometimes disturbing, degree, and the police are simply unable to deal with every complaint which they receive. In the face of the inexorable rise in crime, the reorganization of the force, the tensions over funding and government law-and-order initiatives have seemed at times rather irrelevant.

It is worth reflecting briefly on the notorious image which South Wales had, in some quarters, for much of this century. In 1900–1 Judge Gwilym Williams and others conducted an angry debate over the extent of delinquency in Glamorgan and its major towns. It was claimed that South Wales had some of the highest figures for serious crime, drunkenness and prostitution in Britain. Defenders of 'Black Glamorgan' and 'Black Cardiff' challenged these remarks, or, like D. A. Thomas MP, attributed the delinquency to the exceptional scale of immigration at the turn of the century. It was an extension of Henry Richard's argument of a generation earlier, namely that 'Wales proper' had a naturally lower rate of crime than the other nations of Britain.

Wales in the twentieth century has had a marginally lower crime rate than England, but the figures for South Wales have been consistently higher than those for the other regions of Wales, and for many English districts. Table 2.5 gives the national comparisons in 1989.

Table 2·5: Notifiable offences recorded in England and Wales in 1989, per 100,000 of the population

Classification	England	Wales	South Wales
Violent crimes	352	358	348
Sexual offences	59	57	39
Burglaries	1660	1366	1925
Robberies	69	14	18
Theft and handling stolen goods	4035	3804	4760
Fraud and forgery	270	235	209
Criminal damage	1252	1284	1737
Other offences	56	41	44
Total	7752	6856	9079

Graph 2.3 illustrates the rate of indictable offences within the police districts in Wales. The combined police forces in North Wales at the beginning of the century, and later those in Dyfed-Powys, returned rates that were at or near the bottom of the British crime table. The differences between the Welsh district rates have been explained largely in terms of the nature of their populations and their readiness to commit and report crimes. Although there has been some discussion recently about the rise in rural crime, there have always been fewer offences in the Welsh countryside than in the town, even allowing for a poorer reporting and recording rate. The modern South Wales police district is very different from the rest; it is an unusual mixture of metropolitan centre, industrial valleys, seaports and rural communities. Its chief

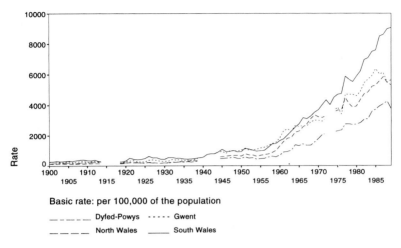

Basic rate: per 100,000 of the population

_ _ _ _ _ Dyfed-Powys   - - - - - Gwent

_ _ _ _ _ North Wales   _____ South Wales

Graph 2.3: Indictable offences recorded by the police in the districts of Dyfed-Powys, Gwent, North Wales and South Wales, 1900–1989

constables in the 1980s and 1990s have insisted that, until governments understand the exceptional character and problems of the district, and provide the necessary resources, a high crime rate is likely to continue.

Graph 2.2, which shows proceedings against people for *non-indictable* crimes is of limited value, as offences were dropped from the lists quite frequently, and others were added. Moreover, the penalty-ticket system has, in the last thirty years, removed thousands of non-indictable cases from the courts. The graph falls into five periods, the first being the high, but falling, rate down to 1932. The decline reflected the reclassification of certain cases as quasi-criminal proceedings, and, more importantly, the reduction in offences like breaches of the laws relating to education, licensing, prostitution and vagrancy. In fact, the chief constable of Cardiff used the latter group of statistics in the inter-war years to defend his city against the 'false allegations' of moral reformers. The new traffic legislation of the early 1930s then made its impact, and the rate of non-indictable proceedings rose again. After a hiatus, brought about by the war conditions, this increase in Glamorgan continued until the late 1960s, when over three-quarters of proceedings were related to motor vehicles. Since then the graph for South Wales has moved somewhat erratically up and down, mainly in response to artificial factors.

The causes of crime

The publication of criminal statistics during the century has stimulated debate about the causes and the location of delinquency. Discussions over the causes of crime have reflected the period in which they took place. Thus, in the very early years of the century, when the official crime rate was low and changed little, people still talked in simplistic terms of delinquency as the responsibiity of a 'criminal class'. This class was composed of habitual criminals and their associates, the drunkards, prostitutes and mendicants, and it was to be found in places like Butetown in Cardiff and the Strand in Swansea. It was widely believed that these people were somewhat different in their physiological and mental make-up from the rest of the population; they were 'outsiders', 'born to crime', who had to be closely watched, and, when necessary, incarcerated. According to R. S. Stewart, deputy superintendent of the Glamorgan Asylum, a proportion of them shared common characteristics with lunatics, and needed similar treatment.

Alcohol was seen as the bonding agent of this class, and the force which also drew respectable people into a life of misery, immorality and crime. Judge Coleridge at the Glamorgan assizes in 1910 claimed that half the crimes were due to drink, and Percy Thomas, the famous Cardiff temperance campaigner, put the proportion even higher. Initially the emphasis was placed on the deleterious effects of alcohol on working-class men and women, but by the 1930s and 1940s attention had switched to the damage inflicted on the young. The chief constable of Cardiff declared in his report of 1941 to the licensing committee that his police had 'on an increasing number of occasions ascertained on arresting young persons of 16 to 20 years of age for crimes ranging from stealing motor cars to burglary, that they have been indulging in intoxicants, which undoubtedly had affected their moral senses'.

Similar statements appeared fifty years later, when a crack-down on drinking establishments and under-age drinking in the capital was regarded as a prerequisite to reducing crime. It was estimated, in a British study of over 2,000 prisoners in 1994, that just over a half had committed their last offence because of an addiction to alcohol or drugs. Certainly the majority of the assaults in South Wales during recent decades have been categorized as 'drink-related', though, as other research has shown, not all of these were actually caused by alcohol. For its part, the drink trade, supported strongly by the *Western Mail*, has for generations stoutly denied any connection between alcohol consumption and delinquency. The message has some point, for the overall rate of indictable crime in South Wales during this century shows no consistent correlation with the number of drinking places, the consumption of beer per head of population, or proceedings against drunkenness.

After the First World War, when proceedings against drunkards, prostitutes and vagrants fell sharply, it became more difficult to blame a criminal class for the evils of society. Other theories now emerged, and one short-lived thesis attributed post-war delinquency to the pyschological problems and social disillusionment of that generation. The subsequent fluctuations in recorded offences during the inter-war years undermined this idea, and encouraged the notion that ordinary people could be drawn temporarily into crime, not by hereditary design or moral decay, but by the prevailing economic and social conditions. Radical journalists, politicians and trade unionists claimed that 'the worse the social conditions, the greater the amount of crime', and Communists like Herbert Hunt of Caerau denounced the system of private property, without which there would be no need for crime.

In the case of 'people of ordinary good character who succumb to sudden temptation' and the 'inefficients in the great industrial army', it was increasingly apparent that economic circumstances were important in their descent into delinquency. There seemed no other way to interpret, for example, the exceptionally high crime rates of 1921, 1926 and 1931. 'There is no doubt', admitted the chief constable of Cardiff in 1924, 'that when industrial prosperity returns, many who now get their livelihood by dishonest means will revert to honest labour.' Stephen Humphries, in a study of the period 1890–1940, has given his support to this thesis; he argues that juvenile theft was essentially 'stealing to survive', and believes that the working class perfectly

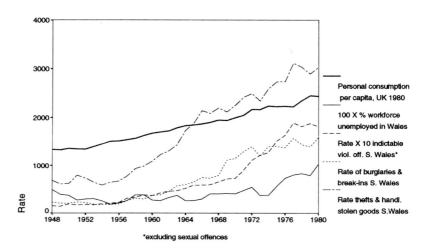

excluding sexual offences

Graph 2.4: Crime and the economy, 1948–1980

understood this. Until the Second World War, such economic analyses of the roots of delinquency remained extremely popular.

The links between crime and the economy have been the subject of extensive research. With some exceptions, these studies show that when personal consumption stagnates or falls, so the number of recorded property crimes rise, whereas the rate of violent offences and those associated with drink move in the opposite direction. Thus in years like 1921 and 1931, and again in the difficult period of the early 1980s, recorded burglaries, theft and criminal damage rose sharply in South Wales, but offences against the person did not. These correlations are not always precise, as can be seen by graph 2.4, but they are close enough to support Simon Field's contention that 'economic factors have a major influence' on criminal activity.

The historical evidence that economic recession stimulates property crime is overwhelming. William Lovell of Cardiff, aged sixty-three, can be taken as representative of thousands who turned to theft when hard times came. After forty-five working years, he lost his job in 1910, and stole sacks. 'It's poverty that drove me', he explained to the court; 'I failed to get work, and I had pawned everything – even the bedclothes – to keep my wife and children from starving.' Both policemen and magistrates anticipated more offences when times were bad, and punished people accordingly.

'Respectable people' caught by the recession were usually regarded with some sympathy, but a few of them, and a greater number of lesser mortals, were selected for punishment 'as an example to the rest'. Everyone knew that, in these periods, court cases were only the tip of the iceberg. In 1921, for example, there were reports from the Rhondda of 'hundreds of men and boys' illegally working the outcropping coal seams, killing the mountain sheep, and taking timber from collieries and advertising hoardings. Even when living standards improved substantially, a sudden economic downturn was always likely to produce a rash of thefts and break-ins.

The precise connection between unemployment and crime has never been satisfactorily established. Many, including the recorder of Swansea in 1932, presumed that there was a direct link, especially with juvenile unemployment. It was one of the reasons why Cardiff and Swansea established juvenile-work committees during the inter-war years. We cannot ascertain the proportion of convicted offenders of that period who were unemployed, but there can be little doubt that a considerable number of people arrested in years like 1921 and 1931 were temporarily without work, and, in the Merthyr district at least, their crimes were overwhelmingly stealing coal and wood. In spite of this, however, other observers were impressed by the 'aversion to crime' amongst the unemployed on the coalfield during this time, and, when asked, the miners themselves attributed this aversion to migration, the common and numbing experience of poverty, and the interest in education and politics which 'kept me from doing something desperate'.

In 1983–4, when about 40 per cent of offenders nationally were without work, the link between job opportunities and delinquency was again a major issue, though there was now more emphasis on juvenile unemployment. A sample of 389 custody records from the Porth police station during the 1980s reveals that half of those arrested, three-quarters of those from the Penrhys estate in the Rhondda, and an even larger proportion of its recidivists, had no employment. Although the employment situation in the Porth

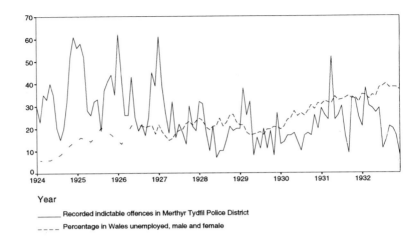

Year

_____ Recorded indictable offences in Merthyr Tydfil Police District

_ _ _ _ Percentage in Wales unemployed, male and female

Graph 2.5: Crime and unemployment, 1924–1932

district was bad, these figures were worse. Police chiefs and Labour politicians, influenced by such evidence and the rising crime rate during the late 1970s and early 1980s, concluded that there was 'a direct correlation' between unemployment and delinquency.

Yet a recent Home Office report on crime since the last war states that 'the fluctuations in the total number of unemployed persons appear to be independent of fluctuations in the number of offences'. Graph 2.4 offers some support for this, though there were periods, especially in recent times, when the rates ran close together. At a local level, it is difficult to make precise connections. H. Mannheim found, in his account of crime between the wars, that in certain towns there was no apparent link between crime and unemployment. Even at a place like Merthyr Tydfil, the monthly totals of recorded crime between 1924 and 1932 did not run exactly parallel with the Welsh monthly unemployment figures, as graph 2.5 illustrates. It is a complex matter; we are constantly reminded by economic historians that most offenders were either in work or at school, and it is difficult to isolate the effects of unemployment from other variables.

The Second World War ended unemployment, and the growing affluence of the post-war years undermined old certainties. 'The pre-war theory that poverty and unemployment were major crime factors, is no longer acceptable in these days of "over-full employment" when real poverty is practically unknown,' said the chief constable of Swansea in 1957. 'No thinking could have been more erroneous', agreed his Cardiff colleague nine years later, 'and what we are finding is the exact reverse – as prosperity increases so does crime.' As we have seen, this is a slight misreading of history, but the existence of a high crime rate in the midst of the comparative affluence of post-war generations forced a reworking of the theories of delinquency.

Three main notions emerged to explain the phenomenon. Firstly, it was suggested that the experience of the Second World War on the home front had 'lowered the standards of honesty' generally. This was, apparently, as true of middle-class businessmen as of working-class consumers, and of adults as well as of juveniles. Faced by shortages, high prices and rationing, 'a substantial proportion of the population' cheated with coupons, stole from their employers, used the black market and turned a blind eye to the thieving of scrap metals, lead, food, petrol and cigarettes. By the early 1950s most 'respectable people' were said to have returned to the 'older standards', but not all. Material improvement, claimed the chief contable of Glamorgan, has 'produced in the community a class, fortunately in the minority', which expected 'luxuries' and turned to crime when they could not secure them.

The war conditions were widely blamed for creating a young criminal generation. The rising figures of juvenile delinquency in the war years were attributed, amongst other things, to fathers serving abroad, mothers working outside the home, inadequate teaching, a decline in religious observance and education, poorly protected property, and greater economic and social freedom for young people. In addition, apprehension grew over the behaviour of infants raised during the war, or in the difficult post-war conditions. They were accused by their betters of 'instability', and of having an obsession with 'excitement and undeserved status and profit'.

However, the long-term rise in the crime rate changed perspectives, and after a while, instead of crime being 'blamed on the war', 'now many social reformers are finding that the source [of the alarming increase in crime] can be traced back to home influence'. This, the second theory of post-war crime, was a more sophisticated version of the nineteenth-century view that criminals were produced by criminal families. Studies of children in the juvenile courts of South Wales in the 1950s and 1960s highlighted the fact that delinquency began at a very young age, and that many of those who appeared in court were from 'unhappy', 'deprived' and 'broken homes'. Some indeed had been placed in care by welfare officers. The chief constable of Merthyr Tydfil estimated that 'a very high proportion' of his juvenile delinquents came from 'broken homes', and the superintendent of the Cardiff remand home proffered the figure of 74 per cent. According to the superintendent, and child welfare and probation officers, a disturbed home background almost invariably produced antisocial and criminal behaviour.

There was, in the pyschological studies of the family, some appreciation of the difficulties experienced by the working class, especially over housing accommodation in the inner-city areas or in the bleak new council estates. At Westminster, Labour Party reformers discussed these connections during the mid-1960s. Alarmed by the survival of pockets of poverty and crime in the welfare state, they sought to improve such areas by giving them priority status and, at the same time, by expanding professional services for families in need of assistance.

Yet not everyone shared their enthusiasm. Many people placed the blame for 'inadequate homes' and 'delinquent offspring' firmly on the shoulders of parents. There was criticism in South Wales chapel, media and police circles of parents who worked all day, were tired or absent from home at night, and allowed their children to miss school and waste their time and money on 'effortless entertainment'. Degwel Thomas in the 1960s led a moral campaign against female neglect of the home, and, with Edmund Davies, recorder of Cardiff, warned of the long-term consequences of bingo and other modern forms of popular culture ousting the place of religious education. They were enthusiastic supporters of the legislation which penalized 'uncaring parents', through their pockets, for the sins of 'socially maladjusted' children who were taken into care or convicted in the courts.

The rise in the crime rate over the last few decades has

stimulated research into the early roots of criminality and the importance of upbringing. Criminologists and social geographers have extended the pioneering work of West, Mays and Downes, and even suggested that one can predict, with reasonable accuracy, the chances of delinquency in the very young. Studies of Cardiff in the 1970s and 1980s revealed, for instance, that there were distinct social and geographical patterns of juvenile crime in the city, which in turn were related to income, housing conditions, family size, parenting, educational aspirations and achievement. According to this work, the classic Cardiff delinquent grew up in a large (skilled and semi-skilled) working-class family in places like Splott and Llanishen, and, with limited opportunities and low aspirations, soon indulged in antisocial behaviour and crime, thus following the example of at least one relative.

The same phenomenon can be seen in Penlan in Swansea and on the Penrhys estate in the Rhondda. Groups of families, often with a history of welfare problems and low achievement, have produced a cohort of unsupervised and restless children, given to drink and rowdyism, drugs and glue-sniffing, vandalism and driving other people's motor vehicles. Many of them, in Penrhys rather than Penlan, were brought up in one-parent families, which has attracted a degree of moral censure and strengthened Charles Murray's brutal image of an irresponsible 'underclass'. As we saw in the last chapter, there were endless complaints to the police about the children on these estates, and currently few job prospects for them. Penrhys, which has an exceptional rate of juvenile crime, exploded into violent anger in 1984–5, and was deemed worthy of Priority Estates status, a national experiment in 'estates renewal'.

Whilst some analysts have found the roots of delinquency here, in the strains and culture of family life, especially amongst the 'underclass', others believed that the explanation for the relentless surge in the crime rate was more simple. Crime was largely a matter of temptation and opportunity; many delinquents, especially of the casual sort, had neither poor family backgrounds nor strong motivations. The third major explanation of the post-war crime wave thus concentrated on the assistance which modern society gives the delinquent. 'Examination of the methods whereby a large proportion of crimes are committed show quite clearly that opportunity is the triggering mechanism,' declared one

South Wales report in 1968. 'This form of opportunity with little or no risk of detection is providing a kind of temptation almost irresistible to increasing sections of the population.'

The post-war temptations were indeed without precedent. The chief constable of Cardiff in the 1950s saw a 'direct relation' between, for example, the sudden increase in registered motor vehicles, the offence of taking and driving away the same, and other autocrime. Others set the astonishing rise in break-ins within the context of the growth of business and industrial parks, and the increasing value of personal possessions and domestic dwellings. In Merthyr Tydfil, where no one seemed immune from the threat of theft and break-ins after the war, the chief constable wanted them all to take a greater interest in crime prevention. 'It is apparent', he wrote in 1959, 'that many property owners depend upon insurance rather than their own protective efforts.'

The police message was simple: if more wealth, more portable property and more private transport were characteristics of modern affluent society, new standards of care and protection were essential to make life difficult for the criminal. In the 1950s and 1960s the public was warned continuously of the dangers of leaving unlocked bicycles and vehicles in the streets, and of sleeping or going on holiday when their homes were insecure. Businessmen were criticized for the same careless attitudes, and for tempting people with unguarded automatic machines and unsupervised shop displays and counters. It was already apparent in the 1960s that the large self-service shops had the highest rate of thefts.

In recent years the easy access to goods, from cars and videos to drugs and alcohol, has undoubtedly increased the temptation to commit an offence. In 1984, for example, the yearly increase of 57 per cent in the numbers of people arrested for the misuse of drugs owed much, we are told, to 'the greater availability of drugs'. International business, computerization and new commercial developments have further extended criminal opportunities. In South Wales there have also been problems with the security of the new city-centre shopping complexes, dockland marinas and out-of-town enterprise parks, especially when linked to fast exit roads and motorways.

The difficulties of committing crime, which apparently deterred a proportion of nineteenth-century offenders, no longer apply, and such is the scale of theft, break-ins and other offences that detection today is unlikely. Many offenders thus have the opportunity of good rewards, 'virtual immunity' from arrest, and, according to one line of argument, 'consideration and clemency' from the courts rather than punishment. In these circumstances, the police have relied increasingly since the 1960s on encouraging crime prevention amongst likely victims, on working with local authorities to design out crime from streets, businesses and houses, and on setting up camera surveillance where possible. On the success of these schemes rest many hopes for the future.

The timing and seasonality of crime

The seasonality and timing of crimes have changed little since 1900. Most occurred in the winter and spring months, during the evening and early morning, and at weekends. This was true of Glamorgan before the First World War, Merthyr Tydfil in the 1920s and 1930s, Cardiff during the Second World War, Swansea in the 1960s, and South Wales subsequently.

The seasonality of the Merthyr crimes in graph 2.5 is shown in table 2.6:

Table 2·6: Seasonality of Merthyr crimes: Merthyr Tydfil Crime Register, 1924–1932

Jan.	324	May	239	Sept.	161
Feb.	311	June	200	Oct.	239
March	255	July	166	Nov.	265
April	245	Aug.	153	Dec.	254
				Month not given	6

Nine out of ten of these recorded indictable offences were against property, and their occurrence illustrates why winter policing, day and night, was given such a priority by chief constables in the early twentieth century.

By the end of our period the basic pattern was similar, though not quite as seasonally distinct. A sample of 472,251 serious crimes committed in South Wales against the person and against property between 1981 and 1989 indicates that they were not reported in great numbers over the Christmas period. These recorded offences were at their height during the month of March, and in the spring and early winter months, whilst June–September was, as at Merthyr in the inter-war years, comparatively quiet (see table 2.7).

Table 2·7: Seasonality of recorded indictable offences, South Wales, 1981–1989

Percentage monthly break-down of 472,251 recorded indictable offences for the years 1981, 1983, 1985, 1987 and 1989

Jan.	8·17	May	8·76	Sept.	7·83
Feb.	8·13	June	8·11	Oct.	8·55
March	9·12	July	7·84	Nov.	8·68
April	8·51	Aug.	8·17	Dec.	8·14

The latest analysis of crime calls from the public has a similar monthly sequence, with Friday, Saturday and Sunday being the days when most 'immediate response incidents' were reported. As a footnote, the number of non-crime incidents recorded on IRIS, the Information, Resource and Information System, in South Wales during the 1980s was spread more evenly across the year.

Each community, and each crime, has its own seasonal pattern of recorded activity. For example, individual council estates to the north and east of Swansea had different monthly graphs in the mid-1980s for burglaries, thefts and autocrime. Burglaries and thefts peaked in some of these localities in high summer. In general, however, over the century the darkest months have tended to be the most criminal. Thus, although 18,086 reports of stolen vehicles received by the Glamorgan police during 1964–7 varied comparatively little from month to month, the busiest period was October–December (28 per cent) with March–April close behind. The majority of these reports, as of thefts from vehicles, were made to the police late at night, or more commonly, at breakfast time.

Shoplifting, like several other offences, has generally peaked in the run-up to Christmas, whilst the threat of burglaries was usually greatest at this time, or in the months immediately afterwards. Reported assaults, domestic incidents, and sometimes public disorder and sexual offences, reached a height in the four hottest months, notably during the hours 8 p.m.–4 a.m. Except in the early decades of the century, when there were notable exceptions, arrests for drunkenness usually followed a similar monthly pattern, and most took place on Friday and Saturday nights, typically between 6 p.m. and midnight.

The location of crime: the urban environment

The location of crime and criminals in South Wales reflected changes in the economy and society, though basic patterns have remained. In the early years of the century, the largest towns had the highest crime rate, and the centres of places like Cardiff, Swansea and Merthyr were regarded as especially criminal and dangerous. Here occurred many of the recorded instances of robberies, assaults, shoplifting, prostitution offences, and drunkenness and disorderly behaviour, though a large number of these crimes were actually committed by people who lived outside the vicinity. Table 2.8 is an example illustrating some of this, but unfortunately the population figures are lacking:

In each of the largest towns, especially those which were seaports, there were designated 'crime spots' or 'criminal areas' where many 'habitual offenders' lived, and where the recorded incidence of assaults and robberies, theft, clashes with the police, and even rioting was high. Swansea had the Strand and its environs, and Cardiff had Butetown. In Cardiff in 1914 there were 149 people under police supervision, 93 thieves and receivers at large, 413 prostitutes proceeded against, and 14 'houses of bad character', and most of these people and places were in Butetown, or nearby in Saltmead, Riverside and Temperance Town.

These 'plague spots' were the target of repeated moral and police campaigns in the early twentieth century, and by the 1930s Butetown was losing some of its reputation for violence, robberies and racial conflict. The chief constable declared in 1931 that 'the majority of the inhabitants of Butetown are respectable people and law-abiding citizens'. Even so, then, and again twenty-five years later, serious attempts were made to change the character of this inner-city area and to scatter its 'criminal population'. Some were moved to the new estates on the edges of the city.

Urban developments in South Wales had a marked impact on where offences were committed, and where criminals resided. Thus the growth, at the beginning of our period, of respectable suburbs like Roath and Whitchurch north of Cardiff and Sketty

Table 2·8: Swansea Divisional Returns 1917: persons proceeded against

	TOWN	NORTHERN	EASTERN	WESTERN	DOCKS
	Central portion of the Borough	Landore, Morriston, Brynhyfryd, Treboeth, Manselton, Cwmbwrla, Plasmarl, Llansamlet	St Thomas, Foxhole, Port Tennant, Bonymaen, Pentrechwyth	Uplands, Townhill, Gibbet Hill, Mount Pleasant, Rhyddings, St Helen's, Sketty, Brynmill, Cockett	
Indictable offences	213	87	70	10	–
Assaults on police	24	–	–	–	–
Common assaults	48	21	4	2	–
Drunkenness	226	13	13	5	–
Prostitution and vagrancy	38	12	–	3	–
Other offences	1642	457	263	106	–
Local acts and by-laws	90	29	17	42	–
TOTAL	2281	619	367	168	–
Robberies					
Burglary, housebreaking and warehouse breaking	56	24	13	12	5
Larceny	305	123	52	48	82
TOTAL	361	147	65	60	87

west of Swansea, was accompanied by many complaints of burglaries and thefts, whilst the building of large council estates between the wars also brought mixed blessings in terms of delinquency. Some, like the estates at Ely and Townhill, which were rather anonymous and lacking in facilities, had a troubled existence from the start. The police had, at first, neither the resources nor the communications to deal adequately with such large estates, and particularly with the newly housed 'problem families'. Commenting on the council estates above Mount Pleasant in Swansea in the mid-1930s, the chief constable claimed that 'if allowance is made for the transference through slum clearance to new Housing Estates, little if any change has occurred in the location of areas where the delinquents resided'.

Examinations of juvenile crime provide further information on the changing geography of urban delinquency. An analysis of 1,373 juvenile offenders charged with indictable offences in Swansea between 1934 and 1940 reveals that already a fifth were living in the new estates on the hill above Swansea. Only a tenth were said to be from 'the centre of town, including the Strand', though many more committed offences there. In Cardiff the official statistics allow us to analyse 8,848 juvenile offences between 1950 and 1965, and these show that, as in Swansea, most were committed in or very close to the city centre (see table 2.9).

Table 2·9: Areas of Cardiff where juvenile indictable offences were committed, 1950–1965

City centre	25·7 per cent	Llandaff	7·9 per cent
Docks	5·4	Rumney	5·8
Canton	10·2	Roath	10·7
Grangetown	5·7	Cathays	9·1
Moors	6·1	Ely	13·4

Each area had its own pattern; thus shop break-ins and shoplifting were very common in the city centre, whilst house break-ins, and thefts from meters and of bicycles were a feature of Ely.

Ten years later, research by social geographers demonstrated firstly, that a large proportion of juvenile offences in Cardiff still took place in the city centre and in Saltmead and Cathays Park, and secondly, that most of the errant youngsters lived in the rough dockside areas of Splott and Grangetown, the declining transitional zone of Riverside, the Llandaff–Gabalfa–Birchgrove area, and Llanishen. In the last two districts many of the convicted youngsters were from council estates. The irony of this was not lost on contemporaries; these estates had been conceived with the intention of improving the quality of life and reducing delinquency, whereas the result was almost a 'built-in crime environment'.

The Cardiff and Merthyr crime registers and charge books for the 1920s to 1950s provide us with more detailed information on the geography of certain types of urban crime. In central Merthyr in the middle of the century, shoplifting and robberies were common in High Street and Castle Street, coal-stealing occurred at the railway sidings and goods yards, and break-ins affected stores, schools, clubs and houses in places like The Grove, Saxon Street and Meyrick Villas. Out in Dowlais, larceny from house meters and break-ins were already a major problem on certain avenues in the new Galon Uchaf housing estate, whilst in the Merthyr Vale district, coal-stealing was endemic at the many collieries and washeries.

In Cardiff during the 1950s Queen Street was the shoplifting centre, St Mary Street was the place for drunk and disorderly behaviour, and bicycle thefts, autocrime and motoring offences were common in Cowbridge, Cathedral and Newport Roads. More criminals arrested in Cardiff's Central police district in the 1950s were outsiders than was the case at Merthyr. One can estimate from a small sample of 250 defendants in the Cardiff Central charge books for 1952–3 that at least a quarter had travelled more than one and a half miles, from Penarth, Porthcawl, Llantrisant, Pontypridd, Newport and other towns, to commit their crime. Many of the others in the charge books had journeyed from the perimeter of the city, from Ely, Llandaff, Roath and other places.

Elsewhere in the capital it was a different story. In the docks division, for example, most of the detected crimes were committed by seamen, dockers, labourers, prostitutes, the unemployed and others who resided, often together, in Bute Street, Loundon Square, Portmanmoor Street and other local thoroughfares, or on ships. According to the divisional charge books for 1951–2, these people committed offences like theft, receiving, smuggling, robbery, assault, loitering with intent, and drunkenness and disorderly conduct, and a large number of the arrests took place in Bute Street.

Other patterns can be seen in the maps of Swansea, drawn by David Herbert from more recent information on crime. They show that in 1975 non-domestic violence in Swansea occurred in the city centre, close to pubs, restaurants and places of entertainment. Burglaries and thefts by contrast were spread more thinly, though there was a vulnerable zone around the edge of the commercial centre, and smaller clusters in council-house estates. Within these general patterns, there were other, more detailed ones, related to the vulnerability of badly sited and poorly protected property. Although the homes of the offenders were not plotted by David Herbert, newspaper and police reports indicate that many of them were from the large estates on the northern outskirts of the city.

The Crime Concern Trust, in a document prepared for the Swansea City Council in January 1994, documented the police sector differences in the recorded incidence of four major types of offences in Swansea at the end of our period. Thus Castle ward in the city centre had high figures of violence, burglary, theft of motor vehicles and criminal damage, whilst the Townhill and Mayhill sector had moderate ones, and in the Pennard and Gower sector they were enviably low. What is not made clear in the document is how, even within these sectors, the experience of

Table 2·10: Recorded indictable offences per 1,000 of the population: thirteen police beats in Swansea, 1985

Fforestfach	128
Mumbles	86
Townhill	72
Blaenymaes	69
Penlan	67
Sketty	66
Gendros	44
Mayhill	40
Derwen Fawr	39
Manselton	38
West Cross	23
Newton	16
Killay	14

crime in the urban environment varies enormously from neighbourhood to neighbourhood. In the most affected city localities,
multi-victimization is depressingly common.

Table 2.10 shows the rates of recorded indictable crime on
thirteen police beats in Swansea during 1985 which illustrate this
variation. Fforestfach is a city community of private and council
houses, superstores, small industries and some dereliction and
deprivation, whilst Killay is a more prosperous western suburb
with a small shopping centre and large private housing estates.
Mumbles and Newton are neighbouring localities in the same
police sector, as are Townhill and Mayhill.

The location of crime: other aspects

Although places like Swansea, Cardiff and Merthyr have always
had higher rates of offences than elsewhere in South Wales, there
have also been significant differences across industrial and rural
districts. Unfortunately, the evidence which has survived from the
first decades of the century does not allow us to make very
detailed comparisons between communities. Yet we can glean
something from the court proceedings and station journals, and
from the comments in official files and newspaper columns.

In the years before the First World War, the highest number of
court cases per head of population in Glamorgan was in the police
divisions of Pontypridd and Merthyr, and the lowest was in the
rural communities in the large Bridgend and Neath divisions. This
was widely interpreted as a true reflection of the differences
in delinquency between these areas. The expansion of the coal
industry at this time, and the opening of new railway lines, was
often accompanied by unacceptable levels of crime and disorder.
Complaints of violence, assaults on policemen, coal-stealing and
other thefts by 'undesirables' (newcomers) in places like Hopkinstown, Penygraig, Treorchy, Abercynon and Mountain Ash
appeared regularly in the reports of the standing joint police
committee. From the station journal for Hopkinstown of 1911–12
we learn that proceedings were begun over a twelve-month period
against one in fifty-nine of its population. The journal reads like an
account of a frontier settlement, with its long list of drunkards,
prostitutes, gamblers, thieving children, uncontrolled dogs, and
people swearing, fighting and urinating in the street. Most of them

were Welsh, intermixed with a small number of English travellers, Irish navvies, and men with no identity fleeing from the obligations of family life. Elsewhere, too, at Caerau near Maesteg, Sandfields (Aberavon) and Tonyrefail, for example, economic growth seems to have attracted similar types and stimulated crime.

During the 1930s and 1940s economic progress was more uneven. Aided by local and central government schemes, the development of the chemical and steel industries, and the new interest in shopping and holiday centres, places such as Aberavon, Bridgend and Treforest expanded rapidly. Building sites, trading estates and caravan parks proved especially attractive to criminals, and the growth of traffic and better roads made life easier for them. The busiest policemen were officers like PC 375 Williams and PC 95 Thomas of the Aberavon area, who daily patrolled the new housing and commercial developments and asked hoteliers, café proprietors, and bus-drivers about people strange to the area and visitors passing through. Much of their time was spent mediating in domestic and neighbour conflicts, checking the authenticity of reports of meter thefts and stolen bicycles, and listening to stories of goods lost from new properties, shops and clubs. According to their annual returns in the middle of the century, policemen in Sandfields (Aberavon) were dealing with about three times the level of crimes per head of population compared with their colleagues in the villages of the Vale of Glamorgan.

By 1945–7 the crime rate in Glamorgan was highest in the subdivisions of Bridgend, Barry Dock and Port Talbot, whilst Aberdare, Tonpentre and Porth, all victims of the great depression, had dropped well down the list, along with predominantly rural subdivisions like Gowerton. This can be seen in table 2.11, and the subdivisional pattern which it describes was to outlast the amalgamation of 1969.

In the 1970s and 1980s the South Wales police sometimes gave details of the types of crime reported in the subdivisions. City centres, and places like Canton and Morriston, had high rates of shoplifting, autocrime, violent incidents and almost all other offences, whilst the police subdivisions of Penarth, Maesteg and Gorseinon had low rates across the board. Other districts were notorious for one or two types of crime. An analysis of crime and incidents for 1978 reveals that the subdivisions of Caerphilly and Ely had high rates of break-ins, whilst the police in Bargoed were

Table 2·11: Crime rate per 100,000 of the population, using the average number of crimes committed in Glamorgan police subdivisions, 1945–1947

Aberdare	561	Pontypridd	855	Bridgend	1334
Mountain Ash	618	Porth	540	Maesteg	703
Abercynon	563	Llantrisant	677	Ogmore Vale	763
		Whitchurch	781		
Port Talbot	1063	Barry Dock	1425	Ystrad Mynach	877
Cwmavon	793	Penarth	762	Bargoed	933
Porthcawl	1104	Cowbridge	1551	Caerphilly	1059
Tonpentre	360	Gowerton	532	Neath	940
Tonypandy	662	Gorseinon	561	Skewen	345
Treherbert	499	Pontardawe	465	Glynneath	861
Ferndale	698				

busy with assaults, domestic disputes and petty vandalism. This area association with certain crimes has continued. Thus the Vale of Glamorgan retains its unenviable reputation for drunken and violent holiday-makers, Abercynon has regained its early twentieth-century notoriety for coal-stealing, Bridgend and Tonpentre have become major centres for autocrime, and Barry was nominated in 1992 as 'the smash and grab capital of Britain'.

Even within these police subdivisions there were wide differences in the experience of crime. The figures for 1986 in table 2.12, of recorded offences per 1,000 of the population in police sections, can be used to identify those communities with the highest and lowest risk factors, though it must be remembered that the small size of the resident population in Cardiff and Swansea city centres makes it an inappropriate comparator.

This, and other evidence, shows that the areas which suffered the most reported crimes and the most reported incidents included the city centres, certain council estates, declining areas of rented accommodation and the vicinities of docks and industrial/commercial premises. Social geographers tell us that the nature of the location and the character of the housing are more important determinants of vulnerability than social class. The most fortunate localities were usually the wealthier owner-occupier town suburbs, rural villages, and a number of small industrial communities.

Table 2·12: Selected high- and low-risk police sections in 1986

High risk	Rate per 1000	Low risk	Rate per 1000
Cathays Park	23590	Blaengarw	1
Swansea city centre	2881	Tondu	10
Merthyr central	975	Dunvant	11
Pontypridd	699	Cilybebyll	11
Roath	403	Bryncethin	12
Docks (Cardiff)	378	St Athan	15
Llansamlet	374	Killay	16
Twynyrodyn	330	Coychurch	16
Pontcanna	290	Bryncoch	17
Splott	282	Pennard	17
Riverside	272	Troedyrhiw	19
Brackla-Bridgend	261	Nantymoel	19
Roath Park (Cardiff)	242	Blaenrhondda	19
Penylan (Cardiff)	242	Loughor	20
Penrhys	238	Llanbradach	21
Morriston	234	Upper Killay	21
Llanrumney East	229	Penclawdd	21
Sandfields (Swansea)	220	Southerndown	23

Some of the second group had, so far as one can tell, low rates of crime throughout the century, but others have changed from being notorious for crime and unruly behaviour to being notable as 'havens of peace', as the population 'settled down', or 'the better class' took over. Such has been the history of, for instance, Miskin, which gradually lost its 'desperate' image and became a quiet terraced suburb of Mountain Ash, and Blaenrhondda. Blaenrhondda is one of those close-knit coal-mining communities which, early in the century, only the toughest policemen could face, but which has, in recent times, reported comparatively few crimes and other incidents.

Other industrial localities in decline displayed different tendencies. Violence, family tension, heavy drinking, disorder and petty thieving were in the 1980s characteristic features of a number of South Wales mining communities suffering long-term economic decay. Such can be found in the Cynon Valley, with its high unemployment, and, to a lesser extent, in the Swansea Valley. In 1987 places like Penrhiwceiber in the Cynon Valley gained national notoriety for coal-stealing, which was as daring, extensive and open as that of the 1920s, and, as the author is writing this book, the people of Abercynon are protesting loudly about the violence and vandalism in the area.

Everywhere, including industrial South Wales, the level of delinquency in the twentieth century owed something to the social constitution of an area. Where, for instance, there was an established, close and elderly community, recorded crime was usually low. This was true of most rural villages; these have traditionally required the fewest police and reported the smallest amount of crime. As we saw in the last chapter, many days passed in the St Nicholas police district in the 1920s without a crime report, whilst in the largely rural Sully station, with a population of a thousand, there were only twenty-seven recorded indictable offences during 1940–2, in marked contrast to the Barry Dock section only a few miles to the west.

The same comparative tranquillity was apparent on the Reynoldston and Peterston-super-Ely police beats both before and after the Second World War. In Reynoldston the rural population posed few problems for the local police, who filled part of every week rounding up stray animals, looking for dog-owners, and catching farm labourers and domestic servants cycling home without lights. The classic daily summary in the rural station journals which have survived since the 1920s is the entry 'all quiet and peaceful', and in their letters to the newspapers the residents of these places boasted, incorrectly, that the majority of their offences were committed by gypsies, tramps, visitors and other outsiders.

Each community deserves to be studied in its own right, for only in this way can we understand the complexities of crime. Council estates provide a good example. Sociologists and social geographers have suggested that, in recent times, the settlements which have experienced perhaps the greatest rise in crime have been the 'problem council estates' with poor facilities, significant deprivation, a continuous turnover of tenants, a young age profile and family difficulties. They are not criminal areas in a full sense, as only a small proportion of the residents are summoned and arrested each year, but the influence of the latter, and their willingness to commit offences close to home, have made such estates notorious.

The classic example in South Wales is Penrhys, the housing

estate set high on a Rhondda mountainside. It was, like the Gurnos estate at Merthyr Tydfil, part of the optimistic socialist planning of the 1960s, but difficulties on the site were soon apparent, and the collapse of heavy industry and mass manufacturers has left its inhabitants terribly exposed. With its thousand dwellings, its high ratio of young, new and one-parent families, and its exceptional levels of unemployment, it has become a byword for a deprived, delinquent and violent community. It has by far the highest crime rate in that part of the Rhondda, but close inspection of the custody records for 1988 confirms that many of those arrested on the estate lived on five streets, often in houses close to one another, and sometimes came from the same family. Their offences, which were typically theft, violence, taking cars, burglary, drunk and disorderly behaviour, and drink-driving, took place equally around the estate and in nearby centres like Llwynypia, Tonypandy, Ystrad, Pentre, Church Village, Treherbert and Williamstown.

In other parts of the Penrhys estate there were few known offenders, and much lower levels of vandalism, autocrime and violence. During the mid-1980s the people in these streets managed, with outside assistance, to limit the criminal activities of the rest. On the huge Ely, Llanrumney and St Mellons estates near Cardiff, the Lansbury Park estate in Caerphilly, the Penlan estate in Swansea, and the Gurnos estate at Merthyr Tydfil, there were similar street differences in delinquency, and ones not due solely, or even mainly, to selective policing and unbalanced reporting.

Criminals

Superficially at least, the character of the criminals has changed little during the century. Most convicted offenders are still male, young and working-class. Even when modern self-report and other surveys are added to the official statistics, these broad characteristics remain. There can be little doubt about the gender ratio. In the early years of the century three-quarters of those charged with crimes, and seven-tenths of the inmates of Cardiff and Swansea gaols were male. The court records exaggerate the differences. About 80 per cent of those apprehended and summoned for indictable crimes in South Wales at this time and an even greater proportion of people proceeded against for non-

Table 2·13: Comparison of numbers of males and females apprehended and summonsed, Swansea 1912 and Cardiff 1913

| | Swansea 1912 | | | | Cardiff 1913 | | | |
| | Apprehensions | | Summons | | Apprehs | | Summons | |
	m	f	m	f	m	f	m	f
Indictable offences	292	47	73	52	426	112	4	0
Non-indict. offences	804	249	1504	285	1622	801	2195	446

indictable offences were male. Thus in 1911–12 Constable Welsby of Hopkinstown gave the names of only fourteen females in his list of 108 people who appeared before the Pontypridd and Porth courts for drunkenness and disorderly conduct and other minor crimes. They were, on average, thirteen years older than the males (whose average age was thirty-two years), and two of them, Minnie McGuire and Maria Ridley, were of no fixed abode.

The most urbanized districts in these early decades had the highest rates of female cases. The returns shown in table 2.13, of people apprehended and dealt with by summons in Swansea and Cardiff, illustrate the point.

In both towns women were also summoned before the courts in considerable numbers, though precise details are not always given. The typical female offences in the indictable list were larceny, larceny by a servant, larceny from the person and attempted suicide, and in the non-indictable list, prostitution offences, drunkenness, assaults, indecent exposure, brothel-keeping and breaches of the Education Acts. Constable Hodge in Cardiff every day confronted people like Mabel Wilkinson of Humphrey Street, a riotous prostitute, Sarah Anderson of Canal Parade, with her coloured boyfriend and colourful language, and Martha Williams of Penylan Hill, a notoriously heavy drinker.

During the inter-war years the proportion of females appearing before the courts fell significantly. By 1936 only 5 per cent of those proceeded against for indictable and non-indictable offences in the county of Glamorgan were female. In Cardiff the proportion was twice that figure, which strengthened the popular belief that only non-Welsh girls of dubious morality had criminal tendencies. The crimes which then brought them before the higher courts were simple larceny, shoplifting, obtaining money by false pretences and receiving, a pattern which has remained to the present day, and, at the lower courts, assaults, and breaches of the revenue laws, Shop Acts and Highways Acts.

Since the Second World War the rate of known female crime has increased, and, over the last twenty-five years, it has matched, and sometimes outpaced, the growth of male crime. In 1989 13 per cent of those proceeded against for serious offences, and 15 per cent of those for other offences, including motoring, were female. Studies of female delinquency have confirmed that these official statistics reflect a real gender difference in criminal activity, though it is not one which is obvious in, for example, shoplifting in 1989. There is no agreement over why women generally commit fewer crimes, except a firm rejection of simple biological explanations and a suspicion that gender attitudes towards law-breaking were not quite as divergent as some contemporaries claimed. As time passes, the emphasis on the special domestic and work situations of females also loses its validity. People do, it seems, still treat and report female crime rather differently from male, but not sufficiently to account for the differential in the statistics.

Table 2·14: Persons charged with indictable offences, Merthyr Tydfil, 1924

Age groups	Males	Females	Age group as percentage of total
0–16 years	111	41	35·5
17–20	54	15	16·1
21–24	24	11	8·2
25–30	46	12	13·6
31–40	47	20	15·7
41–50	21	8	6·8
51+	14	4	4·2
Total	317	111	100

Comparisons over time of the ages of these offenders are doubly difficult because of the raising of the age of criminal responsibility and changes in cautioning policy. There are also the intrinsic problems of the records. Although the information on criminals in registers and charge books is useful, it is not always accurate, and, of course, many offenders do not appear in them. Even so, the age profile in table 2.14 is worth our attention. It was gleaned from the Merthyr crime register for 1924, and is typical of the inter-war period. Each category had its own crime profile. Thus, for example, Merthyr's females were mostly charged with stealing coal from tips, stocks and waggons, whilst the youngest age group of males was accused of breaking into stores, offices and cafés, of stealing coal, and, to a lesser extent, of shoplifting and sacrilege.

Table 2·15: Ages of Cardiff defendants, 1989

Years of age in 1989	*10–13*		*14–16*		*17–20*		*21+*	
	m	*f*	*m*	*f*	*m*	*f*	*m*	*f*
For serious offences	197	8	1597	112	5109	619	10182	1773
For other offences	119	2	1153	37	8047	517	34458	7010

At the courts the age structure of defendants was rather different. In Cardiff and Swansea, just prior to the First World War, a third of those tried for indictable offences were under

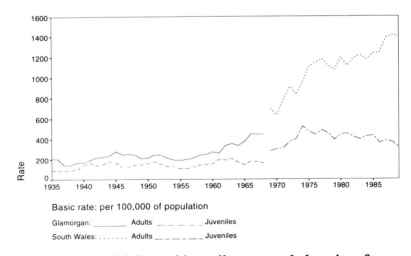

Basic rate: per 100,000 of population

Glamorgan: _____ Adults _ _ _ _ _ Juveniles

South Wales: . . . . Adults _ _ _ _ _ _ Juveniles

Graph 2.6: Adults and juveniles proceeded against for indictable offences in Glamorgan, 1935–1968, and proceeded against and cautioned for indictable offences in South Wales, 1969–1989

Table 2·16: Samples of the rate of juvenile indictable crime: Glamorgan 1947–1949 and Cardiff 1963

Juveniles proceeded against for indictable offences in Glamorgan, 1947–1949

Age	Males	Females
8–10	402	17
10–12	616	48
12–14	745	49
14–16	737	46
16–17	280	23
Total	2780	183

Juveniles charged with indictable offences in Cardiff, 1963

Age	Males	Females
8	17	1
9	22	2
10	41	3
11	54	6
12	61	10
13	83	6
14	127	18
15	94	13
16	99	11
Total	598	70

twenty years of age, and between 40 and 50 per cent were in their twenties and thirties. The average age of the Cardiff defendants at this time was twenty-seven years. Those who were proceeded against for non-indictable crimes were older, at least four-fifths being between twenty-one and fifty years of age. Imprisonment was also reserved largely for the over 21-year-olds. As a comparison, at the end of our period the ages of those proceeded against are shown in table 2.15.

As we have seen earlier in this chapter, juvenile crime has often been a matter of concern during this century. It is impossible to discover the true extent of the problem. The researches of D. J. West and others have indicated that a quarter or a half of modern urban males commit a crime during their teens. Of course, proceedings are begun against a much lower proportion. The official statistics that have survived for Glamorgan and South Wales are set out in graph 2.6.

It was estimated in Glamorgan during the period from 1938 to 1968, that between a quarter and a half of detected indictable offences were carried out by juveniles, with the highest figures being usually in the industrial police divisions. As in Swansea, it seems that the proportion of offences in the county committed by juveniles was high during the early years of the Second World War, and again in the early 1960s. 'I regret to report', said the chief constable of Merthyr Tydfil in 1963, noticing a similar trend in his borough, 'that many of the offences are being committed by youths who have not previously come into conflict with the police.' Youngsters were then responsible for the majority of detected break-ins and sex crimes, and for many of the larcenies and much criminal damage, but for only a minority of serious assaults, motoring offences and white-collar crimes.

The evidence, from the mid-century and later, suggests that fourteen to fifteen years old was the peak age for criminal activity, especially for males. The samples in table 2.16 were typical.

In 1971, of 26,793 people reported or arrested for such crimes in South Wales, 16.4 per cent were aged 10–13 years, 26.2 per cent were 14–16, 22.6 per cent were 17–20, and 34.8 per cent were 21 and over. From all of this, it seems that people were, by their very late teens, committing fewer indictable offences, a trend which becomes more pronounced after they reach their early twenties. David Farrington tells us that a typical criminal career lasts only six years. As people mature they often give up criminal activity and other forms of antisocial behaviour, and this is particularly obvious in the case of males.

Since the early 1970s considerable efforts have been made to keep the youngest offenders away from the courts, and the number and proportion of juveniles proceeded against and officially cautioned has declined. However, the rate of court cases involving 17–21-year-olds has matched that of adults. In 1989 four-tenths of those who appeared in court charged with indictable crimes were still aged twenty years or younger, and many of the rest were in their early twenties. A small number of people in their thirties and forties make a late entry into serious crime, and these tend to be white-collar criminals, shoplifters, dangerous drivers and sex offenders.

Crime, therefore, has been throughout the century a young person's activity. Many people, male and female, seem to have committed their first crime about the age of eight to ten years, and then graduated from petty offences like stealing sweets to more substantial thefts and break-ins. Since the 1930s juvenile break-ins and the violent behaviour of young males have been of considerable concern to society, especially when these teenagers operated in groups. Teenage gangs have always been a feature of town-centre life, and also developed on the large council estates which were built in the inter-war years. In Swansea there were alarming reports in the 1960s of 'small gangs of juveniles breaking and entering' houses in the Blaenymaes, Winch Wen, Treboeth, Townhill and Penlan areas 'where they resided'.

There has been some debate about the nature and career of those juveniles who became persistent recidivists. Many of them reacted badly to their first conviction because they had neither the family background nor the economic security to give them a different perspective on life. In their teens and early twenties they often indulged in heavy drinking, had violent relationships, and committed a wide range of crimes. Only a minority, we are told, followed a particular criminal activity, at least in their early years. One of these was 32-year-old thief, Samuel Wrigley of Cardiff, who left the Cardiff quarter sessions in June 1922 with this record:

Stealing from the person	– 1 day's gaol, and 6 strokes of birch. Sept. 1897.
Beyond parents' control	– industrial school until 16 years of age. April 1899.
Playing pitch and toss	– fined. April 1905.
Desertion: court-martial	– 21 days' gaol. Sept. 1906.
Stealing lead	– 1 month's gaol. April 1907.
Desertion: court-martial	– 6 months' gaol, and discharged. from the forces. May 1907.
Stealing lead	– 12 months' gaol. March 1908.
Stealing brass bearings	– 9 months' gaol. July 1910.
Break-in, counting-house	– 3 years' penal servitude. June 1911.
Break-in, counting-house	– 3 years' penal servitude. Oct. 1915.
Stealing portmanteaux etc.	– 3 years' penal servitude. Jan. 1920.
Stealing portmanteaux etc.	– 3 years' penal servitude, and 5 years' detention 'as habitual criminal'. June 1922.

Table 2·17: Inmates of Cardiff and Swansea gaols, 1903: birthplace, occupations and literacy

	Birthplace						
	Wales	*England*	*Ireland*	*Scot.*	*Foreign countries*	*Colonies & India*	*Others*
Males	56·7%	26·2	11·5	1·3	3·1	1·0	0·03
Females	67·5%	24·9	5·8	1·1	0·4	0·2	0·06

Occupations of male prisoners (percentage)

Labs	*Factory workers*	*Mechanics & skilled workers*	*Shopmen & clerks*	*Shopkeepers & dealers*	*Sailors, marines, soldiers*	*Others*
82·9	0·3	9·8	1·1	3·0	2·0	0·9

Occupations of the female prisoners (percentage)

Domestic servants	*Charwomen & needle-women*	*Shopkeepers & dealers*	*Prostitutes*	*No occup.*	*Others*
2·8	21·4	9·1	35·4	30·8	0·5

Literacy of prisoners (percentage)

	Neither read nor write	*Read, or read & write imperfectly*	*Read & write well*
Males	20·1	77·0	2·9
Females	28·3	70·7	1·0

Wrigley, although a tailor by trade, was regarded as a professional criminal. It is difficult to know how many people were like him. The chief constable of Cardiff said in 1900 that 'the class [of habitual criminals] is now practically extinct', and the number of 'main' card files on 'serious' and 'habitual' offenders since the late 1950s, which are still kept in collators' offices in South Wales, suggests that the total was never substantial. When Wrigley was starting his criminal career, the police estimated that there were over a hundred 'habitual criminals' at large in South Wales, and about the same number were being supervised by the police as convicts on licence. Of course, other well-known characters filled the gaols at this time. As we noted in the last chapter, six out of ten males and eight out of ten females in the Cardiff and Swansea prisons had criminal records, and 40 per cent of these male recidivists, and two-thirds of the female, had at least five previous convictions. Other information on the same prison inmates adds a little to our knowledge of people like Samuel Wrigley (table 2.17).

Another sample of 277 prisoners held at the Treharris police station in 1900–2 fills out this picture. A total of 83 per cent were Welsh, and most of the others were English, chiefly from the West Country. Half lived in the immediate vicinity, another quarter gave an address within three miles of Treharris, and almost one in ten had no fixed abode. Of the prisoners 57 per cent were single, 41 per cent were married, and the rest were widows or widowers. In this mining area, it was no surprise that 38 per cent of the sample were colliers, and 10.5 per cent were hauliers; 12.6 per cent gave their occupation as labourers, and another 5.4 per cent were schoolboys. Females comprised 13.8 per cent, and they were divided into wives, charwomen, servants and prostitutes.

The overwhelming impression from the above is that most of the people taken into custody in that period were from the working class, and often from its lower ranks. This continued to be so for the rest of the century. It was true, for example, of Merthyr during the inter-war period, of Cardiff and Swansea in the 1950s and 1960s, and of the Rhondda during the 1980s. In the charge books for the Cardiff Central district during the early 1950s the six main occupations – almost half the total – were labourer, unemployed, seaman, soldier, hawker/street trader and prostitute, whilst in the docks the charge list was overwhelmingly dominated by seamen, other ship and dock workers, labourers, bookmakers' runners, the unemployed and prostitutes. The dock criminals often lodged together in the poorest streets of Cardiff, or were of no fixed abode; many had criminal records, and three-quarters of them were aged twenty-five years and above.

In 1988 the custody records of Porth reveal a younger profile, but the economic and social status of the accused was again low. Of the sample of 389, 49 per cent were unemployed, 14 per cent were labourers and factory workers, 11 per cent were school-children, 7 per cent were female, and most of the remainder were roofers, scaffolders, decorators, casual labourers and people on youth training schemes. Six of every ten were under twenty-five years of age, and four out of ten were from Penrhys, Treherbert, Trebanog, Maerdy and Tylerstown. In each of these places the people taken into custody lived fairly close together in one or two streets.

The old adage, that the lower the class the higher the crime rate, is borne out by the official records, but it would be wrong to identify delinquency with any one social group. The work of writers like Smithies, Sutherland, Levi and others has shown the extent of corruption by the powerful, the scale of tax evasion and the rewards of white-collar crime. As we shall see in the next chapter, the common sacrifice in both world wars heightened people's sensitivity to offences committed by the privileged members of society, and a number of solicitors, managers and their friends appeared in court on embezzlement and fraud charges. More recently, in 1977, South Wales's reputation for political skulduggery was confirmed by the prosecution of twenty-two former councillors, officials and company directors for corruption and associated offences. The financial return in such criminal activities dwarfed that of other offences. The South Wales fraud squad, which investigated forty major allegations of fraud and three serious complaints of corruption in 1988, estimated that the amount involved was £25 million.

The enforcement of legislation like the Shop and Public Health Acts, and especially that covering the use of motor vehicles, has meant that many trades and professional people have passed through the magistrates' courts during the century. At Peterston-super-Ely in 1935–8, for example, a succession of farmers trooped to Cowbridge, Cardiff and Llantrisant to answer charges of not keeping proper stock records, causing suffering to animals, and offences in connection with the driving, licensing and parking of vehicles. The occurrence books of Nantgarw in the 1960s show, too, that the people most likely to be caught for traffic offences included inspectors, engineers, dealers, managers, and other professional people who travelled in their work.

At the same time, however, those arrested for larceny at Nantgarw were chiefly the unemployed who took coal, factory workers who stole from their employers, and labourers who thieved goods other than coal. It only confirms the general picture: the people charged with indictable offences in the twentieth, as in the nineteenth, century have been very largely of the working class, though it would be grotesque to follow those writers of the past who regarded the working and criminal classes as synonymous.

Convicted criminals have always been a minority of the population, and most of them appeared before the courts only once. Well over half the the defendants at all the Welsh courts in 1900 had no criminal record, and that was still true by the middle of the century. The police record of the 'misconduct' of people living in the Pontyclun area, near Cardiff, between 1923 and 1945, which gives an approximate yearly figure of one person in every thirty-three, shows that most were found guilty of one offence only, typically for a breach of highway regulations and for not having a dog licence. At Taibach, near Port Talbot, where proportionately fewer people were charged each year over a similar period, the pattern was the same; most people had only one or two convictions, for stealing coal, or more commonly for petty misdemeanours like illegal betting and riding a bicycle without lights. On the Trealaw beat in the Rhondda, covering over 4,000 people on the eve of the Second World War, a police officer identified only twenty-four people who were listed in the criminal record office as serious offenders, mostly because of their convictions for stealing coal and metals.

Even on the most criminal inner-city and council estate in South Wales in 1989, only a small minority of people were charged with an indictable offence, and only a minority of these had formidable criminal records. Such 'chronic offenders' are responsible for an exceptional proportion – as many as a half in some regions – of convictions in modern society. This helps to explain why police officers cling to the nineteenth-century notion that most serious offences are committed by a very small number of people. Thus a police sergeant in Bonymaen, Swansea, which is currently regarded one of the most 'criminal areas', claimed in a recent report that 'a significant proportion of crime' in his locality was committed by only 'about 25 young people'. Across the whole South Wales district, one person in fifty-eight was proceeded against or cautioned for an indictable crime in 1989, and one in sixteen for either the same or a non-indictable offence.

The cost and victims of crime

Since the establishment of professional police forces throughout the country the government has made some attempt to estimate the financial cost of property crimes. Each year the police have been required to provide details of the losses sustained in recorded offences, and of the amount recovered. What stands out is the comparatively low value of the goods taken. As the chief constable of Cardiff noted in 1933, 'the bulk of crime today consists of what might be termed systematic petty pilferage'. Both he, and the chief constable of Swansea, emphasized the absence of organized crime 'in which very large and valuable quantities of property were stolen'. The exception was embezzlement and fraud, which occasionally resulted in losses of thousands of pounds.

Over three-quarters of recorded indictable property offences in the early decades of the century were committed 'without violence', and most of these, like simple larcenies, shoplifting, taking from meters and stealing from the person were very minor indeed, as was most juvenile crime. The losses tended to be highest where the victims were of the upper and middle classes, but even then most burglaries, for example, did not produce substantial rewards. The average loss per recorded property offence (excluding white-collar crimes, and malicious damage) in South Wales in the years before the Second World War rose from about £1.50 to £3, and the recovery rate during that period was sometimes as high as 75 per cent, though it was usually nearer a half. In Neath in 1916, for instance, where the annual cost of the police was £2,377 and recorded property losses only £68, 62 per cent of the latter was recovered.

The value of property offences rose with the crime rate after the Second World War. In Swansea the total loss, which had been estimated at over £2,000 in 1938 (almost £3 per crime), increased in 1968 to almost £30 per crime, a rise well above inflation, whilst the recovery rate fell from 32.5 per cent to 11 per cent, the lowest figure in South Wales. The increase in the value of crimes was particularly marked during the 1940s, the late 1950s, and the mid- and late 1960s, and was associated with the increasing number of break-ins and thefts from and of motor vehicles, the folly of carrying large amounts of cash and goods without proper protection, and the improved organization of professional criminals. Even so, one must

Table 2·18: Average cost of property crime in 1989

Kind of crime	England	Wales	South Wales
Burglary	£809	£524	£515
Robbery	£1178	£451	£427
Theft and handling stolen goods	£757	£663	£746

not forget the scale of all this. In the late 1960s the majority of property offences in Swansea were still valued at under £10.

During the next quarter of a century, the cost of crime soared. In 1980 the estimate of property losses made by the South Wales police was over £13 million, and nine years later it had increased by four times. Two-thirds of the losses in 1989 comprised the replacement costs of stolen motor vehicles, and, when thefts from vehicles were added to the figure, it meant that autocrime was responsible for 72 per cent of the total. Together with the most rewarding burglaries, and the organized stealing of expensive goods, these vehicle offences pushed the value of the average property crime as high as £621 in 1989. This was, however, well below the English figures as table 2.18 indicates.

In the light of this, it is perhaps not surprising that the media and public-opinion surveys give the impression that property crimes, like violent offences, are becoming ever more serious, organized and alarming in character. Yet one has to keep a balance. Amongst the most lucrative thefts in 1989 was the taking of motor vehicles, but most of these were reclaimed by their owners, which helped to raise the overall recovery rate for property offences to 42.6 per cent. Moreover, in 43 per cent of cases in that year the crime was valued at less than £100. Many offences at the present time, including burglaries, robberies, thefts from cars and vandalism, remain comparatively small, and are often the result of impulsive and opportunist action.

This situation has caused some academics to question the true character of the crime threat, and to conclude that it has been deliberately exaggerated by those in power for their own purposes, mainly to divert attention from other and more serious social problems. Since the days of Robert Peel, governments have certainly manipulated public feelings on delinquency, but at the end of the twentieth century the general anxiety over property crime derives largely from the experience of such offences. We should remember that the above figures do not take into account all property crimes reported, let alone the dark figure. Many local government losses, including damage to property, are not declared. It is widely accepted that the cost of undisclosed financial and commercial offences runs into millions of pounds a year, or several percentage points of the gross national product. In addition, there are the police expenses of dealing with property crimes, as well as the costs of administering justice, providing probation and prisons, social-service expenses, and the burden of lost trade, unlet properties, increased insurance premiums and higher domestic rates. An independent survey of the cost of Swansea crime in 1992 estimated that it added over £10 million to ratepayers' bills. For the whole of England and Wales, another survey, published in September 1994, put the annual cost of crime at £20 billion.

The new subject of victimology has revealed that people also suffer psychologically from quite minor crimes, and especially from robberies, burglaries and assaults. Violent crimes, which are overwhelmingly trivial in character, leave considerable emotional damage, and sexual ones even more so. Although most of those attacked suffer no more than bruising, they are sometimes permanently scarred by the experience, and their anxiety is conveyed to others. Crime surveys in the 1980s have shown that perhaps a quarter or a third of males over sixty years of age and a larger percentage of women at every age 'feel unsafe'. Victim support groups were formed across South Wales during this decade to bring comfort to those who were burgled, beaten and abused, and more recently the police have inaugurated a scheme of keeping them informed of progress in their cases. Although the state has displaced the victim as prosecutor in this century, there is still a strong desire amongst the latter to be involved.

This interest in victims is comparatively novel, and is worth considering in a historical context. In 1900 it was often assumed that the middle and upper classes were the main targets of the thief and burglar, and that working-class people were the chief victims of violent assaults. This was not strictly true, but research has shown that in late nineteenth-century Wales gentlemen farmers, industrial employers, retailers and hotel proprietors had good reason to complain about losses of property. This continued to be the case in the next century. In the Merthyr police district in the 1920s and 1930s, for example, the crime register indicates that the most vulnerable parties were mining companies like Guest, Keen and Baldwins of Dowlais, Messrs Llewellyn of Cyfarthfa and Plymouth, and Gomer Thomas of Abercanaid, together with merchants, shopkeepers, publicans, the Great Western Railway Company, and the Corporation, especially its education department. The estimated value of property offences recorded by the Merthyr police rose from £398 in 1924 to £7,666 in 1946, and one can estimate that, for much of this period, the above victims lost at least two-thirds of this.

The cost of violent crimes was of a rather different order, and so were the victims. Just over a half of the persons attacked and sexually assaulted in Merthyr between these two dates were female, and, like their male counterparts, they were mostly young and working-class. Typical victims of assaults in the town were children, schoolgirls, domestic servants, shop assistants, housekeepers, wives, boys, labourers and colliers.

According to observers, the targets of crime widened in the 1940s. In the Merthyr charge register for 1944 three out of ten thefts were from private homes, and some of these were in the poorer streets. Speaking of the 114 reported break-ins of dwelling houses four years later, the chief contable of Merthyr declared that 'this type of attack on property is no longer confined to shops and the class of residential property hitherto regarded as fair targets for the thief. Small cottage homes are now entered, particularly in the evenings, and it is suspected they are attacked because the occupiers keep their savings at home.'

Already, therefore, one future pattern was being established: the more vulnerable members of society, with their uninsured property, now suffered as much, if not more, than anyone. In Cardiff this was obvious at an early date. During the mid-1930s more than three-quarters of the victims of recorded indictable crime were individuals rather than companies, and they lived in both wealthy and poor streets. One in five of these individuals were female. The latter were already showing signs of anxiety; Cardiff women were victims of about half the crimes of violence, and of some of the most disturbing property offences. Half of the property offences involving these women took place within the home, or just outside, and in the city centre females had to keep their eyes peeled for young robbers.

Opportunities for criminals increased as everyone became more prosperous and owned more property. In the immediate post-war years there were reports, from Cardiff, Merthyr and elsewhere, of youths on council estates taking cash, jewellery, clothes and radios from their neighbours. As more people acquired bicycles, motor cycles and then cars, so these became popular targets. In 1952, at Merthyr, companies, stores, the Corporation, the Coal Board, British Rail and other organizations were still important victims of crime, but a half were private individuals, and just over a third of these were female. Such people lost, amongst other things, pedal cycles, clothes from their gardens and cash from their homes.

The crime complaint books of Cardiff Central and Docks divisions, Bishopston and Tonyrefail during the 1960s and 1970s show how the composition of victims differed from area to area. In Cardiff Central, where shoplifting, the stealing of bicycles, and autocrime were common, a quarter of the victims were shop-owners and merchants, like James Howell and Jacobs and Son, but most of the remainder were ordinary individuals, of all occupations, from students and salesmen to the self-employed and the unemployed. At the docks it was a different story; here most of the losses were sustained by the Gas and Electricity Boards, the Admiralty, storekeepers, contractors, dealers, and companies and merchants like Western Ground Rents and the Cory Brothers and Co.

Bishopston and Tonyrefail are two very different communities. In the former, a prosperous suburb of Swansea, where most of the offences were autocrime and opportunist thieving, hoteliers, publicans, students, salesmen, managers, builders and housewives were amongst the most common targets. In the district of Tonyrefail prominent victims included garage-owners, shopkeepers, drivers, miners, factory workers and labourers. The sex and age of the private victims, in Tonyrefail, Bishopston and Cardiff, were more balanced than those of offenders. Almost a fifth of the total were female, and a half were over thirty years of age.

Conclusion

A comprehensive crime survey is needed before we can establish the total experience of crime in present-day South Wales. What cannot be doubted, however, is that the concern about delinquency, which grew fitfully before the 1950s, and then steadily afterwards, seems to have been built on solid foundations. By 1989 only eight police forces in Britain returned worse figures of recorded indictable crime, and, when these are combined with prosecutions for non-indictable offences and cautions, the rate was twice as bad in South Wales as it had been twenty years before. More people now experience crime, attend court as witnesses or defendants, and receive fixed penalties than at any time in the century. At the end of our period one serious (mostly property) crime was recorded for every eleven people in South Wales.

The figure is, of course, only an approximation, as many offences are unreported, and many of the recorded crimes are not spread evenly across the population. People living in certain areas, especially if they are of a particular age and sex, are especially susceptible to crime, and a considerable number of these unfortunates suffer several times in a year, thus distorting the proportions given in the last paragraph. According to the British Crime Survey of 1992 the areas with the highest rate of criminal victimization also have the highest rate of multiple victimization. All this helps to explain why, for example, two-thirds of people in a small household sample in Penlan, Swansea, in 1985 claimed that they had never been the victim of a crime. South Wales is still a comparatively safe place for the individual, at least outside the home, though break-ins, autocrime and other thefts are becoming a more common experience.

Hopes of a downturn in the crime rate, based on a fall in the statistics or a slowing down of the increase in the crime rate, have emerged in periods such as the late 1940s, the mid-1950s, the late 1970s, the late 1980s and the early 1990s, but there has been nothing to compare with the great cyclical downturns in previous centuries. No one is very optimistic about future prospects, though a closer look at the incidence and character of different offences helps to place the actual threat of crime in perspective.

3

Crime and Society

As we have seen, it is impossible to discover exactly how much crime existed in twentieth-century society. Even today, the official statistics give only a limited amount of information, and people are divided in their opinions of how bad things really are. As one retreats in time, the situation becomes even more difficult to assess. People who lived through the early 1900s, for example, or the 1930s, gave contradictory accounts of the scale and dangers of delinquency. Much depended on where they lived, with whom they associated, to which class and age group they belonged, and if they were passive observers or active reformers.

It is difficult, even when using the best statistical and literary evidence, to make a balanced judgement on whether we now live in a more civilized, humane and law-abiding society than that of our forefathers of 1950 or 1900. Elderly people, with a few exceptions, are convinced that in their youth people and property were much safer, and that offences then were of a less threatening nature. They are certain in their own minds that the roots of their current anxieties lie in comparatively recent developments. It is an appealing perspective, but it will take many years of research to establish its validity.

What follows is a just a starting-point, a general review of the material on violence, property crime and victimless offences which survives in the government, court and police records, and in the newspapers and diaries of the time. From this the reader should gain an idea of the changing nature of crime, and the beginnings of an answer to the question of whether conditions have improved or not. An attempt will also be made to estimate the numbers of criminals and victims at various moments in time, and to discover what part governments, reformers and the police played in the process of criminalization. By 1989 no family was unaffected by crime, and its influence on politics, policy and community life has become very considerable.

A violent society?

Opinions

The extent of violence in modern society is not easily determined. There are several opinions on this. The general impression, from academic studies, is that society has become more peaceful since medieval times, with the march of civilization, the growth of the middle class, the increasing determination to solve disputes through legal means and better policing. Public behaviour, industrial relations and possibly personal relationships are now less impregnated with violence than in the eighteenth, nineteenth and very early twentieth centuries. The short-term popular view, however, is that society over the last few decades has become more violent, with the main sufferers being young people, females and the elderly. A growing number of the last two groups claim, when interviewed, that they are afraid of being attacked in the street and in the home.

We know, from victim and self-report studies, that violence is massively under-reported in society. No more than a fifth of assaults are today brought to the police's attention, and the proportion was probably even smaller in previous generations. The comments of contemporaries, and the statistics given in this section, must be viewed in that context. Not surprisingly, statements on the subject tended to be rather confused and contradictory. During the 1920s, for instance, the chief constables of Swansea and Cardiff spoke, on several occasions, of the 'orderliness of the public in streets and public places . . .' when compared with the situation at the turn of the century. 'With the exception of the year 1919, Cardiff has been, for many years, remarkably free from numerous acts of violence', was one comment in 1925. Yet, thirty years later, the memory of these times in the capital was rather different. 'I am informed in reliable quarters that life is much quieter than in the old days', said a reporter in 1951. 'Gone to a large extent are those old feuds and quarrels between races. We do not hear of street fights to the same extent as we once did.'

Since the days of the Teddy Boys in the 1950s, such considered historical reflections have been less in evidence. By the late 1960s Cardiff, and other South Wales towns, were said to be sharing in the 'general increase in violence' in the home and in the street, and all against a backcloth of 'anti-police' youth culture, mass demonstrations and acts of terrorism. 'It would seem', wrote the chief constable of Cardiff in 1968, 'that there has been a general lowering of the standard of self-control which has allowed quite small arguments to develop into vicious fights.' Anger over 'brutal thugs' and the effects of excessive alcohol and drugs became a media fixation in the 1970s, with frequent articles in the press on the plight of battered elderly victims and the death of teenagers.

In the 1980s surveys indicated that most people in South Wales, as elsewhere, were convinced that violence was on the increase, and a minority felt under real threat from the mugger, the rapist, the football hooligan and the unrestrained burglar. In 1982 an attempt was made by Chief Constable John Woodcock, his officers and social workers to allay the fears of people on Cardiff's toughest housing estates, and three years later, a judge at the crown court passed long exemplary gaol sentences on two violent men who had started a fight which left a Cardiff man with a fractured skull. Such a judicial policy was welcomed by the public, which had, via the media and various victim-support agencies, become increasingly aware of the evils of violence, sexual attacks and child abuse.

Statistics

The statistics of violence commonly used for the twentieth century have never quite matched the opinions and images described above. They can be seen in graph 3.1. This is the rate of violent indictable offences recorded by the police. Sexual offences have been removed from the total. It includes homicide and wounding, but not, until recent decades, most of the lesser assaults which were either not reported or placed in the non-indictable tables. The rate was low during the first half of the century, which no doubt owed something to poor reporting and to the tolerance with which the police and Parliament regarded violent incidents prior to the 1950s. One has the strong impression in the early years of

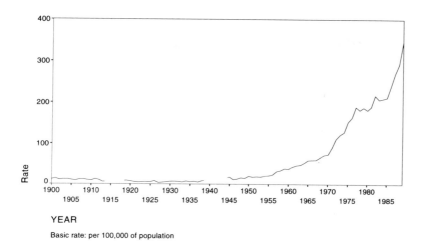

YEAR

Basic rate: per 100,000 of population

Graph 3.1: Violence: indictable offences (excluding sexual assaults) recorded by the police in South Wales, 1900–1989

the century that the police were often content just to separate warring parties, and preferred, if possible, to keep sexual offences out of court.

After a sharp increase in the statistics at the beginning of the Second World War, which was attributed to indiscipline, boredom and the availability of guns, the rate of recorded attacks moved onto a higher plane until the mid-1950s. From then the rate rose consistently until 1970, like recorded crime generally. This in turn was followed by a spectacular ascent, a fivefold increase, temporarily interrupted by the figures for 1977–86. This has attracted a great deal of media attention, and undoubtedly contributed to our anxiety about violence, but part of the explanation for this rise in the statistics is the growing proportion of violent crimes now being returned as indictable offences.

Table 3.1, which gives a more accurate picture of the changes in the recording of violent and sexual offences, is an amalgam of all the cases reported and dealt with in the courts. From table 3.1 we can see that recorded offences were much higher in 1900 than implied by the graph, and fell sharply until the Second World War.

Table 3·1: Reported indictable offences against the person, and persons proceeded against for non-indictable assaults, 1900–1989

Year	Ratio of population to one case
1900	281
1913	524
1923	580
1938	1269
1948	879
1958	814
1969	594
1989	259

This mirrors the opinions expressed by many contemporaries. Similarly, the above statistics confirm the widely held view that things worsened in the second half of this century, though the rise in the table was, like the British Crime Survey figures, less spectacular over the last twenty years than described by graph 3.1.

The superficial impression, from all of this, is that people in 1989 faced the same kind of dangers as their predecessors in 1900. The level of reporting has, however, changed significantly over the century. As we saw in chapter 1, better communications in recent decades enabled people to contact the police when an incident was actually happening. At the same time, the public, police, prosecutors and the courts in the second half of the century took assaults more seriously. If one compares, for instance, the reports and court cases of indictable violence at Merthyr in 1924–46 with those in the same town in the late 1960s, the former contained more stabbings, stonings, glassing and fractured bones, whilst the latter had a higher proportion of assaults by children and cases of minor bruising. According to recent crime surveys only one in five of today's recorded attacks could be described as physically damaging. Most would probably not have come to the attention of the police or the courts in 1900.

South Wales society has, in truth, never been as dangerous as some of its detractors claimed. The rate of recorded violent indictable offences during this century has been lower than the rate of violence in Gwent and North Wales. In 1989 the police figures suggest that one person in 288 in South Wales was the victim of a violent (non-sexual) assault and one in 2,579 of a sexual offence, but only a very small percentage of such people were seriously injured. Moreover, violence and the use of guns is still rare in robberies and burglaries in South Wales. There are signs, too, in the early 1990s that in parts of South Wales open forms of violence, such as late-night drunken affrays, are being brought under control. Even so, we must not forget that all the official statistics should be multiplied several times to capture the actual threat of violence, especially in certain areas and domestic situations.

Violence in the community

The experience of violence in South Wales depended greatly on where one lived. In 1901 it was said that settled rural communities, in which people knew each other well, were the most peaceful areas of Glamorgan, and this remains largely true, at least outside the home. In industrial and urban society conflict was more likely to get out of hand, especially in lodging houses, the workplace, the pub and club, and the street. The growth of the coal and steel communities early in the century and the building of new railway lines brought young and often rowdy workers together. They indulged in drunken weekends and street fights and, at places like Treorchy, Cwmparc, Tonyrefail and Garth, they attacked the police regularly and prevented them from taking violent individuals to the nearest lock-ups.

The seaports also had their problems. At Barry Dock the shipping office was crowded with people of all nations, and violence between them was common, whilst the seafront at Aberavon was described in 1907 as 'an exceedingly rough place'. In Cardiff and Swansea at this time, respectable visitors said that they were appalled by violent knife-carrying seamen, cursing prostitutes and drunken vagrants. In 1913, which was apparently 'much better' than the preceding year, 48 males and 5 females were apprehended for indictable offences against the person in the capital, and proceedings were launched against 312 males and 168 females for non-indictable assaults, more than a quarter being attacks on the police.

Many of these cases were from Butetown, especially Loundon Square, and, as Constable Hodge's notebooks illustrate, there were scores of other violent characters who disappeared before the police arrived, or received an informal warning from them. James Ware (fifty years of age) of Cardiff, with a string of convictions in 1925 for assaults, rape and obscene language, and Patrick McCarthy (forty years old) of Swansea, who made his fifty-first court appearance in 1921, were just two of the 'very vicious' people who instilled fear in everyone who came near them.

We are able, because of the survival of the Merthyr Tydfil records, to examine the nature of inter-war violence in some detail. Table 3.2 gives the recorded indictable crimes only, for 1924–46. Males were thus responsible for the vast majority of the serious attacks in the town, but the victims, in over half the cases,

Table 3·2: Recorded indictable crimes, Merthyr Tydfil, 1924–1946

Type of offence	No. of cases	Persons accused		Victims	
		Males	Females	Males	Females
Homicide, attempted murders, g.b.h. & woundings	101	90	11	71	30
Sexual assaults	112	112	0	25	87
Attempted suicide	67	43	24	43	24

were female. The average age of male assailants was thirty-four, and of female victims of sexual attacks thirteen years. Information on the female victims of other attacks was limited, but most of these women were assaulted by their husbands, and their age, when given, averaged fifty-three years. Stabbing was the most common form of serious assault, and for that a six-month gaol sentence was often given. The usual punishments for other woundings were one month's imprisonment, a small fine and being bound over.

Another sample (ninety-five assaults) from Merthyr's crime register for 1968–9 produces a similar picture, not least of the working-class nature of most attackers and victims, but whilst just over half the victims were again female, almost all the assaults were now carried out by males. Moreover, there was by the late 1960s a fall of eleven years in the average age of those charged with the offences. The growing fear, described above, of the young male thug and rapist was therefore not without foundation, and, if women were more anxious than males in the home and street, this also was understandable. Nor have things changed greatly since; the threat posed by men in their early twenties remains, as we can see from the sex and age statistics given in table 3.3. Along with females, the common victims in 1989 were males aged 16–24 years.

Table 3·3: Persons officially cautioned, proceeded against at magistrates' courts and tried at crown courts in South Wales in 1989

	Violent offences	*Sexual offences*	*Assaults on constables*
Males			
10–16	274	60	12
17–20	854	77	142
21+	2340	322	333
Females			
10–16	67	0	4
17–20	85	0	26
21+	273	5	50

The other important changes were in the places and character of recorded violence. This can also be illustrated by studying the 1930s and 1960s in Merthyr Tydfil. Where once most of the incidents had been in Merthyr's main streets and in various localities in Dowlais, Pentrebach, Pantmorlais and Treharris, the dangerous places in the late 1960s were increasingly the Gellideg, Galon Uchaf and Gurnos estates. Here men and women were punched and kicked rather than stabbed, and here, too, the latter were indecently assaulted.

Each town and city had districts where the rate of recorded violence was comparatively high, and where particular types of assaults predominated. The centres of Cardiff and Swansea, for example, were identified with sexual offences, violent robberies and drunken disorder. The trouble spots, in the early years, apart from the pub and club, were the fish and chip shops and bus stops, and to these were added, after the 1950s, the dance halls, the Chinese and Indian restaurants and the car parks. Besides the participants in the brawls, those attacked were onlookers, police officers who intervened, and hospital workers who dealt with the worst cases.

By 1978, according to the police records, there were four main types of violent community: town centres, poor inner-city areas, a number of large council estates and certain declining industrial localities. Of all of these, places like Llanedeyrn, Grangetown north and Ely in Cardiff have become, since that date, most notorious for domestic incidents and fights between youngsters. Clashes on the huge and isolated estates of Penrhys (Rhondda) and Gurnos (Merthyr) also caught the headlines during the 1980s. The Ely unrest, which exploded in the summer of 1989, received the most publicity, though, as always in such matters, the daily experience of life on that Cardiff estate was less traumatic than the media reporting suggested.

Domestic violence

Although street troubles, at Ely and elsewhere, were occasionally the product of deprivation, boredom and frustration, magistrates and the police have for generations claimed that the main sources of violence are domestic conflict and heavy drinking. Police officers' notebooks and occurrence books take us into the half-hidden world of the family. Constables Welsby at Hopkinstown and Hodge in Cardiff were called to many domestic conflicts in the years before and after the First World War, and, according to their accounts, usually managed to control them. Legal action by the police was taken only when the participants were seriously injured, or if they refused to be quiet when requested by the policemen. It was, and remains, a difficult police activity, one which occasionally provoked greater disorder and official complaints.

The scale of family violence is impossible to ascertain, as the Parliamentary Select Committee of 1975 concluded. Suggestions that it accounts for perhaps an eighth or a quarter of all assaults cannot be fully verified. The term 'domestic incident' was used quite loosely to include conflicts between neighbours as well as those between relatives. Nor were these conflicts always violent. However, they were common. Officers at one police station in Cardiff in the period 1970–2 reported that domestic incidents in their district were twice as common as assaults. In 1978 6,534 'domestic disputes' (almost three times the recorded indictable offences against the person) were included in the South Wales annual record of occurrences, with Morriston and Bargoed police subdivisions returning the highest figures per head of population.

Most of these reports did not lead to prosecution. Frequently the victim wished to let the matter drop, or made a complaint and then withdrew it.

Family conflict was a feature of all classes, but many of the reported cases were from rented private homes, council houses and high-rise flats in areas of social deprivation, overcrowding and heavy unemployment. Throughout the century, most of the documented 'domestics' were of men attacking women, children and in-laws. In the first decades, when several hundred wives each year sought separation orders in South Wales, the court proceedings were full of the iniquities of drunken and violent husbands. In the Cardiff cases there were complaints, which may well have been exaggerated, that men forced their wives into prostitution. Some of the most browbeaten women attempted suicide after finding the courage to call for police assistance.

Divorce became, after the Second World War and notably after the reforms of 1969, a popular solution for warring families, but the period just before and after the legal proceedings remained uniquely dangerous, and problematical for friends, neighbours and the police. In recent years there have been many instances in South Wales of legal or common-law husbands losing control after a separation, kidnapping wives and children, wrecking and burning property, and attacking in-laws, rivals and outsiders. Sometimes, as in the past, such cases developed into long-running feuds, and the police have the unenviable task of breaking up large family affrays.

Women can be violent at such times, but the historical evidence reveals them to be less physically aggressive than men within the home. Although females killed and stabbed brutal and adulterous husbands, and attacked other women after arguments over boy-friends and children, such examples have been comparatively rare. The point is reinforced by table 3.4, which shows the ultimate consequences of family tension. There were on average in Wales twenty-two homicides per year between 1900 and 1989, a figure which changed little from one year to the next. Half of these were in South Wales, mostly in Cardiff, Swansea, and their environs, with a smaller number in Merthyr, Port Talbot and other large towns. The table is a sample of 111 homicides (87 murders and 24 manslaughters), chosen randomly, from each decade of the century.

Table 3·4: Homicides in South Wales, 1901–1990

Offenders		Victims		
Males	Females	Males	Females	Children under 10
96	15	44	52	15

Offender	'Family' relationship between offender and victim Victim	Number of cases
Husband	wife (and co-habitee, ex-wife)	24
Wife	husband	3
Father	child	6
Mother	child	6
Son	father	3
Son	mother	1
Sister	sister	2
Other family	other family	7
Male	girl-friend, lover	7

In addition to the family relationship, another 25 per cent of offenders were known to the victim. These were, mainly, cases involving sailors, foreigners, lodgers and landlords at Cardiff and Swansea in the first half of the century, and youths in the last quarter. In only five instances were deaths the result of robberies and burglaries, whilst in another ten the unfortunate victims were set upon by people later declared to be insane.

The importance of the family in homicides has long been established. The wives and girl-friends in the sample were killed by three main types: the jealous young man, the violent (and often drunken husband), and the elderly companion who was sometimes mentally ill. A handful of men murdered their wives and then committed suicide. Thus in 1982, a fairly typical year, three elderly men 'of diminished responsibility' from Nelson, Cwmavon and Cardiff killed their wives, and one of them tried, but failed, to end his own life. There were also, incidentally, many other deaths of wives and girl-friends in the 1980s, thus undermining a popular view that homicides have now become largely a way of settling non-family differences or the result of drug-taking and violent robberies.

The other vulnerable members of the family were children, and the responsibility for their deaths in the sample was shared equally between fathers and mothers. Early in the century the bodies of babies were found in undergrowth, on tips, in rivers and in boxes and attics, and coroners had problems in deciding whether these babies had expired at birth or whether they had been allowed to die later. Overlaying of young children was common, partly because working-class families had neither the money nor space for cots. Those cases of child-killing which did appear in court were shocking affairs. Mothers beaten by husbands, or unable to cope with yet another child, drowned, poisoned and gassed their babies, whilst young husbands smashed their offspring against chairs and walls in fits of rage. The public in South Wales looked on the death of a newly born baby with some detachment, but reacted angrily to that of a growing child.

The background to a number of these cases was the neglect and cruelty which once characterized the upbringing of a considerable number of children in South Wales. At the turn of the century the NSPCC prosecuted 100–200 people a year for not feeding their children, for not providing them with clothing or bedding, for abandoning them or driving them from home, and for generally ill-treating them. This was, to a degree, a reflection of the poverty of working-class families, but many children were also brutalized by drunken and violent fathers, and by uncaring mothers and stepmothers. It was apparent, from the police and court evidence of the early decades, that such parents were unwilling for anyone to interfere with their right to bring up their children as they wished. Subsequently attitudes changed somewhat, and certainly the court cases of cruelty to, and neglect of, children have become fewer; in 1989, for example, only eighteen men and nine women were cautioned or prosecuted for this in South Wales.

In recent years there has been a new approach to this subject; medical and welfare officials are now trained to spot the physical signs of ill-treatment in the young, the public have been made more aware of child abuse, and a specialist South Wales police family support unit, with three regional branches, was set up in 1991. In 1992 they investigated 1,505 allegations of child abuse (as well as reports of domestic violence), and by 1994 the head of the West Glamorgan branch was able to claim that 'the majority of cases now get referred to us'. But, like so much personal violence, the incidence of child cruelty and abuse remains an elusive matter.

Sexual offences

Over the century assaults of every kind have been treated with increasing seriousness by victims, the police and the media. This was particularly so with sexual attacks. The non-reporting of such crimes was acknowledged to be high in the Edwardian years, and women who brought a court case had a difficult time, both in the dock and in the press. Acquittals were common. The rate of indictable sexual offences changed little between 1900 and 1938, but after the war it reached a much higher level, notably between 1953 and 1963 (see graph 3.2). In that period there was greater Home Office interest in the problem, and more determined reporting and policing, though many observers insisted that there was also a real increase in indecent behaviour against females, most of whom were under seventeen years of age. After the mid-1960s, when homosexual acts between consenting adults in private were decriminalized, the rate of recorded sexual offences fell somewhat, and has since hovered around 38 incidents per 100,000 of the population. However, the latest surveys confirm that, despite the various aids to reporting introduced in the 1980s, a large majority of the indecent approaches made to women, children and men are still not brought to the attention of the authorities.

The police and court information gives us no more than patterns, which are themselves interesting. In Cardiff and at Tonpentre the registers of prisoners show that, on the eve of the First World War, the girls assaulted were very young, and the men who abused them were imprisoned for one month to three years. As we saw earlier in table 3.2, 112 people (all males) were accused of sexual offences in Merthyr Tydfil between 1924 and 1946, and the victims were 87 females and 25 males. In the most typical cases, men in their thirties attacked schoolgirls and boys, at school, in the parks, in the street and near the pits. By the late 1960s there had been a change; most of the people convicted of rape and indecent assault in the town were teenagers, and their punishment was usually a probation order, sometimes with a condition to abstain from alcohol or to seek medical advice.

Officially recorded instances of the rape of adult women have been comparatively rare in South Wales, and the police were, for many years, rather cynical about even these figures. There were indeed examples where complaints were malicious or a cover for

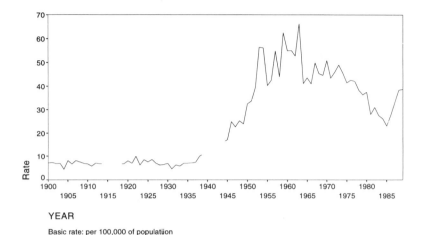

YEAR

Basic rate: per 100,000 of populatiion

Graph 3.2: Sexual offences recorded by the police in South Wales, 1900–1989

an adulterous relationship. Gradually, however, the impact of the feminist movement and of more sensitive policing has brought a more responsible approach to the subject. Although, as we saw in chapter 1, the number of court cases continues to be low, the horrors of rape and the difficulties of persisting with a complaint are better understood. The dangers that lurk within the domestic and work environment, and in the streets, have received much publicity in recent times, which no doubt contributes to the fears described in crime surveys. During the 1970s and 1980s the press in South Wales highlighted almost every court case of women who were dragged through town centres, attacked in taxis and robbed and raped on their way home.

The most vulnerable age for females remains childhood. Sexual abuse of children has been, almost certainly, a major problem throughout the century. The police and court evidence reveals that, apart from members of the family, the most common offenders were those temporarily charged with their care, like baby-sitters, welfare officers and teachers. Much of the abuse took place in secret, and was reported only because of a chance comment or when the child visited a doctor. The family support units, recently established across South Wales, now bring together evidence on such matters and have opened channels for reporting. Of the 1,505 child abuse allegations mentioned above, 994 were of a sexual nature. Court cases remain, however, rare; in 1989, for instance, only 5 people were cautioned or prosecuted for gross indecency with children, 30 for sex with under-age females, and 13 for incest.

Incest is a taboo subject. It was made a distinct offence by the Incest Act of 1908. For years a handful of men were annually charged with this crime in South Wales, and more were saved because of 'insufficient evidence'. When convicted, they received punishment of six months to seven years of gaol. In some cases brothers had sex with sisters for years, and fathers had likewise with young daughters. In several instances the daughters had replaced absent or dead wives. Some offences, committed over years, only emerged after the strain on silenced wives proved too much, or when the victims left home. Very occasionally revenge was taken at a later date, not always through the courts.

In one such incident, in 1989, the sons returned to attack the father who had once indecently assaulted them. Boys were abused less often, it seems, than girls, though the home and school were again the locale of most attacks. Homosexuality between consenting adults in private was a crime until 1967, and thereafter a small number of males appeared in court for affairs in toilets, sidings, sheds and lanes. Sometimes, the offenders admitted to many similar crimes, and the police detection rate, always good for crimes of violence, became even better.

Public disorder

It is not easy to make definitive statements about the history of public behaviour. Contemporaries were divided in their opinions. Thus in the early years of the century some observers wrote about the 'good order' of the population and the 'improvement in morals', whilst others claimed that town life was disturbed almost nightly by parties of drunken men and young hooligans. Such a division of opinion can be found, for example, in Cardiff between about 1916 and 1937. The explanation for these different perspectives must be sought in the location and standards of those who made the statements. Parts of the capital were, at the outbreak of the First World War, comparatively peaceful, but there were other places, like Bute Street, where affrays were a constant problem for Constable Hodge and his colleagues. The fights were of a varied nature; seamen against seamen, women against women, and gypsies, vagrants and prostitutes fighting the police.

Sometimes these disturbances got out of hand. In Swansea trouble often broke out along the mile of road linking the poor working-class quarter of Greenhill to the docks. During the Greenhill riots of 1905, for example, windows were smashed, homes destroyed, and people treated in hospital for their wounds. Family feuding, especially between the O'Connors and the McCartneys, was at the heart of this violence. Superintendent Gill, defending his policemen over their handling of the riots, said that it was virtually impossible to deal with every outburst of Irish anger. The Recorder at the Swansea quarter sessions called it 'a war', and the gaol sentences of three and six months caused 'a sensation'.

In Cardiff there was almost continuous fighting in the dockland communities between resident Blacks, Greeks and Arabs, and between Scandinavian, Chinese and British seamen, and the arrival of the police did not always improve the situation. On 28 March 1907, 'a negro affray . . . a somewhat serious disturbance' broke out in Butetown, and the police officers who arrested the ringleaders were attacked with razors. Two years later the 'long-standing feud between Greeks and Arabs' in Cardiff flared into open hostility, after a fight in a card-school, and similar clashes occurred between Arabs and Somalis.

Such disturbances became less common in Cardiff after 1920, and so, it was suggested, did street violence in the other towns of South Wales. 'Rowdyism' and 'hooliganism' were words constantly used to describe life in many of the industrial and urban communities prior to the First World War. Along the Cynon Valley and the Rhondda Fawr, respectable inhabitants claimed that they 'lived in fear' of disorderly crowds, and policemen thought it wise to travel in pairs. During the First World War, and immediately afterwards, the reduced intake of alcohol was said to have induced a 'marked improvement' in public behaviour in such places, especially on the part of women. In fact, literary and statistical evidence supports the notion that female habits did change in the inter-war years. As one 68-year-old police matron noted in 1948, 'women don't get drunk like they used to. I remember the cells full with 26 in a night. They used to bring them in kicking on hand trucks.'

During the inter-war years opinions varied over whether this improvement in female conduct extended to other groups in society. One has the impression that much of the disorder mentioned in the last paragraphs became increasingly confined to weekend celebrations. From Bedlinog and Bridgend, for example, came reports in the late 1930s of noisy beer-swilling crowds on Friday and Saturday nights, and Merthyr's decision to open the cinemas on the Lord's Day was set in the context of the 'terrible hooliganism' on Sunday nights.

The Second World War was, like the First, characterized by 'good public order', but within a few years of its ending, complaints about behaviour in the streets began to accumulate. In Cardiff, for example, especially in the years 1955–7, and 1960–1, the inhabitants of Gabalfa, Kimberley Terrace, Victoria Road East and Neville Street demanded police action over street fights, drunken hooligans and noisy youths. During the 1970s the protests continued, but it was in the 1980s, and especially 1989, that matters came to a head. The centres of the major towns, certain clubs and pubs on the outskirts of towns and holiday resorts all experienced unacceptable levels of popular violence. One by one the authorities of Merthyr, Caerphilly, Pontypridd, Swansea, Cardiff and other towns placed restrictions on late-night opening and drinking. In several cases this intervention itself produced confrontations between the police and mobs of several hundred people, but the long-term effect seems to have been positive. Riverside in Cardiff and the Kingsway in Swansea have 'been reclaimed' during the late hours for 'decent law-abiding people'.

In this story of public disorder, juveniles have played an important role. Cardiff in 1900 had its hooligans, but not, it was reported, too many of them, and they were strictly observed and punished. At the same time their counterparts were active in Briton Ferry and Pontardawe, and, ten years later, in Merthyr where they used foul language and threw stones at ratepayers and their property. In 1921 young hooligans were blamed for the window-slashing across South Wales towns, a copy-cat offence which originated across the border. Horseplay, smashing lamps and drunken behaviour at dances was reported from the western fringes of Glamorgan in the early 1930s, and even in the war years there were loud complaints of youthful indiscipline.

Since the Second World War the spectre of the young hooligan has grown to ridiculous proportions, a phenomenon wonderfully described by Stanley Cohen. The Teddy Boys of the mid-1950s were a case in point. At Cardiff and Swansea there were fights between gangs, minor riots when rock films were shown, and loud denunciations of declining moral standards. The Porth stipendiary, fining six youths from Pontypridd, claimed that young women were afraid to travel on the railways 'because of the behaviour of youths like you'. Nor did this language disappear. The same extreme opinions were later heard over the activities of Mods and Rockers, and after youth clubs were ransacked and pop concerts disrupted in the 1960s and 1970s.

Popular culture has often been accompanied by violence of some kind. During the 1930s, for example, musical entertainment, boxing and football matches and Guy Fawkes nights were often riotous, though once again this was in part the responsibility of over-zealous police. The most persistent trouble has been at football matches, especially those between Cardiff and Swansea, which have frequently witnessed riot, injuries and, very rarely, death. In the 1920s there were a number of incidents at Ninian Park, though the scale of the violence did not really compare with that of the 1960s–1980s period, nor the police presence. In the 1980s the police were given greater powers and equipment to deal with these trouble-makers, and by the end of the decade these clashes had been reduced.

During the 1980s and 1990s youths have become a symbol of 'the breakdown of law and order' in parts of South Wales. In Rhydfelen (Pontypridd), Nelson, Abercynon, Ely, Pencoed (Cardiff), Manselton (Swansea) and many other communities, inhabitants in these years lectured the police and the media about their declining 'quality of life'. These people described the insults and injuries sustained whilst trying to deal with the 'juvenile problem'. Particularly frightening were the gang fights, which are not a new phenomenon in South Wales, but which were now publicized in great detail. Gangs in the 1980s fought each other with baseball bats, hammers and worse, travelled miles for a confrontation, and damaged buses and cars in the process. The final act of these, and other youthful adventures, was the exciting clash with the police, and there were occasions in 1989 when it became a real battle with petrol bombs and serious injuries on both sides.

Racial conflict

Of all the public order problems, those concerned with race and work have usually been regarded seriously. South Wales has, for most of the century, been seen as 'a model of good community relations'. The police of Cardiff and Swansea, who kept a close eye on their ethnic minorities, were delighted by the lack of racial disturbances in the 1950s and early 1980s. Since 1987 the South Wales force has published information on racially motivated incidents, and these number at the present time some 300–400 per year. They include insults, threats and assaults in the street, the home and at work. In the post-Scarman era, Cardiff and several other towns have established committees and early warning systems to deal with the problem.

One of the reasons given for the comparative absence in South Wales of the kind of rioting that convulsed Liverpool, London and Bristol in the early 1980s was the long and largely peaceful history of immigrant communities in such places as Cardiff and Barry. Yet race relations were not as harmonious in South Wales as is sometimes portrayed. The first two decades of this century were marked by considerable racial tension in the district, and some of this continued until the Second World War.

In Cardiff the presence of hundreds of coloured seamen proved a source of friction whenever economic conditions deteriorated. The years after the First World War were full of suppressed and overt violence, culminating in the Cardiff and Barry race riots of 1919. These were not exceptional in a national sense, for racial conflict was endemic in the docks that year, but the Cardiff riots did leave three men dead, many seriously wounded, and much property destroyed. Bute Street was the centre of the troubles, and here guns and razors were freely used on both sides. From the Whites there was a clear message that the 'foreigners' who had taken their jobs should return to their country of origin, and it was a call which had some appeal, then and later, to the chapels, the Anti-Vice Society, police chiefs and the Home Office. When offered repatriation, however, only about 200 of the settled coloured residents left Cardiff; most regarded themselves as British subjects.

There were smouldering embers of these riots for a number of years, but in 1936 a *Western Mail* reporter claimed that Tiger Bay was 'no more'. Some of its dwellings had been demolished and their inhabitants rehoused. Racial violence had 'gone', inter-marriage was more tolerated, and it was much safer to walk the streets. Nineteen years later the local vicar defended the people of Bute Street from its detractors, and argued that they were 'a living example' to the rest of the world of how races could live together in harmony. In fact, the riots of 1919 had helped to foster a ghetto mentality, and, when attempts were made to move black people to the outskirts of the city in the 1960s and 1970s, this inflamed feelings.

There were, moreover, other lesser racial problems in South Wales. The arrival of Jews fleeing from the pogroms in eastern Europe at the end of the nineteenth century produced a mixed response, but economic conditions again aroused local passions. In 1903 there were attacks on Jews by Dowlais workmen, and eight years later there was a week of destruction in the mining valleys on the Glamorgan–Monmouthshire border. The situation seems to have improved afterwards, but in 1951 and recently, people felt the need to improve relations between Jews and Christians in the area.

Other races have been more fortunate in their reception. Much of the open hostility to the Irish had evaporated by the early twentieth century, though the experience of both wars inevitably heightened national feeling against 'outsiders'. All kinds of foreigners were under suspicion during the First World War; at Neath crowds threatened suspected and actual Germans, and in Swansea Italian shops were the targets. The presence of Americans, at Barry docks in the First World War, and at Swansea in the Second, also caused violent outbursts, and, like the anti-coloured riots described above, this popular anger had a strong sexual strain.

Industrial conflict

Industrial conflict, more than racial confrontation, has been a continuing theme of the modern history of South Wales. It is easy, as Roger Geary's work has shown, to exaggerate the threat posed by industrial disturbances, but there can be little doubt that police chiefs, from Lionel Lindsay to David East, took them very seriously. Lindsay in particular was determined to overwhelm strikers with force, whether that force was his own men or extra policemen and soldiers brought in from outside. The years from 1910 to 1926 in South Wales witnessed some of the worst industrial troubles in Britain, and have been described in detail by Dai Smith, Jane Morgan and Barbara Weinberger.

There was a succession of small but bitter strikes in Glamorgan during the first decade of the century, involving, amongst other industries, the nickel works at Clydach, and the collieries at Aberpergwm and Ynysybwl, but none of this compared with the Cambrian strike of 1910–11. Crowds of miners and their families closed virtually every pit in the Rhondda, provoking a furious response from Lindsay, who was convinced that socialist agitators were behind the affair. After the 'battle' at Tonypandy, which Anthony Mòr O'Brien has recently reinterpreted, extra policemen and soldiers flooded into the area, and, with coal-owners and Lindsay working as one, the men were beaten into submission.

Other industrial troubles followed. The railway strike in 1911 developed into battles with the police in Clydach and Neath, whilst the extended strike of dockers and industrial action by waggon workers, hauliers and colliers in the Swansea and Neath area erupted into violence in 1912–13. Further clashes followed at Swansea in 1917, during one of the wartime domestic explosions, but the next great wave of trouble swept over South Wales in 1919–21.

The coal strikes during these post-war years gave Lindsay the opportunity to confront pickets with large numbers of police officers, and to remove those whom he regarded as 'dangerous agitators'. In 1920, again at Tonypandy, a clash between miners and police produced many arrests, a feature of these years. In 1921 an emergency police committee sanctioned the use of more officers, with soldiers waiting in the wings, and, on Lindsay's orders, processions were broken up and leaders like Arthur Horner and A. J. Cook gaoled. Thereafter, there was little trouble in South Wales, apart from some angry stoppages at certain collieries and refineries, and the overspill of the anthracite strike of 1925.

The General Strike of the following year was more peaceful in South Wales than the Home Office and Lindsay had predicted, though Hywel Francis and Dai Smith tell us that in the Upper Afan Valley 'activities bordered on insurrection'. There were conflicts, too, at Cardiff, Swansea and at places like Treorchy and Maerdy, as people tried to break the strike, but the police were rightly blamed for at least some of the violence. After this, until the coalfield strikes of the mid-1930s, serious industrial disturbances were rare. Even then, the miners in their 'stay-down' protests were anxious to avoid violent confrontations. The records of the standing joint police committee for these years tell of the chief constable's last stand, as he justified actions like the violent dispersal of a crowd at Trelewis, proudly described the extent of police defences, surveillance and arrests, and fended off growing criticisms. The 'arch-thug', as Horner called him, was responsible during the 1930s for some of the biggest trials of industrial workers in our history.

Although the years during and after the Second World War contained their share of strikes, the latter were not on the scale of those described above, nor as violent. Some of the confrontations, such as those involving printers and seamen in 1959–60, were quite hot-headed affairs, but industrial relations throughout this period were generally peaceful, and even polite. The next great battles were the miners' strikes of 1972, 1974, and 1984–5, the last of which deserves a special mention. Chief Constable East claimed in 1984–5 that in his district 'sensitive policing' and the reliance, except for a few days, on local officers, helped to minimize the ill-feeling. Yet there were 479 arrests in 1984, and numerous acts of intimidation, violence and criminal damage, as attempts were made to undermine union solidarity and break the strike. The death of the taxi-driver, David Wilkie, on the Heads of the Valleys Road was the lowest point of this confrontation. The campaign to reduce the sentences on the culprits was in part due to a recognition that, like the miners during the years 1910–26, the strikers had been outmanœuvred and frustrated by the government and the policing authorities. The subsequent trade-union legislation and the gloomy economic situation have further reduced the spirit for open industrial conflict.

Demonstrations and direct action

The history of popular protest is a complex one, though the legislation passed to deal with the crowd gives some idea of its changing intensity and character. Three important Public Order Acts were passed in 1936, 1963 and 1986, each designed to deal with particular problems. Demonstrations in the decades prior to the first Act had consisted, amongst other things, of angry denunciations of pacifists and protests over the scarcity and cost of food during the First World War. The latter protests were carefully monitored, and confrontations with the police and specials were restrained.

A few years later, meetings of the unemployed and hunger marchers had tougher treatment. Lindsay was convinced that 'communists and trouble-makers' were behind the demonstrations, and called on his men to keep the highways clear and to protect government employees from abuse. Between 1929 and 1936 leaders of the protesters were arrested in large numbers for obstruction, unlawful assembly, assaults on the police and indecent language. In the spring of 1935, when the situation looked particularly serious, there were disturbances right across South Wales, sparked by police interference with marches and changes in the payment of relief. The sacking of the Assistance Board Offices in Merthyr Tydfil was the culmination of this discontent. To these protests were added others in these years, for example, those against the British Union of Fascists and the proposed visit of Sir Oswald Mosley to the Rhondda. The government took advantage of this feeling, and extended the powers of the police through the Public Order Act of 1936.

The Public Order Act of 1963, which increased the punishment for offenders, coincided with another bout of public agitation. However, the targets and the nature of protests in this decade were rather different. Amongst the concerns in the 1960s were the apartheid system in South Africa, the nuclear threat, the treatment of the Welsh language and the character of university administration. The chief constable of Cardiff claimed that, in contrast with their predecessors, the new generation of protesters organized processions and other activities which were deliberately intended to break the law. CND (Campaign for Nuclear Disarmament) campaigners marched to Maindy barracks and sat down in the street, students occupied registry offices, and some of the anti-apartheid demonstrators tried to prevent rugby matches.

The law-breaking work of Welsh language agitators in the 1960s has continued down to the present day, as, until the ending of the

SOUTH WALES CONSTABULARY

DAVID A. EAST, Q.P.M., LL.B.
Chief Constable

Our Ref: CC/JW/26/6   26th June, 1984

Dear Prime Minister,

      I wish formally to apologise on behalf of the South Wales Constabulary that you were the unfortunate recipient of an all too well aimed egg during your recent visit to Porthcawl. Despite this regrettable incident, I hope that you feel the policing arrangements were at one and the same time sensitive to the democratic right to demonstrate and yet conscious of the need to ensure your safety in what might have been an extremely tense and difficult policing situation.

      Whilst there has been ill-informed criticism that such an incident could happen, I know that you will appreciate that the police have no right to search for eggs and other such potential missiles. To have removed the crowd even further away would have laid us open to charges of denying the democratic right of demonstration.

      On behalf of the Force, I can only repeat my apology.

Yours sincerely,

David East

Chief Constable

The Right Honourable Mrs. M. H. Thatcher, M.P.,
Prime Minister,
No. 10 Downing Street,
LONDON, S.W.1.

Police Headquarters, Bridgend, Mid Glamorgan, CF31 3SR Telephone: Bridgend (0656) 55555 Telex: 498256

Letter from the Chief Constable of the South Wales Constabulary to the Prime Minister, June 1984.

Cold War, did that of CND, but a feature of the 1980s and 1990s has been the variety of new forms of illegal protest. Many groups, frustrated with peaceful complaints, have turned towards direct action. The 1980s witnessed mothers blocking dangerous roads, students occupying county halls, people breaking the law in the interests of the environment, and shops picketed over animal rights. The police, who have to deal with these and other types of demonstrations, have since the 1970s received greater training in crowd control, support from special units, and the extra powers of the Public Order Act of 1986.

The Special Branch, which assists with this work, has particular responsibility in connection with covert forms of protest. One of their tasks has been to secure 'vulnerable targets' in South Wales, like airports, and another has been to investigate the use of bombs and incendiary devices. There were a number of explosions in Cardiff in 1968, for which language protesters were blamed, and bomb scares and arson campaigns were features of subsequent years. Several bombs were left at forces' recruiting offices and government buildings in the early 1980s, and the police were vilified, as we saw in chapter 1, for 'trawling' for likely suspects. Devices linked with the Animal Liberation Front were also discovered during this last decade in South Wales shops and the post. Fortunately, the threat of terrorism, especially that associated with the IRA, was largely absent from the region.

Comment

The above evidence suggests that the amount of serious violence and disorder declined over the century. The challenge of disturbances of most kinds was greatest in the first decades, when protest had a distinctly political and progressive character. Only rarely in recent times, as during the miners' strike of 1984–5, and in some of the clashes with the police in 1989, have we been reminded of the troubled existence of a bygone era. The Ely and Penrhys disturbances of the 1980s have been described as the painful cry of the neglected 'underclass', and policing and social work have since combined to keep this isolated voice as quiet as possible.

There is little doubt that public behaviour in the streets of South Wales has improved since the 1920s. The number of court proceedings over using obscene language, urinating in public, drunkenness and disorderly conduct, and assaults on police officers, tends to support this view. So does our tabulated evidence on all known violent offences. This suggests that things had changed for the better even before the First World War, and continued to improve until the next war.

Thereafter, the sources indicate that people reported crimes of violence at an increasing rate, partly because of changes in attitude. For example, Stanley Cohen informs us that society generally has become less tolerant of the behaviour of working-class adolescents, whilst, according to Robert and Edward Dobash, 'battered women' are now more willing than their mothers to 'go public' over their ordeals. The public is acutely aware that the rate of recorded violence is still rising at the present time, out of line with some important property crimes, but whether this signifies that society, and even more the home, has actually become more dangerous is a different matter.

The latest crime surveys, which include many offences not reported to the police, still present an optimistic view. The average person can expect to live for many years without even being threatened, let alone attacked. Yet, as we have seen, the people who were most anxious about assaults in 1989 had some justification for their feelings. In parts of the largest towns, at certain times of the day, week and year, the dangers of attack probably increased over the last twenty-five years of the period. Females, who are about the most apprehensive group in South Wales, have reason to fear male relatives within the home and young males outside it.

The lack of protection afforded such victims has sometimes been contrasted with the police emphasis on, and expertise at, containing public disorder. In fact, new forms of private defence, from the acquisition of personal alarms and ferocious pets to neighbourhood patrols, have been adopted in recent years. It reinforces the point that, although the statistical chances of being attacked outside the home remain very small, people have become more fearful about the prospect than their predecessors in 1900.

A thieving society?

The threat of property crime

The present anxiety about crimes against property is not a new development. In 1900 only the well-to-do, and the small minority with insurance cover, could afford to be blasé about thefts. The willingness of the lower-middle-class and upper-working-class victims to report such offences, and to prosecute the culprits, is an indication of their feelings. Robberies and break-ins caused a great deal of anger, not least because females were often the victims of such crimes. Although the statistics of property offences do not suggest a high rate of such crime in the first third of the century, the dark figure was probably considerable.

There was already concern that several types of property crime had become too common and easy to commit. The stealing of coal and bicycles, for example, was said to have reached 'an exceptional' level during the inter-war years, and the police were criticized for not doing more to protect their owners. In the 1930s letters to newspapers conveyed the public's annoyance over domestic break-ins, whilst during the Second World War and its immediate aftermath, there were many complaints about the black market in stolen goods and widespread fraud.

From the late 1950s the feeling of being under threat from the burglar and the thief became even more strong. It seems that the more serious forms of property crime were beginning to affect a wider range of classes and social groups. 'It must be made clear that today', said the chief constable of Merthyr in 1960, 'many people, who in the past never regarded themselves as targets for thieves, now find their homes and pay packets attacked and stolen.' The front page of the local evening papers was often covered in the 1960s with stories and photographs of people subjected to the worst break-ins, and on the inside pages there were depressingly familiar accounts of elderly victims and council-house tenants who had been targeted several times in a year. The young were blamed for much of this, just as they were for autocrime, another blossoming criminal activity, especially in South Wales.

There was, as noted in chapter 1, an improvement in the reporting of these offences, especially of break-ins, across the century, but even when this is taken into account, it seems likely that property has become more vulnerable with the passage of time. The accompanying graphs 3.3 and 3.4 are of indictable property offences recorded by the police, and they are a better guide than the graph of violent offences. The rate of property crime was comparatively low until the Second World War, apart from exceptional years such as 1921, 1926 and 1931–2. After the

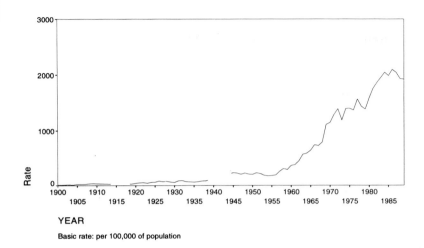

Basic rate: per 100,000 of population

Graph 3.3: Burglaries and break-ins recorded by the police in South Wales, 1900–1989

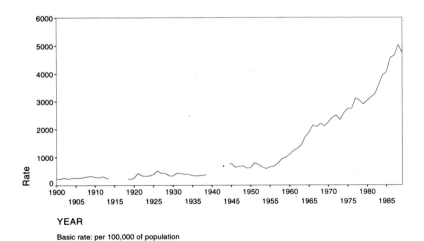

Basic rate: per 100,000 of population

Graph 3.4: Offences of theft and handling stolen goods recorded by the police in South Wales, 1900–1989

war the rate ran at twice this level, and then, in the late 1950s, began a steep incline. By 1969, when the police forces amalgamated, the rate of property offences was three times that of a dozen years previously, an amazing transformation which had a lasting impact on the public, and over the next twenty years the rate more than doubled again. Contrary to received wisdom, the rate of all known property and violent crimes has thus moved at roughly the same pace during the lifetime of the South Wales Constabulary. The overall effect is that in 1989 there was one indictable property crime recorded for every twelve people in South Wales, one of the highest rates in Britain and well ahead of that in the other Welsh districts.

The division of these offences, into those committed with violence and those without, has always been rather arbitrary, and the difficulties of drawing graphs of both are compounded by the way individual crimes were switched across categories and others brought into the tables for the first time. The main offences in the list of property offences committed with violence have always been break-ins and, to a lesser degree, robberies, and there were many fewer of these recorded than thefts and other offences against property committed without violence. The two graphs show that the rate of break-ins rose more sharply than thefts between 1900 and 1938, and that this differential was maintained until the last decades. During the late 1980s the fall in the rate of break-ins was one of the few optimistic trends.

The character and incidence of property crimes varied considerably from area to area. The historical evidence supports the findings of modern crime surveys, namely that urban areas have a much higher rate than rural and other sparsely populated districts. In the last chapter we noted how the police stationed in Cardiff or Aberavon dealt with many more thieves and burglars than their counterparts at Reynoldston and Peterston-super-Ely, though not all the known cases of poaching and fowl-stealing were, it seems, included in the rural returns. The following information in table 3.5, from forty years later, illustrates the continued importance of area differences. It compares the rate of six types of indictable offences across a number of subdivisions in South Wales, incorporating in this order two town centres, an inner- and outer-city district, and two regions which have rural and seaside communities.

Table 3·5: Area differences in the rate of recorded crime per 100,000 of the population, 1978

Sub-divn	Popn.	Acreage	Burglary	Theft from shops	Theft from vehs	Theft of vehs	Fraud & forgery	Criminal damage
Merthyr	61500	27572	1315	496	722	1007	176	322
Morriston	39079	8211	2411	320	939	1336	148	358
Roath	93247	8650	1872	182	786	986	216	288
Llanishen	64885	9326	820	49	487	465	128	160
Porthcawl	34428	12252	1089	145	346	305	154	209
Gorseinon	33480	30844	615	45	343	409	78	116

The police review of 1986, with its examination of crime levels per section, takes us a stage further. It demonstrates that within the centres of the largest towns, shoplifting and autocrime were rife, whilst in the residential outskirts like Roath (Cardiff) and Sketty (Swansea) 'high-value' break-ins were common. In terms of the full range of property crimes, from break-ins to vandalism, the places at highest risk were a number of large and socially deprived council estates. On these in the mid-1980s lived people whose property was targeted twice, three and sometimes more, times a year. The offenders were usually local residents. On other estates the pattern was rather different. At Pentrebane (Cardiff) and Winchwen (Swansea), for example, lived a core of established criminals who worked further afield, travelling regularly to the town centres, the industrial parks and the residential suburbs in search of booty. As we saw in the last chapter, each area has its attractions for the thief.

In a later section we shall establish the precise locale and character of property offences in a number of districts, notably in Cardiff and Merthyr during the 1930s, 1940s and 1950s. This material reveals why there was a growing anxiety over property offences amongst the general public. Firstly, people who felt threatened at home were not imagining things; this was the very place where a large share of recorded crimes occurred. In Cardiff in 1934, the sample indicates that just over half the break-ins were of domestic dwellings, and there were many other instances of goods taken from inside and outside the house. About four out of

ten bicycles stolen in the capital disappeared from within yards of
the home, and two-thirds of stolen cars. Secondly, the evidence
leaves little doubt that individuals, and occasionally very
vulnerable ones, were the primary target of the thief. Eight out of
ten of the Cardiff victims in 1934 were individuals rather than
companies or institutions, and, of these, women often suffered
from the most disturbing of property crimes. In the Cardiff sample
a fifth of the private victims were female, and of these almost a half
were subjected to break-ins and larceny from a dwelling house. In
addition they had handbags stolen from them in the street, and
lost clothes and fowls from back-gardens.

Robberies

The definition of a robbery is felonious plunder. Robberies have
probably caused more anxiety, and received more publicity, than
just about any other crime in modern times. This is a little
surprising, as the recorded offences have been comparatively rare.
In 1900 there were only 9 cases of robbery, extortion and
blackmail in South Wales; and in 1938, 1969 and 1989, 8, 137 and
250 (237 robberies) respectively. They were, from this evidence,
largely a post-war phenomenon. Yet this is not the impression
given in the newspapers, which claimed that people in the earlier
period were sometimes reluctant to report the offence, because of
the poor chances of detection and the embarrassment of some
cases.

The memory of the garrotters of the 1860s and the 1890s was
still important in the early twentieth century, when it influenced
the response to an outbreak of violent robbery in Cardiff. The
robberies of 1907–8 consisted largely of attacks by 'land sharks' on
seamen arriving in the port with money on their person. These
were gangs of robbers, with female associates, who leapt upon
seamen and miners as they walked through the Hayes. Those
prosecuted for this crime in the spring of 1908 received the cat, as
well as imprisonment, and the Home Secretary was heavily
criticized in some quarters for not doing more to prevent this.
Similar debates also accompanied subsequent 'panics' over Cardiff
robberies, notably in 1910 and 1921.

During the inter-war years there were less well publicized
robberies in the industrial communities, and in these cases young
lads and unemployed men took money and goods from women

and children. By the late 1930s some robbers were carrying guns, or imitation firearms, rather than knives, and a number of them already had motor vehicles for a quick get-away. Their chief targets were people known to be carrying large amounts of cash or its equivalent. Amongst those threatened were employees of companies, shops, post offices and banks, as well as car, van and lorry drivers. In the post-war years, as the recorded incidence of robberies rose to its mid-1970s high, petrol-pump attendants, building-society employees, and women walking alone in subways and car parks were also targeted, and a very small number were killed for their possessions.

Fortunately the use of firearms remains rare in South Wales. In 1989 they were used in only 147 offences, the best figures since 1977. Of these eleven were robberies. In the large majority of robberies injuries were slight or non-existent, and the amount taken relatively small. Although this provides little comfort for the victims, their attackers at the present time are not highly trained professionals, but overwhelmingly young males. The latter tend to concentrate their efforts on the vulnerable, the young, the elderly and the female. During the 1980s companies, corporations and the police made life more difficult for these thieves, and, until the sudden rise in the statistics during the early 1990s, there were hopes that robberies, like break-ins, were in decline.

Break-ins

Although break-ins are now well reported, one cannot be sure of the situation for much of the century. Many property-owners were not insured, and probably ignored minor losses, knowing that detection rates for break-ins were comparatively low. As we shall see in chapter 5, unless they were caught in the act, the chances of bringing burglars before the courts were poor, particularly in places like Cardiff. Nevertheless, the common impression, from both literary and statistical evidence, is that before the Second World War the number of break-ins was not a serious cause for concern, except in years like the mid-1920s and the early and late 1930s. The chairman of the Glamorgan quarter sessions said in 1931 that break-ins were becoming too prevalent, even causing people to miss church on a Sunday, and he wanted stronger punishment, especially for the juveniles who were responsible for much of the increase in this crime.

During the war it is difficult to obtain an accurate picture of break-ins. In Glamorgan and Swansea the official figures were high in 1941, and in South Wales generally there was a rise in the reports of this crime towards the end of hostilities. In 1945 2,580 break-ins were recorded, two and a half times the figure of 1931. Merthyr Tydfil, which shared in this, experienced 95 break-ins of shops and warehouses in the last year of the war, and 35 break-ins of houses. Although a few of these were committed by middle-aged professionals, there was then, and for some years later, much anger over the exploits of juvenile burglars and their attacks on 'poor' and 'medium' rather than 'high-quality' properties.

Like many other offences, the rate of break-ins was unusually low between 1953 and 1956, but the rise over the next sixteen years was truly spectacular, helped somewhat by the redefinition of burglary in 1968. Newspapers warned of the dangers to business and domestic premises, and burglar alarms and other crime-prevention measures grew suddenly popular. Between 1972 and 1979 there was some satisfaction with the results, but then the rate of break-ins continued its upward path, reaching its highest point in 1986. In that year the press was full of the terrors suffered by householders; in fact, firearms were used in only two burglaries and the number of offences was about to fall. By 1989, when over 25,000 cases were recorded, the rate had declined for three successive years, only to be reversed again in the early 1990s.

The rates of house and commercial break-ins were somewhat different. The latter were, so far as we know, more common. In the first two decades there were three and a half times as many recorded break-ins of shops and warehouses as of houses. By the outbreak of the Second World War, the gap between the figures had closed considerably, and in some districts continued to do so. In Cardiff and Swansea, on the eve of police amalgamation in 1969, the two types of recorded break-ins were evenly balanced. Over the next twenty years there were, across South Wales, more break-ins of commercial premises than of dwelling houses, but only a third more, and the rates of both types of crime ran along parallel lines.

The seasonality and timing of these offences were also fairly similar. House break-ins, even more than those of commercial premises, were often committed during the winter months, whilst more of the latter type were concentrated in the hours of darkness and at the weekends. In 1900 there were actually more night than day break-ins of homes, but not for the remainder of the century. By the 1940s and 1950s, when people were complaining about houses being left empty by working mothers, eight out of ten break-ins were committed during waking hours, and this situation did not change much in the years that followed.

A good proportion of house break-ins early in the century took place in the more prosperous residential areas. In 1914 mounted patrols were introduced in Uplands, Brynmill and Sketty to reduce this particular crime in Swansea, with, it was said, some success. The offenders, who usually travelled some distance to commit such break-ins, made £10 or more if they were lucky, but the average haul was worth about £2–4. Even so, the returns proved attractive enough in the 1930s for the unemployed adults and the juveniles who between them comprised perhaps 60 per cent of the burglars of South Wales.

In the aftermath of the Second World War gangs of young men preyed upon homes near to their own, or used motor vehicles to travel to new housing and industrial developments on the periphery of the major towns. As we have seen, a feature of the last thirty or forty years was the wide range of people who experienced break-ins. Since 1970 almost every urban family in South Wales has, at one time or another, returned home to find that televisions, radios, cameras, recorders, videos and other items have gone. According to the police figures for 1989, which record one household in forty-six victimized, in a tenth of cases the booty was valued at £1,000 or over, in almost half at £100–1000, and in the remainder at £0–100, though, of course, the criminal realized only a small proportion of this.

The break-ins of non-domestic buildings, which have a lower average financial return, have outnumbered domestic break-ins throughout the century. This is hardly surprising, for until the 1950s shops and warehouses were poorly defended. When, as occasionally happened, employees and ex-employees were parties to the break-ins, the crime was even easier. Jewellers' shops were always popular targets, and, in the austerity of the mid-century, stores selling cigarettes and alcohol were attractive for obvious reasons. A generation later chemists' shops were added to the list. A few of the break-ins of shops, notably recent ones involving large superstores, have netted thousands of pounds, and the chances of non-detection are good.

Offices, warehouses, garages and factories have proved equally tempting for the burglar. In the days before the First World War, railway stations, colliery offices, dock warehouses, and social clubs were regularly set upon. Later, when industrial and enterprise parks became popular, security officers were employed to protect them, and the occurrence books of places like Nantgarw and Aberavon testify to the problems which they encountered. The burglar-alarm systems, introduced after the Second World War, were of limited success. Few intruders were trapped by the silent alarms, and some protected factories were broken into time and again.

Although the takings from warehouses, factories and offices were sometimes high, the owners were surprised that many break-ins did not mean loss of goods. People broke open doors and windows, and did a little damage, or simply ran away. The same was true of break-ins of schools which, as we have seen, were a feature of crime in Merthyr Tydfil in the inter-war years, and of Cardiff and Swansea in the recent past. Like several other popular targets, school buildings were often rather isolated, and their safety was a difficult matter. Crime prevention, which has its roots in the mid-century experience of break-ins, has gone some way to protect these and other buildings.

Embezzlement, fraud and forgery

Such is the reporting and detection of white-collar crimes that a graph of such has limited value, except as an indication of changing attitudes and police priorities. It is widely accepted, in spite of the low figures typically recorded in Wales, that these offences are common, and that their value dwarfs that of most other types of crime. Initially court cases were rare, and a matter of intense public interest. Those of the 1920s, when the defendants were former government officers and ministers of religion, were taken as a sign of a decline in commercial probity dating from the First World War. As evidence of the latter, about 1,500 black-market offences were recorded in South Wales each year of the Great War, most of them of a minor kind and penalized by a £5 fine.

The Second World War, which provided excellent opportunities for unscrupulous farmers, tradesmen, builders and government officials, was also blamed for creating a 'get rich quick' mentality. Commentators had few doubts that business fraud was on the increase by the mid-1950s, when the rate of offences known to the police was more than three times that of thirty years earlier. Between 1959 and 1979 the rate of frauds and forgeries in Wales rose even faster, a fourfold increase, notably during the 1970s. Michael Levi, in his study of commercial fraud, believes that the official figures over the last twenty years have reflected a real increase in such activity, but all statistics of white-collar crimes are strongly affected by changes in policing and prosecution policy.

The 1960s witnessed the first organized police efforts to deal with fraud. Initially, the embryonic fraud squads were small coteries of CID officers, with little training in the work, but in time they benefited from national courses and a national network of information. One must not exaggerate the pace of progress. South Wales in 1972 still had only three officers, based at Cardiff, who were committed full-time to investigating such offences. They examined a small proportion of the 1,533 recorded cases. At the time of the police review of 1986, the fraud squad numbered thirteen, with four divisional detective constables assisting on a permanent basis. It dealt during that year with 23 major allegations of fraud and 5 serious cases of corruption, and made 1,915 enquiries at Companies House, Cardiff. The problems which the squad faced, and the reluctance of some companies and institutions to report offences, have helped to ensure that the rate of recorded white-collar crimes has increased in the last quarter of the century at a slower pace than that of most other offences.

Embezzlement, fraud and forgery were committed by many types of people, but most of the persons charged fell into four categories. One group were those who handled money on behalf of others. Solicitors, agents, clerks, treasurers, insurance representatives, financial advisers and collectors were amongst those convicted of white-collar crimes in South Wales. So, too, were company directors and other businessmen who had the authority, and secrecy, to indulge in dubious transactions and corruption. A third group of minor characters, on the fringes of organized crime, handled forged banknotes, tickets, prescriptions and vehicle-test certificates, whilst the last group were members of local government in South Wales, who personally benefited from deals and contracts. During the 1970s major corruption scandals involving these people were finally brought to court.

Much of the effort over frauds was, however, directed against the lower-middle- and working-class cheats. This, as Edward Smithies informs us, has always been the way of things. Many working people appeared in court for obtaining money by false pretences. Hundreds were fined and gaoled in connection with ration-book frauds, and national assistance and social-security claims. False claims for benefits and the forging of official cheques sometimes cost the taxpayer thousands of pounds, but most were comparatively small in value. Occasionally, magistrates made an example of the culprits, and housewives and labourers were imprisoned for six months. Colonel Ivor Morgan, presiding in a Swansea court in 1962, insisted that unless a firm stand was made against these activities, the welfare state was in jeopardy.

Thefts: kind

Stealing has always been the main form of property crime, and the recorded incidence of it can be found on graph 3.4. This shows that the rate did not change greatly during the first quarter of a century, except in years like 1909, 1912, 1921 and 1926. During the war years, the rate rose significantly and kept on a higher plateau until the mid-1950s. Between 1956 and 1966 there was a staggering threefold increase, which has not been matched since. The fastest rate of growth in the last few years has been during the early 1980s, confirming the links which Simon Field has drawn between this rate and contractions in personal comsumption.

Theft is a general term, which encompasses many types of crime, the popularity of which waxed and waned during the century. Thus the rates of larceny from the person and by a servant have not changed much over the years, whereas those of larceny from shops and of and from motor vehicles certainly have. Table 3.6, of seven stealing offences in South Wales in 1969 and 1989 illustrates the growth in thefts of and from motor vehicles, and larceny from shops. The population grew by only 4 per cent between those years.

It is impossible to recount the history of every type of theft, not least because the changes in the compilation of the statistics during the century make the picture quite confusing. Instead, it makes more sense to deal collectively with thefts under the

Table 3·6: Seven types of theft in South Wales, 1969 and 1980

	Thefts	1969	1989
1.	From the person	175	286
2.	From a dwelling house	418	765
3.	By a servant	306	356
4.	From shops and stalls	2439	5820
5.	Of pedal cycles	1524	2751
6.	Of motor vehicles, and taking and driving away	4673	15676
7.	From motor vehicles	5404	22541

Table 3·7: Types of property stolen in Merthyr in 1944 and 1952

Type	Percentage 1944	1952
Cash (sometimes in handbags, purses and wallets)	18·9	30·7
Clothing, shoes and bedding	16·7	8·4
Food, drink, and tobacco	13·2	8·4
Coal	13·2	2·7
Wood	7·0	5·7
Metal and wire	1·8	11·9
Bicycles	3·9	2·3
Motor vehicles	0·9	5·4
Books and stationery	3·5	0·8
Cutlery, crockery,	3·5	–
Tools, brooms, wheelbarrow	3·1	4·2
Watches, lamps and jewellery	4·8	2·3
Ration and insurance books, coupons, vouchers and tickets	3·9	0·4
Battery, wheels, radiator cap, car seat and petrol	–	4·6
Other items	5·6	12·2

headings of place and type. The lists of recorded crime in Cardiff and Merthyr in the 1930s, 1940s and 1950s provide a useful starting-point. Table 3.7 is a sample of 500 offences of theft, evenly divided between the years.

The stealing of money had obvious advantages, and it had probably become the main type of theft by the middle of the century. As such, it usurped some of the prominence once held by thefts of food, clothing, fuel and metals. Cash was more available now than before, and criminals took it from the person, from tills, from burgled homes and offices, from vending machines and meters, and from armed robberies. Apart from a few cases, notably of robbery, embezzlement and fraud, the amount stolen was fairly small.

The same was true of food and drink. This was removed from from shops, markets, schools, houses and warehouses, especially by the very young. Boys of nine and ten years of age were birched during the First World War for pinching sweets, drinks, eggs and meat, having followed the example of their mothers, who paid weekly visits to markets for free weekend supplies. Others descended upon neighbours' gardens for vegetables, eggs and hens, or took fowls, fish and rabbits from farms and estates in the vicinity. In the 1930s poachers seem to have been very active, with the Margam estate one of the more popular targets. When apprehended, the offenders frequently pleaded poverty, as did so many others who took food illegally.

Clothing was the item most commonly stolen in the nineteenth century, and this was still the situation at the very start of our period. The occurrence books and station journals reveal that much disappeared from clothes lines, and from hotels, public houses and homes. Shops and stall-holders lost innumerable shirts, dresses, trousers, coats, pillows, blankets, boots and shoes. Once again, there is less evidence than might have been expected of organized theft and prominent receivers. According to the Swansea police there were only eight people in that town in 1900 who were interested in purchasing these stolen goods. Most offenders seem to have used the clothes themselves, or to have given them to members of their family.

Fuel was used in the same way, though there was a small trade in stolen coal, oil and wood. Coal vanished from tips, railways and docks. The scale of the crime varied, from a child or woman collecting pieces for the fire, to ambushes of railway trucks near Merthyr in the mid-1920s and in the Cynon Valley in 1987. The police were, on these occasions, sometimes held at bay by crowds of people, shouting about rights and survival. In 1926 and 1931 hundreds of men illegally worked levels in the Rhondda, and in the process annoyed Lleufer Thomas, stipendiary at Pontypridd court. The suspicion that he and his friends harboured was that these miners were not content with cutting enough for themselves. Like Skewen colliers and Port Tennant (Swansea) fuel plant workers of a later date, they were accused of being 'criminal traders'.

Almost by its very nature, stolen metal and scrap metal had to be passed on, and here receivers played an important role. In the first third of the century the evidence suggests that such thefts were typically small, but changes in the scale and incidence of this crime came with the wartime demand for metal, and the shortages that characterized the immediate post-war years. As the chief constable of Glamorgan put it in December 1951:

> amongst the many larcenies recorded there are many cases of thefts of scrap metal from works, factories and yards, and, in addition, there have been several serious cases where thieves have carried out planned thefts of lead from the roofs of buildings (including places of worship) so that they can dispose of the proceeds at high prices in the black market.

Some of the thefts in the 1950s of lead, copper wire and piping, and old machinery, were valued at £7,000–12,000, and in subsequent years this figure grew. In 1971 the South Wales police force established a stolen car and metal squad, based at Cardiff and Skewen. Members of this squad, like the detective officers before them, focused their attention on dealers of a suspicious or criminal character.

The other aspect of the work of this new squad was autocrime, which became, as table 3.6 indicates, a major form of theft. The stealing of conveyances has always been popular. During the inter-war years the police pleaded with workmen, students and children to lock and mark their bicycles, but very few did so. In Cardiff in 1940, where 794 pedal cycles disappeared from outside homes, places of work, shops, libraries and the labour exchange, the losses comprised almost half of recorded thefts. Bicycles were both easy to take and easy to sell, and some criminals specialized in this trade. They were also a casual source of income for unemployed people and gangs of youths. With the replacement of the pedal cycle by other forms of transport this source gradually dried up, but the recent revival in the use of expensive bicycles has once again attracted the thief, not least in Cardiff.

The thefts of motorcycles, cars and other motor vehicles was a cause for concern as early as the 1930s. The taking of vehicles without the owner's consent was said to have reached 'epidemic' proportions in the capital at the outbreak of the Second World War. A total of 407 were taken in Cardiff during 1939, mostly by young people, who often indulged in 'joy-riding' before abandoning the damaged vehicles. For a while after the war, there were fewer such crimes. In the capital in 1960, only 118 motor vehicles were reported as stolen, and 143 driven away without the owners' permission, but things soon changed.

The rate of stealing and taking vehicles quadrupled over the last twenty-five years of the period, the rise being especially marked in the late 1960s and early 1970s, and between 1983 and 1986. Most crimes of this nature were reported to the police. Already in 1971 more than a quarter of recorded indictable crime in South Wales was autocrime, that is, thefts of and from motor vehicles, and twenty years later, in districts such as Tonpentre, Llanishen and Barry, the proportion had increased to well over half. With over 300 vehicles disappearing each week, South Wales developed a reputation for being the worst district for this crime in Britain. The cost of the thefts of vehicles was estimated in 1989 at almost £35 million, of which sum three-fifths was recovered.

Stolen vehicles were sold privately or to dealers, and some were reassembled and given a new identity. In the late 1970s, in a carefully planned operation, a number of the highest-value cars were exported. Many of the vehicles, however, were simply abandoned or destroyed, after the thieves had enjoyed the short-term pleasures of a free drive. This was very prevalent in places like the Bonymaen and St Thomas area of Swansea, where the population was exceptionally young, unemployed and poor. The difficulties of arresting such people, mainly youngsters, for this crime were only too obvious. In the Aberavon area stolen cars were driven at police officers, and chases in the late 1980s sometimes ended in serious accidents and death. For their part the police have tried, by special squads, teams and patrols, and by publicity and education, to control the problem, but after a fall in 1989, the rate of taking and stealing cars is once again rising.

Thefts from vehicles are even more common. From Cardiff in

the 1930s to South Wales in the 1980s, motor vehicles were less at risk than the goods inside them. In 1931 the chief constable of Swansea appealed to motorists to use the 'authorised Parking Places where an attendant is in charge', and to lock their cars if they contained 'articles of value'. During the Second World War the compulsory locking of vehicles sharply reduced such larcenies, but in the 1950s the rate more than tripled. The nature of the goods stolen also changed; car rugs and cases were no longer the main items taken. In the early 1960s there were many accounts of raids on car parks and streets, often by gangs of youths, who removed transistor radios, batteries, wheels and whatever else was required by the car-owning public. At certain times of the year, especially at Christmas, the crime brought good rewards, and, on one notorious occasion in 1982, a deep snowstorm on the M4 turned hundreds of local people into thieves. During the 1980s the city centres saw the introduction of street police squads, observation posts and camera surveillance, but the recorded incidence of the crime rose faster than ever.

Thefts: place

Table 3.8, an analysis of 500 offences, gives some idea of the places where, in an urban setting, thefts occurred in the mid-twentieth century.

As table 3.8 indicates, the home and the street adjoining were the scene of most property offences. Thefts by members of the family were rarely recorded in the police records, but when they were, sons were the usual culprits. Lodgers were, by comparison, more often charged, as were neighbours and passing strangers who took cash and other items from unlocked houses, and clothing, tools, vegetables and poultry from gardens, garages and sheds. The nature of the housing was important in the story; whereas burglars expected rich pickings in places like Roath, the most common domestic theft in poorer districts, such as Swansea's Townhill community and the Penrhys estate in the Rhondda, was the breaking open of prepaid meters and the illegal use of power. Although youths entered council homes to break open meters, the culprits for the illegal use of power were mainly the occupants. Angry magistrates, tired of these cases, blamed the power companies for not checking, and collecting from, their meters at shorter intervals.

Table 3·8: Places of property crime, Cardiff 1934 and Merthyr 1944

Place	Percentage of thefts	
	Cardiff 1934	*Merthyr 1944*
Dwelling houses, garages and gardens	27·3	29·7
Shops	10·1	8·6
Street (bicycle, thefts of and from)	34·9	2·3
Street (motor vehicles, thefts of and from)	11·8	5·0
Offices	3·4	–
Warehouses, stores, workshop	2·1	7·2
Ships, docks and yards	2·9	–
Colliery premises	–	18·0
Other industrial premises	–	5·4
Schools and colleges	0·8	10·8
Public houses, hotels, cafés, cinemas, clubs and dance halls	2·1	6·8
Railway	0·8	2·7
Other places	3·8	3·5

The street was also a vulnerable area. In Cardiff in 1934, as we have seen, four out of every ten stolen bicycles were taken from outside the owner's residence, as were two-thirds of the stolen cars. Most of the others were removed from streets in the centre of the city. This was also the venue for the robberies and larceny from the person. Pickpockets were still working in Cardiff, and other large towns, in the inter-war years, and they were a fixture whenever large sporting and shopping crowds gathered. In the red-light districts of Cardiff and Swansea, prostitutes and their bullies were expert at the art of removing wage-packets and watches. As Assistant Chief Constable Vivian Brooks recalled many years later, this was probably the most lucrative part of their 'trade'.

A large number of thefts were carried out at work. Estimates varied, but it seems that as much as 5 per cent of companies' profits were siphoned off in this way. Most of it went undetected, though employers withheld information on some of these offences from the police. Table 3.8 giving Cardiff and Merthyr crimes contains few of these cases, and even in 1989 the South Wales figure of 356 recorded thefts by employees, valued at a third of a million pounds, was only the tip of the iceberg. In the early twentieth century the coal and steel industry, and other large companies, had their own policemen to assist in the detection of such offences, but even these found the problem a difficult one. So did the British Transport Police and factory security officers at a somewhat later date. Amongst those who regularly appeared before the courts charged with robbing their masters were dockers, colliers, railway porters, postmen, shop assistants, domestic servants and night-watchmen. The temptation for these employees was especially strong when, as during wartime, the demands for certain goods guaranteed them a market. A number of offenders excused themselves by claiming rights to damaged items and other perks, but in some instances the scale of the theft made a mockery of the explanation.

One place which suffered from the greed of employees and outsiders was the docks. In 1914, for example, it was said that 50–60,000 men and women went in and out of the Cardiff dock gates every twenty-four hours, and as they made their way past the numerous warehouses, waggons, tugs and cranes servicing over a hundred ships, some of these people could not resist the goods piled in front of them. Metals, wood, fish, cigarettes and alcohol disappeared in large quantities. The docks police reported eighty-seven cases in Swansea in 1917, an eighth of the town's recorded property crime, and valued at almost £200. Until they were disbanded, the docks police in South Wales handed over several hundred suspicious characters each year to their borough colleagues. The decline of the docks, however, has brought this story almost to an end, though it has been replaced by crime in the marinas.

Unlike this new phenomenon, the security of shops and stalls has been a cause for concern for centuries. The police figures of larceny at these places reflect the policy of shop-owners, the efficiency of the security officers, the support provided by the police, and, to an unknown degree, the scale of the thieving. Each development in the shopping trade in this century, from hanging goods outside doorways to having open counters and self-service, was criticized for helping the thief. D. P. Walsh, the leading authority on shoplifting in the second half of the century, has blamed large companies for making life easy for the culprits, and for budgeting for such losses.

The crime of shoplifting has not changed much over the years. Claims that employees and the drivers who supplied the shops, actually took most of the lost goods were made in the 1930s, and have been repeated in every decade since. Although the police statistics tended to rise in difficult years like the early 1930s and the early 1980s, the increase, especially between 1960 and 1985 was too consistent to permit simple economic analysis. Clothing and food have remained favourite targets, and women and children, together with unemployed males, have always committed a large share of the offences, often travelling long distances to collect the goods.

Minnie Morris, a 29-year-old married lady from St Thomas, who worked her way down High Street, Swansea, in 1940, was representative of one type of shoplifter, and a large gang of teenagers who committed a series of offences in and around Merthyr in 1964 were typical of another. Professional shoplifters were arrested by the Cardiff police in the late 1970s, but, with these exceptions, the crime has usually been small-time activity for limited rewards. In Cardiff and Swansea co-ordinated prevention and detection campaigns, involving truancy patrols, anonymous shop-walkers and plain-clothes officers, have been tried at different times over the last fifteen years, but, as with many other property offences, the lower rate of shoplifting statistics in the late 1980s was not sustained in the 1990s.

Damage to property
Wilful damage differs from all other property crimes because of the character and purpose of the offence. Investigations into vandalism disclose a bewildering set of motivations. In some instances, especially in connection with the smashing and firing of domestic property, the crime usually springs from a personal grudge against the victim. Occasionally psychological disorders are at the root of the crime, made worse perhaps by the influence of alcohol, drugs and solvents. During the two world wars vandalism was sometimes attributed to a mixture of exuberance and aggression, but the most common explanations over the century have focused on the culture of the young, and the lack of work and recreational opportunities for them.

Wilful damage to property covers a wide range of offences, from a pencil mark on a library book to burning down a school. This fact, together with poor reporting and recording, and changes in compiling the statistics, makes any estimate of the real extent of vandalism impossible. The Criminal Damage Acts of 1971 and especially of 1977 increased the proportion of such offences that were returned as indictable crime, and since that time the police figures have moved ever upwards. Although there are some who believe that it is the fastest-growing crime, the British Crime Survey statistics do not bear this out. Moreover, the increase in the police records can be interpreted, at least in part, as society's changing response to such behaviour. Towards the end of the 1970s, for example, politicians, the media and the police made the 'attack on vandalism' a priority, choosing certain areas for special attention. The differences in the figures between communities were indeed very marked. According to one statistical survey of 1978, districts which suffered most per head of population were the centres of Cardiff, Swansea, Merthyr, Port Talbot and Morriston, whilst the quieter residential suburbs and rural communities experienced, or reported, the least amount.

Vandalism is not, in spite of the newness of the term, a modern crime. Damage to trees, common land and animals was a feature of districts such as the Gower and the Vale of Glamorgan in the early twentieth century, but not on the scale of a hundred years before. By comparison, there were more reports after 1900 of the planting of obstacles in the roadway and on railway lines, and of throwing stones at vehicles, street lamps and electricity cables. On a handful of occasions in the 1920s and 1930s, youths at Onllwyn, Briton Ferry and Swansea managed to plunge whole streets into darkness. At the same time the practice of removing and breaking shop, street and traffic signs remained popular, and to the old custom of window-smashing was added the window-slashing craze of 1921 and 1926 in South Wales.

Linked to the last crime, in the inter-war years, was the slashing of car seats – which was extended thirty years later to buses and trains – and the daubing of graffiti. This marking of property, which caused quite an outcry in the 1950s and 1960s, was considered in academic circles as a form of play, defiance, identity and power. Like most forms of vandalism, the people cautioned and charged with daubing on walls, bridges and vehicles were young males. A strong attempt was made, by anti-vandal patrols, and educational and youth work, to restrict their activities but, although graffiti-daubing has declined in popularity, other forms of criminal damage have not.

The targets of the people charged with destroying or damaging property have been both private and public. Elderly residents of

Penarth and Barry in the mid-1980s protested about the damage done to domestic property. Like a number of other groups, they exaggerated its scale, but, as we saw in chapter 1, houses and cars were an attraction to the vandals. On a number of estates, windows and doors were regularly attacked, gardens ransacked, garages broken, and lighted material pushed through letter-boxes. The empty or unfinished home was the perfect playground for the young vandal, and many of the largest building sites since the Second World War have needed watchmen and guard dogs. Outside the home, caravans and motor vehicles have been so often attacked that people are glad to escape just with broken aerials, mirrors and wipers.

Security officers and night-watchmen have battled against vandals for decades. The police journals of the Great Western Collieries at Hopkinstown, just after the First World War, describe the throwing of stones through the lamp-room, the dropping of planks down the pit, and the breaking of panels on trams and workshops. In factories, too, security men in the inter-war period came upon gangs of youths engaged in wanton destruction, and bus garages and depots suffered a similar fate. During the 1930s, as in the 1980s, some of the damage to machines and vehicles was closely related to bitter industrial conflicts, but most of the ransacking of commercial property has not been of this kind.

Public buildings were another obvious target, especially small enclosures like air-raid shelters, public toilets, bus shelters, telephone kiosks and scout huts. Chapels and churches were also easy prey for the vandal, as were cemeteries, though in recent decades the worst excesses have been inflicted on schools, playgrounds, swimming pools, public gardens and parks. In the 1970s, education authorities and councils across South Wales expressed their alarm at the escalating costs of repairing the damage, but the burden shows no sign of diminishing. In 1989 £2 million worth of damage was done to a secondary school at Caerphilly, the culmination of a bad decade, and there has been worse since.

Comment

Apart from malicious damage, shoplifting and white-collar crime, property offences have been during this century much better reported than violent offences. This strengthens the general impression that the extent of thieving increased throughout the century, with the late 1950s and the 1960s being the crucial period of change. By 1989 people were right to feel a little anxious; in that year about one household in nine in South Wales fell victim to a serious property offence, like the loss of a bicycle, autocrime and break-ins, and others experienced petty crime and vandalism which they did not always report to the police. The losses sustained rose faster than inflation during the second half of the century, and, although a large proportion of victims are now covered by insurances, the emotional cost is considerable. So is the expense of protection and policing.

The victims and perpetrators of property crime are a cross-section of society. As we have seen, by the middle of the century everyone had reason to fear the thief, from large companies with cheating employees to the elderly living on the poorest estates. The offenders included professional thieves, like the man arrested at Roath in 1964 for 104 larcenies, who had £1,000 of goods in his home, wealthy fraudsters who were regarded with a mixture of contempt and admiration, and a number of well-known characters engaged in bank robberies and car thefts. They were serviced by a small collection of receivers, some of whom had a respectable trading front. However, the vast majority of property crimes were committed by non-professionals, often by younger males in and out of employment, who kept switching their attention to the least defended and most marketable property. In their early days, some of these people belonged to gangs of juvenile thieves, like the notorious 'K2 gang' at Pontardawe in the late 1930s, but most did not. The bulk of property offences were committed by one or two people, who had short criminal records or none at all.

There has been a tendency, most evident since the Second World War, to place too much of the blame for *all* property crimes on the *very young*. Thus in 1968, only three out of ten persons in Cardiff and Swansea charged with these offences were under seventeen years of age, though they did commit a much higher proportion of the house and shop break-ins. Most of the ten- to thirteen-year-olds in these towns during the 1960s were caught for breaking into shops and shoplifting, and, as they grew a little older, they added house break-ins and autocrime to their repertoire. These, and their exaggerated contribution to vandalism, have greatly annoyed victims and the wider public, and given people a jaundiced view of the younger generation.

Table 3.9 shows that in 1989 both the age structure and the types of offences committed were similar to this pattern. Of the total number accused of burglaries, thefts and criminal damage in the columns, 85 per cent were male, and half were twenty-one years of age or over.

Table 3·9: Ages of persons cautioned and proceeded against for property crimes in South Wales, 1989

Ages	Proportion of property crimes (%)				
	Burglary offences	Theft and handling stolen goods	Stealing from shops	Theft of & taking of m. vehicles	Criminal damage
10–16	26·3	23·1	30·1	18·2	20·4
17–20	34·0	22·6	14·8	35·8	26·9
21+	39·7	54·3	55·1	46·0	52·8

The public's response to property crime has varied, depending on the period, the community, the crime and the criminal. We are told that society has ambiguous attitudes towards shoplifting, employee crime and criminal damage, and there was undoubtedly some support for people stealing food and fuel in the inter-war years. At a later date, these feelings were perhaps less obvious; the widespread experience of property crime in the modern welfare state, and the value of the goods taken, has reduced the interest in, and sympathy for, criminals. In fact, much of people's attention, especially in the last quarter of a century, has been directed towards strengthening the defences. Crime-prevention panels have provided a co-ordinated response, and neighbourhood and other watch schemes have flourished, at least temporarily. Demands for a stronger police presence and for foot patrols have been unrelenting, and, at the present time, beleaguered tradesmen and communities have turned to private security firms and vigilantes for even greater protection.

A controlled society?

Control and regulation

Crimes other than those against people and property have not received their just attention. The public, the police and magistrates spend much of their time with offences that could not be said to be a danger to anyone. The growth of victimless crime was a feature of the second half of the nineteenth century. By 1900 there was, in the view of some observers, 'a policeman state' in Britain; many aspects of life were regulated and supervised. How sinister, planned and class-orientated this was is a matter of debate. For some it was part of a conspiracy to control the masses who had, or were about to receive, political power. Barbara Weinberger and Herbert Reinke argue that in Britain, unlike America, 'class control, in the form of the targetting of certain lower class sections of society, continued to provide the impetus behind much police work' well into the twentieth century. For others the emergence of 'policeman state' was the natural consequence of the growth of a modern, mechanized and civilized society.

Victimless offences were clearly related to the drive for social improvement. Figures were exceptionally high in areas of behaviour which were, at a given time, causing concern. The point was well made by the county accountant of Glamorgan, in his report of January 1937, which compared the nature of magistrate-court cases with those of twenty or thirty years before. 'Whereas drunkenness, public-house offences, prostitution, wounding, assaults, County Bye-law cases, non-attendance at school, and a variety of other more or less serious offences were the rule . . . at the present time, cases of non-payment of rates, Road Act and Motor Licensing offences, Betting, Affiliation and Husband and Wife cases form the major proportion of the Court work.'

As he was writing this, motor vehicles were becoming a vital part of people's lives, and even stricter controls over their use would soon be in place. By 1963 almost three-quarters of the cases dealt with at the magistrates' courts in Glamorgan were proceedings under the Road Traffic Acts and Regulations. Such was the pressure on the courts that the Magistrates Act of 1957 allowed people to plead guilty to minor offences by letter, and this was followed some years later by the fixed penalty system for parking offences, which was extended in 1986 to cover a wider range of misdemeanours.

The public and the police were as concerned about some of these victimless offences as they were about the more serious ones against people and property. Amongst the complaints from ratepayers, businessmen, councillors and ordinary individuals in

1900 were the level of street noise, the dangers of carts, the unpleasantness of obscene language and drunken behaviour, and the nuisance of stray animals. Half a century later the noise of motorcycles and juke-boxes were added to the list, together with the smells of late-night restaurants and the inconvenient parking of motor vehicles. At the present time, as we shall see in the next chapters, the public report such incidents much more frequently than indictable offences.

The police have always been regarded as general servants of the community rather than simply keepers of the peace. At the beginning of the century they acted on behalf of local and national government, as firemen, curators of highways, Poor Law officials, public-health inspectors, liquor-licensing officers and primitive welfare officers. They were responsible for registering pedlars, street traders, aliens and metal dealers, and for the licensing of firearms, explosives, dangerous drugs, hackney carriages, cinemas and dance halls. They were also, until the 1960s, much in demand as traffic wardens and school-crossing patrols. In some communities the police spent well over half of their time enforcing legislation unrelated to violence or property, and occasionally resented it. Amongst the tasks which caused them irritation were assisting with poor relief, truancy, the execution of maintenance orders, the non-payment of rates and the eviction of debtors. It was important work, but it brought criticisms and claims that the police were neglecting their primary responsibilities.

Complaints about the legislation described in this section, and about its enforcement, have gathered during the century around the three issues of control, seriousness and interest. Many people in 1900 resented state interference in the conduct of family life, the education of children, the exercise of leisure and Sunday trade and entertainment. The police and magistrates were told by parents, for example, that 'my children belong to me', and those caught laying a bet in the street replied that 'it is of no account to you'. At this time there were also constant clashes with the authorities over the use of pavements and streets, and this conflict became, with the arrival of motor vehicles, of vital importance and one which the state could not afford to lose.

The debate over the seriousness of victimless offences has a long history. A small number of crimes, like drink-driving, were regarded more seriously in the distant past than we might imagine, whereas some contemporaries felt that playing in the street, spitting, swearing and urinating were not matters which should have been brought to court. Over other minor offences, like obstructive parking, disorderly conduct and keeping savage dogs, people had mixed feelings. Particularly resented were penalties for the sins of 'omission' like failing to keep up-to-date records and riding motor vehicles and bicycles with missing lights and reflectors. The police occurrence and complaint books of the inter-war years contain many protests by motorists over being 'caught out', being refused a second chance, and being 'treated disrespectfully'.

The final issue raised by victimless offences was the interests served by the legislation. The desire for an ordered and regulated society was something which crossed class divisions. There was widespread support, so far as one can now tell, for some of the measures controlling the driving of cars, the sale of food and the treatment of animals. Yet there was a strong feeling that much legislation was rooted in class prejudice and morality. The vagrancy laws, the Education Acts, and those regulating street trading, for instance, were largely targeted at the working class. Similarly the laws against gamblers, drunkards, prostitutes and Sunday traders were, in their execution, heavily weighted against the less prosperous members of society.

One of the popular grievances, especially in Wales, was that as one moral objective was achieved, so another campaign was launched. The crusade against 'the evils of drink' followed this pattern, and so did other chapel-inspired denunciations of Sunday papers and concerts, boxing matches and funfairs, and card-playing and 'A'-rated films. When offenders against this moral code were paraded before the Cardiff courts in the inter-war years, the *Western Mail*, amongst other newspapers, mocked the 'kill-joy' mentality of the city elders. There was, in fact, a perpetual tension between the tight controls demanded by certain members of South Wales society, and the *laissez-faire* attitude of others, seen in a somewhat different context recently in the debate over whether to decriminalize drug-taking and all aspects of prostitution.

Victimless offences and offenders

It is impossible to look at all the controls on people's activities in the twentieth century. We can, nevertheless, note those which

Table 3·10: Prominent victimless crimes in South Wales, a selection, 1900–1975: persons proceeded against at magistrates' courts

Offence	S. Wales 1900	Swansea 1923	Glamorgan 1950	South Wales 1975
Adulteration of food and drugs	113	16	25	108
Betting and gaming	1	31	188	21
Cruelty to animals	210	16	26	39
Diseases of Animals Act	67	2	61	7
Dogs, offences in relation to	2207	177	347	116
Education Acts	2854	590	1031	227
Highways Acts	1648	239	402	409
Indecent exposure	15	30	33	91
Intoxicating Liquor Law	11328	482	479	3356
Labour Law	185	133	185	38
Military, Naval and Air Law	191	5	75	6
National Assistance, or Social Security offences	–	–	13	231
National Insurance Act	–	–	–	473
Police and local regulations, by-laws	4565	372	1460	1364
Poor Law	130	12	–	-
Prostitution	324	48	–	97
Sanitary, Public Health Law	68	3	37	47
Railway offences	275	55	465	697
Revenue Law	352	14	1483	2505
Carriage, public vehicle offences	143	30	89	100
Sunday trading	554	1305	-	2
Vagrancy Acts	433	102	59	192
Weights and Measures Act	69	8	18	14
Wireless Telegraphy Acts	–	–	87	1959
Dangerous drugs, drug offences	–	8	–	344
Aliens and immigration offences	–	7	54	44
Motoring offences	–	–	4804	36127

brought people most often to the attention of the police and the courts. Table 3.10 gives a selection of the prominent victimless crimes dealt with between 1900 and 1975.

The Highways Acts in the table covered offences like causing an obstruction or a nuisance, and the vast majority of breaches of the intoxicating liquor legislation were drunkenness, aggravated and simple. The Poor Law offences included not maintaining one's family, and the Vagrancy Acts outlawed, amongst other things, begging, sleeping out, and being in enclosed premises. There were many categories of offences against police and local regulations, from playing in the street to making excessive noise, but those against the revenue laws were of two main types only, the non-payment of motor and of dog licences. Looked at across the century, there was a contraction in the range of victimless crimes for which people were brought to court in large numbers. By the 1970s there was, apart from maintaining the licensing laws, less concern with people's general behaviour; most defendants were convicted over the licensing and use of motor vehicles, radios, televisions and dogs.

The scale of such offences is probably best seen at a local level. At Cwmgwrach near Glynneath early in the century most of the people locked in the police cells were not charged with indictable offences but with being drunk, drunk and disorderly, sleeping out, neglecting to maintain illegitimate children or the family, and using abusive language. At Hopkinstown, on the industrial east side of Glamorgan, it was a similar story; most of those who appeared before the local magistrates were guilty of driving without lights, being drunk, defiling walls with urine, using indecent language, gaming with cards, begging alms, having unlicensed and uncontrolled dogs, street betting and Sunday trading.

The conviction lists of people living in Taibach and Pontyclun in the first half of this century confirm that there were hundreds of people in these communities who appeared before the courts for victimless crimes. Arthur Veysey, a Taibach butcher, had nineteen convictions between 1907 and 1927 for allowing horses to stray, selling unfit meat and dog offences. George Sigadeli of the Margam café also had nineteen convictions, between 1935 and 1949, for Sunday trading and breaches of the Shops Act, the Food and Drugs Act and Food Rationing Orders. In addition, many others in the area had convictions for bicycle and motoring offences, betting and gaming, drunkenness, and indecent language and behaviour. At Pontyclun, where about one person in thirty-three every year was convicted of 'misconduct' between 1925 and 1945, Richard Morgan and Reginald Williams had, in the last year, twenty-nine convictions between them, mainly for driving offences. Most of their adult neighbours had been trapped for one or more offences in the previous twenty years, often for failing to obtain a dog licence, riding a bicycle without lights and ignoring other highway regulations.

One effect of the vigorous execution of this legislation was the criminalization of a large section of the population. It is impossible to know exactly how many individuals appeared before the court for victimless offences, but it can be estimated that about one person in every thirty-two did so in 1900, and one in twenty-six in 1975. This was three or four times the number of people prosecuted in the same years for crimes against people and property. There were other differences, too, between these two groups; people convicted of victimless offences were older on average, and there were more women amongst them. They were, moreover, a fairer cross-section of society, with more middle-class representatives, though the latter were summonsed and apprehended for only a narrow range of misdemeanours.

Caring for the family

The state has always been interested in reminding people of their family responsibilities. As an illustration, quasi-criminal proceedings in Cardiff in 1914 included 24 bastardy orders, 60 maintenance orders for married women (17 of which had separation orders attached), and 29 orders for the payment of maintenance under the Children's Act of 1908. Over a third of these orders had to be enforced by terms of imprisonment of one to two months. In addition, under the Poor Law Act, 126 orders were made out for people to reimburse the Cardiff authorities for the maintenance of relatives. In Merthyr Tydfil during the previous year the Poor Law guardians obtained as many as 350 maintenance orders, and the chief constable complained of the trouble caused in executing them.

Many men simply ignored the court provisions, preferring to spend a few weeks in gaol. John Evans, a Rhondda man imprisoned for a month in 1910, argued that he felt no remorse as his wife had left him prior to the separation order. Of John Crowley, a 48-year-old coal trimmer who owed £6. 4s. 0d. in arrears and costs in February 1910, his wife said that 'I have had to search the public-houses from the top of Canton (Cardiff) to the bottom every Saturday night for him'. The problem of maintenance became especially acute during the worst economic years of the 1920s and 1930s, when the police were busy across South Wales trying to find missing husbands and fathers. By the middle of the century some of the policemen's leaders were in favour of withdrawing from this arena of domestic conflict.

The treatment of children was another matter about which the police had mixed emotions. Government intervention in the upbringing and education of children was comparatively new in 1900. In fact, much of the initiative, in terms of legislation, was due to pressure from reformers and societies like the NSPCC. As we have seen, the NSPCC was responsible for placing youngsters in private care and the workhouse, and for many of the prosecutions over neglect and cruelty. The police and court papers from the first three decades of the century are full of information on children found burnt, injured, emaciated and wandering. With the passing of the Children's Acts of 1933, 1963 and 1969, more of these children in need of care, protection and control were sent to homes and institutions.

For much of this century, the education and employment of children has occupied magistrates' courts more than the treatment of children within the home. In 1900 2,854 people were prosecuted under the Elementary Education Acts, and almost all of these were parents whose children were absent from school. One attendance officer, who mocked the stubborn independence of some of these parents, said at this time that Wales, far from being a land of education, was 'a bad third for school attendance' in Britain. The offenders, most of whom were prosecuted by School Boards in Swansea, Cardiff, Merthyr, Aberdare and Ystradyfodwg (Rhondda and Pontypridd area), received a fine of 3s.–10s. for non-attendance, and some of their children were sent to the truant schools. During the Second World War, when complaints about poor attendance increased sharply, calls were made for tougher punishment, partly because the connections between truancy and juvenile crime, especially shoplifting, were by then well established.

Prosecutions over non-attendance have, however, generally been in decline since the war, as table 3.10 indicates.

The employment of these children, in a part- or full-time capacity as sellers of newspapers, food and other goods, was a source of much annoyance at the start of the century. People were concerned about the noise which they made, the competition which they offered to rival enterprises, the loss of education and the moral dangers in which they were placed. In Cardiff and Swansea street-trading officers and plain-clothes policemen kept an eye on these youngsters. Several hundred of them, aged 11–16 years, were registered as traders in both places. The parents of others, who worked at a younger age or without a street-trading badge, were prosecuted under the Employment of Children Acts and local by-laws. Eventually, under the Children and Young Persons Act of 1933, everyone under sixteen years of age was prohibited from selling goods in the street.

Dealing with the destitute and homeless

The destitute and the homeless have always appeared before the courts in exceptional numbers, often because of who they were rather than because of what they had done. The scale of vagrancy in the early twentieth century was remarkable. In the years prior to the First World War the police in Cardiff, Swansea, Merthyr and Neath issued annually to vagrants thousands of tickets of admission to the workhouse. Complaints of their behaviour, especially their begging on Sundays, flooded into the watch committees. In 1909–10 great efforts were made, by the Poor Law authorities, the courts and the police in the above towns, to make life difficult for vagrants. A work test was demanded for the receipt of relief, and those who misbehaved in the workhouses were punished severely. Detectives and plain-clothes men were also ordered to arrest people found begging in the streets, and many were ordered from the towns or given short gaol sentences. Some reoffended immediately on release, and added another notch to their formidable criminal records.

The figures indicate that prosecutions for begging declined sharply after their peak in 1909–12, when over 1,200 cases were heard in the courts of South Wales, and they remained low during the inter-war years, but there were many other offences with which people could be charged under the Vagrancy Act of 1924. Some were arrested just for acting suspiciously and for being incorrigible rogues. At the beginning of the century hundreds of vagrants were annually cautioned and convicted for sleeping rough. They slept near brickworks, furnaces, bakeries and breweries, and in derelict and empty properties. In such places the vagrant mixed with the resident down-and-outs. Some of their haunts, like the old Ynysfach works at Merthyr and, later, the squatters' camp at Cyncoed, Cardiff, became notorious, and there were repeated calls to level the sites and move the occupants on. The gypsies at encampments in or near Cardiff, Swansea and Briton Ferry experienced similar harassment and close police supervision.

Controlling animals

Britain's reputation as a land of animal lovers is both illustrated and undermined by the court and police records. The Glamorgan police in the first half of the century spent many hours enforcing the Contagious Diseases Acts and dealing with stray animals. Farmers were required to inform the authorities if their animals had symptoms of scab, swine fever, foot and mouth and other such diseases, and were then subjected to various restriction orders. In addition, farmers were obliged to notify the police of measures taken to prevent these diseases. In spite of many warnings, a large number of farmers and cattle dealers appeared in court for ignoring such regulations, for not keeping records of the movement of animals, and for allowing them to stray onto the roadways. Farmers' sarcasm on these occasions conveyed their feelings about 'officials and their reports'.

Similar attitudes were sometimes evident in cases of cruelty to animals. In 1900, 210 people in South Wales were so prosecuted, the principal grounds being starvation, flogging, kicking and working animals in an unfit state. Once again, voluntary societies like the RSPCA and the Animals' Rescue League did much of the prosecuting, and typical offenders were milkmen, other carriers and farmers. In most cases individuals were charged only once with such crimes, but there were a few sick and unscrupulous people who had several convictions. The statistics suggest that conditions improved for animals during the century. In 1989, for instance, only thirty-three people were officially cautioned and prosecuted for cruelty in South Wales, but, as everyone realized, no more than a small minority of cases came to light.

People did appear before the magistrates in very large numbers, however, over the ownership and behaviour of their dogs, especially at the beginning of our period. The police books that have survived for places like Reynoldston and Taibach reveal that at certain times of the year officers made trawls of the neighbourhood, checking for people without dog licences, and finding embarrassment and resentment at every turn. It was easy work, and brought a fine of a few shillings or a pound. The problem of stray dogs was more difficult, and, until better arrangements were made, those animals captured by the police were usually killed within a few hours or days. The Dogs Act of 1906 made the owners liable for any injuries caused by their wandering pets, and many prosecutions were subsequently brought for 'having a dangerous dog', and for not providing them with collars and muzzles.

Regulating trade
Like many other crimes described in this section, breaches of trading regulations were common, and those people who came to court were only a selection of the most unlucky and wilful offenders. Most of the prosecutions were about the quality, quantity and price of the goods sold, cheating over rationing, unfair competition from street traders, and shop-opening hours. Every week urban magistrates punished people who sold adulterated and impure milk, and underweight bread and coal. In some cases it was obvious that tradesmen were happy to make the profits and pay the fines.

During the war years the temptations to bend the rules were greater, and many businessmen in South Wales fell for them. In the First World War they sold basic necessities above the price set by the Food Controller's Orders, and tried to force customers to purchase other items along with their milk and butter. Popular feeling against this and against food shortages reached a high level in some communities; at Cardiff, for example, the police were instructed in 1917 to break up crowds of protesters. During the Second World War, problems over supplies and pricing revived, and there were numerous infractions of the rationing code, with goods exchanged for too many or too few coupons, and sold to people with no coupons at all. Degwel Thomas, Baptist minister on the Glamorgan Public Health and Housing Committee, criticized magistrates at Caerphilly and Bargoed for being too lenient with traders who exploited the war situation, and was supported in his remarks by other councillors and trade-union bodies.

None of this, however, compared with the continuous saga over where and when people could sell goods. By the early twentieth century street trading had been curtailed and licensed. Even so, the complaints from shopkeepers about street vendors continued, and attempts were made to remove them altogether in some places. In Cardiff, which will be taken as our example, the battle was long and hard, with the law being broken by all parties to the dispute. The street traders claimed that they had sold fruit, vegetables and other goods in the city centre for generations, but in 1914, for much of the 1930s, and again in the late 1950s and early 1960s, they found themselves under great pressure. In 1933 the city council, after representations from businessmen and the police, made an order preventing hawkers from using a number of streets. This, and later additions to the list of prohibited thoroughfares, was fiercely resisted, and street sellers were regular visitors to the Cardiff courts.

For their part, shopkeepers were often prosecuted for having their premises open after hours or on a Sunday and public holiday. There was a succession of important Shop Acts in the first half of this century, which affected working hours and the sale of goods on licensed premises. The police were required to check these and other trading conditions, and one of their discoveries was that many shopkeepers supplied small items after closing time. On a Sunday it developed into a farce. Hundreds of shops were open on the Lord's Day; in Cardiff alone one estimate in 1938 put the number at a thousand. Typically in the first four decades of the century, 500–3,000 shopkeepers in South Wales were prosecuted each year for Sunday trading, especially in Swansea, where the determination on both sides was legendary. The familiar names of the recalcitrant appeared each year on the charge sheets and in the newspaper columns. The police grumbled about the difficulties of enforcing 'the obsolete Act'. It lacked public support, and – said the police – it penalized the poorer rather than the wealthier shopkeepers, but the chapel lobby was more vocal and influential.

Restricting the sale and consumption of alcohol
Liquor licensing laws in 1900 were based on Henry Bruce's legislation of 1872, modified in Wales by the Sunday Closing Act

of 1881. At the turn of the century, a time of revivalism in South Wales, chapel and temperance leaders pressed for further restrictions and fewer public houses. With the assistance of the Licensing Act of 1904, which made provision for compensating publicans who lost their licences, the number of such premises fell dramatically over the next quarter of a century.

One of the complaints of the Free Church Council and the temperance and improvement societies was that the owners of licensed premises did not experience the full rigours of the law. In numerical terms this claim was correct. The police paid thousands of daily visits to these places, but found it much easier to arrest a drunkard than an erring publican. A small number of the latter in each town were prosecuted annually, but cases were often dismissed. The most common charges were selling alcohol without a licence, serving under-age youths and habitual drunkards, permitting drunkenness on the premises, and selling beer during prohibited hours, including Sundays.

Selling beer without a licence, or shebeening, was a Cardiff speciality, but it was one which occupied the courts less and less. In 1908 83 people were convicted in the capital for the offence; five years later the number was 3. 'Presumably', said the chief constable in his annual report, 'high fines have made the business unremunerative, or else the clubs and the flagon trade have reduced the temptation to resort to shebeens.' Some of the legitimate publicans, faced with the same competition, were prepared to flout the new legislation which banned children and convicted drunkards from bars and prohibited the sale of off-licence beer to young people. The usual excuse was that the youths who had been illegally supplied looked older than their years, but selling drink to the 'habitual drunkard' was harder to explain away, as publicans were given court lists of individuals banned from their premises.

The selling of beer and spirits outside opening hours, and on a Sunday, was a very common crime. The police organized raids on pubs and clubs which were suspected of serving after hours, and watches were kept on the people who called at the back door for a jug of beer to have with their Sunday dinner. Those who were caught protested that, whilst they were harassed, the better-off were imbibing in hotels. During the war years, when the production of alcohol was curtailed and hours of sale reduced

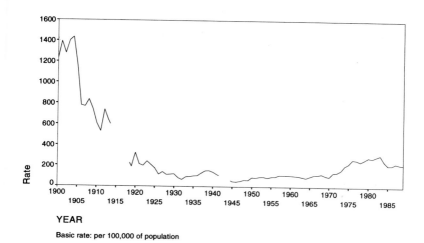

YEAR

Basic rate: per 100,000 of population

Graph 3.5: Proceedings for drunkenness in South Wales, 1900–1989

even further, it was said that almost everyone obeyed the new rules, but the improved statistics may have been due to the lack of policing as much as to patriotic sacrifice.

The *Western Mail*, ever the opponent of the temperance lobby, claimed that throughout the century most people in urban Wales simply ignored the Sunday drinking legislation, and it welcomed its repeal in the 1960s. If anything, however, checks on licensees have since become tighter. In 1989 proceedings were instituted against them for 425 offences, mainly for selling liquor outside permitted hours and to under-18-year-olds for consumption on licensed premises. It is, of course, impossible to estimate the scale of under-age drinking in public houses. The statistics, such as they are, reached one peak in the early 1960s when over 400 youngsters per annum were convicted of the offence in Glamorgan alone.

The most commonly recorded breaches of the licensing laws were simple and aggravated drunkenness, the latter alternatively described as drunk and disorderly. The rate of court proceedings over drunkenness owed something to changes in police procedures, the work of pressure groups and the directives of police committees, but it provides, nevertheless, a general guide to the extent of heavy drinking outside the home in the twentieth century (see graph 3.5). The broad outlines are clear. There were very high figures of recorded drunkenness until the outbreak of the First World War, a continuation of the late nineteenth-century trend. This was the era of the classic drunkard, of females like Mary Coase, who made at least 121 court appearances and went to a home for inebriates, and of John Leary of the Swansea workhouse who claimed, on his 125th appearance in the dock, that he could no longer take beer as he used to.

The number of proceedings against such people fell during the war, and remained comparatively low until the late 1930s. In the 'best' year, which was 1932, the rate per 100,000 was more than sixteen times better than the figure in 1900. Lleufer Thomas, stipendiary magistrate and temperance reformer, told the Royal Commission on Licensing of 1929–31 that the main reason for this was 'the wonderfully tactful, kindly and conciliatory' behaviour of police officers, but another witness, the chief constable of Cardiff, had no doubt that 'for some years' the native population had been 'sober and well-conducted'.

The subsequent rise in the rate was ended by the wartime conditions, and thereafter the rate fluctuated somewhat. By 1973 the rate was more than twice that of 1932, and it contined to rise until its peak in the early 1980s. On 1 June 1985 a system of cautioning most of the adults arrested for simple drunkenness was introduced throughout the South Wales force area. In 1989 the rate of proceedings per 100,000 was close to the rate of the early 1920s, and, even allowing for the 993 adults and 45 juveniles cautioned, it was historically a much better situation than many people imagined. However, the other popular myth that associates drunkenness with affluence has a stronger factual basis: throughout the century the rate often rose when people had more to spend.

The figures suggest that South Wales had a lower rate of proceedings over drunkenness than many parts of England, and the evangelicals claimed the credit for this. Within the region, places like Cardiff, Swansea and Merthyr had high rates, and the centre of Cardiff, the docks area (with Bute Street prominent) and Mynachdy had, in the middle years of the century at least, an even higher level. The country areas, by contrast, had much lower rates. There were also significant sex and age differences that fluctuated over time. In the years before the First World War, as many as a quarter of Cardiff's convicted drunkards were women, but afterwards, as we noted in the last chapter, 'women did not get drunk as they used to'. The change was sudden, and such was the fall that by 1968 only 5 per cent of Cardiff's proceedings were against females. In recent times, the trend has reversed a little; in 1989 the figure for South Wales was 9 per cent.

Most interesting of all perhaps have been the shifts in the age of those charged with abusing alcohol. In 1912 three-quarters of the people convicted in Swansea were over thirty years of age, and they were often seamen arrested down at the docks and in High Street and Castle Street. In the mid-century, in Cardiff and Merthyr Tydfil, that proportion of over-30-year-olds in court had fallen to two-thirds, and in Swansea in the 1960s it was about a half. In the last town, where cautions were often administered to under-age drinkers, between a fifth and a quarter of the prosecutions in that decade were against people under twenty-one years of age.

Subsequently, perhaps because of the relaxations on the sale of alcohol, there has been a rise in the number of teenagers charged with drunkenness. Table 3.11 for South Wales in 1989, or rather the publicity given to these statistics, illustrates once again why young people in their teens and early twenties have become associated in people's minds with some of the most unpleasant forms of crime. During the 1980s, when town centres and popular

Table 3·11: Age of persons proceeded against for simple drunkenness, and for being drunk and disorderly, South Wales, 1989

Ages	Males	Females	Proportion of total (%)
Under 18 yrs	187	20	7·4
18 and 19	455	37	17·5
20–9	1210	113	47·0
30–9	319	50	13·1
40–9	236	22	9·2
50 and over	156	8	5·8

out-of-town venues were crammed at weekends with lager-drinking juveniles, great efforts were made by the licensing authorities, the police and other agencies to restrict the hours of opening and to control under-age drinking. The immediate results, and the continued fall in the statistics, seem promising.

Keeping the streets respectable; indecency, gambling and prostitution

The interest in what could be regarded as indecent behaviour has waxed and waned over the century. In the early 1900s evangelicals strongly pressed watch committees to act over foul language, lewd songs, bathing naked in canals and rivers, and urinating in public. The last practice led to the building of public conveniences in several towns, but the offence remained one of the most common weekend misdemeanours. Much of this was fairly innocuous, but there were many cases, found in early station journals rather than court records, of people exposing their person to passing females and worse. Children and teenage girls were the frequent target of this kind of exhibitionism, and in some instances they were lured into houses to see pornographic photographs, books and films which had been illegally supplied by local shops.

Another activity which took place in the street was betting and gambling. Young men in the years before the First World War were often charged with playing pitch and toss in the highway, and with 'gaming with cards'. In 1913, for instance, Constable William Roberts discovered card-schools on the mountainside at Trealaw, a welcome diversion for an officer who was usually weighed down with cases of drunkenness, 'defiling of pavements' and sex in the urinals. At Trealaw, too, and in most other sizeable communities, there were bookmakers' runners 'loitering to receive bets'. The scope of this was extraordinary. In each town runners had their own strictly defined operating areas. At the Cardiff docks there were some twenty people collecting bets in 1951, and, in spite of hefty fines of £10, £15 and £30, they were able to make a living. The police complained, justifiably, that the legislation governing betting was widely condemned and ignored, and the court statistics simply reflected the number and effort of the officers in plain clothes.

When betting and gaming in the street were checked, people moved indoors. Publicans and hoteliers took racing bets and were periodically visited by the police. Other houses were turned into gambling dens. Police raids on such places had to be carefully planned. In Cardiff, during the famous raids of 1913, a dozen officers barricaded the exits, and arrested scores of Asians and West Indians who were amongst the keenest card-players of Butetown. Crowds attended the court cases, which resulted in very large fines, and cheered the participants. During the war years the battle continued, with official and moral denunciations of money wasted on unproductive enterprises.

A series of Betting, Gaming, and Lottery Acts attempted to clarify and reduce the restrictions, but popular resistance continued. In the 1950s, about 200–300 persons per annum were prosecuted for breaches of the Acts in the capital city. Butler's Betting and Gaming Act of 1960, however, virtually ended street betting; it also relaxed the conditions on commercial amusements in public places, and began the system of registration which, by the end of the decade, had embraced all race-tracks, bingo halls, casinos, bookmakers and pools promoters. As a result, one prolific source of non-indictable crime had been removed.

For many people, immoral and indecent behaviour in the street was embodied in the prostitute. The number of prostitutes had fallen since the mid-nineteenth century, but Cardiff and Swansea still had hundreds on parade at the start of our period. They were targeted by various groups, from the Vigilance Society and the Forward Movement to the police vice squads of the modern era. The legislation used to check the activities of prostitutes was the Vagrancy Acts of 1824 and 1898, the Criminal Law Amendment Act of 1885, the Street Offences Act of 1959, and the Sexual Offences Act of 1985.

The policing of prostitution was a difficult business. Watch committees, under pressure from reformers, demanded firm action, but catching the organizers and landlords of prostitutes was never easy. In 1927 the *Evening Express* alleged that Cardiff was the worst centre in the British Isles for white-slave traffic, with scores of innocent Welsh girls shipped off to continental Europe and South America. An official investigation found no truth in the story. Nor was prostitution in Cardiff quite as controlled as was sometimes suggested; many of the women were managed by female brothel-keepers, but there were others who worked independently, often with a male bodyguard, and used small hotels and private houses. It took days of surveillance before the police confirmed the claims of angry neighbours that such houses were being frequented for sex, and then the courts threw out about a quarter of the cases.

The police were acutely aware that the penalties for soliciting and disorderly conduct were hardly a deterrent. Mary Sullivan, down the Strand in Swansea, and Margaret Probert of Cardiff dockland, appeared dozens of times in court at the turn of the century, and there they poured scorn on the police, the magistrates, the social missionaries and the rescue homes to which they were sent. They quickly returned to the life of sex, larceny from the person and drunken revelry. In 1902 proceedings were brought against 341 prostitutes in Cardiff, 6 people were charged with living off their earnings, and another 74 for keeping disorderly houses used by them. The highest figures for the century were reached during the purge against prostitution in the capital in 1908–9. The number of cases fell to a lower level during the war, and again, even more sharply, after the mid-1920s.

After the Second World War the number of prosecutions increased somewhat; in 1968, a typical year, there were 105 cases relating to prostitution in the capital, and 64 cautions administered to women under the Street Offences Act. Twenty years later Riverside in Cardiff was still a problem area. A combined uniform and plain-clothes police presence in that district during 1989 produced 77 arrests (40 being of five prostitutes only), and 24 cautions, some for the second time. During that decade, as more women once again sought an income from prostitution, the Sexual Offences Act was passed to curb the menace of men driving around looking for sex. In Cardiff prosecutions under the Act were rare, though the main purpose of the legislation, to improve the quality of street life, was partly achieved.

Regulating the use of motor vehicles
Motoring offences have been the real growth area in twentieth-century crime, and one which had a major impact on policing and public attitudes. Nowhere was the debate over the 'policeman state' more fierce. Some reformers, anticipating the trouble to come, wished to remove the police altogether from the regulation of traffic, and to establish instead a separate system of civilian

A policeman on point duty, regulating traffic in Cardiff in 1938.

supervisors and courts. For their part, the police were determined to retain control over traffic, and the Road Traffic Acts of 1930 and 1934 confirmed this. From that date a substantial part of their work has been connected with the problems of motor transport. The appointment of traffic wardens and school crossing officers in the early 1960s, and the regular use of special constables at busy times of the year, have eased the burden, but it remains a formidable undertaking.

The context is the astonishing increase in the use of the roads during the century. In 1900 road transport consisted of horse-drawn vehicles and pedal cyles, and a few hundred motor cycles and other motor vehicles. By 1938 the situation had changed significantly; in Cardiff and Swansea during that year 23,077 vehicles were registered, and the problems associated with such numbers were discussed in Parliament, council rooms and police committees. Lingering public claims to the free use of the highways were swept aside. Speed limits, one-way streets, parking restrictions, pedestrian crossings, frequent road accidents and deaths were already a familiar part of modern life.

The Second World War brought some respite, but afterwards, with the increased affordability of motor vehicles and an end to petrol rationing, the need to improve the quality and policing of highways became ever more important. By 1958 the number of vehicles registered in Cardiff and Swansea was almost three times the figure of twenty years previously; town centres were full of traffic, and other roads were congested during the summer months. Then, over the next thirty years, the situation in South Wales was transformed by the extraordinary popularity of the family car, the threatening presence of heavy-goods vehicles, and the building of motorway and dual-carriage roads. In 1989, 19,887 road accidents were reported to the South Wales police, and, to add to the burden, they had to deal with 81,200 offences relating to motor vehicles.

Since the middle of the century, there has been a proliferation of motoring regulations. The Road Traffic and Improvement Acts of 1956 and 1960, and council by-laws and orders over traffic flow and parking, were followed by stricter controls over the roadworthiness of vehicles and the drinking habits of drivers. There was some resistance to aspects of this legislation, and initial suspicion of the technical equipment used by the police, but in time this faded, as did the concern over the compulsory wearing of seat belts in the 1980s.

Of the motoring offences only a very small number, like causing death by dangerous driving, came within the indictable category. The great majority were defined as lesser crimes, and in the days before the First World War they comprised fewer than 5 per cent of non-indictable proceedings. During the 1950s the proportion rose to a half and more, and the pressure on the courts grew excessive. The extensive use of cautions, the Act of 1957 which allowed guilty defendants to plead by letter, the subsequent fixed-penalty arrangement, and the vehicle-rectification scheme of the late 1980s, were all attempts to reduce the burden, but motoring prosecutions have continued to dominate the magistrates' courts. In 1989 the motorist was still the archetypal criminal, much as the drunkard had been in 1900 and the thief in 1800.

One of the common complaints across the decades was that motorists were not dealt with in a consistent fashion. Informal cautions were handed out by the police in large numbers during the early years of the century, but, as we saw in chapter 1, this policy had its problems. Chief Constable James Wilson of Cardiff was against 'too much leniency', whereas his counterpart in Merthyr in the 1960s felt that 'many of the problems are created not so much by the motorists themselves' as by outmoded roads, and he therefore wanted his men to be considerate. Written warnings were, in fact, given during the 1960s to several thousand people each year in South Wales, chiefly for ignoring traffic directions, obstruction, illegal parking and lighting offences.

Even so, the increases in prosecutions for motoring offences were sometimes staggering. In 1967, according to the national statistics, 38,228 persons were prosecuted in South Wales for 51,713 offences relating to motor vehicles, three times the rate of only ten years before. After reaching a peak in 1975, the rate of prosecutions fluctuated, but if one adds the incidents dealt with by fixed penalties, the rate of offences relating to motor vehicles more than doubled in the last twenty years of our period. In 1989, the main court prosecutions were over car insurance, driving licences and vehicle tests, and most of the fixed penalties were for parking offences.

The character of offences on the highway underwent some interesting changes during the century. At first the typical crimes were leaving horse and cart unattended, riding furiously, having no lights, and driving on the wrong side of the road. By the 1930s the pedal and motor cyclist, and the car, lorry and bus driver were the common offenders, and they were charged with lighting and licensing offences, speeding, and having too many passengers. Later came more parking offences, cases of causing obstruction, and having defective means of transport. The records show that a wide range of people were charged with these misdemeanours, though the class and residence of the offenders were important determinants of the type of crime. Thus in Swansea during the 1960s many people from the council houses on Townhill were convicted of driving without licences and insurances or in defective vehicles, whilst the middle class of Mumbles and West Cross were caught for speeding and disobeying traffic signals.

An extra word is required on those motoring offences which were both potentially and actually dangerous, and for which people sometimes found themselves in the higher courts. In 1900 prosecutions of this kind were difficult. There were endless arguments over 'speeding on the highway'; it was a subjective measurement, of 'about 15 or 20 m.p.h.'. In January 1914 Police Constable George Young of Cardiff told the stipendiary magistrate that he had witnessed 'the fastest car that I have ever seen on the road. It was travelling more like an express than a motor car.' The occupant, who collided with another driver, claimed that he was doing about 20 m.p.h., not 35–40 m.p.h. as Young stated, but he was fined £5 for endangering the public and £2 for not sounding his horn.

In 1922 the Glamorgan police were ordered to make greater efforts to catch such drivers, and the next ten years witnessed some exciting car chases. Campaigns were also launched in the 1930s against drink-driving. Persistent offenders were fined a large amount, or given a month in gaol and a disqualification from driving for a year. If they killed someone at the same time, the sentence was typically three times as severe. Police chiefs then, and in the 1950s, campaigned for a more serious attitude to be adopted towards dangerous driving and drink-driving, but the impact of the tougher sentencing proved initially disappointing. The Road Safety Act of 1967, and the use of the breathalyser, marked a new departure, and over the next twenty-two years the increase in drink-driving charges outpaced almost every other motoring statistic. This increase in charges, together with improved car design and road-safety publicity, has helped to make driving better and travel safer.

The control of drugs

According to some observers, the motor car has, over the past few years, been replaced as the major social evil by the menace of drugs. Prime Minister Thatcher claimed in 1985 that the drugs trade was the greatest threat to western civilisation, and proceeded to make life more difficult for its organizers. South Wales then had less of a drugs problem than the English metropolitan police districts, though cannabis and heroin were more available in places like Cardiff than they had ever been. In 1986, 741 people were proceeded against for drug-related offences, only 144 more than the figure for 1972. Many of these were from the police subdivisions of Cardiff Central, Llanishen, Roath and Barry.

The misuse of drugs was, of course, not new. Laudanum was a popular sedative at the turn of the century. During the First World

War attempts were made to control the intake of drink and narcotics, and, in the police records of the inter-war years, there are occasional references to the stealing of drugs from chemists. However, the bulk of the evidence on the trafficking in, and abuse of, drugs dates from the late 1950s. Cardiff was the centre of the trade in South Wales, and in May 1967 its chief constable formed a drug squad, which attempted to cut the supply of cannabis into the city. Very soon afterwards, LSD and heroin replaced cannabis as a major cause for concern, as, twenty years later, did amphetamines and crack.

Throughout the period the criminal statistics reflected the vagaries of law enforcement. In recent times the police have had more resources and greater powers to catch offenders. In 1989 1,084 people were arrested for drug-related offences in South Wales, 821 persons were stopped and searched on suspicion of possessing illegal drugs, and 328 warrants were issued under the Misuse of Drugs Act of 1971. Almost nine of out ten persons cautioned and proceeded against in that year were male, and four out of five were twenty-one years of age or over.

The illicit trade in drugs required planning and organization. In some instances this amounted to forging prescriptions and stealing from doctors' cars and pharmacies; in other cases dealers had to obtain their goods from elsewhere in Britain and abroad. In 1981, working with the Metropolitan police, the South Wales constabulary broke up three major drugs organizations. About the same time, the police and community bodies worked hard at prevention, for these years were marked not just by experiments with new and more dangerous drugs, but also by the phenomenon of solvent abuse. After a number of deaths from glue-sniffing in South Wales during the early 1980s, a campaign was launched there to persuade Parliament to outlaw the activity. Others, of a different ideology, sought to decriminalize the whole business of using drugs. As they pointed out, some drugs were non-addictive, many of the arrests were for comparatively minor infringements, and these anyway bore no relationship to the size of 'the problem'.

Conclusion

The purpose served by taking such people to court has been a point of contention throughout the century. Whereas there was probably widespread support for regulating behaviour in public, especially in the streets, and a belief that much had been achieved in this way by the 1930s, the invasion of the private world of morality and responsiblity was a more complex matter. In some areas of personal behaviour, the statistics of victimless offences only highlighted the ineffectiveness and class dimension of the constraints, and popular resistance to controls on betting, drinking and trading ultimately proved to be a force for change. Today the missionary zeal, which once sought to civilize and educate the 'lower orders' in society through legislation, has largely evaporated; the great majority of victimless offences in 1989 were confined to a few areas: motoring, the licensing of televisions and radios, and the sale and use of drink and drugs. Occasionally, however, in some of the thousands of telephone calls to the police, elderly callers – working-class as well as middle-class – recall with longing the olden days when adults and children appeared regularly in magistrates' courts for petty misdemeanours like swearing and playing in the street.

Society draws a line between most of these offences, which are discovered by officials, and those against people and property, which the public usually report themselves. Yet the links between them were significant. For example, many young people, who were often poor school attenders, were led into violence, theft and vandalism as a result of their passion for drink, drugs and cars. In some communities, too, such as those at Penlan, Penrhys and Ely in the 1980s, there were comparable levels of antisocial behaviour and criminal activity. For both of these, youths were widely blamed. As we have seen, the prominence of young people in crime has probably been exaggerated, but after the middle of the century they were responsible for many of the offences which annoyed society, and were punished and controlled accordingly. They committed more than their fair share of break-ins and autocrimes; were guilty of many acts of indecent assault and vandalism; were warned for many drinking offences; and were accused, probably wrongly, of committing most drug offences.

Looked at in the long term, South Wales society has become more civilized in the twentieth century, but, almost certainly, more criminal. This is not always how very old people remember it. In 1900 there were many complaints about standards of behaviour in public, and in parts of the large towns heavy drinking, hooliganism and violent conduct, by men and women, were only too common. Despite the claims of the increase in violence since the Second World War, there has been little to compare with that of the Edwardian era. In 1989 certain city streets were regarded as 'no-go' areas during the evening by the apprehensive members of society, and tensions were evident on some of the most deprived housing estates, but robberies, assaults, and crowd and industrial disorders have not returned with the same regularity and threat as those in the early years of this century. People born mid-century can expect to reach old age without being attacked by an individual or a crowd, at least outside the home.

The experience of property crime, especially after the late 1950s and 1960s, has been rather different, and rendered people more crime-conscious than ever before. By 1989, people's anxiety over delinquency was understandable, if a little exaggerated. Although the inhabitants of South Wales were still comparatively safe, females had some reason to worry about violence and break-ins, and, in the worst-affected districts, every adult knew that sooner or later he or she would become the victim of a property crime. Such crime, however, was likely to be of a minor kind. In 1989 no more than 1 in 125 people reported a house burglary to the police.

There is, too, another side to people's experience of crime in the twentieth century. People in 1900 appeared before the courts in larger numbers than one might suppose from the graph of indictable crime. There were communities in South Wales, like Taibach, where a good percentage of the inhabitants knew what it was like to face the magistrates. Those convicted of indictable and non-indictable offences at that time were mainly of the working class, but even before the outbreak of the Second World War this was changing. During the second half of this century, motoring, trading, licensing, drugs and other offences have brought hundreds more of the middle class before the courts, though, as in the nineteenth century, comparatively few of them were indicted for serious white-collar crimes. Altogether, in 1989, one person in eighteen in South Wales was proceeded against, almost three-quarters of them for non-indictable offences.

This criminalization affected people's attitudes towards legislation, delinquency and the forces of law and order. In some ways it lessened respect for the law, and worsened the relationship between the public and police. It seemed, especially to certain middle-class motorists, that the protection of life and property was less of a priority than keeping up the numbers of victimless offences. The police were caught in the middle of this; they have always been general servants of the state and controllers of public conduct as much as crime fighters. In some harassed communities in South Wales the police have been seen as ineffective in the last task, and perhaps too effective in the others.

4

The Police

In the chapters to date, the missing element in the story of delinquency has been the police. The history of the British police has been transformed in recent years, except in Wales where Ken Birch ploughs a lonely furrow. In the new writings, the volumes of Charles Reith, the official police histories, and the reminiscences of retired officers have been criticized for their lack of objectivity. In their place have appeared studies by Robert Storch, Ben Whittaker, Robert Reiner, Clive Emsley and others which have shed new light on the roots, character, reception and impact of the professional police forces. Some of these works have been written from a left-wing perspective, and others have been neo-Reithian, but all the writers seem agreed that the British police over the past 150 years have never been primarily a crime-fighting force, nor have they been as popular or as efficient as was once claimed.

The role of the police was established in the second quarter of the nineteenth century. The stated aim of the Metropolitan police, formed in 1829, was to prevent crime, but the men in blue also had other functions, chiefly to preserve order and to act as general servants of city government. The nature of the first forces was carefully planned; the British police, unlike some of their foreign counterparts, were to be essentially a 'low-profile' civilian body, committed to 'open policing' and minimal force, subject to the common law, under the control of local committees and jointly financed by central and local government. These new police were intended to be different from their predecessors; they were to be professional and efficient members of a bureaucratic structure, separate from the public and yet dependent on it for co-operation and consent.

By 1900 many of the hopes of Edwin Chadwick and other police reformers had been fulfilled, and in South Wales, as elsewhere, the forces faced the future with some optimism. In the event, important population and community changes, the advent of the motor car, and economic unrest soon provided serious challenges for the police. So did the inconsistent, and then consistent, rise in the crime rate from the middle of the century. By the late 1950s and early 1960s the police had lost a degree of credibility and public support, and governments inaugurated fundamental revisions in the numbers, control and activities of the forces.

During the last quarter of a century, the changes in policing have been unprecedented, and so, too, has been the level of debate and criticism. The modern police forces have become large bureaucratic institutions, controlled by managers, and heavily dependent on civilians and computers. The profession has, to quote one academic, become 'de-mystified'; its traditional image has gone, its effectiveness, independence and integrity have been seriously questioned, and its functions and work are being reassessed, possibly with a view to limited privatization.

The character and control of police forces

The establishment of the South Wales police in 1969 brought together five forces which had once been independent, namely those of Glamorgan, Cardiff, Swansea, Neath and Merthyr Tydfil. The last had been created in 1908, on the incorporation of Merthyr as a county borough, and was to remain a separate entity for sixty years, whilst Neath, which had a smaller police force, merged with the Glamorgan constabulary in 1947.

Each force had its own character. The Glamorgan police had a conservative, even backward image, which owed something to the fact that for almost a hundred years (1841–1937) it was run by chief constables of a military-gentry lineage. Henry (1867–91) and Lionel Lindsay (1891–1937), father and son, with a family estate at Glasnevin near Dublin, mixed naturally with the Glamorgan gentry at race meetings, shoots, shows and clubs, and displayed an old-fashioned paternalism. They exerted an exceptional control over their men, and, under their influence, and that of their successor, Joseph Jones (1937–51), the Glamorgan police trod a well-worn path. By comparison, Cardiff and Swansea had a reputation for being efficient and innovative, which was often attributed to the appointment of 'outsiders' as chief constables, men like James Wilson, a Yorkshireman with a legal mind, who became chief constable of Merthyr and then Cardiff (1920–46), and Thomas Rawson at Swansea, who introduced police boxes as early as 1927. Each force brought its traditions and practices into the South Wales Constabulary (1969–), and influenced it in different ways.

These forces, prior to the reforms of the 1960s, were controlled by watch committees and, in the case of the Glamorgan constabulary, by the standing joint police committee. These were composed of representatives of local élites, in their capacity as councillors, aldermen and justices of the peace. Each committee was dominated by a handful of regulars, who attended almost every meeting and who held key positions over long periods. In Glamorgan, in the first half of the century, they included magistrates Lieutenant-Colonel (Sir) Rhys Williams of Miskin Manor, Sir John T. D. Llewelyn of Penllergaer estate, J. Blandy Jenkins, squire of Llanharan, Oliver H. Jones of Fonmon, Colonel W. H. C. Llewellyn, Alderman (Sir) William Jenkins (MP) and Councillor George Gethin.

These 'stalwarts' had an important role as intermediaries, working with the chief constables, representing vested interests in agriculture, industry and commerce, and acting for local government committees and pressure groups. In the early days the landed interest was to the fore on the county's police committee; the location of the police courts, stations (often built on their land) and beats reflected something of the world of half a century before. The Tredegar, Margam, Penrice, Penllergaer, Bute and other landed estates still hired constables from the force, as did fishing associations, and the regular officers spent much of their time dealing with animal diseases, stray cattle, sheep-worrying, poaching and the like.

Even so, Glamorgan's police had other forms of property to protect, and one of the main tasks of the county's police committee after 1900 was dealing with requests for assistance from the coal-owners' association and from chambers of trade, ratepayers' associations and other respectable bodies on the coalfield. Guest, Keen and Nettlefolds Limited, the Crawshay Brothers, Powell Dyffryn Steam Coal Company, David Davies and Sons, and other companies hired several dozen constables from the county, not always to the delight of other 'influential inhabitants' of the industrial towns and villages who complained that they were 'left to the disorderly'. In fact, in the early years of the century new stations and courts were rapidly erected at places like Blaenclydach, Seven Sisters, Llanbradach, Bargoed and Abercynon.

Other requests for more public and private constables came from parish, district and county councils, and from various local government committees. These bodies wanted the police to perform a wide range of administrative tasks, such as collecting rates and checking licences, and to provide traffic control and school crossing patrols at dangerous places. Increasingly, too, councils sought police protection for their property, against the burglar and the arsonist. During the inter-war years, and afterwards, the policing of the new council estates and schools became a priority matter, and one increasingly considered by councillors at the planning stage.

In Glamorgan the chief constable had a good measure of independence from his police committee, though Lionel Lindsay was censored on occasions by new Labour members for an over-vigorous defence of the interests and property of his landed and industrial friends. In the towns the watch committees met more often, and kept a closer eye on the management and spending of the police. In Merthyr and Neath, for instance, councillors and magistrates had a strong influence on crime and service policing at the time of the First World War. At Cardiff, too, chief constables found it wise to bring major policy and disciplinary matters before the committee. Nor was this the end of the matter, for agreements in police committees over men and money were sometimes overruled by parsimonious and angry borough councils.

The central government, which paid half of the police costs, and inspected the forces annually, had a growing interest in their condition. In this process of centralization, the industrial troubles in South Wales played an important part. Jane Morgan, in her book *Conflict and Order*, describes how there evolved from the conflicts of 1900–39 'the concept of a national police force designed to counter either a local or a nation-wide threat from labour'. The exigencies of the wartime situation also strengthened inter-force links. During the First and Second World Wars the police were an important arm of defence, working under regional commands and emergency committees. In Cardiff they had the mammoth task of defending key military and naval installations, and co-ordinating civil-defence measures. Significantly, after both world wars, greater central direction and standardization were brought to police training and methods, but the idea of a truly national police force, which was discussed in the 1940s, found little favour in South Wales.

In post-war Britain the character and control of the police forces became major political issues. The first stage of this debate, which was concerned with police corruption, efficiency and accountability, culminated in the police commission of 1960–2 and the Police Act of 1964. The decisions to reduce the number of forces and to change the composition of the local police committees, had a mixed reception in South Wales. Each police force had already embarked on its own programme of station building and technical development, and was sceptical of the value of one huge bureaucratic organization servicing well over a million people. The chief constable of Merthyr Tydfil added a note of cynicism: 'the burning desire to form large units to provide greater opportunity for promotion and experience is being overdone.' Cardiff mounted the most vigorous opposition to the amalgamation, and won a parliamentary investigation into their claims. Tasker Watkins, QC, on behalf of the objectors, claimed that the amalgamation was in reality 'a complete take-over' by Glamorgan, which ignored the importance, size and problems of the capital, and threatened the quality, technical expertise and efficiency of its existing police force. The argument failed to convince the government, and on 1 June 1969 the South Wales Constabulary was born.

The years since 1969 have seen the gradual erosion of effective local control over the police. From the start, when economies were enforced on the new amalgamated forces, central government was determined to increase its influence over policing. The involvement of the Home Office has been manifest in stricter inspection, more intervention in the appointment of senior officers, and the growth of regional and national forms of policing and intelligence-gathering. At the same time, chief constables have gained greater independence from the police committees, and have more control over their officers and their deployment than was once the case. One member of the South Wales Police Authority claimed in 1984 that his colleagues had no influence on the chief constable and were 'totally impotent' in matters of strategy and operations. The co-ordinating work of the Association of Chief Police Officers during the miners' strike of 1984–5, and its subsequent discussions of a possible FBI agency for dealing with serious crime, has revived early nineteenth-century fears of a 'government police'. However, when Michael Howard, the latest Home Secretary, attempted the final act of creating a *de facto* national police force with minimal local accountability, the resistance was formidable and the appeals to history eloquent. In South Wales, where the years 1993–4 have witnessed a bruising and much-publicized battle over police numbers and finance, Mr Howard's campaign has been particularly resented.

Structure, organization and ranks

The police forces of South Wales at the start of the century were simple institutions. Glamorgan had a staff of only six people at headquarters, with the rest fairly evenly spread across its five divisions of Merthyr, Pontypridd, Bridgend, Neath and Barry Dock. Each division had, on average in 1902, one superintendent, three or four inspectors, eight sergeants, six acting sergeants (of which rank the Home Office disapproved) and seventy constables. The management of the force was in the hands of the chief constable, with some assistance from his deputy and two chief clerks, and with advice from the four divisional superintendents. All but a handful of the force were engaged in operational duties, manning the fifty county stations, patrolling several hundred well-established beats, doing occasional plain-clothes work, and, when the occasion demanded, riding horses to quell serious crowd disorder.

The police command had similarities with that of the armed forces; control was exercised from the top via a series of printed orders and instructions, and by occasional visits and checks on rank-and-file officers. It was recognized from an early date that the small group of senior people was overburdened with administration and court work, and 'unable to give the amount of supervision they would have liked to their men in their numerous out-stations, etc.'. Communications between headquarters at Canton in Cardiff and divisional offices were reasonably good, but the outlying cottage-stations had to manage largely on their own.

Thirty years later the police organization in the county had changed, though not drastically. The major alteration had been the decision, at the time of the coal strike of 1911, to break up the over-large territorial divisions and create eight new ones which reflected more accurately the density of the county's population. The three new units were based at Treharris, Tonpentre and Gowerton. By 1936 there were 76 county stations and 216 police cottages in these divisions, almost all of which were connected by private police telephone.

In the same year the county police had a staff of 819, almost double that of 1900. Rank structure remained unchanged; each division still had only one superintendent and three or four inspectors, and most of the men under their command would now be labelled 'response officers'. Only fourteen officers were employed at headquarters, though a departmental structure had begun to emerge there, to co-ordinate the work of the nine men engaged in detective work, to supervise the mobile police patrol which had been created five years before, and to organize the extensive criminal records. Formal specialization was, however, at the primitive stage. In contrast with the borough police forces, Glamorgan had been able to say in March 1932 that it had 'no plain clothes staff, neither have we a detective staff'. For years the force had relied on hastily collected teams for 'detective duty', which included checking breaches of the Sunday Closing Act, and countering the threat of 'sedition', possible attacks on royal visitors, and industrial disorder.

By contrast, the Cardiff and Swansea police forces had more complex and permanent structures, and reputations for introducing new systems. Cardiff in the mid-1930s had 92 of its police staff of 316 employed in the administrative division, and, as the organizational (Figure 4.1) chart shows, these were located in the detective, court, training and related departments. In addition, there was a motor patrol section, and three foot-patrol divisions covering the city centre and the docks, the districts to the west of the River Taff, and those to the east. A Home Office committee in

CARDIFF CITY POLICE – ORGANIZATIONAL CHART 1935

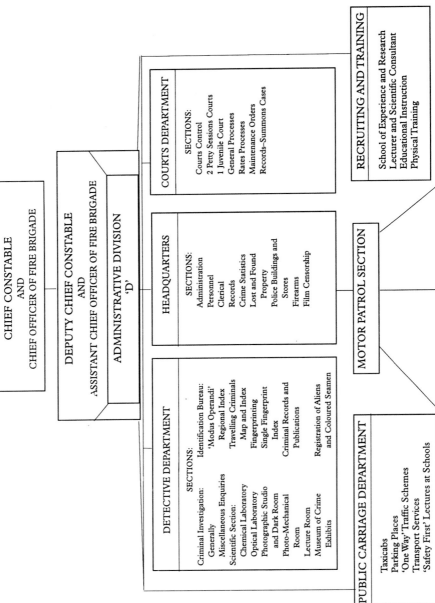

CHIEF CONSTABLE
AND
CHIEF OFFICER OF FIRE BRIGADE

DEPUTY CHIEF CONSTABLE
AND
ASSISTANT CHIEF OFFICER OF FIRE BRIGADE

ADMINISTRATIVE DIVISION 'D'

DETECTIVE DEPARTMENT

SECTIONS:

Criminal Investigation:
Generally
Miscellaneous Enquiries
Scientific Section:
Chemical Laboratory
Optical Laboratory
Photographic Studio and Dark Room
Photo-Mechanical Room
Lecture Room
Museum of Crime Exhibits

Identification Bureau:
'Modus Operandi'
Regional Index
Travelling Criminals Map and Index
Fingerprinting
Single Fingerprint Index
Criminal Records and Publications
Registration of Aliens and Coloured Seamen

HEADQUARTERS

SECTIONS:

Administration
Personnel
Clerical
Records
Crime Statistics
Lost and Found Property
Police Buildings and Stores
Firearms
Film Censorship

COURTS DEPARTMENT

SECTIONS:

Courts Control
2 Petty Sessions Courts
1 Juvenile Court
General Processes
Rates Processes
Maintenance Orders
Records–Summons Cases

RECRUITING AND TRAINING

School of Experience and Research
Lecturer and Scientific Consultant
Educational Instruction
Physical Training

MOTOR PATROL SECTION

PUBLIC CARRIAGE DEPARTMENT

Taxicabs
Parking Places
'One Way' Traffic Schemes
Transport Services
'Safety First' Lectures at Schools

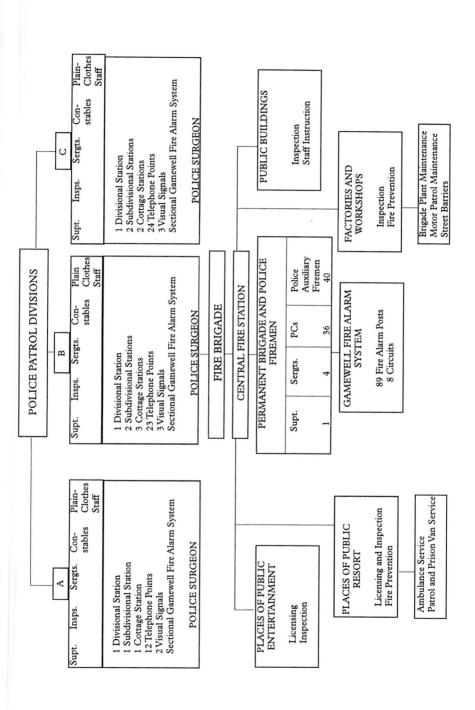

1933 was said to have been impressed by 'the organization at Cardiff', not least by the training of probationer detectives and by 'the well-equipped photographic studio at the Detective Department, and its bureau work'.

In the post-war years new ranks were introduced into the forces, and greater emphasis was placed on administration, training and specialized policing. In South Wales, traffic, prosecution, communications, administration and science departments became much more important, and licensing and crime prevention departments were created in each force, usually from existing manpower. Cardiff, of course, had unique policing problems, and decided in the 1950s and 1960s to appoint separate vice, dangerous drug and fraud squads. The 1950s also witnessed the establishment of team policing to supplement the work of the beat constables, and the experimental beginnings of motorized unit-beat policing which became universal with amalgamation. Special police groups were another feature of these years, sometimes being created just to deal with particular crime or public-order crises.

In 1968, on the eve of amalgamation, Glamorgan had 1,189 members of the regular force (only 31 of them women), 44 cadets and 205 civilians. There were then nine divisions, Neath having become part of the county force in 1947. In each division one or two chief inspectors had been added to the traditional ranks, along with an average of nine detectives. The position of acting sergeants had disappeared, but otherwise there was little change from the rank structure of 1936. The main difference was in the size of the combined traffic and communications department (128), and the number of people (58) devoted to administration, crime intelligence and detection at headquarters. At Bridgend, and in the divisions, 119 of the regular staff were attached to the county CID. Cardiff, with 678 police (19 female), 30 cadets and 102 civilians, had a traffic division of 89, and a slightly larger criminal investigation department. Swansea in 1968 had 383 (8 females) on the regular staff, and Merthyr had 132 (6 females).

Amalgamation was intended to improve the management, organization and efficiency of the police in the face of the rising crime rate. However, the South Wales Constabulary was born at a time of financial stringency, and from the start some of the plans for growth and reorganization had to be postponed. The centre of the police district was established at Bridgend, which had been the headquarters of the Glamorgan force since 1947, but Cardiff retained a special status as the 'support headquarters', the home of the No. 8 regional crime squad, the drugs squad and the fraud squad, and the centre of one of the three traffic sectors. It also had two of the most important territorial divisions, out of the eight formed.

The South Wales force covered one of the largest non-metropolitan police districts in Britain, and, as we have seen, its character was unique. From the start its chief constables had to introduce a command and control structure which would cover this large area and integrate the constituent elements of the old forces. Communications were upgraded, management services reorganized, and standard practices gradually laid down. The size and importance of the headquarters grew apace, whilst the eight divisional centres were given new buildings, a larger and more senior supervisory staff, and extra civilian administrative assistance.

Running parallel to these, and other developments was a half-suppressed debate about the nature of the new force. For many ex-Glamorgan officers, still ensconced at Bridgend headquarters, it was important to keep the traditions and practices inherited from the days of Joseph Jones and even Lionel Lindsay, whereas chief constables like Thomas Gwilym Morris, newly appointed from Cardiff in 1971, and John Woodcock (1979–83), the first genuine outsider, were determined to bring in new men and methods, and carry out comprehensive reorganization.

Since amalgamation, several major establishment reviews were executed, in 1972, 1979 and 1986, and one has been recently completed. Apart from justifying demands for more police and civilian recruits, these reviews noted areas of pressure and weakness, and promoted key developments. These developments were many. A single tier of command and control was introduced, traffic administration was separated from communications, a completely new computer network was installed, crime prevention and public relations were given a higher profile, training was restructured, administrative support groups formed in all divisions, and a growing proportion of unit beat officers were switched to foot patrols and community policing.

The chart of the organization of the South Wales Constabulary in 1989 reveals the size and complexity of the modern police

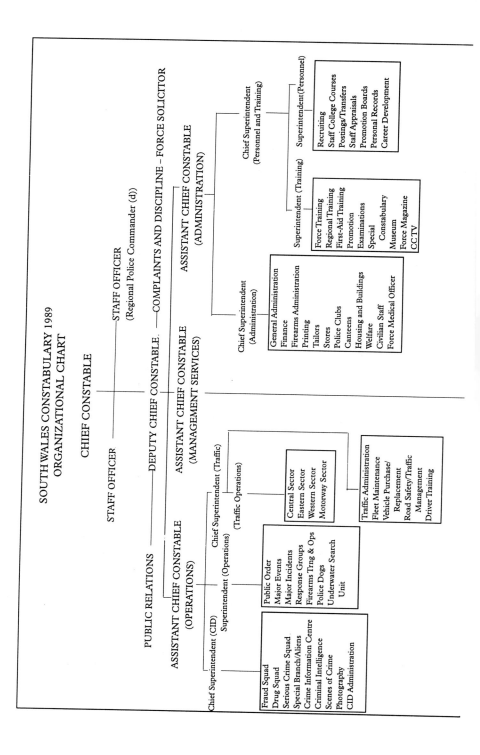

SOUTH WALES CONSTABULARY 1989
ORGANIZATIONAL CHART

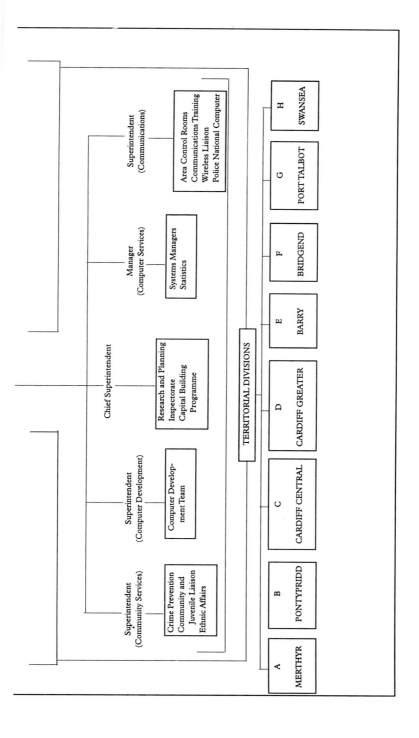

Chief Superintendent

Superintendent
(Community Services)

Crime Prevention
Community and
Juvenile Liaison
Ethnic Affairs

Superintendent
(Computer Development)

Computer Develop-
ment Team

Research and Planning
Inspectorate
Capital Building
Programme

Manager
(Computer Services)

Systems Managers
Statistics

Superintendent
(Communications)

Area Control Rooms
Communications Training
Wireless Liaison
Police National Computer

TERRITORIAL DIVISIONS

A	B	C	D	E	F	G	H
MERTHYR	PONTYPRIDD	CARDIFF CENTRAL	CARDIFF GREATER	BARRY	BRIDGEND	PORT TALBOT	SWANSEA

force. Of the 3,118 staff, 387 were in the headquarters division, 283 in traffic, and 64 in communications. The separation of administrative and operational officers was more complete than ever before, making it a very different force from that of 1900. As the chart in Figure 4.2 shows, assistant chief constables were responsible for operations, management services and administration. Chief superintendents played a key role, being in charge of various sectors of activity at Bridgend, and of each division, and they were supported by over a hundred superintendents and chief inspectors. An average territorial division, with its own headquarters staff, had 1 chief superintendent, 3 superintendents, 5 chief inspectors, 16 inspectors, 51 sergeants and 219 constables.

The biggest change was in the number and significance of the civilian staff. These had been employed during, and after, the First World War, as telephonists and typists, and their number increased sharply during the next war. They were initally regarded, and dressed, as part of the police establishment, although second-class in terms of numbers, pay and conditions. Even in 1961 there was only one civilian for every ten officers in the South Wales forces. Then a large intake of clerical staff, and the appointment of traffic wardens, increased the proportion, and by 1970 it had reached a quarter.

The government policy of supporting civilianization, especially in areas such as police buildings, transport, communications and photography, gave the process added impetus, and ultimately changed the relationship between regulars and 'civvies'. The latter became more of a separate entity, distinct from the officers, and favoured by ministers of the Crown because they were a cheaper substitute. As their numbers grew, so did the demands that they be given their own training and career structure. By 1989 there were 1,198 full-time and 233 part-time civilians in the South Wales force, and whatever the future holds for the police, civilianization up to a high-ranking level is one of the most likely and potentially important elements.

Subsequent developments, outside the period of this book, were the creation in September 1991 of fourteen smaller police divisions, and greater decentralized control and budgeting. More stringent procedures for assessment, quality control, consultation and complaints have also been put in place. It is, as the chief constable stated in 1991, part of a 'major upheaval', the full impact of which has yet to be felt. With the approach of local government reorganization, there is evidence that the police are moving in the same direction. Administrative ranks such as chief superintendent are disappearing, headquarters staff will probably be scaled down, and future territorial divisions might well resemble independent unitary authorities, recalling past structures of the mid-twentieth century.

Although the South Wales Constabulary has not yet been the subject of a major sociological enquiry, studies of other forces have identified organizational problems which have been inherent in large police forces from an early date. One of these is vertical integration, and another is horizontal integration. The London survey of the early 1980s, carried out at the request of the Metropolitan police by the Police Studies Institute, concluded that vertical integration was the chief weakness in the management of the force. If policy is laid down by the people at the top, as it is in the police and armed forces, it is important that contacts and controls work lower down. In the early years of the century, when supervision was minimal, there is evidence that some outlying stations of Glamorgan acted almost independently of the centre, and out-of-date procedures were carried on without headquarters knowing it.

Constables in smaller stations were obliged to act on their own, and adopted work practices which suited them, sometimes in contravention of central directives and legal requirements. Some of the entries of 'insubordination' on the records of Cardiff and Glamorgan constables were angry expressions of resentment as new inspectors and sergeants sought to change these customary ways of proceeding. Standing orders, which have been distributed to all police officers since the beginning of the century, together with chief constables' circulars and orders, were intended to weaken this mentality. Later contributions to better vertical integration, especially post-Scarman, have been the emphasis on closer supervision, on the middle-management role of people like inspectors, and on more rigorous assessment of operational staff. Whether this has actually improved relationships between the various levels of the force remains to be seen. An internal opinion survey in the South Wales force in 1993 reaffirmed the 'need to enhance communication and consultation within the organization'.

Horizontal integration is rather different, and became a problem when specialization bred new departments and separate management structures. Certain branches of the force grew apart from each other. Amongst the difficult relationships were those between the uniformed officers and CID, between the operational units and headquarters, and between regulars on the one hand and civilians and specials on the other. Tensions between the first pair began to emerge once the detective departments grew in size. Although the detectives in the Cardiff and Swansea forces in mid-century had heavy case-loads, they had a higher status and better pay and promotion prospects than their colleagues in the uniform branch. Records from the 1930s to the 1950s reveal that the latter were responsible for about 38 per cent of the detections in Swansea, and in Glamorgan and Cardiff it was sometimes higher, thus stoking the rivalry between them and the CID men.

According to market research, the present-day officers walking the beat find much of their work dull and unrewarding. They are repeatedly told of the value of uniformed and CID officers working in tandem, but the former are largely deprived of the satisfaction of dealing with crimes reported to them, or discovered by them. Although the public wishes to have more foot patrols, it is regarded internally, in the English forces studied, as a job for young and unambitious individuals. Car patrolling has a greater attraction. Sociologists tell us, however, that whatever their differences, all these front-line officers are united in a common disdain of career 'pen-pushers' at headquarters, of the liaison work of community policemen and women, and of the civilians and specials who 'are not real policemen'.

Technical developments

The backwardness of the Glamorgan force, which we have already noted, was underlined in September 1937 by the inspector of constabulary, and, more than twenty years later, by the Home Secretary in his response to county requests for augmentation. The former stated that the general efficiency of the force was remarkably good 'when it is realised how handicapped the several departments at Headquarters have been for the years during which other forces have been developing on modern lines'. The most obvious of these developments was in transport, buildings, communications, scientific investigation and record-keeping.

Prior to the First World War, all of the forces used horses. In

Glamorgan, Lionel Lindsay had his own horse and driver, and his superintendents had horses and traps. In 1913 Captain Alfred Thomas, the new chief constable of Swansea, established regular mounted patrols in the outlying western parts of the borough. At Cardiff, in the same year, the police had a mounted contingent of fifteen. All the forces kept the equipment of mounted police, and borrowed horses from tradesmen and the gentry on ceremonial occasions and in an emergency. Horses were used, for instance, until the 1930s to control crowds and escort carts during industrial conflicts. The First World War, however, ended Glamorgan's plans to build stables and coach-houses right across the county, and police transport became increasingly a matter of pedal and motor power.

Constables on the most extensive beats had used their own bicycles since the late nineteenth century, and were given allowances to meet their costs. In 1919 the Glamorgan force paid 158 such allowances, together with 20 for officers who owned motor cycles. In 1931, after the Home Secretary's insistence that each force should have a mobile patrol, partly to enforce new traffic legislation, the county bought ten motor-cycle combinations, and five years later these were replaced by cars. Lindsay resented the charge that his force was backward in this regard, but in Cardiff James Wilson stated in 1934 that all of them had 'fallen far behind the times in respect to mobility. Increased mobility means increased efficiency.' His motor patrol in that year arrested 28 people, summoned 480 others, and cautioned 299.

The post-war growth in vehicles for the traffic police was fairly rapid, though progress in most South Wales forces was slower than in Britain generally. They were used at first during the daytime, but then at night as well. The traffic police responded to emergency calls, accidents and other occurrences, as well as helping foot patrols on occasions, but their main task was dealing with breaches of the highway regulations. 'Although the work of the police has increased in every sphere', said the Cardiff chief constable in 1965, 'no single item matches the gargantuan problem which road traffic poses.' The traffic police were grateful for the automatic signals, which had been first used in Swansea in 1918, for the wireless sets fitted to cars during the Second World War, for the radar meters added during the 1960s, and, indirectly, for the comprehensive adoption of unit-beat policing in 1967–8.

The arrival of panda cars revolutionized the way that policemen worked their beats. One patrol vehicle was able to manage an area six times as large as that covered by an officer on foot and, moreover, they could respond more quickly to calls and had instant access to information in the control rooms. Nevertheless, as we shall see in the next chapter, criticisms of this new system began early and expansion was curtailed. In 1969 the South Wales Constabulary had 459 motor vehicles (almost three and a half times the number of 1961), and twenty years later the number was 556, a quarter of which were for traffic duties. By 1989, the traffic police were organized into western, central and eastern sectors, with a fourth covering the M4 motorway. All, of course, were in contact with each other, and with their sector base.

Communications have always been an essential part of modern policing. At the beginning of the century telegraphy kept forces and stations in touch with each other, though men on the beat, or their wives, had to pass on messages by hand. The Glamorgan force had its own, highly prized, private phone service at an early date, whilst Swansea introduced the box system in 1927, which permitted policemen on the beat and the public to contact headquarters. A few years later, transmitting and receiving stations were built to enable a police wireless system to be operated in Cardiff and Swansea; this delighted James Wilson who made patronizing comparisons with the situation in the adjoining county. Glamorgan erected its own two-way communications network during the 1950s, and, as unit-beat policing drew near, personal radio sets were issued to area constables. The operations room at Glamorgan's headquarters became, as a result of all these developments, 'the nerve centre of the working of the force in dealing with traffic duties, crime and all types of emergency and routine work'.

Communications between the public and the police were improved with the arrival of the 999 facility in Swansea in the mid-1940s, and elsewhere in the 1950s. By 1963, 2,208 emergency 999 calls were being received at Swansea, leading to 53 arrests; and 12,401 wireless messages were received and broadcast, 62 per cent of which concerned crimes. Other information on offences and offenders was communicated by telex, and after 1973, via the terminals of the police national computer. Finally, in 1983, after much planning, IRIS, a computerized incident, resource and information system based at headquarters and linked to all stations, became operational, and half a million incidents were entered on the system annually.

The use of science in the detection of criminals was, in 1900, less important than the extent and speed of police communications, and has remained so. The Home Office was concerned about the lack of fingerprinting and photographic facilities in the Glamorgan force at the start of our period, and even the urban police were rather slow to realize their importance. By the 1930s, however, Swansea and especially Cardiff claimed to have a 'standard of crime detection . . . not surpassed in this country'. The Cardiff facilities, which included a forensic science laboratory, were taken over by the Home Office in 1938 and converted into a regional centre for South Wales and Monmouthshire. Eventually the forensic work done at Cardiff and at Bristol was combined in a new site at Chepstow.

During the post-war period all the forces in South Wales had fingerprinting and photographic departments. Units of officers trained in these techniques visited the scene of all serious crimes. In Glamorgan the amount of this work carried out by seven officers – who were soon to be trained in identikit – was said in November 1960 to be 'overwhelming'. There was subsequently an increase in their numbers, but not an exceptional one. In 1972, just prior to partial civilianization, there were 30 scenes-of-crime officers in South Wales, who made 12,350 visits and helped to identify 708 people responsible for crimes.

In 1959 the Western Criminal Record Office was established at Cardiff to cater for nine forces. It was an extension of the record-keeping and crime information work which had, for decades, been carried out in the individual forces. The WCRO housed large collections of fingerprints and photographs, together with indexes of wanted and convicted persons, a *modus operandi* analysis of certain types of crime, and lists of stolen property. Each year, on behalf of the Welsh forces, the office made thousands of searches through its files for individuals and vehicles, and disseminated daily information on wanted and missing persons, and selected crimes, to policemen, dealers, shopkeepers and others. The Record Office moved to Bridgend in 1964, and back to Cardiff ten years later. It closed down in 1989, being replaced by a crime information centre for the South Wales force alone, which, together with other regional and national networks, provides a comprehensive science and intelligence service.

Training and promotion

For over forty years training varied a good deal from force to force. The urban police had the most advanced kind, though in 1900 it amounted to only a few weeks' instruction in law, first aid, drill and general education, before recruits were placed on the beat with older officers. Lionel Lindsay, who grew exasperated with talk of police education and colleges, was convinced that the 'hard school of practical experience' rather than 'reading law books, etc.' was the best form of training.

At first, training had something of a military character; men were expected to keep their uniform smart and to be disciplined and deferential. They were required to be in good physical shape, and were taught how to drill and to control disorderly individuals. Lindsay, who was given a gold medal for his recruiting services during the First World War, welcomed the character-forming opportunities offered in those years to teach his younger recruits a little about military bearing and the handling of swords.

The Desborough Committee, in its reports of 1919–20, attempted to bring more central direction and standardization to police training and recommended the appointment of a training officer in each force. A small number of training schools were quickly established, and for a few years Swansea sent its recruits to the training school in Birmingham. Then, in 1929 and 1933 respectively, Swansea and Cardiff started their own police schools, where recruits from several forces were given thirteen weeks' basic training with fortnightly tests. In the Glamorgan force, less structured training was provided for recruits, and, to complaints, these probationers were transferred in 1934 from headquarters to the crowded Barry Dock station, with the overspill going to Cadoxton. Although Lindsay was probably aware of the advantages of having a more educated and trained force, he was eloquent on the inconvenience which it caused, and the loss of so many working hours.

The decision was taken towards the end of the Second World War to establish district centres which would provide training for probationer constables and short refresher courses for officers returning from the war and for those in service. Initially, these centres had an aura of the military barracks and were disliked by a considerable proportion of the recruits. Dyffryn House during the war, then Bryncethin (1946), Bridgend (1947) and finally Cwmbran (1974) acted as the training centre for forces across South Wales. About the same time, police colleges also made their appearance, including that at Ryton-on-Dunsmore in Warwickshire in 1948. These offered training courses for ambitious young officers and specialist courses for senior staff.

The growth of crime, the requirements of new legislation, and the changing nature of society have all obliged the police to become more professional and specialized. First Glamorgan, and then the other forces, provided training in motor driving, firearms and civil defence, and sent officers away for instruction in crime prevention, computer work, photography, fingerprinting, the misuse of drugs, and much more. During the 1970s the South Wales force developed a number of in-service schemes, and public-order and firearms training were given a high priority.

South Wales, like other police forces, was much affected by the restructuring after 1975 of probationers' training, and by the government economies that followed. A comprehensive teaching programme was introduced only after the Scarman Report highlighted the need for better trained and supervised police officers. Much of the training thereafter was done 'in-house', according to national guidelines. In 1989 the force's training department was extended and given responsibility for three grades of instruction: the revamped 'on-the-job' training of probationer constables, the dual-rank development course for sergeants and constables, and internal and external learning opportunities for inspectors and above. In this, as in most forces, the training of civilians and specials has been rather neglected.

One of the outstanding features of the policing profession, which has marked it out from certain others, has been its meritocratic character. Although the county forces in 1900 still had a semi-military character, with non-commissioned officers being appointed to the best posts, this quickly changed. Most of the men who became chief constables in this century, like James Wilson and Joseph Jones, rose from the ranks. North Walian Jones began his working life as a railway porter. Moving down a grade, it was claimed that farming and industrial applicants who joined the

Glamorgan force about the turn of the century 'reached high ranks in later years'. Most of the superintendents were, in fact, ex-colliers and miners, labourers, railwaymen, farmers and clerks, as table 4.3 shows.

Their progress through the ranks was steady rather than rapid. Superintendents appointed in the years 1883–1930 had taken nineteen years to become inspectors and another eight years to reach their final rung on the ladder. There was a small number of notable exceptions, like Cecil Watkins, the young lad from Pentre in the Rhondda, who became a superintendent at the age of thirty-six years (and chief constable at fifty), and William Jones, the collier from Newquay in Cardiganshire, who matched these achievements until his dismissal for embezzlement. The other ranks took longer to gain promotion. The typical progress for a Glamorgan inspector in the first half of the century was thirteen years as a constable, three years as acting sergeant, and eight years as a full sergeant. Others moved through the force even more slowly, their progress halted by the the non-retirement of senior officers, which happened during the First World War, and by failure in examinations.

Examinations for entry into the force and later for promotion became the norm. In Glamorgan in the 1920s and 1930s about 150 applicants sat the basic entry examinations each year, and a similar number took the promotion examinations on law and general knowledge begun in 1924. In April 1933, for example, 167 officers sat the qualifying examinations to become acting sergeants, sergeants and inspectors; 38 passed all papers, 50 passed one paper, and 79 failed. J. M. Judd of Penarth Intermediate School, who set and marked the papers, said that the candidates 'reached, on the whole, the highest level yet attained'. After the war, these examinations became organized nationally, and several exceptional candidates in South Wales, like Edward Ronald Baker, progressed rapidly through the force.

One of the complaints that was increasingly heard after the Second World War was that there were not enough people of Baker's quality in the police forces. In 1955–9 the educational level of police recruits in Glamorgan, which was slightly better than the national average, was as in table 4.1. The poor educational standards of recruits became a major issue in the 1960s, when, as the royal commission put it, 'a better educated public'

Table 4·1: Academic qualifications of police recruits, 1955–1959

Without GCE	With GCE	No. of subjects at O Level							No. of subjects at A Level		
		1	2	3	4	5	6	6+	1	2	3
305	65	10	10	6	10	15	5	7	1	1	–

was entitled to expect a better-educated policeman. Efforts were made both to attract graduates into the forces, and to give serving officers the chance of higher education. The South Wales force was ambitious in sending bright recruits on polytechnic and university courses, and in the 1980s, due to a combination of circumstances, the graduate intake rose. In 1990, when almost two-thirds of new recruits had good educational qualifications, there were 205 graduates in the force, many in key management posts.

Mrs Thatcher and her advisers expressed concern during these years about the quality of the 'officer class' within the police forces, fearing its inbred nature, fixed attitudes and capacity to obstruct the best intentions of government. Robert Reiner, who has researched the recent history of chief constables, finds evidence of a concerted Home Office drive to encourage the appointment of men at the top with a different set of values. It is a very far cry from Lionel Lindsay, who carefully nurtured his own élite, and poured scorn on the grand schemes of governments and intellectual outsiders.

Police numbers

The increase in the number of policemen and women across South Wales has been an inconsistent one, as graph 4.1 illustrates. In 1900 the authorized establishments of the four forces totalled 782, or about 1 officer per 1,081 of the population. Glamorgan had one of the poorest ratios in Britain of one policeman for every 1,391 of the population in 1902, the worst figures being for the Pontypridd (1: 1,592) and Merthyr (1: 1,456) divisions. In the former there were industrial communities like Hopkinstown (with a population to be policed of 3,789), Cwmparc (3,080) and Blaenclydach (2,942) which had only one officer, which explains the requests for more police mentioned above. By contrast, in the more rural Barry Dock division, (1: 1,144), fortunate inhabitants of places like Rhoose (population policed of 454), and St Fagans (675) also had, in 1902, one policeman.

Thirty-six years later, the force establishments had almost doubled in size, and the ratio of the actual number of officers to population in South Wales was about 1: 794. Cardiff had the highest ratio of the five forces, and Swansea and Glamorgan usually the worst. In the Glamorgan force, which had an overall figure of 1: 824 in mid-1938, the ratio varied from 1: 632 in the Barry Dock division to 1: 950 in that of Tonpentre. By 1968 the number of officers in South Wales had increased to 1 per 530 of the population, and in 1989 it was 1 per 419.

These figures have to be set against developments such as the reduction in working hours, the weeks lost through training, and the civilianization of the police. Even so, they reveal some interesting trends. The line on graph 4.1 showing Glamorgan police numbers, which covers the years prior to amalgamation, shows that there were three distinct periods: the first ten years, when the rate of police to population in the county did not change much, a sudden rise to a higher level which moved gradually upwards until the Second World War, and the take-off during the 1950s and 1960s.

The reports and police-committee minutes of the early decades were full of requests from parishes and townships for extra constables. In Cardiff, where there had been no increase in the police establishment since 1899, the chief constable stressed the new problems caused by the granting of an extra rest day for the police, by the growth of population, street mileage and traffic, and by people flooding into the city centre during the evenings. Eventually, in 1909–10, he got approval for fifty more men. In Glamorgan, where industrial disorder posed an additional threat, the increase in the police establishment in the years prior to the First World War was similarly dramatic, and, in view of Lindsay's political anxieties, essential. Between 1909 and 1914, 228 extra men were recruited in the county, many of them for the mining areas; and, to complete the picture, there were 60–100 members of the national police reserve, and another 63 constables working for private (mainly industrial) companies in the county. In Cardiff and Swansea there was also the harbour police.

These, together with the special constabulary, formed a useful

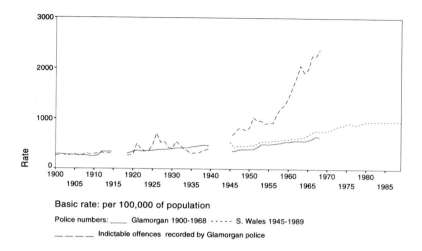

Basic rate: per 100,000 of population

Police numbers: ____ Glamorgan 1900-1968 · · · · · S. Wales 1945-1989

_ _ _ _ Indictable offences recorded by Glamorgan police

Graph 4.1: Police numbers in Glamorgan and South Wales, 1900–1989

reserve force when the regulars were stretched by major disorders, disasters and war. During the First World War Cardiff, being a prohibited area, and Glamorgan, with its Admiralty coalfield, faced considerable policing problems as their men left to join the armed forces. Regular officers were refused retirement, extra work-hours became the norm, beats were doubled in size, large numbers of specials were paid to patrol and watch, and more would have been used had the working class responded more readily to the call. When the war ended, the regular force of Glamorgan was 38 per cent down on the 1914 total.

After the war it took a few years to re-establish the police forces in South Wales, but further improvement in the number of recruits was curtailed by the government economies of the early 1920s. During the worst years of the inter-war depression, the police forces hardly expanded at all, and the chief constable of Glamorgan, in report after report, expressed his 'grave apprehension' at this situation. Even when the 'dangers' of communism and disorder declined, his successor stressed the difficulties of controlling motor traffic and of policing those areas where commerce was flourishing. A number of young males and females had been appointed as clerks and telephone operators in each division, but only enough to release a few regular officers.

During the Second World War the place of the many policemen who joined the armed forces was taken by the First Police Reserve (mainly police pensioners), the Police War Reserve (middle-aged men, often unemployed, who were excused war service), the Women's Auxiliary Police Corps, and large numbers of special constables, working in a part-time or unpaid capacity. Even so, these proved insufficient to perform the variety of police, ambulance and civil-defence tasks required, and in 1941 the Home Secretary lifted the ban on recruiting young men. When the war ended the number of regular police in Glamorgan was 300 under the authorized establishment.

Contrary to expectations, there were major problems attracting and keeping recruits after men returned from fighting. The Glamorgan chief constable, writing in 1948, warned of the operational consequences of large numbers of experienced officers taking retirement, and of young men filling their place and then leaving to find better-paid jobs. In December of that year he reported that there had been 123 resignations from the force since 31 January 1946, for the reasons outlined in table 4.2. Nor were

Table 4·2: Reasons for resignations from the Glamorgan force, 1946–1948

	Probationers	Men with more more than 2 years' experience
Housing problems	8	–
Domestic problems	12	10
Police work uncongenial	16	3
Rejoined HM forces	1	4
Obtained more remunerative work	31	34
Other reasons	4	–

there enough new applicants of 'sufficient' physical, medical and educational standard. From 1946 until 1952 there was an average annual shortfall of 180 officers in the Glamorgan force, and, reluctantly, the county kept a few of its war reservists and appointed the first policewomen. Swansea, which needed more police to cover its new housing estates, was in a comparable situation, but Cardiff and Merthyr had fewer vacancies.

As the line on graph 4.1 showing South Wales police numbers indicates, only in the years after the Oaksey Report did the increase in appointments make a significant difference to the rate. Then followed a gradual improvement, until the major addition of men and women in the mid-1960s, which was matched by a substantial rise in civilian staff, of typists, cleaners, school crossing officers, traffic wardens and the like. Even in Swansea there was some optimism over the quality of recruits and about the future prospects, but in 1968 these hopes were dashed by government economies. The coming of amalgamation was accompanied by a freeze on new appointments which was to have a lasting impact.

The next big increase in the regular force was in the early 1970s, a short burst before the next round of cuts in public expenditure and a rare drop in police numbers. In 1978 Lord Edmund-Davies's report and the pay award was well received by the police, and the following year was designated 'the best ever' from the point of view of recruiting and retaining new officers. In that year, when there were almost 3,000 regulars, and just over 1,000 full- and part-time civilians in the South Wales force, the density of serving officers varied from 1 per 36 of the (exceptionally low) resident population in Cardiff's city centre subdivision, to 1 per 908 in the centre of Maesteg. Since then the story has mainly been one of stagnation, with the emphasis on civilianization and the redeployment of officers to operational duty. In 1989, when the regulars numbered 3,118, the figure was not that different from ten years earlier, nor has it increased much since that time. As we shall see in the next chapter, the Home Office and the Tory government are convinced that numbers alone are not the answer to the modern law-and-order problem.

Profile

The great majority of police recruits during the century have been male. Women were employed from the start as police matrons, to deal with female prisoners, and others worked closely with the police as probation officers, but there was much resistance to the notion of policewomen. After a number of requests from

**A Glamorgan policewoman on school crossing patrol in
Barry in the late 1940s.**

feminists, including the Aberavon and Port Talbot branch of the
National Union for Women's Suffrage, Lindsay declared in 1924
that policewomen were neither necessary nor efficient, and his
counterpart in Cardiff replied in similar vein to Lady Astor and
the Cardiff Women's Citizens' Association a few years later. When,
in 1931, James Wilson made the second of his reports on the
matter, there were already 167 policewomen in England, but he
was convinced that the experiment had been 'a complete failure'.

The Second World War highlighted the value of women as
clerical workers and staff-support officers in police forces, and
soon after its ending all four of the South Wales bodies appointed
members of the WAPC as their first policewomen. In Glamorgan,
where there was a short delay before representatives on the
standing joint police committee overcame their prejudices, there
were problems in getting female recruits and persuading them to
stay for more than a few years.

Part of the explanation for this was their pay, which was set at 10 per cent below that of their male counterparts, the lack of promotion, and the nature of the work given to them. Their work consisted at first of dealing with female criminals, prostitutes and juvenile delinquents, interspersed with traffic duties, but gradually they were given a fuller range of duties. At Cardiff in 1956 the one female inspector, one sergeant and fourteen constables patrolled in all three divisions, and worked in the CID and court departments, being responsible for 'the advancement of charges' in 178 indictable offences and for 295 prosecutions over summary offences.

In Cardiff, Merthyr and the other forces, chief constables praised 'the excellent' contribution of these policewomen, but their number remained small. In December 1969, after amalgamation, there were only 65 of them compared with 2,326 males. Six years later, with the passing of the Sex Discrimination Act, the separate policewomen's section was broken up, and their work subsequently cannot be disentangled from that of their male colleagues. By 1989 their number had grown to 268, still fewer than 10 per cent of the regular force, and, in sharp contrast to the males, 70 per cent of these women had under ten years' service. Some feel today, like their predecessors in the 1940s, that real equality has not yet arrived.

Apart from being a largely male profession, the police force has been, for much of the twentieth century, dominated by working-class recruits who joined in their early twenties, and retired after thirty or more years of service. In Glamorgan at the turn of the century, 'the rural counties of Wales provided a fruitful source for suitable candidates', as did the 'mines and other industries', whilst tradesmen with special skills were always appreciated. In 1913, however, the chief constable of Glamorgan noted a change in the area and occupation of the recruits: where once robust farm workers from west Wales filled his force, now a greater share came from Ireland and (about a seventh) from the army. In fact, he underestimated the recruitment of local people, and exaggerated the Irish connection, as can be seen in table 4.3 showing three chronological samples, 1865–93 (officers all types), 1883–1930 (superintendents) and 1912–41 (inspectors). Of the third group (inspectors 1912–41), 32 per cent were either soldiers, or had previously served in the armed forces, usually in the Welsh

**Table 4·3: Geographical and occupational origins of
recruits: three samples of the Glamorgan force
(percentages of total)**

	Recruits 1865–93 (officers of all types)	Recruits 1883–1930 (superintendents)	Recruits 1912–41 (inspectors)
Geographical			
S.W. Wales	34	30	20
Glamorgan	32	32	60
Monmouthshire	4	12	4
Somerset and Devon	16	0	2
Brecon and Rads.	4	6	4
Shrops., Herefs. and Glos.	6	6	4
Ireland	0	8	0
Others	4	6	6
Occupational			
Farmer	4	6	4
Labourer/farm labourer	30	12	4
Collier/miner	14	20	24
Railway worker	6	16	0
Soldier	2	0	12
Clerk	0	10	6
Others	44	36	50

Guards. The chief constable was thus reasonably accurate when he
told the Glamorgan police pay committee in September 1937 that
a third of the appointments in the previous three years had been
ex-soldiers. One suspects that they were welcomed here, though
not by Will Paynter and the miners, with open arms.

In Cardiff it is possible that there was, in the early years, a policy
of appointing outsiders to the force. Prior to the First World War,
Englishmen made up 62 per cent of the recruits. Most of them
originated from Bristol, Somerset, Gloucestershire, Devon and
Herefordshire, whilst many of the Welsh recruits (32 per cent) had
a Monmouthshire upbringing. Three out of ten Cardiff policemen
who joined the force at the turn of the century gave their previous
occupation as labourers, and the rest were a mixture of estate

workers, farmers, gardeners, craftsmen and, to a lesser degree, industrial workers and seamen. They took up their new appointments when they were in their early twenties, three out of ten were married, and a similar proportion resigned or were dismissed from the force within five years. By 1913 things had improved: 53 per cent of the 294 police officers in the city then had ten years' service or more, and one in five had at least twenty years' service.

By the 1930s there had been a significant change in the background of the Cardiff force. The great majority still joined in their early twenties, but a small sample of new appointments, compiled by Jeremy Glenn, shows that six out of ten had been born in Cardiff. Most of the remainder were from elsewhere in Glamorgan and Monmouthshire, and in their previous employment they had often been clerks, railwaymen and motor mechanics. The same group completed an average of twenty-three years' service in the force. Six out of ten of them were promoted to sergeant, an exceptionally high ratio, after an average of sixteen years in the force, but only one in ten of the sample progressed further. Annual snapshots of the whole force give a rather different picture: thus in 1938, 60 per cent of the Cardiff police were of Welsh origin, and 37 per cent were from England, 69 per cent of the force had served for ten years or more, and the average service period was thirteen years.

In Swansea in 1920, 59 per cent of the force were Welshmen, 32 per cent were English, and just over a third of the police recruits had been previously employed as soldiers, railwaymen, colliers and policemen. As in Cardiff, the rate of local recruits rose in the inter-war years, and the lack of job opportunities encouraged the Swansea men to stay in this career. In 1938 the average age of these officers was thirty-five and they had spent, typically, thirteen years in the force. Thirteen years later both figures had fallen, but only slightly. Over three-quarters of the Swansea force were married.

After the Second World War people continued to be recruited into the forces largely from the skilled manual and low-grade non-manual workers, but the conditions of age, sex, marital status, height and accommodation for new appointments were modified or removed. Although twenty years was normally the minimum age for a regular officer, Swansea employed teenage boys as clerks as early as 1928. Then, in the immediate post-war years, each force developed its junior police corps (cadets), many of whom eventually became senior policemen. In the 1960s these cadets were at last removed from clerical tasks, put into uniform, sent on residential courses, and attached to patrol divisions and headquarters departments. It thus became possible to join the police profession directly from school, or, in time, directly from college and university.

In Glamorgan, as befits a force initially run on semi-military lines, the declared preference was for unmarried recruits, who would live on police premises. Nine out of ten recruits in the county before the First World War were unmarried, and were obliged to remain single for three years. The requirement was increased on Lindsay's bidding to five years, but reduced to four years in 1938, and removed altogether in 1945, though officers were still obliged to notify the chief of their wedding plans. By 1951 things had changed significantly; about half the new appointments in the county were already married, and most of the others became so during their mid and late twenties. Yet the interest in policemen's wives and their employment remained, for they were, as matrons, station-keepers and unpaid messengers, a vital part of policing in many communities.

Conditions of service

One of the factors which delayed marriage and held back possible applicants was the accommodation situation within the forces. Originally many recruits were accommodated at headquarters, station houses and police lodgings. Lindsay, who strongly approved of young men being in quarters, believed that it fostered camaraderie and efficiency. In December 1913 he declared that all men should live at stations, or very close to them. The costs of lodgings were deducted from the officers' wages, but, after the Desborough Report on the service, all police accommodation became rent-free.

The provision of such accommodation was, however, inadequate for the growing number of recruits, and unpopular with those about to marry and on the verge of retiring. After the Second World War, the Welsh police forces embarked on extensive building programmes, sometimes with the aid of urban authorities which were anxious to have police officers residing on their new estates. In August 1959 the Glamorgan police committee reported that 364 police houses had been built since the war, 62 premises had been converted into flats, and 79 houses purchased for police use. The same policy, on a smaller scale, was executed in the boroughs. Ultimately, it proved to be unnecessary, for men and women in the police, as in other professions, preferred the security of buying their own homes, using the accommodation allowance to pay off the mortgage. By 1989, 83 per cent of officers in South Wales had become owner-occupiers, and police houses were being sold off in considerable numbers.

Conditions of service changed markedly over the century. In 1900 policemen worked long hours for low pay; it was ten years before they gained one rest day in seven and a week's annual leave. Such was the problem of getting additional officers over the next decades that Welsh forces frequently delayed the execution of national police regulations, like that of 1920 defining eight hours as the 'normal period' of duty for constables and sergeants. Glamorgan had an exceptional level of 'overtime and excessive hours of duty performed'. Lindsay argued that until county forces were given more equality with urban, it was the only way that he could handle the increasing burdens of road traffic, 'extraneous' duties and crime.

In truth, this particular chief constable believed, like his nineteenth-century predecessors, that 'apart from sleeping' his officers should spend all their time at the station where they would be 'ready' for action. At Hopkinstown, Constable Welsby usually came on duty at 9 or 10 a.m. in 1912, and, except for a couple of hours' break, stayed until the early hours of the next morning. The same was true of Constable Brooks at Peterston-super-Ely before he became ill in 1936, though, unlike Welsby, he had a weekly rest day. Gradually, however, the nominal 48-hour week was reduced to 44 in the mid-1950s, to 42 in the 1960s, and 40 by the 1970s.

The non-salary perks of the job were few; officers had, as we have seen, free rent after 1919, as well as certain clothing, transport and travel allowances, but after the early years of the century they were not allowed to keep gratuities offered by a thankful public. Of them all, the rent allowance (which also covered rates) was the most important extra for the men and women of the forces, and demands for increases in the rate were frequent. As the response to the government's examination of that allowance in 1990 shows, it has remained a vital issue for serving officers.

So have the pension and insurance schemes which have been part of force life since the 1890s. Small pension deductions were made from the weekly wage, and for that in 1900 a policeman received, after completing a lifetime in the force, about £400 a year as an ex-chief constable of the Glamorgan force, or £54. 12s. 0d. as an ex-constable. In addition, under the Police Act of 1896, the standing joint committee was empowered to grant a policeman's widow a gratuity related to her husband's service, and the Glamorgan Police Mutual Benefit Association, formed in 1903, paid out up to £100 on the death of a member or his wife. Lindsay, who organized charity rugby matches to raise money for the widows of young policemen, was adamant that all these forms of support kept alive the *esprit de corps* so essential in his force.

A policeman's job also had another advantage; it was, in the context of South Wales society, a comparatively healthy and even safe profession. Deaths in service were rare. The police doctors rejected a lot of applicants on health grounds, and many resigned early, finding the work too physically demanding. 'Apparently the night duty during the winter is too much for them,' said Lindsay in 1913 of some of his young recruits. He expected high levels of commitment, and rather despised sick notes. Days lost through sickness and injury in his force were, for most years, surprisingly few prior to 1948, though individual examples of hardship are easy to find. Samuel Hocking is an obvious one; selected to take charge of the Blaenclydach beat, 'a very rough one, on account of his exceptional strength and vigour', he never recovered from the injuries sustained there before, and during, the strike of 1911.

'One has the impression', said the chief constable of Swansea, after comparing the days lost in 1958 with those of twenty years before, 'that since the advent of the National Health Service in 1948, people have become more conscious of minor ailments, and possibly take longer over convalescence than was once the case. With certain exceptions, it might be said, too, that one misses the keen personal interest in a man's early return to duty, which was evident in the days when the Police Surgeon attended to all sickness within the Force.' When the Home Office carried out its surveys into 'non-effectiveness' in the early 1970s, the South Wales force was losing on average thirteen days per officer a year because of 'sickness'.

Since then the situation has changed, though this has been magnified somewhat by the attention given in recent years to the dangers of violent assaults and injuries at work. By the end of our period as many as one in four police officers suffered an attack, usually a minor one, each year. This aspect of policing will be discussed in the next chapter, but the result has been that 2,374 working days were lost through assault in 1989, and to these must be added 3,949 lost because of injury on duty, as well as 35,633 working days from certified and self-certified illness. The last, at just over 11 days per officer, marks a small improvement on the figure of 1971–2.

The pay of policemen and women has often been a contentious issue. It began from a very low point, in every respect. There were many demands for increases in pay at the beginning of the century, including several from Lindsay and other chief constables, as well as complaints of the differences in rewards across the South Wales forces. Cardiff in 1900 had the highest rates of pay for police constables, and Glamorgan, with £65–82 p.a. for constables, the worst. Chief Constable Lindsay had £550 per year, with £150 for travel expenses, and his superintendents £160–240. Expenditure on salaries, at well over over £40,000 a year, comprised the vast bulk of his force's costs.

After 1911 there was more standardization of salaries across the forces, but the payment, or non-payment, of various bonuses and allowances fed a growing discontent. The tension was barely suppressed during the war years, as the cost of living escalated. Although there were no sympathy strikes in South Wales for protesting colleagues in Liverpool, Birmingham and London, feelings ran high, especially in Cardiff. In Glamorgan Lindsay, who supported many of his men's wage demands, could barely conceal his contempt for the police union and refused to allow his men to attend its mass meetings.

The award of April 1919 gave his men more than twice their pre-war payments, but this was to be the last increase for a long while. For most of the 1920s and 1930s the pay of police officers in the South Wales forces stagnated. There were, however, few problems recruiting people because of the shortage of other employment and the long-term attraction of a police pension.

When the economy improved, especially in the industrial sector, the police authorities were in difficulties. Pay rises then became vital to boost recruitment and recover morale, and supplements were necessary during the Second World War. By November 1946 the minimum pay of a Glamorgan constable, at £274 p.a., was about 50 per cent above the pre-war level, and other ranks benefited proportionately.

After the favourable Oaksey Report of 1949, there was a series of major pay awards. At the end of 1955 the salary scale for a constable in the Glamorgan force was £475–640, and for a superintendent £1,225–1,285. In the years 1955–9, only 156 men left the Glamorgan force with under twenty-five years' service (that is, without a pension), about 15 per cent of the force. Substantial improvements in pay and pensions followed in the early 1960s, when the *South Wales Echo* expressed a popular sentiment that a better-rewarded profession was justified and cost-effective, if it improved efficiency and lowered the crime rate.

Further annual pay increases followed in the late 1960s and early 1970s. Soon after amalgamation, males newly appointed to the post of constable and superintendent (class I) were receiving just over £1,000 and £3,000 respectively. Chief Constable Thomas Gwilym Morris, writing in 1973, announced that the morale of his force had reached a new height, with 'improved promotion prospects, . . . payment of overtime at the option of the individual, the freedom of house purchase, and the minimum of transfers . . .' Within a couple of years the mood had changed, to one of some bitterness, and only with the Lord Edmund-Davies Report, did this disappear.

Thereafter the police did as well as any group in the public sector in terms of securing salary improvements. By 1989, when £80,793,000 (85 per cent) of the South Wales force's expenditure was spent on employees, the police had comparatively few problems in recruiting officers, including graduates. Conditions of service and the rewards of the profession now bear little comparison with those of a century ago. No doubt this is one of the reasons why people stay in the force longer; in 1989 69 per cent had served for ten years or more, whereas twenty years before, in the first year of amalgamation, the figure had been only 51 per cent.

Police image, values and culture

A great deal has been written about the image, values and internal life of police forces. Most of these writers begin with the statements of the first metropolitan police commissioners in the nineteenth century. Faced by a deep popular suspicion of 'government police', they declared that their force would be civilian and non-political in character, fair and legal in its procedures, courteous when dealing with the public and prepared to use only minimum force. These standards have been constantly reinforced in training manuals and standing orders, and most recently by the Statement of Common Purpose and Values issued by the South Wales Constabulary (1991).

How much the police have, or can, conform to these basic principles are questions which have been asked, at intervals, throughout this century. There were justified complaints, for instance, that Lionel Lindsay, who had been in charge of the gendarmerie in Egypt, saw his Glamorgan men as a semi-colonial force, subduing the natives and separate from them. He led the fight against political and industrial 'sedition' in the county, and worked closely with the military. During the 1920s and 1930s, prominent, and even suspected, Communists in the county were watched, weekly reports on their activities were made by senior officers, and secret files were kept on them at headquarters in Canton. This was political, semi-military and largely unaccountable policing of a high order.

Other chief constables, including McKenzie in Cardiff at the beginning of the century, were accused of being particularly hostile to the 'underclass' of petty criminals, beggars, prostitutes and 'down-and-outs'. The discipline books of the Cardiff police provide some evidence to support this. Officers were cautioned for using bad language and excessive violence towards hawkers, people of no fixed abode and 'ladies of the *pavé*'. In the 1930s, 1940s and 1950s, perhaps because of the early example set by Chief Constable Wilson, there were many complaints, and some reprimands, over the behaviour of his officers when dealing with motoring offences and road accidents. There were also a few references in the discipline books of this period to police corruption and the abuse of power. With the benefit of hindsight, these last charges now appear comparatively innocuous, and we are assured by various writers that until the middle of the century the national image of the policeman as a 'fair, peaceful and honest George Dixon figure' was hardly dented. As we shall see in the next chapter, this was not strictly true.

According to police sociologists and historians, the character and attitudes of the police changed a good deal after the mid-century, and especially in the last twenty-five years of the period. They became, to paraphrase Robert Reiner, less constrained and accountable, and more political and militaristic. The debate over amalgamation, the battles over police pay, the rising crime rate and the threat of disorder, demonstrations and terrorism, have all helped to give the police a higher profile. Since the 1970s chief constables and representatives of the Police Federation have become media figures and political lobbyists, and for a while worked closely with members of the Conservative Party.

Alongside this politicization has gone a kind of militarization which has some similarities with that of Lindsay's period. Like other forces, the modern police in South Wales have become more proficient in crowd control, and increasingly armed when dealing with criminals. Moreover, the events of 1984–5 and the nationally co-ordinated activities of specially trained police units finally shattered the image of the British police as a 'reactive civilian force'. To quote the critical Robert Reiner: 'Dixon is out, and Darth Vader is in.'

In the battle against disorder and rising crime, the modern police have been armed with extra powers and better surveillance techniques, whilst at the same time losing some of the local accountability which was once a feature of British policing. According to John Osmond, John Davies and other radical observers of the South Wales scene, the most insidious threat in the 1980s was not the criminal but the police – aggressive, powerful, sometimes above the law and largely uncontrollable.

These comments tended to reinforce the 'police culture', which has always had a distinct 'us' versus 'them' mentality. Although the police were instructed to be open and courteous to the public, they were from the start expected to live as a separate entity. Social contacts were to be kept to a minimum, and constant 'removals' of officers disrupted even these. Thus Charles Clifford Vaughan, a perfectly representative policeman, trained at Canton and Barry Dock in 1929, and then had nine postings or transfers, moving from his early days in Mountain Ash to retirement at Gorseinon on the other side of the county.

Lionel Lindsay wanted these men to make their profession and their families the centre of their social lives. The families of policemen were encouraged, in Glamorgan and in the boroughs, to think of themselves as providing support and future recruits for the force. At the same time, these families benefited from pensions, life insurance and payments to cover enforced early retirement, whilst serving officers were provided with recreation and billiard rooms, sports and music facilities, and their own libraries and magazines. Deputy Chief Constable E. R. Baker, who retired in 1972 after a lifetime in the Glamorgan and South Wales forces, epitomized the commitment to welfare and education. Accounts of early twentieth-century policing suggest that drink and rowdy behaviour were other vital ingredients of this police culture. Accusations by superior officers of drunkenness, bad language and brawling in stations were common. Other traits, according to sociological studies, were male chauvinism and racial prejudice. James Wilson, chief constable of Cardiff in the inter-war years, with his cynical remarks on drink reformers, female inadequacies and inter-race liaisons, was a classic stereotype. Wilson and Lindsay believed in the virtues of teaching recruits by example, and no doubt many of the above cultural traits were passed on from older to younger officers. Certainly, there were many female complaints in the first half of the century of 'uncivil behaviour', suggestive language and sexual advances by Cardiff's police officers. Since the Second World War, and more particularly since the 1970s, official efforts have been made to extinguish the white-male-heterosexual prejudices that inhabit the traditional police culture, but others remain, such as an unswerving internal solidarity and an instinctive suspicion of academics, do-gooders, politicians and others who do not have to man the battlements.

One of the dangers of a separate professional mentality is that it can sometimes justify and disguise activities which ultimately undermine the best interests of the wider community. It has been suggested that in their 'mission' to reform a morally weak state, the police have sometimes been prepared to bend the rules. They portray themselves as men of action, caught between the pressure to get results and the restrictions imposed on their actions by an over-sensitive society. We are told that 'verballing' and physical threats have always been part of British policing, whilst recent cases have highlighted the manner in which rules of evidence and procedure in the forces have been ignored. As we saw in chapter 1, some policemen in the South Wales forces used physical intimidation against the young teenager, the 'street nuisance' and the obstructive defendant. Thus, for instance, one officer was severely reprimanded in Cardiff in 1948 for ordering a bookmaker's runner into a patrol car, and promising him a beating if caught again. There were also examples of the police making false statements and otherwise manipulating evidence, though few major cases of this have come to light before the 1980s, at least in the sources seen by this writer.

Attempts were made from the beginning of the century to ensure mimimum standards of behaviour in the forces. Cardiff can be taken as our example. Of 100 men recruited in the 1890s, one in five had reports of misconduct on their career file, and the charges reached a peak (71 men accused in divisions A, B and C) on the eve of the First World War, before dropping to much lower levels thereafter. During the 1920s and early 1930s the number of officers disciplined was about half the figure of 1913–14, and the rate then fell even further. Most charges were for having a drink and resting when on duty; others were for not attending court, failing to report an incident or insecure premises, being dirty, making improper overtures to females, laying wrongful charges, assaulting prisoners and stealing. Punishment was commonly a fine of 2*s*. 6*d*., a drop in pay, and a severe reprimand. Where the offence was bad or repeated, the police officer faced dismissal and the loss of a good-conduct certificate. In the Glamorgan force, in the difficult days before the First World War, 'inefficiency' and 'insubordination' figured more prominently in the lists of faults than in Cardiff, and dismissal was the usual result.

Dismissals, like resignations, became less common during the inter-war years. There were a few spectacular cases, like the embezzlement charges against John D. Jenkins at Cardiff headquarters in 1919 and against Deputy Chief Constable William Jones of the Glamorgan force in 1933, and the £200 damages won by William Morgan of Loughor for assault, unlawful arrest and false imprisonment in 1941, but most accusations against the police were fairly mundane.

During the Second World War the impression, in Cardiff

especially, was that the temporary police officers were more 'insubordinate', and more willing to accept gifts, hide stolen property and take goods from unoccupied premises than the constables whom they replaced. In the post-war years the records suggest an improvement in conduct; no more than eight police officers a year were normally punished for misconduct in each of the South Wales forces, the main charges being neglect of duty, disobedience, discreditable conduct, and being guilty of a criminal offence. During the first full year after amalgamation, formal disciplinary charges were proved against only nineteen officers, and the figure did not change significantly over the next twenty years. There were, however, as we shall see in the next chapter, other complaints against officers and civilians, mainly from the public, which were dealt with by other means.

Police work: history and perceptions

Each generation, and each commission and committee on the police, has claimed that the work of the police has increased. When Robert Lawrence declared in 1990 that 'today's officer carries a far greater workload than his colleague of ten years ago', he was not saying anything new. Every chief constable, often in requests to the Home Office, has documented the growing burdens on his force, the widening range of police work, and its increasingly sophisticated and complex character.

In truth, the duties of the police have, from the start, been more diverse than many police histories indicate. The first professional police had the triple functions of fighting crime, keeping order and serving the community, and the first of these was not always the most important. Officers, especially in small boroughs like Neath, were essentially servants of the ratepayers. They were called upon to perform tasks like collecting rates and fines, fighting fires and driving ambulances. In 1900 they were often assistant poor-relief officers, auxiliary census and truant officers, and inspectors of weights and measures and public health.

In the twentieth century the role of the police has contracted in some areas and expanded in others. The Cardiff police, stung by the charge that they were under-utilized, published early in 1914 a detailed account of the 'miscellaneous duties' performed during the previous year. This gives us some idea of their work-load, and of the manner in which it grew. In 1913 the force comprised 294 men, with another 21 forming a fire brigade. The officers served 6,950 summonses and executed 1,894 warrants, conveyed 1,449 prisoners to gaol, dispatched 11,969 letters, watched 2,594 premises during the absence of owners, reported 8,558 premises insecure, found 683 street lamps defective, restored 543 children to their parents, seized 342 stray dogs, authorized 265 pedlars' certificates, and did much more besides.

Twenty-five years later, when the force was 342 strong, with a fire brigade of 41, all the above tasks were completed, but now more than twice as many summonses and warrants were served and executed, and twice as many letters dispatched. In addition, £33,218 was collected by the police court department upon warrants of distress for non-payment of rates, 25,962 informations on crimes and criminals were circulated, 443 persons were finger-printed, and 657 were photographed. In the same year, too, 1,306 resident aliens and 1,025 coloured alien seamen reported their movements to the Cardiff police, 436 deaths were reported by the police to the coroner, 1,125 cinema film posters were approved by the police, and 4,339 rounds of ammunition were surrendered at police stations.

Other duties in Cardiff included checking public houses, lodging houses, shops, hackney carriages, street traders, pedlars and dog-owners, whilst in the county Lindsay claimed in 1933 that the extraneous 'duties which entail the greater part of the time' of his police were those 'performed under the Diseases of Animals Acts and the Road Act of 1920'. One can see therefore why both chief constables insisted that more officers were needed 'to keep pace with (these) demands' and to provide an 'efficient service', as well as for crime and 'the protection given to the community'. Lindsay, in particular, resented the Home Office's formula of approving or disapproving requests largely on the basis of population numbers, sometimes set against crime figures.

The First and Second World Wars brought extra burdens, which ranged from air-raid duty, ambulance service, and the guarding of strategic and vulnerable points, to supervising aliens, and enforcing regulations concerning food and drink, lighting and transport. Such was the intensity of the work, especially in bombing areas, that the Home Office arranged for transfers of officers between forces. After the Second World War the police also

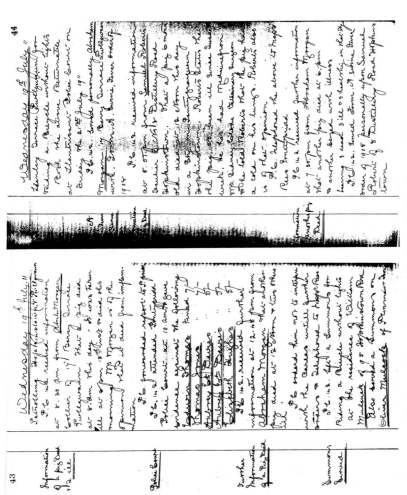

Extracts from the Hopkinstown Police Journal of 1911 showing notifications of swine fever as part of the duties of the police.

played a major role in organizing civil defence, and in licensing the domestic use of firearms and explosives.

One extra responsibility which began because of war conditions was the registration of aliens, something which was both tiresome and yet acceptable, for it gave the police control over people whom they frequently despised as much as the criminals, and whom they regularly blamed for violent disorder and racial troubles. Under the Aliens' Restriction Act of 1914, and subsequent amendments and orders, the police kept a watchful eye on these 'outsiders', and, when necessary, recommended deportation. In 1928, for example, when there were 2,552 aliens (1,370 males and 1,182 females) resident in Cardiff, 72 of them were repatriated and 9 criminal ones deported. The Special Restriction (Coloured Alien Seamen) Order of 1925 was then still in force, and the Cardiff police had 7,127 notices of their movements during the year. 'The police', said James Wilson in 1928, 'attach considerable importance to this Order and they would like to see it made more restrictive. The mingling of the white and coloured races in the Shipping Quarter of this Port is giving rise to problems which require solution.'

Wilson was also concerned about traffic in the city, for the expansion of the road network and of private motor transport was transforming the life of the police. In the 1930s there were already complaints that point duty, road accidents and the parking of cars were consuming too much of a constable's time. Some commentators wanted to remove traffic completely from the hands of the police and establish civilian traffic patrols and traffic courts. In 1963 the chief constable of Glamorgan, who approved of neither proposal, claimed that 'crime and traffic vie for place of prime importance for the police', and his colleague in Cardiff found it 'almost impossible . . . to deal satisfactorily with all the complaints relating to motor vehicles received by them'.

However, relief was already on its way. School crossing officers, and then traffic wardens, were appointed, special constables assisted with point duty, and other civilians took over clerical work from regular officers. The Magistrates' Courts Act of 1957, and the fixed-penalty ticket system, also gave the police more time for operational matters. Yet the changes proved less beneficial than was hoped. Firstly, the police were given new responsibilities as, for example, juvenile-liaison and community-relations officers, and secondly, as we shall see in the next section, they were overwhelmed at this time by reports from the public of non-crime incidents. One South Wales officer said in 1970 that people liked nothing better than to have their 'own personal police', giving them advice, solving their problems and dealing with their neighbours. More than a half of the police's time in South Wales during that year was spent following up 100,000 telephone calls from the public, the majority of which were of the non-crime variety. It was, traditionally, an important service function, but one which could now be accurately recorded for the first time.

Two work areas which have undoubtedly expanded since the 1960s have been public order and crime, though, as we shall again see in the next section, the police spend much less time on these than we assume. Certain writers have suggested that minimizing conflict at all levels, from the domestic to the state, has always been the prime function of the police, but this role was given a higher profile after the 1960s. As an example, during the amalgamation year of 1969 the new force felt it necessary to publicize the hours devoted to royal visits, investigations into Welsh extremism, and the policing of anti-apartheid activities. Fifteen years later, during the miners' strike, the public-order contribution was even greater, and ordinary patrols and community services had to be restricted. By 1989, when over seventy marches and demonstrations were policed, as well as sporting crowds and other mass gatherings, the chief constable stated that the public-order work of his force had become 'a major commitment', though only a small percentage of total police time was actually spent on it.

A second major problem for the police in the second half of this century has been the spiralling crime rate. The chief constable of the Merthyr borough force said, in his reports of the early 1960s, that the 'marked upward trend of crime in the past ten years has led to a sharp re-appraisal of police functions in terms of priorities'. His force decided to make the prevention of crime one of these priorities, though it is difficult to establish just how much effort this entailed, and, for that matter, what effect it had.

The commitment to the detection of crime is easier to calculate, and it appears that the police spent less time on this than is sometimes suggested. The occurrence books of the Glamorgan force show that in the mid-century only a small number of criminal cases were handled during a typical week at a medium-sized station, and, in isolated rural districts like Llanmorlais on the Gower, weeks passed without any crime complaint at all. At Peterston-super-Ely, a larger semi-rural community, one indictable crime was reported every fortnight in the years 1964–6, whereas reports of straying animals, sheep-worrying, lost property, road accidents, noisy motor cycles, and malicious phone calls were more of a daily occurrence. In Tongwynlais, on the northern fringes of Cardiff, it was slightly different; in 1960 Constable Howell received information on 37 local indictable crimes during the year, and reported on 104 non-indictable (mainly traffic) offences, but dealt with fewer occurrences than his Peterston-super-Ely colleague.

In 1961 the number of recorded indictable crimes per serving officer in the forces was 15.3 in Cardiff, 11.5 in Glamorgan, 9.4 in Merthyr Tydfil and 9.4 in Swansea. In 1986 the rate had risen to 34 crimes for each member of the South Wales force, though the more realistic figure of cases per response officer was 77.

The burden of this fell especially on the CID. By 1971 the case-load of detective constables and sergeants had reached 286 crimes per person, almost twice the nationally recommended rate, and overtime was common. The investigation of homicides took such an effort, in time, cost and manpower, and so disrupted routine detective work, that it was decided in 1975 to leave murders, and the most serious assaults and thefts of motor vehicles, to the two serious-crime squads. Even so, as we shall see in the next chapter, the pressure on CID officers in South Wales has continued to be unrelenting.

Although certain sociologists claim that the image of the 'over-worked crime-fighter' is largely a myth, the burden of crime on the police in recent years has never been greater. Ironically, the South Wales force has, via its community constables and other related activities, rediscovered the importance of the service and community role of the police at the very time when dealing with the crime wave has become a political and public priority. To add to the mental stress, the pressure to 'get results' in the battle against crime has come when the Home Office insists that it must be done by deploying existing officers more wisely.

Deploying the police

From time to time historians are provided with accounts of how the police were employed, and the proportion of time actually devoted to various tasks. These provide an interesting check on popular perceptions of police work. It was estimated, during the first quarter of the century, that the Cardiff and Swansea police spent about two-thirds of their time on patrol duty. One critic, writing in the *Western Mail* in 1902, said that of 70–80 policemen on duty at any one time in the capital, 'there are fifty constables engaged in doing absolutely nothing else than sauntering leisurely through the streets'.

Table 4.4 shows the deployment of the Cardiff men in 1920 by comparison with their duties in 1912.

Table 4·4: Deployment of Cardiff force in 1920 (1912 in brackets)

Patrol and traffic duties	224	(240)
Station duties	22	(22)
Headquarters dept.	12	(6)
Detective dept.	12	(11)
Court dept.	7	(6)
Coroner's court	1	(1)
Aliens' registration dept.	5	(0)
Stores dept.	3	(2)
Drill instructor	1	(1)
Fire brigade	2	(0)
Total	289	(289)

In 1957 the Cardiff chief constable bemoaned the increase in police traffic and service activities, which meant little time was left for actual supervision and crime prevention 'on the beat'. In Glamorgan it was estimated that the 'actual force establishment engaged in beat coverage only' had fallen from 63.6 per cent in 1938, to 54.9 nine years later, and 52.4 in 1959. The chief constable of Swansea produced a report in 1958 which showed that whilst 72.5 per cent of his force were still employed on beat and patrol duties, only a third of the increase of manpower since 1938 had been assigned to this work. Moreover, when account was taken of the hours lost over the previous twenty years through extra leave, sickness, training courses and the like, 'it may be fairly said that the manpower position has remained static, despite the greatly increased work in all branches of the Force'.

It was considerations such as these which explain the initial enthusiasm for unit-beat policing. By 1972 at least four out of ten constables on outside duties were patrolling beats by car, a similar proportion were on town-centre patrols, and the rest were area constables. Motorized patrolling was, however, neither as 'efficient' nor as popular as expected. During the later 1970s and 1980s more and more officers were returned to foot patrols, and other operational staff were employed as community constables. In 1981, under John Woodcock's regime, it was estimated that, with 365 community officers and 612 beat men, almost a third of the force's strength was 'on foot patrol duties'. Yet this figure is rather deceptive, for these constables performed a variety of tasks. Comparative studies in England have shown that only a relatively small amount of total police time is spent walking the beat.

The deployment of manpower in the modern forces is perhaps different from that imagined by the public. In 1985, for example, the men and women of the South Wales force were deployed in the proportions shown in table 4.5, which highlights the strong commitment to patrolling, and the limited amount of time devoted solely to crime and public-order incidents.

Analysis of how policemen and women actually occupy their time is a difficult business. The Glamorgan station journals of the

Table 4·5: Deployment of South Wales force (percentages) at 31 December 1985

General deployment	
Total operational	88·94
Support	8·81
Training	2·26
Area of work	
Patrol	57·91
Crime	13·19
Traffic	8·22
Community relations	1·41
Public order	1·18
Other areas	18·09

1960s, which do not record details of every activity, give the general impression that about a quarter of a constable's time at the smaller stations was spent on the premises, and the same proportion on visiting and conferring with people, including witnesses at their homes and fellow officers in other stations. The rest of a shift was devoted largely to patrolling, with a smaller amount of time spent at the scenes of crimes, in court and eating meals. This account of PC 157 Howell's shift at Tongwynlais on Tuesday, 10 January 1961 was typical:

On duty	2.00 p.m.
Station	2–3.00
Patrolled Merthyr Rd. and observed traffic and people leaving licensed premises	3–3.35
Visited road-crossing patrol	3.35
Patrolled to Rhiwbina and visited station at	4.00
Patrolled beat, and came off duty for meal at	5.15
Resumed duty	6.00
Station-inspector confers with Howell at	8.30
Patrolled beat	9.00
Patrolled to Rhiwbina and conferred with PC	9.45
Returned to Tongwynlais and came off duty at	10.00 p.m.

The response officers in G (Port Talbot) division were questioned in 1986 about the timing of individual duties per eight-hour shift. An examination of 684 tours of duty over a two-week period produced table 4.6. If one compares the analysis in table 4.6 with other areas, it is obvious that the amount of time given to 'pro-active' patrolling in the Port Talbot division was exceptionally large. The figures on the right in table 4.6 represent a similar return from the Clifton Street section in Cardiff Central division, which gives a very different picture. As can be seen, much less of an average 7 hours 48 minutes tour of duty was available for 'free' or 'pro-active' patrolling in the Cardiff section, and much more time was spent on responding to incidents, arrests and clerical work. According to the Audit Commission's report on policing in 1990, this was more in line with national practice.

There is no similar information from the 1980s on the work done by the CID, but an analysis of a very detailed officer's diary for 1965–6 reveals that 47 per cent of a divisional detective constable's time in a typical month was spent in the home station

Table 4·6: Timing of individual duties in Port Talbot section and Clifton Street, Cardiff, 1986

Duties	Time spent, Port Talbot division	Time spent, Clifton Street section
Normal patrol	3 hr.39·90 min.	1 hr.18 min.
Report writing	1 hr. 10·00	1 hr.25
Responding to incidents	59·57	1 hr.57
Other duties, like enquiries, statements and transport	53·51	1 hr.34
Meals	40·90	35
Escort/charge room relief	13·94	9
Arrests	8·92	34
In court	8·53	0
Reporting offenders	4·31	3
Relieving IRIS operator or enquiry desk	0·43	13

(Skewen), and 53 per cent outside, patrolling the district, attending at scenes of crime, visiting witnesses and so on. The break-down according to task is provided in table 4.7. Two points should be added here. Firstly, the detective often worked from 9 a.m. until late in the evening, doing two, three or more hours' overtime. Secondly, he actually did more clerical work than the table indicates, but, unlike the modern image of detectives trapped under a mountain of paper, this constable devoted a commendable amount of time to investigating, and occasionally solving, crimes.

Until current analysis of work schedules in the South Wales force is completed, the above information takes us only so far. Comparative research takes us a little further. Studies have shown, for example, that about half of police time in the Metropolitan and Merseyside forces was spent on the premises, and half outside. A large amount of time in the Merseyside force was given to non-crime-related administrative duties and paperwork, which, when added to crime-related paperwork, meant that clerical duties consumed very nearly a quarter of all police effort. Another quarter of police time was spent on patrolling and special duties (largely connected with public order), but only a relatively small amount of 'outside work' was devoted to reported, anticipated and

Table 4·7: Tasks of a divisional detective constable, Skewen, in a typical month, 1965–1966

Task	Time spent %
Clerical office work at station (reading messages, crime information bulletins, etc. and doing reports on cases, statistics, etc.)	21
Interviews (inside and outside the station)	15·4
Patrolling (sometimes making observations and checks whilst doing so)	21·3
Attending at scenes of crime and incidents	11·4
Making enquiries into crimes	13·3
Other duties, including serving notices, and attending court	6·4
Having meals	11·3

discovered crime. It seems, from these studies, that external response officers occupied many hours simply 'passing time', on 'uncommitted work'. 'Police officers', write David Smith and Jeremy Gray in their survey of London police officers during the 1980s, 'whether in cars or on foot, are inactive for much of the time.' Police sociologists, like the *Western Mail* reporter of 1902, are deeply suspicious of the value of this 'uncommitted' patrolling.

Criticisms of the police for 'waiting for things to happen', for 'not going after crime', and for 'wasting hours' on 'non-crime activities' betray some confusion over the history, value and reception of police work. This is precisely how policing has always been, and how it appeared in Martin and Wilson's pioneering study of police work in 1969. Officers have spent most of their time since 1829 patrolling on foot and in cars. This was welcomed by the public, and reduced their fear of crime, even though it was well known that men and women on the beat discovered few indictable offences, and might have been engaged 'more profitably' in other areas of crime work. It was, after all, 'open policing' rather than the secretive continental-style version; a 'true Briton' preferred liberty to over-zealous interference from plain-clothes men. The police officers, on their patrols and in their stations, waited for offences to be reported to them, and whilst they did so, they were also the recipients of information about innumerable, but important, non-crime incidents.

The last contribution was, and remains, very significant in terms of police work. The public of South Wales, in contrast with that of Merseyside, for example, has always regarded its police as much more than crime fighters. In the first chapter, we noted that most of the telephoned requests for police action in Abercwmboi and Swansea in mid-century were over lost property, stray dogs, naughty children, parking and other minor incidents. Since that time, as the occurrence books for Peterston-super-Ely and Sully in the 1960s confirm, much police time has been spent in reacting to similar calls. If one looks at work-loads in the South Wales force for 1974 and 1978, these indicate that the police had to deal with more than four and a half times as many 'occurrences' as reported indictable crimes. The former included road accidents, sudden and suspicious deaths, missing persons, lost property, domestic disputes, minor acts of vandalism, fires and burglar alarms. In some places, like Canton and Ely, such was the extent of these occurrences that by the end of our period 'all officers were engaged on incidents rather than being available for foot patrol'. Ironically, those who demand such patrols, especially at the weekends, are often the very people who reduce, by their 'incident calls', the police time for patrols.

Conclusion

In the recent drive towards efficiency, it is worth remembering that most policing during the century has involved activities unrelated to crime, though none the less important, especially for the general public. As the *Western Mail* noted in 1914, when commenting on Cardiff's policemen, they offered 'a surprising range of public services' and a high degree of 'usefulness'. The police have never properly educated the public about their various roles, nor has the manning and financing of the forces always reflected the multifarious character of their work. Like several other professions, including university teachers, the police know that there are advantages to having a number of functions, and being able to play one off against another, but there are disadvantages as well. In a period of belt-tightening, unpleasant choices have to be made. 'No police force has, or will ever have, the resources necessary to fulfil all its possible functions,' concluded the Audit Commission in 1990.

For almost as long as we have had professional police, there have been people who have asked the question 'what should and should not the police be required to do?' There was considerable discussion early in the century over whether some of their services, like collecting rates and maintenance payments, could be better performed by other professionals, and this debate was later extended to include matters such as dealing with road traffic and family conflicts. Significantly, the crime-fighting duties performed by the police were less of an issue. People recognized the wasted man hours that patrolling sometimes incurred, and the ineffectiveness of many traditional responses to certain offences, but were unwilling, until very recent times, to support a major switch in police activities or to seek assistance from private crime-fighting agencies.

The latest controversy over the nature and efficiency of policing, instigated by the Adam Smith Institute, and dramatized by Group Four transporting prisoners from courts to gaol, is potentially of the greatest importance. The prospects, now being discussed, of privatizing (wholly or in part) vital operational services like motorway and neighbourhood patrols, and developing local-government or civilian-run systems for other types of police work, have aroused strong feelings. One concern is that new forms of private protection and policing will, like their eighteenth-century counterparts, be poorly regulated and available only for the fortunate few. For this and other reasons, the notion of a slimmer police body, geared to dealing with only the most serious forms of public disorder and crime, has not appealed to many, though it remains a possibility.

Over the century the character of police work has changed less perhaps than the police forces themselves. By 1989 the latter would still have been recognizable to the men of 1900, but the degree of centralization, of specialization, of change in management structures, of technical advances, of training and civilianization would have surprised them. The developments since 1989, which include the creation of more police territorial divisions, greater local control and practical training, are, superficially, a return to older systems. Whether all these changes have made the forces more efficient as a crime-prevention and detection agency, and whether indeed they were ever 'efficient' in this regard, is problematical.

5

The Police, Crime and People

The functions of the police have, since their establishment, been many, though their main contributions have been as a service force, an order-maintenance agency, and a crime-fighting unit. The last has not been the dominant role, but it is the one that has always caught the eye, and which now preoccupies the media and naturally interests the potential victims of crime. It is, moreover, the function by which the police have usually been judged. In the early nineteenth century there was much debate over the efficiency of the police as crime-fighters. Some ratepayers argued that the old watchmen, private associations for the prosecution of felons, and the wider community had dealt with crime just as well as, if not better, than the new men in blue, and certainly more cheaply. In the 1980s and 1990s, as police costs and the crime rate have risen simultaneously, issues of quality of service and value for money have again surfaced. The effectiveness of the police as crime-fighters is currently being analysed with an intensity never before experienced.

Police views of crime and criminals

The police response to crime is partly a reflection of attitudes which have changed little over two centuries. Policing in the nineteenth century was, to a considerable degree, based on the notion that crime was mainly the responsibility of a criminal class, which either lived in particular 'crime spots' or moved across the country on circuits of delinquency. The police were expected then, as now, to know these people and to trace their movements. 'The police stationed in the Bute Town area [of Cardiff] exercise a firm check upon the criminal and vicious section of the inhabitants of the area,' said Chief Constable James Wilson in 1931. 'They know their haunts and their ways.'

To assist in this work, the police were given special powers under the Habitual Criminals and Prevention of Crimes Acts of 1869–71, and this surveillance continued into the early twentieth century. In Cardiff in 1913 the police table of supervised persons included 8 from the previous year, 110 persons who had been released that year from Cardiff gaol, and 70 who had entered the city from other districts. In Swansea, in the same year, 40 men and women were officially placed under police supervision, and another 38 thieves, 2 receivers and 40 suspected persons were listed by the police as being 'at large' in the town. In 1914 both the Swansea and Cardiff police also compiled parallel registers of aliens, who were often regarded as little better than criminals, whilst in Glamorgan Lindsay had his large index of Communists. For that chief constable, someone like Fred Thomas of Caerau, secretary of the local branch of the Communist Party in the 1930s, was, if anything, worse than the 'thieves and other persons of low type' with whom he associated, and on whom the police were obliged 'to keep an eye'.

Joseph Mason, a 45-year-old fireman who spent almost half his life in gaol, and Joseph Woodfield were two of those who complained about the levels of supervision. The former said, at the Glamorgan assize of 1902, that he was never allowed any freedom, even when out of gaol. In 1909 Woodfield, who was charged with burglaries at Barry, protested to the jury at the Glamorgan quarter sessions that since being convicted seventeen years before 'he was under the constant surveillance of the police, and had several times been arrested, but discharged. In consequence of this he had had to communicate with the Home Secretary.' He was found guilty in 1909 of receiving only, but the police were adamant that since his return to Barry in 1901 he had committed break-ins every weekend.

The relationship between these people and the police was a familiar and symbiotic one. The former were known by nicknames, which gave a clue to their physical character and criminal expertise. They were identified collectively by terms such as 'villains', 'vermin', 'rubbish', and, most recently, 'toe-rags', thus marking them off from the rest of the working class to which they and the police largely belonged. When offences occurred, officers were concerned to know where these 'villains' were, and who had seen them recently. To keep track of them, the police were assisted by numerous files, registers, and photographic and fingerprint books. Much, however, remained in the heads of local policemen, who passed this information on, verbally or in written form, to their successors. Thus, in the late 1930s, a constable retiring from the Trealaw beat left behind him a booklet, containing the names of twenty-four people in the area who were worth observing or who had previous convictions.

These systems of recording and labelling suspected and known criminals were to become more sophisticated after the appointment of area constables and collators in the 1960s, and the introduction of new computer techniques. 'The main function of an area constable's work', ran one job description of that period, 'is that of keeping in close touch with the activities of known and suspected criminals, and the associates, vehicles and premises used by them . . .' By 1970 the South Wales force and Western Criminal Record Office had indexes of 'local active criminals', convicted and suspected drug users, and people who committed indecency offences, together with street maps of the homes of thieves and dubious characters. How much these, and the daily bulletins and crime-information sheets produced by collators and the CID, were actually used by the police is another matter.

There are two different modern perspectives on this. One group of sociologists, which includes Simon Holdaway and Mike Stephens, claim that the police, with their strong moral vision and insistence on territorial control, have continued to think in terms of a distinct criminal class at war with society. When asked to describe their job in 1970, foot-patrol officers, area constables and detectives in the South Wales force said that their first duty was to discover 'the movement of known criminals or those suspected of crime', and to become familiar with those inhabitants who could give information about them. Probationers and constables posted to new stations in the 1960s were, we are told, 'as soon as possible shown the local criminals'. One of the primary tasks of Glamorgan detectives, as evidenced by their diaries, was to keep an eye on 'likely suspects' for each type of offence, and to interview them regularly '*re* outstanding crime'.

It has been argued, by Stephens and others, that the separation of the police from the public with unit-beat policing distorted the former's view of society and of the criminals within it. Where once the police had been 'part of the community' (an exaggerated claim), and dependent on it for information, the separation left the police in a more isolated and embattled position. They felt increasingly that they were 'the thin blue line', the last defence against the 'rough element' and the criminally minded. According to this group of sociologists, these beleaguered police officers concentrated their work in the 'worst areas', where their mobile patrols made large numbers of easy, though 'marginally legitimate', arrests of the disorderly, the drunkards and the homeless, and of teenagers suspected of crimes.

In Britain's big cities the 'main clientele' of today's police is the 'underclass' ('the policeman's property') of young, unemployed and often coloured people. In South Wales there are areas of Cardiff and the Rhondda where this picture is familiar, and where 'lads' on motor bikes and in cars are stopped almost as a matter of course.

Other researchers question these assumptions about priority or selective policing. Scholars like Rob Mawby have found that, when interviewed, police officers have a poor idea of the names of known and likely criminals and of the streets which they inhabit. Morning briefings from sergeants and the contents of crime bulletins often pass over their heads. Patrols in Sheffield did not, according to Mawby, spend extra time in streets where most offenders lived or where most crime was committed. In Liverpool in 1985, Richard Kinsey found that, although patrol officers were told to make the maximum use of the collator and of records of local criminals, this was not usually done, nor was their knowledge of their areas very profound. In fact, patrols in Liverpool and in London during the 1980s spent much of their time on 'uncommitted' activity or responding to public requests, and showed little initiative in seeking out crime and criminals. It seems, as we noted in the last chapter, that the scale of present-day crime, the number of first-time offenders, and the heavy reporting of delinquency by the public, all make the business of crime-fighting more reactive, pragmatic and frankly chaotic than many critics suggest.

Police opinions on the causes of crime and the punishment of offenders have always been closely related to their work experience, their view of the world as a hostile and unstable place, and their ideas of what constitutes a criminal. The police claimed to be in a unique position to reveal 'the truth' about delinquency and offenders. 'It is generally admitted that the Police', said James Wilson, the chief constable of Cardiff, in 1932, 'by their close contact with those possessing criminal tendencies, are in the best position to speak as to the causation of crime . . .' His views, and those of his successor, were typical of those held by many senior policemen of that period. They argued that police numbers alone could not 'check the growth of the criminal classes', for the latter had its origins in the materialism of modern society, the gradual breakdown of family life, and the lack of responsibility shown by victims and those in authority.

James Wilson believed that his work would be of limited value until business people and the public generally made life more difficult for the criminal, and until the courts dealt effectively with offenders. In his opinion, better education and 'second-chance' forms of punishment had not 'eliminated nor subjugated' the criminal instinct. Bail, probation and fines were often followed by a repetition of the original offences. A stubborn juvenile delinquent should, he believed,

> receive an exemplary sentence, which would give those responsible for custody the opportunity and the means to convince him that the Law must be respected, that he must be disciplined to resist temptation and that he must labour to rehabilitate himself and become a law abiding citizen. These observations are also in a measure applicable to the adult offender.

Opinions such as these were repeatedly expressed, and elaborated, by the police over the next sixty years. In the 1950s they reached a crescendo, as police leaders denounced the changes in family life, especially in the role of women, the effect of corrupting entertainment on the young, the growth of new opportunities to steal valuable property, and the inconsistencies of penal policies. Thirty years later the exasperation of the police over some of these matters was just as evident, not least over 'the disproportionately large amount of crime committed by a relatively small number of persons who had already entered the criminal justice system . . .' (Robert Lawrence, chief constable, 1989).

As part of the process of politicization described by Robert Reiner, a number of senior policemen campaigned in the 1980s for changes to laws, procedures and punishment to sustain the police in their crime-fighting role. However, as the Royal Commission on Criminal Procedure (1981) concluded, it seems unlikely that such changes would make much difference to the extent of crime or to police detection of it. There is now, in the post-Scarman and Alderson era, a greater awareness amongst everyone, from chief constable to officers on the beat, that the problem of delinquency cannot be solved by policing and punishment alone.

Traditional forms of crime policing, 1900–38

In the early twentieth century, methods of preventing and detecting crime had hardly changed since the 1850s. Beat patrolling by foot was, as we saw in the last chapter, the main policing activity, and it had the advantage that, whatever its efficiency, it gave people the security of a regular police presence. The beats varied in size, the largest being in the areas of least population. In the Glamorgan county force, where the ratio of police to population was low, some of the rural beats in 1900 covered many hundreds of acres, and were often patrolled for only part of the twenty-four hours.

Reynoldston on the Gower peninsula was then by far the largest beat in the county, being eight miles long and five miles broad, with only one constable for 3,000 people. This was ideal territory for the watchful ex-farm labourers in the force. The impression gained from early notebooks is that sergeants and constables on these large rural beats performed the full range of police duties, including the inspection of dog licences and farmers' stock books, but soon learnt which matters were 'important', and kept others away from their superiors and the courts. Many days passed before a crime was entered in their brief daily reports.

The following is a typical report from such places in the years before the Second World War:

PC 485 Clark, Peterston-super-Ely Station, Monday, 20 September 1937

Conferred with inspector	3.35 p.m.
On duty	4.00

Patrolled Peterston, St Brides, and Pendoylan Rd.	4–5.30
Tea	5.30–6.00
Patrolled district, and visited places to examine	
stock movement record books	6–8.30
Off duty	8.30–10.00
Patrolled Glyn Cory and visited Kingsland	No time given
Conferred with sergeant at St Nicholas station,	
gave him declarations of sheep dipping, and a report	
of halt signs at Pendoylan	11.50
Visited railway station and sidings	1.00 a.m.
Visited the Grange, St Brides, and Tynewydd House	
Off duty 'leaving all quiet and apparently correct'	2.00 a.m.

In Swansea, only a short distance from the Reynoldston beat, there was, in 1900, one policeman for every fifty acres, and one per 900 of the population. By 1931 the town had grown to a population of 164,797, and, on the eve of the Second World War, it had 197 road miles, 191 police officers, 30 urban beats and 8 rural. Its urban beats were patrolled throughout the twenty-four hours by constables working in eight-hour shifts, whilst the rural beats were covered by two shifts of eight hours each. Each Swansea beat had its boxes and conference points, where messages were exchanged, and reports handed in. The ideal in beat working was to have the whole of the beats fully covered; 'unfortunately this ideal is seldom attained', said the town's chief constable, 'as sickness and other causes have constantly to be considered.' Working overtime was common.

Beat policing was carefully planned and supervised; beat directories listed the roads that had to be walked down, the people to be contacted, the periods for breaks, and the fixed points which had to be reached at certain times. In the notebooks of Constable Hodge, who worked from the Cardiff Central and Docks stations in the inter-war years, his two- or three-hour patrols were laid out with stop-watch precision, as were his anticipated arrival times at the 'specially watched premises' which had to be checked six or eight times over twenty-four hours. Hodge and other urban policemen moved from one beat to another at regular intervals, and changes were made, too, in the geography of the patrols if the state of crime warranted it.

The police officer was expected to know the people on his rounds, and the criminals who lived there. As one of them stated, in his job description in 1970, 'a wide and varied knowledge of this beat and surrounding beats is demanded in the course of daily police duties. This knowledge is made up of personal contacts and observations – people and what they do, criminals and how and where they operate, works, factories and other concerns – what is done inside them and who does it.' Policemen established contacts with magistrates, councillors, employers, doctors, welfare workers and other officials, and built up a network of reliable informants. The last were often the classic 'observers' in society: night-watchmen, cab-drivers, licensees, roundsmen and the like.

Although the beat officers were occasionally criticized for their 'leisurely' approach, they performed a wide variety of duties other than preventing and detecting crime. At Hopkinstown on the eve of the First World War, Constable Welsby, who dealt with very few indictable offences, studiously attended meetings of miners, and gave his superiors and the coal-owners early warnings of strike action. He and his colleagues also doubled as community advisers and helpers: reporting on accidents, broken drains and diseased animals, attending to domestic disputes, fires and sudden deaths, and collecting fines, rates and lost dogs. Already their dislike of paperwork can be seen in their hurriedly scribbled notes on these and other matters.

Beat policing was physically hard, and required considerable initiative, especially in the rural and urban out-stations. Some beats, like St Thomas in Swansea and Blaenclydach in the Rhondda, were regarded as particularly difficult, and even dangerous. Men were relieved there after six months on duty, or sent away for hospital recuperation if they were seriously injured. In the Glamorgan force, short-distance interchanges of staff were common; early in February 1912, for example, fourteen constables were exchanged, one going from Skewen to Port Talbot, another from Port Talbot to Cowbridge, a third from Cowbridge to Skewen, and so on.

One of the patrolman's complaints was that, because of the rigidities of the system, there was little time to follow leads and respond to emergencies. In a large rural beat like Reynoldston, the report of a serious crime totally disrupted a constable's normal schedule. Similarly, the records of industrial and urban stations reveal that officers often failed to appear at fixed points and conferences for meetings with their colleagues. At Deri, where conveying people to the nearest police cells in 1905 took three hours out of patrol time, there were usually good reasons for such absences, but in Cardiff and Swansea the missing constables were sometimes discovered in public houses, restaurants and private homes.

The nature of the beat-work in the early years varied from day to night-time. Daylight hours were spent 'maintaining order and checking offences in streets and public places', keeping the highways clear, and dealing with enquiries. Men on patrol received information on crimes and incidents directly from the public or via the *Police Gazette*, daily information sheets and weekly reports, the latest details being passed to them at the morning parades and at the conference points. In Swansea, from an early date, it was also possible to receive and give such information via the police boxes.

In the Glamorgan force, night-time patrolling in 1900 was regarded as even more important than day-time. Village constables frequently worked until 12 midnight, or, in some more populated rural areas, did a 10 p.m.–6 a.m. shift. During that time they examined farm buildings and fences, patrolled favourite haunts of fowl thieves and poachers, visited the public houses, and called at the village shop, the school, the big house, the rectory and the railway station.

In towns during the hours of darkness the chief duties of the beat constable were enforcing the drink licensing laws, and, according to a Swansea report of the mid-century, checking 'the security of premises, deterring would-be thieves by his presence, examining shops and houses to see that they are secure, and stopping and questioning persons who may be in possession of stolen property or housebreaking implements'. Night constables were expected to be alert, as the Cardiff police default books for the inter-war years illustrate. In a typical case, two policemen were cautioned for failing to detect a shop in Penarth Road being entered on the night of 4 October 1929, when they were in the vicinity.

The observation of property and persons by beat officers was extensive, and occasionally rewarding. The police notebooks and journals show that much of their time was spent visiting shops, banks, warehouses, public and refreshment houses, railway stations and sidings, garages, building plots, unoccupied houses, electric substations, explosives stores and all manner of industrial premises. Thousands of owners were warned each year that their doors and windows were insecure, and that the police had found signs of attempted break-ins. Perhaps, as we shall see later, many crimes were prevented in this way.

Very occasionally a patrolling constable came upon a crime in progress, and, when resources permitted, intensive watching of vulnerable property brought good results. Police Constable John Rees, on his rounds at Swansea, twice arrested burglars 'on the job' in 1910, and was warmly praised for it, whilst in the same town other officers waited for hours to grab people responsible for damaging urinals, and for stealing from orchards, sidings and sheds. In Cardiff Constable Hodge, who secured the conviction of about two or three people per month for indictable offences, caught some of them in the act of smashing windows in St James Street in the early hours, and tackled others as they fled from their victims.

Close and sustained observation of individuals was a different matter, and the first beat men did only a small amount of this. Hodge at Cardiff and Welsby at Hopkinstown squeezed a few hours of plain-clothes work into a week of patrolling. They watched 'habitual offenders', followed the unemployed to the coal stocks, waited for people to lay a bet, and noted others acting suspiciously. The last might have been a newcomer to the district, a poor person carrying expensive goods, a workman with a bulge under his jacket, and a person out at night in the vicinity of a warehouse. Amongst the people taken into custody by Hodge were men of no fixed abode 'loitering with intent' or selling shirts and wearing silk scarves. Stop and search was the instinctive police reaction in such cases, and for certain periods, as in the spring of 1907 at Neath and in the winter of 1909–10 at Cardiff, it developed into a very popular form of policing, though one which caused some protests. At the other extreme, there was a surprising number of poor and depressed individuals in these early years who committed thefts and burglaries, and then walked straight into the nearest police station.

Beat constables exploited their knowledge of the community, and of its 'bad characters', to discover vital information about the most serious crimes when they did occur. Those on duty at Sully and Peterston-super-Ely in the inter-war years were able to rely on 'trustworthy inhabitants' for assistance, whilst in Cardiff good contacts were maintained with certain publicans, merchants and ex-criminals. In 1918 Detective Sergeants Thomas Little and John Pugsley used an informant to catch those responsible for three cases of robbery with violence in the capital, and, after other tip-offs, fellow officers like Hodge were directed to warehouses being robbed, and houses crammed with stolen goods.

The official detection rate was very impressive in the first decades of the century, as we shall see, but the limits of this kind of policing became only too apparent. 'Success' as crime-fighters depended largely on being on the spot at the right time. Although the Cardiff chief constable was possibly correct when he said in 1938 that beat patrolling, when done in sufficient numbers, often deterred open street crimes like robbery, break-ins and assaults, those thieves who gave beat officers the slip in the capital were unlikely to be caught. Moreover, it was an inappropriate form of policing for hidden offences, like embezzlement and fraud. No doubt the public were aware of these realities, and it is probable that the low figures of indictable crime recorded in the first third of the century owed something to the character of a policing system based largely on slow-moving foot patrols.

Some writers look back upon these days with a good deal of nostalgia, and are convinced that one of the virtues of traditional beat policing was the close and harmonious relationship that developed between the officers and the residents. There is some truth in this, but it can be exaggerated. As we noted in chapter 4, the men on patrol were busy doing things other than investigating serious crimes, and some of these activities brought them into conflict with a sizeable proportion of the community. An examination of the convictions returns for Hopkinstown, Taibach, Pontyclun and Peterston-super-Ely over the first decades reveals that policemen trapped hundreds of local people for allowing horses to stray, having unlicensed dogs, failing to record the movement of animals, riding bicycles without lights, ignoring road signs and obstructing roadways, illegal betting and gaming with cards, foul language and drunken behaviour, and many other misdemeanours. Although this kind of policing varied in intensity from area to area, its existence reminds us that close surveillance, positive law enforcement and a willingness to make 'marginally legitimate arrests' were not as new as some writers have suggested.

Criticism of beat policing was, on investigation, rather greater than we imagine. In the 1920s, and especially in the 1930s, all the traditional forms of policing were under pressure. As Melbourne Thomas, Glamorgan's chief constable, observed some years later (in 1963), 'the historic role of the policeman . . . served well for the static life of the last century', but communities and police tasks were being transformed. The changes in the urban environment, the development of large housing estates, the siting of new industries, and the movement of the population had an important impact on the policing described above. So did the extra responsibilites placed on the police, the growth of road traffic, and the increased mobility of the criminal. In Cardiff James Wilson had, by 1935, 'reached the conclusion that foot patrol constables in residential areas were now obsolete. Their work could be more efficiently performed if they were provided with either pedal or motor-cycles.'

In his review of the force in 1929 the chief constable of Swansea agreed that thirty-year-old methods of policing were no longer suitable. New beats were needed for suburban development, more men were required for traffic duties, and improved communications within and into the force were essential. He continued:

> In these days, when criminals are often not the least intelligent members of the population and employ modern means of quick transport, the police must correspondingly keep pace with them, both in intellect and in methods, and it is imperative that some means should be adopted to enable the public to get quickly in touch with the police in emergencies, and for assistance to be sent immediately by motor transport, when and where it may be required.

Changes in crime policing 1938–68

Changes were made, though they did not improve crime-fighting quite as much as anticipated. Amongst the major developments after the 1930s were greater specialization, notably with the growth of detective and traffic police, better communications and extensive mobile patrols. As we saw in the last chapter, all the South Wales forces developed criminal investigation departments in this period. Men were selected from the uniformed patrol staff, and those able 'to cope with the very much increased work of crime investigation' were sent on national training courses. By

November 1960 the Glamorgan force, the slowest starter, had fifty-two men in the CID, a chief superintendent and chief inspector at headquarters and the rest scattered in the nine territorial divisions.

CID officers had numerous duties, but the main ones were working with informers and the criminal fraternity, taking charge of serious crime cases and preparing court actions, circulating crime information lists and compiling crime returns, communicating with record offices, other forces and Scotland Yard, and dealing with aliens, firearms, drugs and matters of national security. It was, from the beginning, regarded as a difficult vocation, needing patience, a tolerant family and 24-hour commitment. Detectives often worked in cramped conditions, and were burdened with a heavy mix of cases and paperwork. In Glamorgan the case-load in 1960 was 205 for each detective officer, whilst in Swansea it was much better, at 76 cases in 1938, and 92 twenty years later, when the force had twenty-one detectives. The CID had to rely on uniformed officers and the public for many detections, and was able to deal with only a very small proportion of white-collar offences which, said the Merthyr Tydfil chief constable in 1955, 'have become a marked feature of post-war crime'.

The improvement in communications, which was another key development in policing after the Second World War, has been described in the last chapter. At its heart was uniformity of networks across the forces, better communication facilities for ordinary patrolmen, and greater access for the public via the expanding telephone system. In 1944 the chief constable of Neath believed that his force was 'in the forefront as a modern well-equipped unit'; it had wireless receiving and transmitting stations, police boxes, street pillars, and patrol vehicles with field telephones. By the time of amalgamation, twenty-five years later, systems of communication had become standardized, full details of crimes and criminals could be transmitted rapidly across South Wales, and many people had direct contact with the police via their own private telephones.

These developments improved the reporting of crimes, and response times, but it is easy to exaggerate the impact of better communications and intelligence-gathering on the prevention and detection of offences. According to the published statistics of this middle period, one hundred '999' calls produced, on average, no more than five apprehensions, and of every hundred cases referred for fingerprint and photographic identification, only a handful of arrests resulted. In the final analysis detection still depended greatly on the speed of reporting by the public, and the amount of information which they were able to give the police. An examination of message books reveals that members of the public frequently identified the person who physically injured them, and, on a few occasions, also suggested the names of people who took goods from their homes, shops and factories. All of this information proved to be extremely useful to the CID.

The revolution in communications was matched by changes in the methods of policing, which improved mobility and contained the promise of greater efficiency. Rural policemen were the first to use bicycles and motor bicycles for their patrols, and their example was followed by officers who had to cover large beats on the residential outskirts of towns. In Swansea, which was to the fore in this, cars soon replaced bicycles. After the Second World War it was reported in that town that 'experiments have been made in covering two, three, or in emergency four, outlying beats with light cars'. 'Whilst effective up to a point', declared the chief constable, 'it must be conceded that this method cannot hope to reach the same standard of efficiency as a beat constable on foot patrol.'

Nevertheless, mobile patrols proved attractive for towns with policing problems. Merthyr Tydfil in the mid-century had an auto-cycle patrol of fourteen men to fill the gaps caused by a deficiency of foot patrols on the edge of town, where new council houses and industry had sprung up. In Cardiff and Swansea during the late 1940s and early 1950s mobile teams, usually comprising one sergeant and three constables in a wireless-equipped car, were superimposed on groups of foot-beats. 'In addition to making the work of beat constables much more interesting', wrote the chief constable of Swansea in his report of 1954, 'the teams create an element of surprise, ensure quick action at scenes of crime and help to bring about a greater percentage of successful investigations.' Since that time the speed of police response has been regarded as one of the hallmarks of a force's efficiency.

Another response, adopted in several places in the 1950s and 1960s, was to allocate police accommodation and offices on the largest housing estates. In Swansea, where the chief constable attributed many of his problems in the post-war years to the under-policing of new estates and industrial areas, police offices were erected in Townhill, Sketty Park and other expanding communities. On the Gurnos and Galon Uchaf housing estates of Merthyr Tydfil, officers placed there in the 1960s were carefully chosen 'for knowing the people re-housed . . .' 'Traffic patrol cars and beat patrol cars also make frequent visits to the section,' added the town's chief constable, and here, as in other large towns, foot patrolmen were offered the assistance of team and support groups, trained to deal with offences like burglary and public disorder.

The comprehensive adoption of unit-beat policing in 1968–9 was a natural consequence of the above developments. Several beats were grouped together, and each of these territories had a resident area constable, equipped with a personal radio, and a beat patrol car. The task of the area constable, who worked independently but alongside traditional foot-beat officers, was to get involved with the community, and to discover as much as possible about the local criminals. The car patrol men, on a 24-hour circuit, were expected to render help to these officers, as well as dealing with other reported crimes and emergencies.

With its new panda cars, its own sergeants and detectives, the benefit of excellent communications, access to collators and their files, and the promise of a four- or five-minute response time, this unit-beating scheme seemed to offer much. The chief constable of Swansea declared in 1968 that, with unit-beat policing, the detection rates for offences such as assaults were bound to improve, and there was a general expectation – though not one shared by the Association of Chief Police Officers – that it would 'bring the police into closer contact with the public'.

Unit-beat policing also allowed other patrol cars to concentrate on their primary task of traffic control. The period 1938–68 saw the traffic police emerge as a separate entity, with their own training and *esprit de corps*, and their own sectors of operation. The huge rise in the number of motor vehicles using the roads of South Wales in these years, and the growing concern with road safety and town-centre traffic, made specialization inevitable. The anxiety, often expressed in the late 1950s and early 1960s, was whether the police 'were being withdrawn from their legitimate (criminal) duties' to deal with such matters.

'Such random talk should be discouraged', wrote the chief constable of Swansea in 1961, 'as in my view traffic regulation and accident investigation claim an importance equal to that of crime investigation . . .' It was part of a general responsibility to protect life and property, and the statistics reveal just how important this aspect of policing had become. In 1966 the 92 traffic-patrol officers of the Glamorgan force reported 12,630 offences, including 4,200 cases of breaking the speed limit, and 1,386 of dangerous and careless driving. They arrested 553 people, gave out 32,812 cautions, recovered 284 stolen vehicles and dealt with over 2,000 accidents.

Modifications, 1969–89

In the twenty years after amalgamation, the policing of crime was modified in the light of a spiralling crime rate, an anxious public, the constraints of government expenditure, and experience on the ground. Unit-beat policing proved to be 'no more effective in reducing crime than foot patrols', and it was less popular than anticipated. There were three main areas of criticism. Firstly, the scheme required a major commitment of manpower and resources, and in Cardiff, for example, this was not always available. Area constables were continually having to help out on the car patrols, and communications between the officers, cars and headquarters were not always of the best. Secondly, unit-beat policing increased the distance which had already developed between communities, which were themselves in a process of change, and their police officers. Contacts between the UBP men, who covered wide areas, and local residents were restricted. Thirdly, this form of policing reduced the status of constables beating on foot, and turned mobile patrolmen into the real 'crime-fighters'; 'Z Cars' had replaced 'Dixon of Dock Green'. As the chief constable of Merthyr Tydfil admitted in 1968, the men in the panda cars liked the conditions of work and the excitement. They responded to the 999 calls, and dealt with many of the incidents once left to the local bobbies. However, although unit-beat officers provided a quick response, it was sometimes a more confrontational one. Sociologists tell us that for many people, especially the young, the panda car became a symbol of a rather distant and unsympathetic authority.

An early panda car: the introduction of unit-beat policing in 1968.

The pace of the disillusionment with unit-beat policing was remarkable; in many urban areas of Britain it was quickly abandoned. In 1972, when the South Wales force had 461 car beats and 206 area constables, as well as 468 town-centre patrols, the decision was taken to reduce the car beats, and to increase the number of area constables and, in particular, the number of constables walking the beat. This policy was confirmed in a major review seven years later. Thereafter 'traditional methods involving beat patrols' were reintroduced in many places, and additional area constables were deployed in urban as well as rural districts. The public seemed to appreciate the changes, and where they took place, as at Dowlais, the police claimed a marked improvement in the reporting of crime and the levels of vandalism and hooliganism. Yet, ironically, research at this time by J. A. Bright in Britain and by scholars in America found little evidence that increasing the number or frequency of foot patrols actually reduced crime.

By 1981 South Wales had almost a thousand policemen and women on foot patrols. Of these 365 were designated as community police officers, whose task was to liaise with representatives and institutions of the locality. Much of their work, brought under a new comunity services department in 1984, was of the crime-prevention kind; they spoke to schools and societies, got involved in leisure and welfare programmes, and encouraged people to fit door-chains and mark their possessions. They were an important catalyst, too, in the creation of community watch, and other similar schemes. Chief Constable John Woodcock believed that the immediate consequence of this community policing would be a rise in the crime rate, as offences were more readily reported, but he hoped for long-term benefits. Anticipating future criticisms, he said in 1982 that community constables were as important in the fight against crime as the officers on the front line. Taking up this theme, Home Office researchers have argued that 'if community policing succeeds in improving confidence among groups where this is lacking, reductions in crime might follow'.

In spite of the pressures upon them, the South Wales police have tried since that time to keep a balance between community policing, crime prevention and specialized crime-fighting activities. Crime prevention was not new; the chief constable of Swansea, for example, when replying to complaints about disorderly juveniles in 1911, wanted crèches for working mothers, better education, new out-of-school activities, improved work training for the young, and less exposure of shop goods. At a more practical level, his policemen checked that house, shop and warehouse owners had secured their property, and left warnings for the 'worst offenders'. In Swansea this work was again given a high profile just after the Second World War, whilst Merthyr Tydfil in the same period witnessed a number of important crime-prevention innovations, including making use of the press to provide regular warnings and information. However, the 1960s was the major turning-point in this story; during that decade the Home Office became actively involved in this area of policing, and one force after another appointed crime-prevention officers and created departments for them.

In the new South Wales force, crime prevention meant several things. It meant, for example, greater effort in obtaining information on criminals and their plans, and using the car-patrol system to deal with disorder before it got out of hand. At a different level, it entailed working closely with business people, persuading house and car owners to protect their property, distributing leaflets, giving talks, and initiating or assisting with the establishment of watch schemes and crime-prevention panels. By 1989 there were 214 neighbourhood watch schemes, with 3,900 members in the Cardiff Greater police division alone, 80 in the Pontypridd division, and hundreds more across South Wales. Crime prevention also meant encouraging companies and architects to design out the opportunities for crime. Finally, prevention was interpreted as offering alternatives to delinquency, especially for youngsters; police and social workers organized everything from non-alcoholic discos to summer vacation activities.

One of the justifications of the national commitment to crime prevention in, and after, the 1960s was that it would reduce the burden of petty crime, and allow the police to concentrate their main efforts on professional and organized criminals. These were the targets of the detective branch, and of the specialist police groups which began to appear in the 1960s. As we have seen, it took a little time for the CID of the new South Wales force to reach national standards of size and efficiency, and to eliminate the practice of seconding foot-patrol officers to help with its work. By 1972, the CID staff at headquarters numbered 46 policemen and women and 39 civilians, whilst just over 250 CID officers were located in the divisions.

In that year an average of 170 crimes per operational officer was taken as the basis for determining 'a realistic detective establishment' for each subdivision, but only Gorseinon, with 142 cases per detective constable and sergeant, met this target. An internal report on the CID in 1973 found that the number of its officers was dangerously low. On occasions divisional detectives had to be withdrawn to help with major investigations of serious crimes at headquarters, whilst the size of the drugs and fraud squads meant that outside the main towns and seaports only a very 'limited degree of effectiveness [was] possible'.

By 1986 some growth had occurred, though much less than was desired. More than one hundred officers then worked for the CID at headquarters. The drug squad had 22 members, the fraud squad 13, the scenes-of-crime squad 34, special branch 35, and the serious crime squad 17. There were 293 detectives distributed across the subdivisions. The case-load of the latter varied considerably, though it was generally well above the recommended levels. In Llanishen and Aberdare subdivisions the load was 471 and 467 cases per detective sergeant and constable, whilst in Bargoed and Bridgend it was 270 and 312 respectively. The work of these officers, including the thousands of scenes-of-crime visits, was often routine and tedious. As we saw in the last chapter, the exciting business of investigating truly serious crimes in 1986, like the task of protecting national security, had been hived off to special units, which operated for much of the time on an inter-force basis.

Intensive policing and specialization also spread during this period to the uniform branch. Special units were created in the 1960s to deal with, for example, alarming outbreaks of burglary, shoplifting, autocrime and vandalism, and a few of these, like the stolen vehicles and metal squads, became permanent. Later, in 1976, divisional support groups were formally established to give assistance where required to officers on the beat. Other units emerged in the 1980s, including special patrol and area-response groups, the latter of which comprised twenty-three officers each and appeared in Cardiff, Swansea and Pontypridd in January 1986 to provide the force 'with a more co-ordinated approach to the increasing problem of disorder'. Recently, too, there have been joint uniformed and detective experiments with 'priority policing', 'saturation policing', 'targeted surveillance' of criminals and areas like Riverside in Cardiff, and 'stop-and-search policing' under the Police and Criminal Evidence Act of 1984. In 1989 1,967 persons and vehicles were searched under the Act in South Wales, many of them in the centre of Cardiff. A total of 440 arrests resulted, often of young people. According to Home Office research, such forms of policing can, in the right conditions, be quite successful, but they raise the question of just how pro-active and intrusive the police should really be.

In summary, the policing in South Wales in 1989 could be described as more professional, differentiated and flexible than that at the beginning of our period. The police in 1989 had immediate and unprecedented access to all the latest information on crimes and criminals. Command and control structures were able to analyse crime patterns and plan the best strategies for dealing with them. Patrol groups, community policing and support services were in place, and the operational skills of special branch and public-order units were demonstrably impressive. At the same time, government pressure and the interchange of senior officers between forces have produced in recent years a greater willingness to adopt new and controversial crime-control measures, like camera surveillance. All this is very far from the largely open and non-specialized policing of 1900.

Research suggests, nevertheless, that the effectiveness of some forms of modern policing is open to doubt. Much of the collation and computerization of information, for example, has not produced noticeably improved prevention and detection, and we are assured that 'increases in detective manpower and technological improvements yield only marginal gains in clear-up rates'. Nor are the immediate prospects good; in fact, as the crime rate has continued to rise and the demands on the police have increased, day-to-day policing is now moving towards the 'fire-brigade' variety, of graded response and case-screening. In 1984 the force admitted that it could not deal with all the reports of crimes and incidents as quickly as people expected, and there have been times since when it has been stretched to provide even basic services. Inevitably effort and expense have to be concentrated on the worst life-threatening crimes and accidents, and on the most serious challenges to public order, and other aspects of policing and public relations have had to be curtailed.

Police efficiency and effectiveness

Police efficiency and effectiveness mean different things, and they mean different things depending upon which police functions and objectives are being considered. There were calls in the 1980s for 'more informed discussion about the tasks which the police should and should not perform' and for 'output measures' to be established by which to judge 'the efficiency and effectiveness of their non-crime work' as well as their ability as crime-fighters. In 1990 the Audit Commission dismissed the traditional indicators of police success, the crime and clear-up rates, as inadequate. Instead it called for more PBO (policing by objectives) and better management techiques as recommended to chief constables several years before. During the early 1990s, in the South Wales force as elsewhere, attempts were being made to evaluate police efficiency in terms of set objectives, work practices and value for money. As yet, the results of this internal evaluation have not been published.

The criteria of both efficiency and effectiveness in the police force, are difficult to establish. Two traditional standards for judging the former have been the work-load of police officers, and the manner in which they have responded to public reports and requests. We have already examined the former in a little detail, but the figures only tell some of the story. An inquiry into policing in Swansea in 1958, which looked at tasks, manpower and hours worked over the previous twenty years, found that whilst the rate of crime had precisely doubled, other developments had reduced 'available manpower' in 1958 'actually to the level of 1938'. There had, concluded the chief constable, been a 'great increase' in productivity. The same point was made in 1972, when a survey showed that the South Wales force had to face unprecedented levels of recorded crime and occurrences with officers who were away for almost half a year because of leave, holidays, sickness, courses and secondments.

The claims of increased productivity have continued. In the establishment review of 1986 the South Wales force showed that, when compared with South Yorkshire, Lancashire and seven other large forces, its officers dealt with more crimes than most, with less overtime and at about the cheapest cost. In addition, South Wales had one of the best detection and arrest rates of the ten forces, well above the national average. The detection rate fell subsequently, but Chief Constable Robert Lawrence attributed this directly to the increased work-load that made his officers the busiest in Wales.

Since the 1960s, comparisons have also been drawn between response times in the various forces. The first mobile patrols set high standards, which the public quickly regarded as the norm. The Merthyr Tydfil force in 1968, for example, promised an 'attendance time' anywhere in the borough of four minutes. This now seems incredibly prompt. When the graded response system was introduced in 1984, to the 'immediate response' time were added 'delayed' (within an hour) and 'scheduled' (over the hour). Subsequently, about 20 per cent of incidents were responded to immediately, that is, within about fifteen minutes, and most of the rest have fallen into the second category.

The force has also succeeded in its recent Charter target of answering most 999 telephone calls within ten seconds, and non-999 calls in twenty seconds. The police, and the public, set great store by these time contracts, but criminologists tell us that they have more to do with the image of efficiency and good public relations than with the real effectiveness of the police as crime-fighters. The latter is discussed below.

Effectiveness: police numbers and crime

Historically, a sudden rise in the crime rate and outbreaks of serious disorder have led to calls for more police and better methods of detection. To take just one example, there were frequent complaints in the early years of the century that the Glamorgan force was inadequate, considering the services it provided and the problem of crime and social protest in its urban and industrial areas. After admitting that the 'thin blue line' only just held during the worst industrial disturbances, Lindsay reminded the government in December 1925 that keeping a force 'up to strength, by nipping matters, which may become serious, in the bud, is no doubt an economy in the long run'. It was a typical comment, which could have been uttered by any chief constable this century.

We can make several observations on the relationship between police numbers and delinquency, using the information in the graphs and tables in this volume. Firstly, there has always been a connection of some kind between the availability of officers and the reporting of crime, not least in the era before people had telephones. 'It is a fact of life', said one senior South Wales policeman, 'that more policemen produce more statistical crime.' The truth of this statement can be considered geographically and chronologically. Looking at the detailed crime statistics, for Glamorgan and then for the amalgamated force, these reveal that the most policed subdivisions did occasionally return the highest rates of recorded crime, but not consistently so. Barry Dock in the years 1945–7 was a good example of the former, whilst Cowbridge was not. The small (11) number of policemen in the Cowbridge subdivision handled many more reported crimes per officer than, for instance, their more numerous counterparts (36) in Aberdare.

Table 5.1, which gives figures for incidents as well as crimes, confirms the difficulties of establishing direct and universal connections between policing and crime levels. The subdivisions in the groups which had the most or fewest response officers per population and area did not always produce the highest or lowest rate of offences and incidents. The nature of the communities in these subdivisions, their natural level of delinquency, and relationships between the public and the police are just some of the variables that have to be added to any equation.

Table 5·1: Police numbers, recorded crime and incidents in 1986

| | Group 1 | | Group 2 | | Group 3 | |
	Bargoed	Llanishen	Roath	Swansea City	Aberdare	Lliw Valley
Pop. per response officer (RO)	614	1505	875	425	1017	956
Acres per RO	130	82	31	15	272	246
Crimes per RO	42	94	117	118	57	52
Incidents per RO	157	317	392	351	200	213

The same point, about the dangers of simple analysis, must be made over the chronological correlations between the rate of police per head of population and crime. In Glamorgan between 1900 and 1968 both rates moved upwards, but the fluctuations in the rate of recorded crime during the first half of the century were more pronounced, and the subsequent rise much sharper, than that of police numbers. Nevertheless, connections between the two rates seemed, at times, perfectly obvious to contemporaries. During the Second World War, for example, when the soaring crime rate heralded the drama to come, many people blamed the phenomenon on the difficulties experienced by the reduced, inexperienced and overworked police forces.

Comparing the number of police officers across South Wales after 1945 with the crime rate, it seems that for part of the immediate post-war period, and for much of the 1960s and 1970s, the rates moved upwards together, though at a different pace.

Chief Constable Cecil Watkins was acutely aware of this differential in the late 1950s, and used it repeatedly to underline his requests for more men and equipment. He argued that the problem of manpower had dogged his county since the end of the war and had finally reduced his force 'below the level necessary for efficiency'. However, the relatively high detection rate in Glamorgan did not fully support Watkins's view, unless the figures had been doctored.

There were several exceptions to the joint upward march of both police numbers and the crime rate. In the optimistic years 1951–3, there was an inverse correlation between the two trends, whilst during the 1980s, when police numbers per 100,000 of the population held steady, the rate of recorded indictable crime continued to rise. Seeking an explanation for these two examples, those offered by the forces themselves in the early 1950s were the recruitment of police officers of high quality (linked to better pay), the adoption of new methods such as team policing, and improvements in the social life of the nation, chiefly the benefits of a more settled family life after the trauma of the war years. In the 1980s three main reasons were offered internally for the way in which the escalating crime rate seemed to move independently of police numbers: the economic and social problems of the time, better reporting of crime and occurrences, and the growing difficulties encountered by an overworked force.

The assumption, therefore, which lay behind the many police and public requests for extra officers over the century was that more crime necessitated more police. Yet this has never been a popular reaction with governments, especially in periods of recession. The Home Office often turned down demands for more officers in these circumstances, and called on chief constables to economize through greater mechanization and the employment of civilians as cheaper substitutes. In the late 1950s and early 1960s, and again in recent years, the phenomenal surge in the crime rate prompted a more vigorous political response, and anxious governments intervened more decisively in the make-up, methods and control of the police forces.

On the first of these occasions, the Royal Commission on the Police of 1960–2 acted as a focus for reformers and politicians who wanted a change. Roy Jenkins, in the new Labour government, saw police amalgamations and modernization as the answer, with the Home Office co-ordinating the introduction of unit-beat policing, computer technology and crime prevention. None of it worked as well as was hoped. 'Centralisation of the police force', said a nostalgic Superintendent Welford at an Aberdare liaison meeting in 1983, 'destroyed a system which stood the test of time.' Yet, as graph 4.1 shows, these changes in policing were hardly underresourced. For much of the Labour-dominated 1960s and 1970s the number of police officers rose sharply, only to fall, with the crime rate, during the premiership of James Callaghan, once a spokesman for the police in Parliament.

In the Thatcher years there was a very short honeymoon period, when the Tories fulfilled their election pledges to strengthen the police forces in their battle against crime. In spite of more policemen and better pay, however, the crime rate continued to rise rapidly, and the clear-up rate fell. The government, in its new austerity phase, demanded better value for money, and for the rest of the 1980s the rate of police officers to population hardly changed. In a Home Office research study of 1984 on police effectiveness, Ronald Clarke and Mike Hough gave ammunition to the Tory government by showing statistically that 'crime will not be significantly reduced simply by devoting more manpower to conventional police strategies'. Since that time, forces have had to work within tighter budgets, and adopt new management techniques and policing methods recommended by the Home Office, but so far this has made little difference to the effectiveness of the police as crime-fighters.

Effectiveness: the police and the prevention of crime

Effectiveness is a difficult concept, and even more difficult to measure. People have, since 1829, said contradictory things about the contribution of the police towards a crime-free society, and the historian finds it difficult to decide between them. The prevention of crime has, until modern crime and self-report surveys, been unquantifiable, whilst the official detection rate has long been recognized as unreliable. The chief constable of Merthyr Tydfil declared in 1964 that 'the number of arrests and clear-up percentages . . . is not the yardstick of a successful police force. In my view, the yardstick is still the same as that laid down by Richard Mayne in 1829, that is, the absence of crime shows best whether or not the efforts of the police have been successful.' For much of the 1950s and early 1960s, his Merthyr police made crime prevention a 'principal feature' of their effort.

One of the main functions of foot-patrol men from the earliest times was to prevent crime. In places like St Nicholas and Ely at the turn of the century, they were apparently 'a great check' on fowl-stealing and poaching, especially in the run-up to Christmas, and their patrols of ricks and outbuildings were evidently appreciated. Propertied people in urban and industrial communities also believed that the presence of the police made a significant difference to their security. They claimed that patrolling the beat inhibited open violence, robberies and thefts in and about houses and shops.

Nightly police checks on business and domestic premises were regarded as an insurance against burglaries. Over the years, the number of offices, shops, warehouses and homes added to the police surveillance lists indicates that people were indeed convinced of the value of this crime prevention. In Merthyr the minority of careless property-owners were sent warning letters and given verbal advice. Writing in the winter of 1958–9, the chief constable of that town argued that the rising tide of stealing and break-ins could have been prevented 'to a large degree by the efficient patrolling of beats by uniformed constables', especially at night, but they had 'been whittled down considerably since the war by reason of man-power problems'. Increasing the detective staff, in these circumstances, was 'like putting the cart before the horse'.

From time to time, police chiefs in South Wales gathered their resources in short-lived operations to reduce the level of certain property offences which were causing concern. Thus attempts were made to prevent autocrime in Cardiff at the onset of the Second World War, and break-ins in the capital a few years later. However, the efforts of the Cardiff and Swansea police to get car owners to lock their vehicles had a mixed reception, as the reports of autocrime in the 1950s and 1960s clearly illustrated.

In the mid-1960s the Swansea force tried to assess what crime prevention could deliver in terms of reduced statistics. It estimated that 'had reasonable attention to security been paid by complainants', about 1,500 crimes (one in three of the total) could have been prevented, and of these the majority were autocrime and 'miscellaneous larcenies'. The pleasing hiccup in the rising crime rate in the town during the late 1960s was attributed to the efforts of the new crime prevention officers, the introduction of automatic alarm systems and similar precautions, but, as always with these matters, it was difficult to ignore other factors.

Generally, the benefits of crime prevention were regarded as long-term, and this is how the policy was sold in the 1980s. In places like Penlan in Swansea, intensive 'safe neighbourhood' campaigns brought immediate results, but the latest studies reveal that too often community programmes have a short life. Similarly, many watch schemes have folded after initial enthusiasm. Misgivings have been expressed about the role of the police in some of these, and there is more concern that the latest versions, with their heightened surveillance and computerized information, represent the unacceptable face of crime prevention. To achieve permanent benefits for crime prevention across South Wales, sustained public support is essential, together with a gradual process of education and costly collaborative projects designed to displace as well as prevent crime in the most vulnerable areas.

Effectiveness: the police and order

One of the most important functions of the police from the beginning was to impose order on society. This order had several facets. At a very basic level, the police were expected to prevent domestic disputes, both within families and between neighbours, from getting out of hand. They were further required to monitor standards of behaviour in the streets and public arenas, and to contain industrial disputes and mass protests. There is some evidence that the police in the later nineteenth century were quite successful in this regard, helped no doubt by the spread of education, political democracy and other civilizing influences.

As we saw in a previous chapter, this work continued in the early twentieth century. Strong police patrols in towns and industrial communities, under the leadership of tough characters like Edward Gill at Mountain Ash, were regarded as the *sine qua non* of a more peaceful street life. At Hopkinstown in 1911–12, for instance, Sergeant Evans, Constables Welsby, Batten, Edwards and others dealt with a constant barrage of obscenities, stone-throwing and pub fights, and in that time sent scores of truculent youths, miners, women and vagrants before the Pontypridd magistrates. In addition, they kept angry workmen away from each other during the strikes and lock-outs.

Such work was praised by the Cardiff and Swansea chief constables, though in the 1920s and 1930s they also acknowledged the importance of changes in public attitudes. Constable Hodge in the 1920s was, after all, *called* by angry passers-by and residents to deal with many of the foul-mouthed prostitutes, urinating drunkards, fighting sailors, stone-throwing children and argumentative relatives in the capital. Gradually, things improved. 'The orderliness of the public in the streets and public places of the Borough has been excellent; this was particularly so during the General Election,' said the chief constable of Swansea in 1923. 'It reflects the greatest credit on the inhabitants of the Town and I have much pleasure in taking this opportunity of expressing my appreciation of the ready assistance at all times rendered to the Force.'

Such was the change by 1944 that the chief constable of Neath said that the daily foot patrol had become 'merely the symbol of safety, whilst it does little or nothing to prevent or detect crime. In bygone days patrols were fully occupied in dealing with affrays and such like breaches of the peace. Nowadays occurrences such as these are rare.' With a few half-exceptions, such as the Teddy-boy fights of the 1950s, and the Penrhys and Ely confrontations of the 1980s, all of which the media exaggerated, the police have proved capable of controlling disorder in the streets.

Although the police have often been criticized for turning industrial protest into violent conflict, and for dealing insensitively with demonstrations, they generally became more adept and professional as the years passed. There were occasions in the first twenty years of the century when riots between the Irish and against coloureds and Germans in Swansea, Cardiff and Neath stretched police resources, whilst the parallel industrial troubles on the coalfield necessitated external police and military assistance. In a revealingly modest phrase, Lindsay admitted, after the coal strike of 1921, that with a depleted, new and unfit police force 'the County had got somewhat out of hand . . .' Further conflicts were to follow with the unemployed movement and the anti-Fascists in the 1930s, culminating in the sacking of the Assistance Board offices in Merthyr. The policing of these demonstrations did precipitate, as well as contain, violence, and brought protests from the miners' union, councillors and the National Council for Civil Liberties (NCCL), but the retirement of Lindsay in 1937 coincided with an easing of tensions.

After the Second World War, there were fewer public-order crises. Roger Geary, in his study of twentieth-century industrial disputes, claims that relations between the police and pickets became almost respectable in the post-war generation, with 'push and shove' the only confrontation. Even so, the power of the police, and the policing of the crowd, gradually changed over the next decades. The demonstrators of the 1960s were faced with much strengthened police forces; strikers were later confronted by Mrs Thatcher's riot-control reforms; and the hooligans in the football crowd found life was harder after the Public Order Act of 1986. In 1984–5, the South Wales police were able to confront the biggest challenge, the miners' strike, without parading all the riot gear used elsewhere, and with a degree of confidence. The charges then, and later, were not about the effectiveness of the police, but over the use of excessive force and the arrival of 'unaccountable military-style policing'.

Effectiveness: the police and the detection of crime

The police, the public and, increasingly, modern governments have kept a wary eye on the detection of crime. It was used, from the start, as a hallmark, the proof that the professional police were better than their amateur predecessors, and more effective than their counterparts overseas. Studies of the nineteenth century have shown that official clear-up rates were set artificially high. Looked at more closely, it seems that whilst offenders were easily apprehended for crimes of violence prior to 1900, burglars, robbers and fraudsters were much more difficult to catch. Much depended on the assistance given by the public and the proximity of the police to the crime. The story in the twentieth century is rather similar, despite the growth of detective departments and new scientific methods of identifying criminals.

The official detection rate can be found in graph 5.1. At the beginning of the century, the rate was typically well over three-quarters of indictable offences recorded by the police, but there is

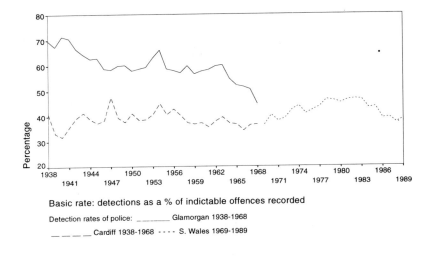

Basic rate: detections as a % of indictable offences recorded

Detection rates of police: _____ Glamorgan 1938-1968

_ _ _ _ Cardiff 1938-1968 - - - - S. Wales 1969-1989

Graph 5.1: Detection rates, 1938–1989

evidence, summarized in chapter 1, that police statisticians at this
time ignored many reports of crimes which were unlikely to lead to
a court case. In Cardiff, where greater elasticity in compiling the
crime rate became the norm after the First World War, the clear-up
rate fell to about a half by the early 1920s, with house break-ins
and larcenies of bicycles and from motor vehicles a major problem.
'However efficient a Police Force may be', said the chief constable
of the city in 1924, 'its vigilance cannot equal the astuteness of
criminals, plus the negligence of those who have lost their
property.' By 1940 the detection rate in the capital had fallen to 32
per cent, and it only improved a little in the years that followed.

In Glamorgan, Merthyr, Neath and Swansea, by contrast, the
detection rate remained very high until the last years of the
Second World War. In Merthyr the official rate was 72 per cent in
1925, rose even higher on the eve of the war, but dropped to 55–6
per cent in 1945–6. It had fallen again to 42 per cent by 1956, but
improved in the early 1960s when men were released for detective

work from traffic duties and out-district patrols. From 1945 onwards, Swansea's rate also plunged, to about half or less, and remained like that until amalgamation, whereas that of the county force was still 58 per cent in 1949. The problems were, nevertheless, the same across all the forces; in 1949, for example, the county police failed to detect a large percentage of bicycle thefts and shoplifting, and the majority of reported break-ins, simple larcenies and thefts of motor vehicles.

The detection rate in Glamorgan remained, at around 60 per cent, well above the average for Britain and the rest of South Wales until the early 1960s. It was not consistently good across the force, for stations like Sully returned uneven performances. Yet chief constables of the county were proud of their county's record, and attributed it, amongst other things, to the quality and spirit of their men, their willingness to work long hours, and the improvements in the force since the inter-war years. During the mid-1960s, however, the county detection rate began to fall, in spite of rising police numbers, and in 1968, the last year before amalgamation, it stood at 45 per cent. Chief Constable Melbourne Thomas, in his report for that year, said that there was 'no single cause for the drop', but felt that 'the increase in crime, the need to adjust from the conventional method of policing to Unit Beat Policing, [and] the number of resignations followed by the poorest recruiting figures for many years, must go a long way to explain this decline'. In Cardiff, as graph 5.1 shows, things were worse, and had been so since the war, the rate hovering for much of the time between 35 and 40 per cent.

In the light of this, and bearing in mind the greater willingness to report crimes in recent decades, the performance of the South Wales constabulary has been better than at first appears, and above that of many English forces. The clear-up rate has been close to 42 per cent throughout its life, the best period, 1978–83, coinciding with an improvement in police numbers and conditions, and the worst being that of very recent years. In 1989 the force had a detection rate well above the English average, but it had the worst figures in Wales (see table 5.2).

Although different in degree, the pattern of clear-up rates in 1989 across categories of crimes is similar to that of a century ago. Maximum resources have been committed to solving serious offences like homicide, and much less effort has been devoted to

Table 5·2: Notifiable offences recorded by the police: clear-up rate by offence group for 1989 (percentages)

Area	Total	Violence against the person	Burglary	Theft & handling stolen goods	Fraud & forgery	Criminal damage
Eng.	33	76	27	30	66	23
Wales	43	89	34	41	82	31
Dyfed-Powys	52	97	42	43	87	47
Gwent	54	92	45	49	89	44
North Wales	44	90	31	40	91	32
South Wales	39	85	32	39	71	25

finding the perpetrators of minor crimes. Figures are excellent for crimes such as assault, where the offender is usually known, and for crimes like fraud and drug offences, where the police initiate most of the proceedings, but otherwise it is a depressing story. No more than a third, at most, of the victims who report break-ins, theft and criminal damage are likely to have their crime solved, and in some areas the chances are much less. Within the South Wales force in the 1980s the divisions of Bridgend and Barry, for instance, usually returned good detection figures whereas Cardiff Central did not, something that has been reversed in the early 1990s.

At a subdivisional level, the selection given in table 5.3 gives the worst and best performances during 1986, with the accompanying case-load per detective constable and sergeant. They cast doubt on the common statement in annual reports that detection rates and the level of crime are closely linked.

The figures tell us only a limited amount about the performance of the police as a detective agency. The police relied heavily on the public for information to secure an arrest, and where assaults and rape were concerned, this was a major factor behind the high clear-up rate. In the case of property offences, too, the CID benefited again from names supplied by the public, from information given by the British Transport Commission Police and similar bodies, and from the work of their own uniformed colleagues. In the cottage stations the last factor remained important for a long while. At Sully in 1958–9, for example, where the detection rate was 53 per cent, the local constable devoted many hours each week to crime investigation.

Table 5·3: Rates of detection in 1986: best and worst performances

Sub-division	Population	Reported crime	No. of cases per officer	Detection rate %
Group 1				
Bargoed	27610	1893	270	54
Barry	78400	6263	417	51
Merthyr	59200	4727	364	49
Group 2				
Maesteg	41139	2084	417	33
Swansea W.	118365	6178	363	33
Roath	81407	10894	351	32
Ely	74200	5017	456	28

The situation was rather different in the urban forces. We have already noted the contribution of the uniform branch in the Swansea force in the 1930s and 1940s. They were responsible for almost half the detection rate of 61 per cent in 1938, but twenty years later, when Swansea's CID had doubled in size and the rate fallen to 49 per cent, the men on patrol played only a minor role in solving crimes. This was the way of the future; by the 1960s everything, including reports of stolen milk bottles and sweets, was handed over to the town's detectives.

Contemporary research suggests that detectives spend much of their time filling in forms and doing other clerical work rather than investigating crimes, and the latter anyway is less productive than viewers of *The Bill* might suppose. Crime investigation takes time, resources and a willingness to absorb criticism and disappointment. Records of the CID from the 1960s show the importance of co-operative victims and witnesses, and the value of an early breakthrough, for prolonged enquiries frequently ended with the phrase 'no useful information gained'. Nor, it seems from notebooks and diaries, were suspects as willing to admit crimes to a Skewen detective in the 1960s as they were to Constable Hodge in Cardiff in the 1920s. 'Denied knowledge of the offence' is a recurring theme in the detective's diary.

Given the recent work-load of the CID, case screening according to solvability (which the public dislike) and other forms of selectivity are essential. At present about one in seven indictable crimes in South Wales are detected at the time of reporting, half of the total are screened out, and the rest referred for further investigation. The policy has its merits. Thus intensive campaigns to catch those involved in organized car-stealing, vice and corruption in South Wales have, from the 1970s until the present day, brought satisfactory results, but questions are then asked about the lack of success in other fields. The competition for resources is endless. One study funded by the Home Office in 1982 concluded that a 10-per-cent increase in manpower, devoted solely to CID work, would raise the clear-up rate by less than 1 per cent.

Many of the offences cleared up are, indeed, not the result of the efforts of either the public or the police, in a narrow sense, but of confessions made by people before and after conviction for another crime. Thus Graham Davies, who was charged with sixteen offences of larceny and fraud in July 1965, asked the Neath court for 138 other crimes to be taken into consideration. In 1992, for the first time, the annual report of the chief constable revealed that just over a third of his force's detections were achieved by 'secondary methods', which included crimes taken into consideration and not previously reported to the police, and offences admitted by persons serving custodial sentences and recorded as detected under Home Office guidelines.

The police and the public

One of the truisms of policing, which has been borne out throughout these chapters, is that the effectiveness of the police as crime-fighters depends heavily on public co-operation. A great deal has been written in recent years about the relationship between police and public, and this has modified the earlier picture drawn by Charles Reith. The revisionists remind us that opposition to the new police was stronger than once surmised, and it was only in the later Victorian period that relationships improved significantly. Thereafter, so we are told, contacts between the friendly bobby and the community were generally good until the late 1950s, when publicity over police corruption and a deterioration in public confidence helped to precipitate the Royal Commission on the state of the police.

The Commission's public-opinion survey found that the

overwhelming majority of the people still had 'great respect' for the police, but since that time, so it is claimed, the emergence of unit-beat policing, the implementation of stricter traffic and drug laws, the policing of demonstrations and strikes, the spiralling crime rate, and evidence of doubtful convictions have all brought a further erosion of respect for the police. Robert Reiner and others have noted how, for some young groups in society, notably the coloureds and the growing numbers of unemployed, disillusionment with the police has turned into outright hostility. And this has been reinforced to a degree by middle-class people who have themselves been criminalized or who have become alarmed by the politicization of the police and their lack of accountability. The post-Scarman developments in community policing and consultation are, in part, a conscious policy to redress this balance.

The historical sources of the twentieth century do not fully support either the Reithian or revisionist interpretations. There were, it is true, demands for a police presence from ratepayers, councillors and others in the early years, and official thanks and leaving presents for officers who had guarded them for long periods. Yet there was also considerable hostility in the industrial valleys of South Wales for at least some of this time. Police constables were attacked at regular intervals, criticisms of their attitudes and violent conduct were heard after each wave of strikes, and attempts were made by miners' representatives to change the composition of the police committees. 'It has been the invariable custom', ran one report in December 1911, 'to resist an arrest by the police, and there are certainly more assaults on the police in proportion to the population in this district [Ynysboeth and Matthewstown], than in any other district in the Aberdare division.' It is difficult to estimate the number of assaults in that year, but in 1901 there were 315 court cases in the county concerning attacks on the police, a situation comparable with that of a generation before.

In the largest towns and seaports there were many complaints of police harassment and misconduct in the early twentieth century, and annoyance, sometimes leading to crowd troubles, with the police over the execution of the Betting, Licensing, Sunday Trading, Vagrancy and Highways Acts. This was, as we saw in the last chapter, the time when official complaints against the police in

Cardiff were at their height, and the same is true of violent clashes between constables and members of the public. In 1903 there were 174 court cases concerning assaults on Cardiff police officers. This was equivalent to attacks on three out of four policemen, or one case for every thousand of the population. Perhaps the most notorious assailant was Mary Jane Martin, who made her 160th appearance in the dock during the following year.

Although the level of complaints and assaults dropped in Cardiff and several other forces with the outbreak of the First World War, the heads of the borough police forces continued to plead with the public for greater assistance, especially once better communications were provided. There was some disappointment with the response. In industrial areas, too, more help was requested, and, during the worst troubles of the inter-war years, policemen were stoned, stations stormed, and lessons in self-defence given to Glamorgan officers.

The Second World War was widely regarded as marking an improvement in police–public relations. The chief constable of Glamorgan caught the mood of excessive optimism, which grew from shared experiences and police wartime services. 'Obviously', he stated in February 1943, 'a large number of citizens have through the war made close contact with the Police, which they had never done before; consequently, it can reasonably be assumed that after the war the Police Officer will be regarded with a greater degree of mutual understanding between himself and the community in which he serves . . . (and) the Police Station will become the centre to which the public will naturally go for information and guidance on matters in which they think the Police Officer can help them.'

The state of police–public relations in the middle of the century is a complex matter. There were certainly criticisms during the late 1950s of the police forces, especially of their failure to stem the rising tide of crime, and of their apparent obsession with parking and speeding offences. Even so, senior policemen at this time in Cardiff and Swansea praised the co-operation between the public and their officers. 'Greater co-operation has become evident in recent years', said the chief constable of Swansea in his annual report for 1961, 'and the public appears to be more conscious of the value of giving assistance than was formerly the case . . . In crime problems the Police are greatly dependent upon information given by members of the public.' Amongst the rank-and-file police officers, however, as the Royal Commission of 1960–2 made clear, there was a distinct feeling that public standards and respect for the police had declined. One exaggerated claim in November 1960 was that in the county 'cowardly assaults upon Police Officers, particularly when a lone Police Officer has been involved, are now far more frequent than they have been at any time during the period for which records are available'. In Glamorgan and in Cardiff young males were the principal offenders.

Since the early 1960s the police have been very conscious of the value of public support, and public relations departments were created to improve their image, as well as effectiveness. In the South Wales force such a department was created in 1979. It established close links with the press, TV and radio, distributed information on the force, and helped to organize police lectures in schools, and public visits to police stations. Some of this work was taken over in 1984 by the community services department, and the divisionally based community service teams. There is little doubt, from all the research studies, that the public appreciate community policing and the permanent presence of officers in their localities, together with the opportunity to express their feelings about what he or she should be doing. In general, they want more foot patrols, if necessary at the expense of other kinds of policing, like dealing with petty motoring offences.

The activities of community policemen, the reappearance of foot patrols, and the introduction of free 'crime-stoppers' and other 'hot-lines' of the 1980s have probably improved the level of reporting crimes, but whether they have changed public feelings towards the police is a different matter. Public-opinion surveys suggest that today a small but significant and growing proportion (possibly a quarter or more) of the population, across all areas and classes, is suspicious of the police and critical of their methods. In its reports and its establishment review during the 1980s, the South Wales force identified certain mining, inner-city and council-estate districts, where 'apathy' reigned, and hostility towards the police was expected. In 1989, in one of these, the Ely estate in Cardiff, petrol bombs were thrown, police cars set on fire and the police station attacked.

The number of recorded attacks on the police increased

throughout the 1970s and 1980s. In 1990, when the force establishment was 3,123, there were 793 attacks, about 1 for every 1,500 of the population, and double the rate of 1969. Such figures, it was suggested, were about the worst in Britain, and, wrongly, without historical precedent. A survey of 1988, carried out by the force and the University College of Cardiff, revealed that these attacks were especially heavy in the Pontypridd and Cardiff divisions. The nature of the assaults, mostly by young men of a drunken and violent reputation who believed that the police were overly aggressive, were very similar to those committed throughout the nineteenth and twentieth centuries. Unfortunately, they tell us only a small amount about general changes in public attitudes.

Complaints against the police can be found in every age, and they have usually coalesced around issues of conduct, veracity and physical assault. As we saw earlier in this chapter, the level of complaints by both the public and colleagues was high in Cardiff during the early years of this century. The city police were accused of intimidating women and the homeless, taking bribes from licensees and hush-money from prostitutes, stealing from clients, inventing charges, false imprisonment, and beating people either at the time of arrest or later in vehicles and cells.

Not all the complainants in Cardiff were working-class. Tradesmen grumbled about the manner in which the Shop and Public Health Acts were executed, and upper- and middle-class drivers disliked being warned for motoring offences. In 1927, for example, two of the latter, Colonel Kyffin of Radyr and Major Parry Brown of Newport, told the chief constable of Cardiff that they expected officers to be 'more discreet' in future. Some of the policemen accused of more serious indiscretions were dismissed from the force, and even taken to court, though the number of the latter was small.

During the middle years of the century fewer complaints from the public were recorded in the Cardiff police files, an index perhaps of improved relationships, and one which can be found in London and elsewhere. 'Incivility to the public', 'rudeness', 'victimization' and 'unnecessary violence' were common gripes in this period, especially by motorists, but the accusations were frequently dismissed by senior officers as 'unjustified' or 'frivolous'. This itself proved a source of annoyance, and the police commission of 1960–2 recommended an official complaints procedure, which police chiefs disliked but which they still controlled. In Cardiff the immediate effect of the publicity surrounding the new procedure was to increase the number of public complaints from 23 in 1963 to 81 three years later, with the road traffic police a common target, but by 1968 the number had fallen to 59.

Since the establishment of the South Wales force the number of complaints by the public that have been investigated has grown from 216 in 1969, to 320 in 1974, 900 in 1978, and 892 in 1989. This pattern probably owes more to changes in public sensitivities and the complaints procedures than to the actual growth of police misconduct. Reports for the early 1990s have shown that complaints are heavy in places like Merthyr and the Cynon Valley, and about 60 per cent of them are of violence, unnecessary exercise of authority and incivility. The majority of the complaints over the last twenty years have been withdrawn or not substantiated, up to a quarter have been informally resolved, and a handful of complaints have resulted in formal reprimands and more serious disciplinary measures.

It is impossible to make a final statement about police–public relations. The status of police officers has, one suspects, changed less over the century than is sometimes suggested. The 'policing by consent', which is said to have characterized the early decades, was never as romantic and unquestioning as it is fondly remembered by some. The police have always been viewed with a mixture of respect and suspicion, and there has been a long-standing, if quiet, cynicism about their effectiveness in dealing with crime.

According to the latest police and crime surveys, whilst most people continue to respect the police, and think they are doing a good job, cynicism and suspicion have spread, especially amongst the most anxious and the most criminalized members of the population. Lesley Noaks, in her thesis on Bettws in Gwent, tells us that about half the population in 1988 were unhappy with the local police service. If this is correct, it is a cause for concern. 'Where the police have lost – for whatever reason – the confidence of those they police', it has been said, 'there is probably very little that sheer numbers can do to contain crime.'

Conclusion

This, and the last, chapter have shown that police efficiency and effectiveness are complex notions, and our understanding of them is limited because few attempts have been made properly to identify and evaluate all the functions which the police carry out. Crime-fighting is only one of these; the police are also a service industry, and an order-enforcement agency. All of their functions react on each other, all require large resources, and all are important. For the first thirty years of the century the maintenance of public order was a clear priority, whereas over the last thirty years the growing problem of crime has taken more of the police's attention. Even so, the present burden of controlling road traffic, dealing with thousands of non-crime incidents, coping with emergencies, and defusing threats to public order has ensured that fighting crime remains, as it has always been, a minority activity.

Criticisms of this activity have never ceased, and the methods and claims of the police were, to a degree, responsible for this. The spiralling crime rate of recent years has revealed problems which have been present in British policing for a very long time. Police effectiveness in dealing with crime, like the detection rate, has never been as good as assumed, and, when this became apparent after the late 1950s, 'paradoxically the very policies of increased technology, centralisation, specialisation and professionalism as a means of (improved) crime fighting may have aggravated the police ineffectiveness which motivated them'. As John Woodcock said of unit-beat policing, some developments are conceptually good, but 'do not produce the goods'.

All of this has become more serious in recent years. The police are confronted by an unprecedented crime problem, which has been magnified by the pressures coming from politicians, media obsessed with crime and a vociferous and increasingly anxious public. There was a growing feeling in society by the 1980s that the forces of law and order were unable to cope with the level of delinquency, either because they were too few and underfunded, or because the nature of the policing was inappropriate. As one Home Office report of 1984 put it, 'more of the same' policing will not do. The South Wales force, like many others, has begun to experiment with alternative forms, like community policing, and acknowledges the value of a more comprehensive and multi-agency response to the present crisis, in which policing and punishment have important but not exclusive roles. Whether the new-style forms of policing, including closed-circuit television surveillance and possibly access to information on 'smart' identification cards, can make an impact remains to be seen. The fact that large numbers of people seem ready to support such innovations is a break with history and a sign of their anxiety.

The public, who have long feared crime, have begun at last to be alarmed about the state of policing, and not simply about its modern public-order strategies which preoccupy so many academics. According to the Metropolitan and Merseyside crime surveys, a quarter of the victims of crime became dissatisfied with the police after reporting an offence, and an even higher proportion believed that no action was taken in their case. The present public image of a profession understaffed, overworked and often ineffective in its response to crime may prove extremely damaging, for the public, who have traditionally supported extra police resources and supplied the police with invaluable assistance, may take their custom elsewhere. Some individuals and estates in South Wales have already half-turned their backs on official forms of policing, and have lauded the virtues of community self-help, vigilantes, private security firms and council-run civilian patrols.

Epilogue

The value of any historical study is limited by the impossibility of recapturing the total past. The historian of modern crime is always aware of this; he or she can only guess at the real extent of crime, and has restricted access to the records which can throw light on this and other aspects of the subject. This book is, partly for this reason, no more than an introductory account of crime and policing during this century, which others will no doubt develop and modify. All one can claim for the present publication is that it has cast a little light on our present social anxieties, and given a basic historical framework to the current enquiries by politicians and social scientists into delinquency and policing.

There have been a number of collective panics about delinquency since the late eighteenth century, and these have sprung from sources not always related to the experience of crime. In the nineteenth century, governments, reformers and the media sometimes stimulated public interest in crime for their own ends, and the temptation to do this at moments of political crisis remains a strong one. In the twentieth century there has been less need than there was in Robert Peel's time to create a popular interest in crime; since the Second World War people have been 'crime conscious' to a remarkable degree, and fascination with the subject is now at an unprecedented level. The press, radio, television and the cinema, as well as popular and serious fiction, are saturated with stories of crime and policing, and public-opinion surveys leave us in no doubt as to the extent of people's interest and anxiety.

Although the press and politicians have been prepared to exploit this concern, they did not create it. It springs from a strong and common historical instinct that, in some important respects, things have deteriorated. We noted the problems in establishing the evidence for this. People in the past held conflicting views of the state of the nation, and the public's response to delinquency has changed over time. The reporting of crime, of all types, improved after the middle of the century, and so did the police recording of crime which in the past hid a great deal of known, as well as hidden, delinquency. The rising crime rate thus contains an element of 'success' as well as 'failure', and it has to be modified in the light of national and local crime surveys.

Yet, when every conditional clause is added, it seems indisputable that criminal behaviour has increased since the late 1930s, with a sharp upswing in recorded property offences for a period after the late 1950s, and a similar, if less spectacular, trend in recorded violent crimes over the past twenty years. People's experience of both depended largely on where they lived, though sex and age were also important factors. In 1989 one indictable offence was recorded for every eleven of the population, but there were 'crime spots' in urban districts where inhabitants were much more vulnerable than their friends in neighbouring or rural communities. For these victims, the term 'hyper crisis' has a real significance, and the worsening statistics since 1989 suggest that South Wales is deeper in this crisis than most regions of Britain.

Popular myths and anxieties over crime have, therefore, some grounding in historical fact. When elderly people tell us that life and property were safer fifty or sixty years ago, it was true, though they exaggerate the absence of crime in the 1930s, and forget to mention that South Wales was notorious for violence and disorder for generations before that. What is interesting is the way in which particular anxieties, held by the elderly and others in our society, can be related to subtle changes in the nature of crime and criminals. Since the Second World War, individuals have had more reason to feel threatened in their homes, as burglars targeted domestic dwellings. Females especially, who half expected assaults within the family, became rightly more aware of the dangers outside, especially from young males. Even so, the neurosis that afflicts some members of the public, especially over the current behaviour of the young, is hardly justified. Some of this feeling, like the mass reporting of crimes and incidents described in chapter 1, is related to changes in modern society, when close neighbourhoods gradually disintegrated and new ones seemed more unfriendly and anonymous.

Historical comparisons help us to keep a sense of proportion about such matters. There are today communities in South Wales where crime is not an everyday occurrence, and where, contrary to popular opinion, no robberies have taken place within living memory. Street life in the towns of South Wales is more civilized now than it was at the beginning of the century, and violence outside the home still affects only a small minority of people. In the longer historical perspective, the level of violence in today's society does not match that of the mid-nineteenth century, though the extent of property offences is now probably without equal in modern times.

We have been assured by Vic Gatrell and other writers that the dangers of crime have been exaggerated. This seems to have been true for much of the twentieth, as for the nineteenth, century. Until recent years, recorded crime was often of a petty nature; it hardly threatened the economy or the stability of governments. There was no large black or criminal market, as existed, for example, in American states. Nor was the threat of a 'criminal class' as serious as was sometimes stated. Most of the people caught by the police for indictable offences in the twentieth century were casual criminals, often of a fairly young age, who took advantage of the increasing opportunities for theft. Until the late 1960s one has the impression that political parties were not too bothered about these or the small group of recidivists, but members of Parliament *were* sensitive to the public outcry over their activities.

What governments, and the police, took seriously were the threats to public order and the state. At the Home Office Winston Churchill, Edward Troup and their successors carefully monitored the clashes between protesting miners and Lionel Lindsay's forces. Central direction was increased, temporary assistance given, and long-term strategies considered. After Lindsay's retirement, more sensitive policing was introduced, but threats to public order were still quickly suppressed. Some critics, then and later, claimed that the real dangers to society actually lay in the political response to the problems of protest, as exemplified by the Criminal Justice Act of 1994. During the century the role of local magistrates in the maintenance of order has been reduced to a minimum, and the machinery has been centralized and co-ordinated in a manner which would have shocked most of its originators. The Special Branch of Wyndham Childs widened its net, much as Lindsay had requested, and forms of riot control and surveillance were created which alarmed civil-rights groups. We know, despite the destruction of evidence, that Special Branch followed the example of Lindsay's inspectors and continued to make regular intelligence reports on 'political extremists'.

Over very recent years, with the ending of the Cold War, much of this has abated. Similarly, serious dangers to public order and the state are now few and far between. The most likely sources of open violence in 1989 were the antics of young men high on weekend alcohol, and the suppressed tension of people living on estates where poverty and disillusionment matched the crime figures. Some of the acts of defiance, burning and vandalism in places like Ely remind one a little of the activities in Merthyr's China district and other 'no-go' urban enclaves of the early nineteenth century, but today's rioters are more of an isolated and temporary phenomenon, and heavily policed.

There are concerns in contemporary society about the costs of dealing with such violence and delinquency, and about the other effects of a high crime rate on governments, local authorities and a demoralized public. Since the 1970s governments have become more aware of the rising costs of the police, criminal justice administration, the prison service, legal aid and victim compensation, and, at the present time, efforts are being made to control and evaluate such expenditure. As in a number of other areas of social responsibility, ministers of the Crown would like to privatize certain of these services and to make local government pick up more of the bill. For their part vulnerable communities in South Wales have grown ever more frustrated by what they regard as political indifference. In neglected housing estates and industrial valleys, angry people in the late 1980s and early 1990s took matters into their own hands and, through direct action, sought dangerously simple answers to complex problems. Thus although crime is often petty in character, a perpetually rising crime rate is, as Edwin Chadwick said in 1839, ultimately damaging to society and to constitutional forms of law and order. The hope must be that, as it has always done in past centuries, the graph of crime will turn downwards. In parts of Wales, as in England, this has begun to happen, but the only sign of it in South Wales was a very slight improvement in 1993.

It is a depressing picture, though not without its ironies. Crime has been, in some respects, a productive activity, helping to oil the wheels of capitalism, change unpopular legislation, and identify problems in modern society and its materialist culture. Amongst the recent suggestions, one tentative and the other long-standing, have been that certain high financial irregularities might be ignored in the wider economic interest, and that drug-taking regulations could be relaxed without adversely affecting social mores. Crime, too, has influenced a variety of other developments, from the design of vehicles to the architecture of streets and houses. It has shown, and cemented, the strength of some communities and the weaknesses of others. A high crime rate encouraged governments, from Harold Wilson's in the 1960s to John Major's in the 1990s, to look again at child care, poverty, and job and leisure provisions in some of these communities. At the present time, the work of multi-agency groups in places like Penrhys, Lansbury Park, Penlan and Ely is one of the few forms of interventionism still given political approval.

The South Wales experience of crime in the twentieth century can be compared with that of English and other Welsh districts. Wales in the nineteenth century had a somewhat lower indictable crime rate than England, and a slightly higher acquittal rate at the assizes and quarter sessions. The former was still true in 1989, though the South Wales police district ranked high in the British tables of crime statistics. This is not surprising; since statistics were published in the early nineteenth century Glamorgan and Monmouthshire had much higher crime rates than the rest of the Principality. We have seen that 'Black Glamorgan' and Cardiff in 1900 were linked with the worst English areas, and the continued concentration of population and industry in this region of Wales has helped to sustain the comparison.

South Wales has always been less rural than the Home Office acknowledged when dealing with the requests of Lionel Lindsay and Robert Lawrence for more police officers and better funding. In fact, the region has undergone huge economic changes during the century, from the explosive growth of the coal industry in 1900 to its almost complete demise ninety years later. Towns such as Aberdare and Maesteg have declined or grown only a little, whilst Aberavon, Porthcawl and other new industrial, business and leisure centres have expanded greatly. The story of delinquency and policing naturally reflects all of this; each community has its own history of crime, which might be very different from that of its neighbour.

The Welsh element in such a history is not easy to disentangle. There was evidence, for a time, of anti-coloured and anti-foreigner hostility in a few places, and exaggerated claims that outsiders made up a large proportion of criminals, habitual drunkards and prostitutes. Moreover, the appointment of Englishmen as policemen at the turn of the century, and the use of police reserves from across the border at the height of industrial unrest, increased the sense of being treated like wayward colonials. It was felt during the inter-war years, and again in the 1980s, that one reason for the crime and protest in Glamorgan's industrial communities was the manner in which distant Whitehall mandarins ignored their unique plight. In a more direct way, the post-war anger of Welsh nationalists and language activists sometimes took a criminal form. Their bombings, arson and criminal damage were a mixture of protest and publicity, and each victory over the 'political police' was a celebration. With these exceptions, however, there was not a permanently and distinctly Welsh character to the delinquency described in this book.

The reasons why people turned to crime were complex, not least because of the varied nature of criminals, but, as we have seen, the explanations offered by contemporaries were fairly general and reflected the conditions prevailing at the time. The economic context has always been important, more so than governments are willing to admit. Poverty and unemployment were the experience, and the excuse, of many delinqents, from the vagrants of 1900 to the 'underclass' of 1989. Although the conection between unemployment and crime was not precise, the rate of property offences in South Wales often peaked in the worst economic years. In fact, socialists in the twentieth century, like their predecessors in the nineteenth, have argued that this situation was almost welcomed by those in power, as it gave greater moral authority and control to the rulers of an unequal society. Rates of violent crimes and drink offences were, by contrast, usually higher when job opportunities and income improved. Nevertheless, there were important exceptions to all of this; many people became criminals for reasons which had little to do with economic considerations.

Similarly, the environmental explanation for crime was only partly sustained by the evidence. There was some irony in this, for in mid-century political and social leaders expected positive social results from town-planning legislation, and the dispersal of the inner-city 'residuum' to clean new housing estates. As David Herbert and other geographers have shown, much depended on how these places were peopled, and the facilities provided for them. There were parts of Ely (Cardiff) and Townhill (Swansea) where problems arose at an early date, just as they did with Gurnos (Merthyr) and Penrhys. However, as we saw in chapter 2, there were streets on these estates, and in other poorer districts of South Wales, where crime and criminals were comparatively rare.

From the 1950s onwards, pyschological studies were made of groups of people who, in the welfare state, still displayed criminal and antisocial tendencies. It was discovered that what distinguished such individuals from their neighbours was not their housing conditions, economic circumstances, social position or intellect, but their willingness, already apparent by the age of ten years, to ignore the moral and social codes. According to the child pyschologists, welfare officers and policemen on the new council estates in the 1960s, this instinct owed much to family background and domestic attitudes. It is, as David Farrington's Cambridge studies have shown, a persuasive analysis of the origins of chronic offenders, but 'problem adults' do not exist in a vacuum, and many other families now find themselves on the wrong side of the law.

The indictable crimes of which these people were convicted changed more during the last third of the century than before. Acts of violence probably changed least, though the court records give a rather different picture. People in recent decades have been prosecuted for less serious forms of violence than in the past; fewer than 5 per cent of today's victims attend hospital. Victims are now hit by fists and feet rather than by knives, axes, pokers and stones, whilst the use of firearms is still a very rare occurrence. Guns were used in 1989 in only thirty-nine recorded cases of violence. Property crimes have changed in character rather more, because of the type of goods which people purchase and the places where they are stolen. Whilst typical offences in 1900 were stealing clothes, fuel and food, the message books and crime registers since the middle of the century have been full of break-ins, autocrime, thefts of bicycles and cash, and criminal damage, and much of this has happened inside or just outside the home.

The changes in the profile of victimless offences reflected the modernization and mechanization of society, and the class priorities of governments, reformers and respectable citizens. At the start of the century attention was focused on the drunk, the homeless, the prostitute, the man who neglected his family, the parent with a child at school, the owner of a dog, and the person who traded on a Sunday. By mid-century these people were causing fewer problems, or they, and their children, were being controlled in other ways. More of the courts' time in recent decades was devoted to other forms of licensing and to enforcing new legislation, such as that controlling the sale of dangerous drugs and, especially, the use of motor vehicles. In one way or another, the motor car has been the greatest influence on the changing character of twentieth-century crime.

It also had an impact on the nature and organization of criminals. The notion of a separate criminal class, moving across the country, was still prominent in Edwardian times, but the inadequacies of that notion were already obvious. There were professional criminals, and indeed families, who made a living out of crime. Amongst them were a few notorious robbers, burglars and shoplifters, as well as groups of shady characters who ran some of the gambling and prostitution dens in Cardiff. During the Second World War, certain businessmen, shopkeepers and drivers were very active in the black-market economy, and since that time a number of prominent people in South Wales have obtained large sums through corruption and fraud. Car-thieving and drug-dealing have become similarly rewarding for the fortunate few. Yet large-scale criminal organizations and conspiracies were much rarer in South Wales than in America and a number of European countries. The researches of Dick Hobbs, Dermot Walsh, Mary McIntosh and others have shown that 'thieving is not organised into large businesses' in modern Britain; most full-time criminals act independently of one another. The distribution of stolen goods, however, has become more sophisticated; where once thieves in South Wales used local pawnbrokers, dealers and shopkeepers as their receivers, now the outlets for high-quality goods, expensive cars and illegal drugs are national and even international in character.

In comparative terms, only a small proportion of people have made a lucrative career out of crime. The majority of those who appeared in court for indictable offences during this century were local people with few, if any, previous convictions, and a short criminal life. Like David Farrington's small élite of chronic offenders, they were chiefly males, aged 15–25 years and working-class. Women in the inter-war years dropped out of crime and heavy drinking in public, and only in recent years has this trend been reversed. The reasons for this have been much debated, but so far there is no agreement, other than a rejection of a simple 'blame-the-feminists' theory.

Many of these females, and their male counterparts, broke the law at an early age, and were most criminally active in their teens. As we saw in chapter 2, the young age of criminals was even more apparent in the 1920s, 1930s and 1940s than it is today. In mid-century juvenile delinquents were, it seems, very prominent in the crime story, and were later rightly blamed for some of the most unpopular offences. Yet the recurring anxiety which makes the terms 'youth' and 'criminal' seem almost synonymous has not always been justified. In recent years, for example, the obsession with the punishment and control of juveniles has reflected their bad public image rather than the criminal threat which they now pose. John Major's remarks in September 1994 about a 'yob culture' reinforce long-held prejudices.

On the whole, those convicted of serious offences were from the same social groups that were regarded as potentially or actually criminal in the nineteenth century. This was, to a degree, predetermined; in the case of some crimes, like assault and fraud, working-class culprits were easier to detect and more likely to be targeted and gaoled than those of the middle and upper class. They also posed fewer problems, at least for the first decades, being more ready to admit charges and less able to afford representatives in court than other social groups. The result is that Cardiff and Swansea prisons were then, as they are today, full of working-class people. When this situation changes, declares Michael Levi, we shall know that the offences of the rich and the middle class are at last being taken seriously. Nevertheless, the trading legislation, the laws controlling the sale and use of drugs, and especially the Traffic and Road Safety Acts, did criminalize many more middle-class people than in the nineteenth century. The 1960s was an important decade in this respect, and, by the end of our period, most families in South Wales had a member who had received a caution, a fixed penalty or a court conviction. This has been a matter of concern to some observers, though society is careful not to apply the term 'criminal' to the majority of victimless offenders.

Until recently the victims of crime have received much less attention than criminals. One of the interesting aspects of our research has been an examination of the material which contemporaries themselves ignored. As we saw in chapter 2, victims have always been from all ranks of society, but an exceptional number in the early decades of this century were people such as shopkeepers, merchants and farmers, as well as industrial and shipping companies. Since that time a much larger section of society has been personally touched by crime. Examinations of crime complaint forms from the 1950s to the 1970s show that, in the most affected urban communities, hardly anyone escaped for long without falling victim to a small or large property offence. Sadly, in recent times, it has often been the most vulnerable and the least protected and insured in our society, including the poor, the unemployed and the young, who have suffered the most. In the most criminal locations, multiple victimization is common. Victim support groups and compensation schemes are a welcome innovation, but they can help only a selection of those robbed and attacked.

It should not surprise us that, in all the circumstances, the public hold strong views about crime and the police. At the start of our period they were still prosecutors in their own cases. If they have been ambivalent about some victimless offences, and about illegal activities such as employment (including white-collar) crime which do not directly affect them, they have nevertheless been keen supporters of most of the laws protecting individuals and their property. The public place robbery, rape and burglary at the top of their list of policing priorities. According to modern crime surveys, they are much less bothered about the policing of unruly behaviour, football hooliganism, prostitution and petty motoring offences, but, as we have seen, people in South Wales were quite prepared to inform the police about these matters.

The police have always relied heavily on the public for information about the more serious offences, and received it from members of all classes and social groups. Some violent and property offences were reported better than others, but the reporting of all of them seems to have improved with the communications revolution after the Second World War. A study of telephone message books confirms that people in many different types of community were willing to contact the police not just about crimes, but about petty acts of spite and vandalism, the street games of children and the parking habits of their neighbours. At the present time between a third and a half of the population speak to the police each year. Certain residents are good watchers, though what they see is often determined by age, class, self-interest and fear. Constables of previous generations made use of such people, and the modern forces now realize, in their public-relations, crime-prevention and victim-counselling work, the scale of their contribution.

The relationship of the public with the police has never been an easy one. In the first half of the century it was probably less good than historians have claimed, at least over large parts of South Wales. For example, the control of industrial protests and the suppression of 'street nuisances' was obtained at a social cost. After the 1950s the relationship again became more difficult because of the rising crime figures. The criminalization of society, via motoring, drink, drug and other offences, reduced respect for the police amongst groups who had traditionally given it. More victims of crime also meant more anger, more demands on the police, and a wish, in some quarters, for greater public control over the machinery of law and order. The growth of a more centralized, motorized and specialized police force has been paralleled by calls for greater accountability, extra foot patrols, and a permanent police presence in 'neglected' areas. There are even signs that, as the crisis has deepened, people have begun to accept the need for alternative forms of policing, and some sacrifice of liberty in the interests of efficiency.

The police were placed under increasing pressure during the century, as communities changed, responsibilities increased, communications improved, and politicians and the public sought a more effective response to the latest crime wave. The latest debates over policing, and the Audit Commission's report of 1990, highlight the confusion which still exists over the original functions of the police and over what society requires of them in terms of services, the maintenance of order and fighting crime. Historically the new police have always given a high priority to order enforcement, and have performed a wide variety of other duties, from dealing with emergencies to rescuing lost children and animals. They have, in South Wales at least, spent only a limited amount of time on crime work, something which society, governments and supporters of privatization have never fully appreciated.

If one takes into account the changes in numbers, duties, conditions of work and work practices, the improvements to the police as a crime-fighting force during the century were less than the Home Office claimed. Moreover, the use of scientific methods, better communications and transport, civilianization, new management structures and specialization have all disappointed their most ardent supporters. Nor did the informal contract between the police and the new Tory government of 1979 prove ultimately rewarding. At present the police are being asked to consider further amalgamation and new efficiency targets, without being convinced that their tasks and problems are fully appreciated in London. The current mood is one of caution, cynicism and demoralization. Threats to cut back on policing targets, appeals for public and political support, and a bitter dialogue over funding with the Home Office are indications of a profession under strain.

The police have, however, been partly responsible for their current difficulties. For generations they used the crime rate as an index of police efficiency and the need for more officers, and they claimed higher standards of prevention and detection than were probably ever achieved, at least outside small and stable communities. As we saw in the last chapter, the official rates of detection in the largest towns were already low at the onset of the Second World War, and became so in the county a quarter of a century later. Since that time, the police forces have been obliged to be more realistic in their predictions, and careful with their promises. Chief constables' reports of the modern age have lost much of the optimism and missionary quality of their predecessors.

There has been, since the disillusionment with unit-beat policing, a greater wariness about the likely outcome of new forms of specialized and intensive policing, and an appreciation of the time needed for crime-prevention and community policing to have a chance of success. Initial results from these experiments in other forces have been mixed. The police can, it seems, affect one type or district of crime by having clear objectives and focusing resources, but there is little confidence now that these alone can make a sustained and comprehensive impact on the general level of criminal behaviour.

In the light of the pressures, it is not too surprising that a few officers cut corners when looking for those who committed very serious crimes. The historian knows that this has always been done, and was occasionally revealed in the early police complaints and punishment books, but in recent years the closer media and political scrutiny, the formal complaints procedure, the Police and Criminal Evidence Act and an independent prosecution service have forced more things into the open. Whilst most officers welcome this, others see themselves as overly restrained and exposed, holding the 'thin, blue line' against an increasingly wicked and cynical world and a succession of smooth-talking Home Secretaries.

The question which the Home Secretary of this, and any age, has to consider is a deceptively simple one: what is the most rewarding response to the problem of crime? To assist him there is the guidance of opinion polls, reports of experts, the recommendations of the police and the studies of academics. The long-term prospects are not encouraging, apart from the projected decline in the proportion of people in the population aged 15–24 years and a possible rise in personal consumption. This book has shown that modern industrial society offers great scope for crime. Much of it takes place in companies, shops and places where the authorites have limited access, and in communities where formal and informal controls are weak. Many of the criminals described in these chapters form part of an 'underclass' which has been marginalized by rapid economic change and looks out onto a bleak future.

This book offers a few historical clues to what might or might not be useful ways forward. Changes to the existing police forces would probably be of limited value, and are likely to be costly. Further amalgamation, internal reorganization, better computers and an increase in numbers do not by themselves promise an answer to the crime problem, nor does the current passion for privatization of police services. Crime prevention, if taken seriously, interpreted widely and financed properly, should help to reduce the rate of property crime. A large proportion of such crime in the nineteenth and twentieth centuries has been of goods which were poorly protected. Better security for homes, motor vehicles, bicycles, radios and the like is a sensible precaution and is already well advanced. For several years the most active councils and communities have adopted, with government money and police advice, carefully co-ordinated safety measures in places known to be 'at risk'. Together with 'targeted policing' of such districts, this can have satisfying results, as the chief constable's report for 1993 indicates.

It is not a complete answer, for criminals continually seek out the weak points, and society as a whole has never adopted a fortress mentality. Compulsory locking of vehicles during the Second World War virtually stopped autocrime overnight, but owners resented being threatened with prosecution for failing to take these and other security precautions. The same balance of interests is raised by CCTV surveillance, possible introduction of identity cards and the activities of the most ambitious watch schemes. It is important for the police and governments to work closely with the public on these and other initiatives, for one of the themes of this book has been the crucial importance of public attitudes and actions in the story of both crime and policing.

So far as punishment is concerned, this book has not considered this in any detail, but a word is in order. The twentieth century has witnessed the victory of the reforming penal policy, with the abolition of the death penalty, the removal of the youngest offenders from the criminal justice system, and decisions to caution, fine, place on probation, and give other non-custodial sentences to more of the remaining offenders. The reforming consensus just about held, as Victor Bailey has shown, down to the 1960s, but the rising crime rate and the anxiety over delinquent juveniles brought it to an end. In the subsequent era of 'penological pessimism', when law and order returned to the top of the political agenda, conflicting voices competed for attention. Some professional associations still insisted that cautioning and progressive forms of probation were both more effective than their alternatives and comparatively inexpensive, but the dominant mood of the 1980s and early 1990s was in favour of 'real punishment', either in the community or in custody. In an increasingly competitive and unequal world, coercion and discipline seem to be the most direct way of dealing with social problems.

At the beginning of our period, there were serious doubts about the value of retributive and deterrent punishment, and the use of imprisonment declined for much of the century. Yet in recent decades custody has recovered some of its old popularity, even for the treatment of fairly young offenders, and gaol sentences have been lengthened. Home Secretary Michael Howard told a Tory Party conference in 1993 that imprisonment can reduce the crime rate by taking sufficient numbers of the 'criminal class' (chronic offenders) out of circulation, an argument which had lain almost dormant for several generations. Howard has also given his backing to other historical throwbacks, like privately run penal institutions and secure units for young children. In truth, the effectiveness of the prison as a reforming or deterring organization has never been established in Wales, but for the last two hundred years it has fulfilled other than these basic functions. It is, to paraphrase Michel Foucault, the detestable solution which we cannot do without.

From time to time people in this century have advanced the idea that, as the roots of crime are well known, so vigorous efforts should be made to change the soil in which they flourish. The socialist press in South Wales in the 1920s and 1930s clamoured for environmental, educational and political initiatives which would 'make men seek better paths'. In the post-war Labour honeymoon, there were similar expectations, across all parties, of the social benefits that would flow from the establishment of the welfare state, urban planning, community renewal and greater family assistance. The long-term disappointment, when crime refused to disappear as anticipated, has been only too obvious. The Labour pamphlet, *Crime – A Challenge to Us All* (1964), was ultimately answered by John Major's comment in 1993 that 'we should understand less and condemn more'. In the intervening years much was tried, from psychological, educational and recreational programmes to giving priority status to districts and estates with exceptional problems. During the 1980s the level of crime, hooliganism and violence prompted 'community revitalization' schemes, with places like Penrhys, Penlan and Ely the beneficiaries.

Whether a successful Labour government under Tony Blair might go further than this with its 'tough on the causes of crime' policy remains to be seen. It seems unlikely. The present climate is hardly conducive to economic and social policies of a radical and expensive nature. The final legacy of a crime problem which has outlasted so many different political and social regimes is a lack of popular sympathy for the criminal and a deep cynicism about any solution.

Note on Graphs

The term 'South Wales' covers the district policed by the South Wales Constabulary, and, prior to 1969, the districts policed by the forces of Glamorgan, Cardiff, Swansea, Merthyr Tydfil and Neath. In graph 2.3 the police districts of Dyfed-Powys, Gwent and North Wales have been similarly extended backwards in time to include the same geographical components as the modern force areas.

The population figures used in the graphs are a problem. The figures given in the chief constables' reports, the reports of inspectors of police and various parliamentary papers, are on occasions clearly inaccurate. They have been modifed in the light of information in the census returns, the Registrar General's annual reports, the annual *Digest of Welsh Statistics* (produced yearly by the Welsh Office), and J. L. Williams (ed.), *Digest of Welsh Historical Statistics*, 2 vols. (Cardiff, 1985). Changes to the police districts, in terms of mergers, extensions and lost territory, have also been accommodated.

The statistics of crime used in the graphs have been taken from the last source mentioned, and from the annual criminal statistics published as command papers, the supplementary statistics and tables produced by the Home Office since 1945, the annual reports of the chief constables of Glamorgan, Cardiff, Swansea, Merthyr Tydfil and Neath, and the *Digest of Welsh Statistics*, published by the Welsh Office since 1954. Further detail on these is supplied in the Bibliography. The Home Office figures have been mostly used, with a number of additions.

This applies to both indictable and non-indictable offences. The

South Wales figures for indictable crimes during the Second World War, which are not available nationally, have been added from local sources. The chief constables' reports have also been used to alter the number of indictable offences recorded in the command papers for 1972–4. The Home Office return of 1974 covers April–December only, and the missing figures have been reinserted. Moreover, for the years 1972–4 thefts of under £5 were not recorded in the national lists of indictable offences. These have also been re-entered in the Wales and South Wales totals, though not in those of the other Welsh police districts.

Other changes have been made by the author for the sake of consistency. For the years from 1934 to 1969, the non-indictable crimes akin to indictable, like taking motor vehicles without consent, have been included in the Welsh totals of indictable crime. So, after 1977, have the cases of criminal damage under £20, which explains over a third of the increase of that year. There were, of course, other technical amendments to the indictable statistics, which were mostly of a minor character, and are discussed in some depth in chapter 2. Graph 2.2, of persons prosecuted for non-indictable offences, is the result of even stronger influences, notably changes in the classification of motoring offences, and the modern policy of dealing with certain of these crimes out of court. The rate for Wales is an amalgam of annual returns in the command papers, the supplementary statistics produced by the Home Office, the chief constables' reports, and the *Digest of Welsh Statistics*, whilst the rate for Glamorgan and South Wales is based on the figures in the chief constables' reports, 1900–89.

Police statistics of numbers and detection rates can be found in the annual reports of chief constables, the reports to the watch and standing joint committees, and the reports of inspectors of constabulary. The actual police numbers have been used, rather than the size of the authorized establishment. This presents certain problems, as the number often fluctuated considerably within a year. Prior to 1947, when Neath merged with the Glamorgan force, the police numbers for the latter were taken from the mid-summer figures in the chief constables' reports. Thereafter, for the Glamorgan, Cardiff, Swansea, Merthyr Tydfil, Neath and South Wales forces, the police numbers are conveniently provided by the *Digest of Welsh Statistics*. The rate of indictable offences recorded in

Glamorgan, which is included with that of police numbers in graph 4.1, is based on the criminal statistics given in the parliamentary papers for 1900–38, and in the chief constables' reports 1939–68.

Finally, the economic statistics in graphs 2.4 and 2.5 are taken from J. L. Williams (ed.), *Digest of Welsh Historical Statistics*, 2 vols. (1985), B. R. Mitchell (ed.), *British Historical Statistics* (Cambridge, 1980 edition), and *Economic Trends* for the figures of personal consumption.

Select Bibliography

The following is a selection of the sources examined in the preparation of this book. Not all have catalogue numbers. Some of the material, like that from Porth and Tonyrefail stations, actually arrived as the manuscript was being prepared, and more has yet to be properly catalogued and made available for researchers. Jeremy Glenn, curator of the Police Museum at Bridgend, and Jayne Pucknell of the Glamorgan Record Office in Cardiff are the persons who should be contacted for the latest acquisitions. In the interests of brevity, I have included in the list of publications only books, chapters of books, and reports, together with a few exceptional articles and theses on South Wales.

Primary Sources

A. Official papers published by central government

1. Command papers
Annual criminal, judicial, police and prison statistics for England and
   Wales, 1900–89
Annual statistics relating to drunkenness and motoring offences, 1900–89
Reports of inspectors of constabulary, 1900–89
Reports of the commissioners and inspectors of prisons, and of the work
   of the prison service, 1900–89.

2. Supplementary statistics, produced by the Home Office
Annual statistics of indictable crime, and proceedings over non-indictable
   crime, per police district, 1934–79

3. Supplementary tables, published by the Stationery Office
Annual statistics of indictable crime, and proceedings over non–indictable
   crime, per police district, 1980–9

4. *Reports, etc.*

Colliery strike disturbances in South Wales: correspondence and report, 1911

Report of the (Desborough) Committee on the police service, 1919–20

Report of the Royal Commission on police powers and procedures, 1928–9

Report of the Royal Commission on licensing, 1929–31

Report of the police post-war committee, 1946

Report of the (Oaksey) committee on police conditions of service, 1948–9

Report of the Royal Commission on the police, 1960–2

Report of an inquiry in respect of the objections to the proposed amalgamation in South Wales, 1968

Report of the Select Committee on violence in marriage, 1975

Report of the Royal Commission on criminal procedure, 1981

B. *Police Museum Archive, Bridgend*

Amalgamation proposals, and working party reports, 1969

Beat policing: various Glamorgan and Swansea directories and maps, 1967–8

Blue Print, 1975–89

Cardiff city police personnel:
    Cardiff police register, 1856–95 (compiled by Jeremy Glenn and Sharon Davies)
    Selected details taken from service records of police officers who joined in the 1930s (compiled by Jeremy Glenn)

Charge books, Cardiff Docks, 1951–2

Charge books, Cardiff Central, 1950–3, 1956–7

Chief constable's circulars, Glamorgan, 1941–68

Chief constable's reports for Cardiff, 1913, 1954, 1960, 1963, 1964–8

Chief constable's quarterly, and then annual, reports for Glamorgan, 1900–68, and for South Wales, 1969–89

Chief constable's report for Neath, 1944

Chief constable's reports for Swansea, 1933, 1937–68 (with gaps)

Complaint or discipline books:
    Cardiff, A division, 1923–61, 1962–9
    Cardiff, C division, 1923–69
    Cardiff, D division, 1926–64
    Cardiff, all divisions, 1963–9

Crime complaint books:
    Bishopston, 1967–8
    Cardiff Central, 1963
    Cardiff Docks, 1961
    St Nicholas, 1940–5
    Tonyrefail, 1973

Crime registers, Merthyr Tydfil, 1924–46

Custody records, Porth station, 1988

Establishment reviews of the South Wales police force, 1972, 1979 and 1986

General orders and circulars, 1911–68 (with gaps)

Glamorgan crime information files: stolen bicycles, jewellery and other items, 1961–2, and wanted and missing persons, etc., 1964 and 1967

Glamorgan Police Magazine, 1954–72, continued as the *South Wales Police Magazine*

Home Office circulars, 1939–93

Joint working party on rank structure, 1970. Various job descriptions.

Morning summaries, taken from IRIS, 1987–93

Notes on the Glamorgan Constabulary, compiled by J. Gill and E. R. Baker

Photographs and particulars of persons on the Trealaw beat, from 1938 to uncertain date

Police notebooks and diaries. Those examined included:

Notebook of W. Roberts, Trealaw, 1913

Notebooks of C. C. Hodge, Cardiff, 1921–37

Notebooks of Douglas Jones, Port Talbot, 1946 and 1952

Detective officer's diary, Neath, 1947

Detective officer's diary, Skewen, 1965–8

Notebooks of A. Bowen, 1962–85

Press release files, 1979–80

Pro-file, a compilation of police press cuttings, for 1982–7, 1992 and 1993

Report on the civilianization of the scenes-of-crime squad and driving school, 1974

Report on the review of the overall size of the force CID, 1973

Salaries and pay book, Glamorgan Police, 1841–1972

Section and out-station message books and diaries, Porth station, 1988 and 1990

Skewen police station records of weekly intelligence reports on Communists, etc., 1925–43

Standing joint committee minutes for Glamorgan, 1900–68

Standing Orders of the Glamorgan and South Wales forces, 1967 and 1977–8

Station journals, occurrence and duty books. Those examined included:

Bishopston, 1971–4

Cardiff Central – station uncertain, 1968–9, 1970–2

Hopkinstown and Great Western Collieries, 1911–23

Nantgarw, 1959–64

Peterston-super-Ely, 1935–7 and 1964–7

Pontypridd, 1969

St Nicholas, 1923–4, 1924–6, 1937–8, 1938 and 1939–41

Sully, 1940–3, 1958–60 and 1967–9

Tongwynlais, 1960–2

Summary of undetected crime, Neath, 1944

Weekly orders, South Wales Constabulary, 1969–93

Western Criminal Record Office, daily information files, 1967

Work outstanding books, Tongwynlais, 1983–90

C. Glamorgan Record Office, Cardiff

1. Glamorgan records

Unlisted. Reports of the chief constable, and standing joint committee minutes, Glamorgan, 1900–63

D/DCon/3/1, and 10–13. Registers of Glamorgan police officers

D/DCon/52. Strike duty journal, Llanharan, 1926

D/DCon/74–81. Diaries of Lionel Lindsay, 1889–1941 (with gaps)

D/DCon/82. Letters to Lionel Lindsay, 1920–32

D/DCon/90. Newspaper cuttings, Aberdare and Mountain Ash, 1911–13

D/DCon/96/1. Register of convicts under licence and supervision, 1877–1938

D/DCon/101. Station journal, Bridgend, 1930–1

D/DCon/119. Register of prisoners, Cwmgwrach, 1905–42

D/DCon/147. Register of prisoners, Tynewydd, 1885–1935

D/DCon/151. Station journal, Pontardawe, 1909–11

D/DCon/162. Station journal, Treharris, 1908–9

D/DCon/163. Information book, Treharris, 1908–11

D/DCon/165. Prisoners' book, Treharris, 1900–8

D/DCon/193/1–23. Notebooks of J. Gill, Tonpentre division, 1913–15

D/DCon/210–19. Scrapbooks of cuttings on policing, 1910–39

D/DCon/220/1–4. Scrapbooks of E. R. Baker. Some of this has been returned to the Police Museum, Bridgend.

D/DCon/282/2/1–2. Minutes of a conference of superintendents, Glamorgan, 1937–44 and 1959

D/DCon/282/3. Minutes of the Police Federation, Glamorgan branch board, 1961–9

D/DCon/283/4/1–9. Unit-beat policing records, Glamorgan, 1967–9

D/DCon/283/7. Telephone message book, Glamorgan Police, 1937–8

D/DCon/285/1/1–2. Personnel records, 1955–70

D/DCon/288/1/1–48. Warrants for the arrest of criminals, 1900–30

D/DCon/290/1–3. Newspaper cuttings, Glamorgan Police, 1939–69

D/DCon/291/5. Home Office instructions for the preparation of statistics relating to crime, 1964–8

D/DCon/291/10. Calendars of prisoners tried at the Assizes and Quarter Sessions, Glamorgan, Cardiff, Swansea and Merthyr Tydfil, 1922–5

D/DCon/C292/2/1–2. Telephone message books, Abercwmboi, 1945–7
D/DCon/292/3/1. Occurrence book, Abercynon, 1966–7
D/DCon/292/7/1. Occurrence book, Miskin, 1937–42
D/DCon/293/1/1. Divisional discipline book, Pontypridd, 1921–65
D/DCon/293/3/17–18. Record of convictions, Pontyclun, 1923–46
D/DCon/295/3/14. Occurrence Book, Cwmavon, 1945–6
D/DCon/295/7/13. Occurrence book, Pyle, 1966–8
D/DCon/295/8/1. Occurrence book, Sandfields, 1954–5
D/DCon/295/9/30–1. Previous convictions, Taibach, 1922–51
D/DCon/298/1/1. Return of prisoners for trial, Tonpentre, 1912–14.
D/DCon/299/3/20–2. Telephone message books, Llangyfelach, 1963–70
D/DCon/299/5/4. Crime complaint forms, Llanmorlais, 1962–6
D/DCon/299/6/1. Police notebook, Mumbles, 1911–17
D/DCon/299/10/1. Occurrence book, Reynoldston, 1937

2. Cardiff records
D/DCon/C1/1/1, 2, 3, 4, 5, 6, 7, 8, 10, 11. Reports of chief constable,
  Cardiff, 1900–6, 1906–10, 1910–13, 1913–16, 1917–18, 1918–21,
  1926–30, 1930–4, 1937–43 and 1944–9
D/DCon/C1/2/1–15. Reports of the chief constable, 1955–68
D/DCon/C3/1/1. Crime register, Cardiff, 1933–4
D/DCon/C3/2/1. Fingerprint and photographic register, 1904–8
D/DCon/C3/5/2. Habitual criminals register, England and Wales, 1925
D/DCon/C5/14, 17, 18, 20, 23, 29, 32, 36, 44, 48, 50, 55, 59, 66, 69, 72,
  74, 77, 78, 83, 84, 85, 86. Newspaper cuttings, Cardiff Police,
  1900–62. Other volumes were also quickly examined.
D/DCon/C7/1/1–2. Reports of the chief constable to the licensing
  justices, Cardiff, 1914–64
D/DCon/C8/4/2. Police notebook, Cardiff, 1934–5
D/DCon/C9/4/1–2. Divisional discipline books, Cardiff A, B, and C
  divisions, 1912–35
D/DCon/C9/5. Divisional discipline book, Cardiff B division, 1923–69

3. Merthyr Tydfil records
D/DCon/MT1/1–3. Reports of the chief constable, Merthyr Tydfil,
  1908–10, 1911–13 and 1939–42
D/DCon/MT2/1–23. Reports of the chief constable, Merthyr Tydfil,
  1946–68
D/DCon/MT3/1–18. Reports of the chief constable to the licensing
  committee, 1949, 1952–68
D/DCon/MT5/1/1, and 10. Crime register, Merthyr Tydfil, 1951–5 and
  1968–9
D/DCon/MT5/4. Notes relating to crime in the area, Merthyr Tydfil,
  1961–2

4. Neath records
D/DCon/143/1–2. Reports of the chief constable, Neath, 1905–18
D/DCon/N/1. Reports of the watch committee, Neath, 1923–5
D/DCon/N2. Scrapbook of cuttings, compiled by J. Davies, 1896–1919

5. Swansea records
D/DCon/S2/2/1. Reports of the chief constable, 1920–36
D/DCon/S2/3/2–4. Reports of the chief constable, 1908–15, 1921–7, and 1929
D/DCon/S2/5. Minutes of meetings of Swansea Police Force members, 1908–25
D/DCon/S2/6/1–4. Minutes of branch boards of the Police Federation, 1928–69
D/DCon/S7/1. Newspaper cuttings, Swansea, 1939–50

6. Newspapers
The following, together with other newspapers, have, since my first visits, been moved from the Glamorgan Record Office to other repositories, chiefly to the National Library of Wales, and the Central Library, Cardiff.
Cardiff Times, 1926, 1934–40
Glamorgan Gazette, 1900–68, 1980–9
Merthyr Express, 1964–5, 1980–9

D. Cardiff City Council

Police records, chiefly correspondence, and some prosecution briefs. The full catalogue of these has been compiled by Jeremy Glenn and the late Sharon Davies, of the Police Museum, Bridgend.

E. Central Library, Cardiff

Minutes of the City Council and Watch Committee, 1900–68
Reports of the chief constable, Cardiff, 1914–18 (with gaps)
Cardiff Times, 1941–51
South Wales Daily News, 1909–17
South Wales Echo, 1901, 1938 and 1958
South Wales News, 1921, 1926
Western Mail, 1931–89

F. Central Library, Swansea

Reports of the chief constable, Swansea, 1946–68

South Wales Daily Post, 1901–32, continued as the *South Wales Evening Post*, 1932–89

G. City Record Office, Swansea

Reports of the chief constable, Swansea, 1912, 1917, 1923, 1924, 1930, 1931 and 1933
Council minutes, 1950–68
Watch Committee minutes, 1913–49

Secondary Sources

A. Home Office research publications

1. British crime surveys published by HMSO
M. Hough and P. Mayhew, *The British Crime Survey of 1982: The First Report* (1983)
——, *Taking Account of Crime: Key Findings from the 1984 British Crime Survey* (1985)
P. Mayhew, D. Elliot and L. Dowds, *The 1988 British Crime Survey* (1989)
P. Mayhew, N. A. Haung and C. Mirrlees-Black, *The 1992 British Crime Survey* (1993)

2. Other books and booklets, published mainly by HMSO in London
S. R. Brody, *The Effectiveness of Sentencing* (1976)
——, *Screen Violence and Film Censorship* (1977)
D. Brown, *The Police Complaints Procedure: A Survey of Complainants' Views* (1987)
——, *Investigating Burglary: The Effect of PACE* (1991)
J. Burrows and R. Tarling, *Clearing up Crime* (1982)
R. V. Clarke and M. Hough, *Crime and Police Effectiveness* (1984)
J. A. Ditchfield, *Police Cautioning in England and Wales* (1977)
P. Ekblom and K. Heal, *The Police Response to Calls from the Public* (1982)
S. Field, *Trends in Crime and their Interpretation* (1990)
E. Gibson, *Homicide in England and Wales, 1967–1971* (1975)
M. R. Gottfredson, *Victims of Crime: The Dimension of Risk* (1984)
R. Harris, *Welfare, Power and Juvenile Justice* (1987)
W. H. Hammond, *Persistent Criminals* (1963)
K. Heal, R. Tarling and J. Burrows (eds.), *Policing Today* (1985)
T. Hope and M. Shaw (eds.), *Communities and Crime Reduction* (1988)
M. Hough, *Uniformed Police Work and Management Technology* (1980)
M. Maxfield, *Fear of Crime in England and Wales* (1984)

D. Moxon, *Sentencing Practice in the Crown Courts* (1988)

K. Pease, *Community Service Orders* (1975)

G. J. O. Phillpotts and L. B. Lancucki, *Previous Convictions, Sentence and Re-conviction* (1979)

D. Riley and M. Shaw, *Parental Supervision and Juvenile Delinquency* (1985)

L. J. F. Smith, *Concerns about Rape* (1989)

——, *Domestic Violence* (1989)

P. Southgate (ed.), *New Directions in Police Training* (1988)

P. Southgate and P. Ekblom, *Police–Public Encounters* (1986)

R. Tarling, *Sentencing Practice in Magistrates' Courts* (1979)

——, *Unemployment and Crime*, Research Bulletin (1982)

M. Tuck, *Drinking and Disorder: A Study of Non-Metropolitan Violence* (1989)

R. Walmsley, *Personal Violence* (1986)

B. Welsh Office publications

Digest of Welsh Statistics, nos. 1–35 (Cardiff, 1954–89)

J. L. Williams (ed.), *Digest of Welsh Historical Statistics*, 2 vols. (Cardiff, 1985)

Welsh Social Trends, vols. 1–7 (Cardiff, 1977–91)

C. General publications

J. Albanese, *Organised Crime in America* (Cincinnati, 2nd edition, 1989)

A. Albrow, 'The fears of the elderly in Cardiff in 1982', SRU Working Paper, 12 (1982)

J. Alderson, *Policing Freedom* (Plymouth, 1979)

——, *Law and Disorder* (London, 1984)

H. E. Alexander and G. E. Caiden (eds.), *The Politics and Economics of Organized Crime* (Aldershot, 1985)

R. W. Anderson, *The Economics of Crime* (London, 1976)

C. Andrew, *Secret Service: The Making of the British Intelligence Community* (London, 1985)

D. Archer and R. Gartner, *Violence and Crime in Cross-National Perspective* (London, 1984)

Audit Commission, *Effective Policing: Performance Review in Police Forces* (London, 1990)

V. Bailey, *Delinquency and Citizenship: Reclaiming the Young Offender, 1914–48* (Oxford, 1987)

J. Baldwin and A. E. Bottoms, *The Urban Criminal: A Study of Sheffield* (London, 1976)

M. Banton, *The Police in the Community* (London, 1964)

H. Becker, *Outsiders* (NewYork, 1963)

G. K. Behlmer, *Child Abuse and Moral Reform in England, 1870–1908* (Stanford, Calif., 1982)

T. Bennett, *Evaluating Neighbourhood Watch* (Aldershot,1990)

J. Benyon (ed.), *Scarman and After* (Oxford, 1984)

J. Benyon and J. Solomos (eds.), *The Roots of Urban Unrest* (Oxford, 1987)

V. T. Bevan and K. Lidstone, *The Investigation of Crime: A Guide to Police Powers* (London, 1991)

H. Blagg and D. Smith, *Crime, Penal Policy and Social Work* (London, 1989)

D. Bochel, *Probation and After-Care: Its Development in England and Wales* (Edinburgh, 1976)

V. Bogdanor and R. Skidelsky (eds.), *The Age of Affluence, 1951–1964* (London, 1970)

A. K. Bottomley, *Decisions in the Penal Process* (Oxford,1973)

A. K. Bottomley and C. Coleman, *Understanding Crime Rates* (London, 1981)

A. K. Bottomley and K. Pearse, *Crime and Punishment: Interpreting the Data* (Milton Keynes, 1986)

A. Bourlet, *Police Intervention in Marital Violence* (MiltonKeynes, 1990)

S. Box, *Power, Crime and Mystification* (London, 1983)

——, *Recession, Crime and Punishment* (London, 1987)

P. Boyer, *Urban Masses and Moral Order in America, 1820–1920* (Cambridge, Mass., 1978)

D. Bradley, N. Walker and R. Wilkie, *Managing the Police* (Hemel Hempstead, 1986)

M. H. Brenner, 'Effects of the economy on criminal behaviour and the administration of criminal justice in the United States, Canada, England and Wales and Scotland', *Economic Crises and Crime* (Publication no.15 of the United Nations Social Defence Research Institute, May 1976)

D. T. Brett, *The Police of England and Wales: 1829–1979* (Bramshill, 3rd edition, 1979).

I. Bridgeman and C. Emsley, *A Guide to the Archives of the Police Forces of England and Wales* (Cambridge, 1989)

M. Brogden, *The Police: Autonomy and Consent* (London, 1982)

——, *On the Mersey Beat: Policing Liverpool between the Wars* (Oxford, 1991)

M. Brogden, T. Jefferson and S. Walklate, *Introducing Policework* (London, 1988)

A. Brown, *Watching the Detectives* (London, 1988)

S. Brown, *Magistrates at Work: Sentencing and Social Structure* (Milton Keynes, 1991)

D. Brushett, 'Difficult, deviant and delinquent: an appraisal of the effectiveness of intervention in the lives of deviant adolescents in South Glamorgan' (unpublished University of Wales thesis, 1989)

T. Bunyan, *The Political Police in Britain* (London, 1977)

M. Cain, *Society and the Policeman's Role* (London, 1963)

A. Campbell, *Girl Delinquents* (Oxford, 1981)

R. Carr-Hill and N. Stern, *Crime, the Police and Criminal Statistics* (London, 1979)

J. Carrier, *The Campaign for the Employment of Women as Police Officers* (Aldershot,1988)

S. Chibnall, *Law-and-Order News: An Analysis of Crime Reporting in the British Press* (London, 1977)

S. Christopher and L. Noaks, *Assaults upon the Police: The Assailants' Perspective* (Cardiff, 1989)

A. Clarke, *Television Police Series and Law and Order* (Milton Keynes, 1982)

R. Clarke and M. Hough, *The Effectiveness of Policing* (Farnborough, 1980)

R. L. Clutterbuck, *Britain in Agony: The Growth of Political Violence* (London, 1978)

S. Cohen, *Folk Devils and Moral Panics* (Oxford, 1972)

——, *Visions of Social Control: Crime, Punishment and Classification* (Cambridge, 1985)

S. Cohen and A. Scull (eds.), *Social Control and the State* (Oxford, 1983)

J. J. Collins (ed.), *Drinking and Crime: Perspectives on the Relationship between Alcohol Consumption and Criminal Behaviour* (London, 1982)

D. Cowell, T. Jones and J. Young, *Policing the Riots* (London, 1982)

G. Crandon, *The Police and the Media: Information Management and the Construction of Crime News* (Bradford, 1992)

A. Crawford, T. Jones, T. Woodhouse and J. Young, *The Second Islington Crime Survey* (London, 1990)

I. Crow *et al.*, *Unemployment, Crime and Offenders* (London, 1989)

R. Dahrendorf, *Law and Order* (London, 1985)

R. N. Davidson, *Crime and the Environment* (London, 1981)

J. Davies *et al.*, *Political Policing in Wales* (Cardiff, 1984)

R. E. and R. P. Dobash, *Violence against Wives* (Shepton Mallet, 1980)

——, *Women, Violence and Social Change* (London, 1992)

D. Downes (ed.), *Crime and the City* (London, 1989)

D. Downes and P. Rock, *Understanding Deviance* (Oxford, 1992)

S. M. Edwards, *Policing 'Domestic' Violence* (London, 1989)

D. Elliott, *Gender, Delinquency and Society* (Aldershot, 1988)

C. Emsley, *Crime and Society in England, 1750–1900* (London, 1987)

——, *The English Police: A Political and Social History* (London, 1991).

——, 'Mother, what did policemen do when there weren't any motors?', *Historical Journal*, 36, no.2 (1993)

D. Englander, 'Police and public order in Britain, 1914–1918', in C. Emsley and B. Weinberger (eds.), *Policing Western Europe: Politics, Professionalization and Public Order* (London, 1991)

N. Evans, 'Regulating the reserve army: Arabs, Blacks and the local state in Cardiff, 1919–1945', in *Immigrants and Minorities*, 3, no.2 (July 1985)

——, 'The South Wales race riots of 1919', in *Llafur*, 3, no.1 (Spring 1980)

D. P. Farrington and J. Gunn (eds.), *Reactions to Crime: The Public, the Police, the Courts and the Prisons* (Chichester, 1985)

N. Fielding, *The Police and Social Conflict* (London, 1991)

B. Fine and R. Millar (eds.), *Policing the Miners' Strike* (London, 1985)

R. Fine *et al.* (eds.), *Capitalism and the Rule of Law* (London, 1979)

J. Foster, *Villains, Crime and Community in the Inner City* (London, 1990)

M. Foucault, *Discipline and Punish* (Harmondsworth, 1977)

D. Francis, *Report on a Survey of Assaults on Officers of the South Wales Constabulary in 1986.* Internal police report.

H. Francis and D. Smith, *The Fed* (London, 1980).

M. Freeman, *The Police and the Criminal Evidence Act 1984* (London, 1985)

V. A. C. Gatrell, 'Crime, authority and the policeman-state', in F. M. L. Thompson (ed.), *The Cambridge Social History of Britain, 1750–1950*, vol. 3 (Cambridge, 1990)

R. Geary, *Policing Industrial Disputes, 1893–1985* (London, 1985)

R. Graef, *Talking Blues: The Police in their own Words* (London, 1989)

T. R. Gurr *et al.*, *The Politics of Crime and Conflict* (London, 1977)

S. Hall, *Drifting into a Law and Order Society* (London, 1979)

S. Hall and T. Jefferson, *Resistance through Rituals: Youth Subculture in Post-War Britain* (London, 1976)

S. Hall *et al.*, *Policing the Crisis: Mugging, the State, and Law and Order* (London, 1978)

J. Hanmer, J. Radford and E. A. Starkey (eds.), *Women, Policing and Male Violence* (London, 1989)

J. Hargreaves (ed.), *Sport, Culture and Ideology* (London, 1982)

F. Heidensohn, *Women and Crime* (London, 1985)

——, *Crime and Society* (London, 1989)

D. T. Herbert, *Social Problems and the City: A Geographical View.* Inaugural lecture (Swansea, 1981)

——, *The Geography of Urban Crime* (London, 1982)

D. T. Herbert and D. J. Evans, *Urban Environment and Juvenile Delinquency: A Study of Cardiff*, a report prepared for the Home Office Research Unit (Swansea, 1973)

—— (eds.), *The Geography of Crime* (London, 1989)

D. T. Herbert and D. M. Smith (eds.), *Social Problems and the City* (Oxford, 1989)

S. Holdaway (ed.), *The British Police* (London, 1979)

S. Holdaway, *Inside the British Police: A Force at Work* (Oxford, 1983)

T. Holden *et al.*, *Crime Reduction and Community Safety in Swansea* (Swindon, 1994)

R. R. Hopkin, 'The Llanelli Riots, 1911', *Welsh History Review*, 11, no.4 (1983)

C. Horton and D. Smith, *Evaluating Police Work* (London, 1988)

C. Hughes, 'The Tredegar Riots of 1911', *Welsh History Review*, 11, no.4 (1983)

———, *Lime, Lemon and Sarsaparilla: The Italian Community in South Wales, 1881–1945* (Bridgend, 1991)

S. Humphries, *Hooligans or Rebels? An Oral History of Working-Class Youth, 1889–1937* (Oxford, 1981)

———, 'Steal to survive: the social crime of working-class children, 1890–1940', *Oral History*, IX, 1 (1981)

W. W. Hurt, *To Guard My People: An Account of the Origin and History of the Swansea Police* (Swansea, 1957)

K. Jeffery and P. Hennessey, *States of Emergency: British Government and Strike-Breaking since 1919* (London, 1983)

L. Johnston, *The Rebirth of Private Policing* (London, 1992)

D. J. V. Jones, *Crime in Nineteenth-Century Wales* (Cardiff, 1992)

———, ' "Where did it all go wrong?": Crime in Swansea, 1938–1968', *Welsh History Review*, 15, no.2 (December 1990)

I. G. Jones and G. Williams (eds.), *Social Policy, Crime and Punishment: Essays in Memory of Jane Morgan* (Cardiff, 1994)

M. F. Jones *et al.*, *The Penlan Project: A Report* (Swansea, 1987)

S. Jones, *Policewomen and Equality: Formal Policy and Informal Practice?* (London, 1986)

T. Jones, B. McLean and J. Young, *The Islington Crime Survey* (Aldershot, 1986)

M. Kettle and L. Hodges, *Uprising! The Police, the People, and the Riots in Britain's Cities* (London, 1982)

R. Kinsey, *Merseyside Crime Survey: First Report* (Liverpool, 1984)

——— (presenter), *Survey of Merseyside Police Officers: First Report* (Liverpool, 1985)

R. Kinsey, J. Lea and J. Young, *Losing the Fight against Crime* (Oxford, 1986)

L. A. Knafla (ed.), *Crime, Police and the Courts in British History* (London, 1990)

J. Lambert, *Crime, Police and Race Relations* (Oxford, 1970)

———, *Police Powers and Accountability* (London, 1985)

M. Levi, *Regulating Fraud: White-Collar Crime and the Criminal Process* (London, 1987)

J. Littlejohns, *Black Glamorgan* (Swansea, 1901)

J. Lock, *The British Policewoman* (London, 1979)

M. Maguire, R. Morgan and R. Reiner (eds.), *The Oxford Handbook of Criminology* (Oxford, 1994)

S. Mainwaring-White, *The Policing Revolution: Police Technology, Democracy and Liberty in Britain* (Brighton, 1983)

H. Mannheim, *Social Aspects of Crime in England between the Wars* (London, 1940)

G. Mars, *Cheats at Work* (London, 1982)

J. M. Martin (ed.), *Violence and the Family* (London, 1979)

J. P. Martin, *Offenders as Employees* (London, 1962)

J. P. Martin and G. Wilson, *The Police: A Study in Manpower: The Evolution of the Service in England and Wales, 1829–1965* (London, 1969)

R. Matthews and J. Young (eds.), *Confronting Crime* (London, 1986)

R. Mawby, *Policing the City* (Farnborough, 1979)

R. I. Mawby and M. L. Gill, *Crime Victims: Needs, Services, and the Voluntary Sector* (London, 1987)

J. B. Mays, *Growing up in the City* (Liverpool, 1954)

S. McCabe, P. Wallington, J. Alderson, L. Gostin and C. Mason, *The Police, Public Order and Civil Liberties* (London, 1988)

F. H. McClintock, *Crimes of Violence* (London, 1961)

F. H. McClintock and N. H. Avison, *Crime in England and Wales* (London, 1968)

M. McConville and J. Baldwin, *Courts, Prosecution and Conviction* (Oxford, 1981)

M. McIntosh, *The Organisation of Crime* (London, 1975)

M. McMurray and C. R. Hollin, *Young Offenders and Alcohol-Related Crime* (Chichester, 1993)

P. J. Milton, 'The Cardiff race riots of June 1919' (unpublished dissertation, Polytechnic of Wales, 1988).

B. R. Mitchell (ed.), *British Historical Statistics* (Cambridge, 1980 edition)

A. Mòr O'Brien, 'Churchill and the Tonypandy Riots', *Welsh History Review*, 17, no.1 (June 1994)

J. Morgan, *Conflict and Order: The Police and Labour Disputes in England and Wales, 1900–1939* (Oxford, 1987)

J. Morgan and L. Zedner, *Child Victims* (Oxford, 1992)

R. Morgan (ed.), *Policing, Organised Crime, and Crime Prevention* (Bristol, 1990)

R. Morgan and D. J. Smith (eds.), *Coming to Terms with Policing* (London, 1989)

T. Morris, *Crime and Criminal Justice since 1945* (Oxford, 1989)

J. Muncie, *'The Trouble with Kids Today': Youth and Crime in Post-war Britain* (London, 1984)

C. Murray, *The Emerging British Underclass* (London, 1990)

G. F. Newman, *Operation Bad Apple* (London, 1982)

L. Noaks, 'The perception and fear of crime and its implications for residents of the Bettws community' (unpublished M.Sc. (Econ.) thesis, University of Wales, Cardiff, 1988)

J. Osmond, *Police Conspiracy?* (Talybont, 1984)

G. Pearson, *Hooligan: A History of Respectable Fears* (London, 1983)

M. S. Pike, *The Principles of Policing* (London, 1985)

J. Pitts, *The Politics of Juvenile Crime* (London, 1988)

B. Porter, *Origins of the Vigilant State* (London, 1987)

P. Pyke, 'Unemployment and crime' (unpublished M.Sc. (Econ.) thesis, University of Wales, Cardiff, 1988)

L. Radzinowicz, *Ideology and Crime* (London, 1966)

L. Radzinowicz and J. King, *The Growth of Crime* (London, 1977)

P. Raynor, *Social Work, Justice and Control* (Oxford, 1985)

——, *Probation as an Alternative to Custody: A Case Study* (Aldershot, 1987)

P. and J. Raynor, *The Work of the Cadle Intermediate Treatment Centre 1984–1985* (Swansea, 1986)

R. Reiner, *The Blue Coated Worker: A Sociological Study of Police Unionism* (Cambridge, 1978)

——, *Chief Constables: Bobbies, Bosses or Bureaucrats?* (Oxford, 1991)

——, *The Politics of the Police* (London, 2nd edition, 1992)

R. Reiner and M. Cross (eds.), *Beyond Law and Order: Criminal Policy and Politics in the 1990s* (London, 1991)

C. Reith, *The Police Idea* (Oxford, 1938)

——, *Police Principles and the Problem of War* (Oxford, 1940)

——, *The British Police and the Democratic Ideal* (Oxford, 1943)

G. Robb, *White-Collar Crime in Modern England: Financial Fraud and Business Morality 1845–1929* (Cambridge, 1992)

P. Rock, *Helping Victims of Crime* (Oxford, 1990)

M. Rutter, *Juvenile Delinquency: Trends and Perspectives* (Harmondsworth, 1983)

P. Scraton, *The State of the Police* (London, 1985)

—— (ed.), *Law, Order and the Authoritarian State* (Milton Keynes, 1987)

J. Shapland and J. Vagg, *Policing by the Public* (London, 1988)

C. Smart, *Women, Crime and Criminology* (London, 1976)

D. Smith, *Aneurin Bevan and the World of South Wales* (Cardiff, 1993)

D. J. Smith and J. Gray, *Police and People in London* (Aldershot, 1985)

E. Smithies, *Crime in Wartime: A Social History of Crime in World War II* (London, 1982)

——, *The Black Economy in England since 1914* (Dublin, 1984)

F. Snyder and D. Hay (eds.), *Labour, Law and Crime: An Historical Perspective* (London, 1987)

South Wales Miners' Video Project, *Whose Law?* (1985)

R. F. Sparks, H. Glenn and D. J. Dodds, *Surveying Victims* (London, 1977)

P. J. Stead, *The Police of Britain* (New York, 1985)

M. Stephens, *Policing: The Critical Issues* (London, 1988)

E. H. Sutherland, *White Collar Crime* (New York, 1961), and uncut version (London, 1983)

C. Townshend, *Britain's Civil Wars: Counterinsurgency in the Twentieth Century* (London, 1986)

——, *Making the Peace: Public Order and Public Security in Modern Britain* (Oxford, 1993)

A. A. Vass, *Alternatives to Prison: Punishment, Custody and the Community* (London, 1990)

R. Vogler, *Reading the Riot Act: The Magistracy, the Police and the Army in Civil Disorder* (Buckingham, 1991)

P. A. J. Waddington, *The Strong Arm of the Law* (Oxford, 1990)

N. Walker, *Crime and Punishment in Britain* (Edinburgh, 1965)

D. Walsh, *Heavy Business: Commercial Burglary and Robbery* (London, 1986)

D. P. Walsh, *Shoplifting: Controlling a Major Crime* (London, 1978)

M. Weatheritt (ed.), *Police Research: Some Future Prospects* (Aldershot, 1989)

B. Weinberger, 'Police perceptions of labour in the inter-war period', in F. Snyder and D. Hay (eds.), *Law, Labour and Crime in Historical Perspective* (London, 1987)

——, *Keeping the Peace? Policing Strikes in Britain, 1906–1926* (Oxford, 1990)

B. Weinberger and H. Reinke, 'A diminishing function? A comparative historical account of policing in the city', *Policing and Society*, 1, no.3 (1991)

D. J. West, *The Young Offender* (Harmondsworth, 1967)

——, *Delinquency: Its Roots, Careers, and Prospects* (Cambridge, 1982)

J. Whetton, *Towards a Community Strategy for Criminal Justice* (Swansea, 1978)

B. Whitaker, *The Police* (London, 1964)

——, *The Police in Society* (London, 1979)

M. J. Wiener, *Reconstructing the Criminal* (Cambridge, 1990)

G. P. Williams and G. T. Brake, *Drink in Great Britain, 1900 to 1979* (London, 1980)

J. Q. Wilson, *Thinking about Crime* (New York, 1975)

J. Woodcock, 'Overturning police culture', *Policing*, 7, no.3 (1991)

M. Zander, *The Police and Criminal Evidence Act 1984* (London, 2nd edition, 1991)

Index

Aberavon 117, 140, 146, 152, 287
  Sandfields 91
Aberavon and Port Talbot branch of
  National Union for Women's
  Suffrage 214
Abercwmboi 16, 25, 238
Abercynon 4, 30, 42, 90, 92, 94, 129,
  190
Aberdare 91, 92, 167, 259, 262, 263,
  265, 275, 287
Adam Smith Institute 239
Afan Valley 133
age
  of criminals 95, 97–101, 118–19,
    160
  and drunkenness 175
Age Concern 4
Albrow, M. 3
alcohol
  cause of crime 74–5, 76, 114, 120,
    124, 127, 285
  drink–driving 38, 52, 162, 182
  drunkenness/drink offences 22, 32,
    71, 85, 86, 92, 119, 128, 165,
    173–6, 184, 287; by police 225
  regulation 163, 171–6; see also
    licensing regulations
Aliens' Restriction Act (1914) 230
Andrews, Elizabeth 52
Animal Liberation Front 136
animals, controlling 169–70, 228
  see also dogs
Anti–Vice Society 130
antisemitism 131
Association of Chief Police Officers
  192, 254

Audit Commission 235, 238, 260, 292
autocrime 63, 71, 82, 84, 92, 106, 107,
  141, 142, 151–3, 154, 157, 158,
  159, 266–7, 270, 271, 289, 295
  fear of 2
  reporting 17–18, 19

Bail Act (1976) 31
Bailey, Victor 295
Baker, Edward Ronald 208, 225
Bargoed 91, 92, 120, 170, 190, 259,
  263, 273
Barry 92, 130, 152, 158, 182, 241
  fear of crime 2, 4
Barry police 200, 272, 273
Barry Dock 91, 92, 94, 117, 131
  magistrates' court 42
Barry Dock police 192, 206, 210, 224,
  262
Bedlinog 128
betting 11, 176–7, 184
Betting and Gaming legislation (1950s
  and 1960s) 62, 177
bicycles 9, 44, 138, 142, 151–2, 154,
  159, 270, 271
  police 253
Birch, Ken 187
Bishopston (Swansea) 21, 110
Black Cardiff 72, 286
Black Glamorgan 2, 72, 286
black market 67–8, 138, 146, 289
Blaenclydach 190, 209, 220, 247
Blaenrhondda 93
bombs 25, 136
  explosions 41, 136
break-ins 63, 66, 71, 82, 88, 91, 101,

106, 109, 138–42 *passim*, 143–6,
159, 185, 266, 270, 271
non-reporting 6
Bridgend 90, 91, 92, 128
magistrates' court 42
Bridgend police 192, 196, 200, 207,
259, 272
centre for archives and information
57–8, 205
Bright, J. A. 256
British Crime Surveys 2, 7, 8, 12, 111,
116, 157
Briton Ferry 128, 157, 169
Brooks, Constable 20, 219
Brooks, Vivian 154
Brown, Major Parry 278
Bryncethin 93, 207
burglary 56, 66, 72, 84, 87, 89, 139, 272
fear of 2, 283
reporting 12, 26

Cadoxton 206
Caerau (Maesteg) 91
Caerphilly 91, 92, 128, 158, 170
Lansbury Park 95, 286
Callaghan, James 265
Cambrian strike (1910–11) 132
Campaign for Nuclear Disarmament
134, 136
Cardiff
Butetown 74, 85, 88, 89, 117, 127,
130, 131, 177, 241
causes of crime 75, 77, 80, 81, 82
cost and victims 106, 109, 110
courts 40, 45, 46, 66
crime rate 65, 67, 68, 69, 70, 73, 286
criminals 96, 98–9, 101–2, 103, 289
Ely 3, 11, 87, 91, 95, 120, 129, 184,
238, 266, 273, 277, 283, 285, 286,
288, 297; riots 71, 136, 268
evidence for crime in 55, 56, 57
Llanishen 88, 141, 152, 182, 259,
263
Llanrumney 3, 11, 93, 95
location of crime 85, 87–95 *passim*
perception and fear of crime 2, 3, 5,
7, 11
prison 47, 53, 57, 95, 102, 103, 290
property crime 8, 140–6 *passim*,
149–59 *passim*
Riverside 85, 88, 93, 178, 259
Roath 85, 93, 141, 153, 159, 182,
263, 273

sentencing 49–50, 51, 52
sexual offences 124
Tiger Bay 131
timing and seasonality of crime 83,
85
victimless crime 163, 166–83 *passim*
violence 113–14, 117–22 *passim*,
126–33 *passim*
Cardiff, Penarth and Barry branch of
NSPCC 37
Cardiff police
archives 3, 57–8
and causes of crime 75, 79, 82
Central division/district 21, 88, 103,
110, 182, 200, 213, 235, 236, 246,
272
character and control 188, 189, 190,
191
conditions of service 221
and crime 23–35 *passim*, 56, 73, 85,
106, 113, 140, 241, 243, 248–53
passim, 255, 258, 259, 266, 268,
270, 271, 276, 277, 278, 279
deployment 233
Docks division 88, 110, 246
image, values and culture 223, 225,
226–7
numbers 210, 211, 213
profile 13, 214, 215, 216–17
and prosecution 37, 38, 39, 41, 43,
45; alternatives to 33, 34
role and functions 16, 227–30, 232,
238
structure and organization 193–7
passim, 200, 201, 202, 220
technical developments 14, 29, 203,
204, 205
training and promotion 206, 224
see also Hodge, Constable
Cardiff Temperance Association 32
Cardiff Three 41
Cardiff Women's Citizens' Association
214
cautions 32–6, 39, 49, 51, 100, 119,
174, 180, 295
Chadwick, Edwin 188, 285
children
abuse, violence and neglect 7, 71,
122–3, 125–6, 167–8, 176
treatment in custody 31
Children and Young Persons Acts 49,
63, 167
(1933) 31, 49, 63, 66, 168

(1969) 31, 33, 35, 49, 50
Children's Act (1908) 166
Childs, Daisy 49
CID 27, 28, 29, 30, 147, 196, 202, 215, 232, 235–6, 251–2, 258–9, 272, 273–4
Citizens' Union 37
civil liberty groups 41, 42, 269, 285
Clark, Constable 28, 30
Clarke, Ronald 265
class 11, 103–5, 148, 161, 163, 185, 289, 290–1
  and non-reporting of crime 11
  victims of crime 108, 109
  see also working class
Clydach 132
CND 134, 136
coal
  stealing 9, 65, 66, 77, 88, 92, 94, 104, 105, 138, 150–1
  see also industrial unrest; mining communities
Coase, Mary 174
Cohen, Stanley 36, 48, 129, 137
Coleridge, Judge 74
communications, police 14, 204–5, 252
Communists 57, 66, 75, 223, 241
community service orders 46, 48, 51, 53
compensation 32, 291
conditional discharge 47, 48, 51, 53
Conservative Party
  penal policy 52–3, 296
  and policing 213, 224, 265, 293
Contagious Diseases Acts 169
Cook, A. J. 132
corporal punishment 50, 52, 142
council estates 80, 81, 84, 87, 88, 89, 94–5, 101, 105, 119, 120, 141, 254, 277, 285, 286, 288
  fear of crime on 2–3, 70
  police and 190, 253–4
courts 42–5, 57
  acquittal rate 286
  crown 31, 39, 45, 46, 47
  see also magistrates' courts; sentencing
Cowbridge 92, 262
  magistrates' court 22, 40, 48
crime 282–97
  causes of 72, 74–83, 243–4, 287–8
  changes in nature of 288–9
  clear–up/detection rate 8, 250, 254, 260, 265, 269–74, 293

costs 106–10, 159, 285
dark figure 6–11, 59, 108, 138
definition 1
evidence 55–8
legal framework 61–3
location 85–95, 119–20, 140–1, 145, 283
non-reporting 6–11, 12
police and *see under* police
positive influence of 286
possible responses to problem of 294–7
timing and seasonality 83–5, 144–5
Crime – A Challenge to Us All (Labour Party) 296
Crime Concern Trust 89
crime prevention 5, 13, 70, 82, 83, 144, 146, 160, 257–8, 265–7, 294, 295
crime rate 59, 60, 61, 63–74, 110–11, 112–13, 260, 286, 293
  and dark figure 7
  rise in 3, 4, 14, 54, 59, 69–72, 188, 231, 257, 263–5, 280, 283, 285, 295; causes 79–83
Crime Stoppers 14, 277
crime surveys 5, 56, 71, 113, 137, 279, 281, 283, 291
criminal class 74, 75, 79–80, 284, 289, 296
  police and 102, 240, 244
criminal damage 62, 63, 71, 72, 92, 94, 156–8, 159, 256, 272
  fear of 2, 158
  reporting 14, 17–19
  sentencing 48
Criminal Damage Act (1971) 62, 156
Criminal Damage Act (1977) 156
Criminal Justice Acts 47
  (1948) 49, 50, 62, 69
  (1972) 48
  (1982) 62
  (1991) 49
  (1994) 284
Criminal Law Act (1977) 63
Criminal Law Amendment Act (1885) 177
criminal statistics 55, 58–61
  see also crime rate
criminals 95–105, 288, 289–91, 294
  evidence 57–8
  police view of 240–5, 246–7
  treatment in custody 30–2
criminology 4, 81, 262

Crowley, John 167
crown courts 31, 39, 45, 46, 47
Crown Prosecution Service 41–2, 45
    Director of Public Prosecutions 40
custodial sentencing 46–7, 50–1, 52–3,
    99, 114, 148, 296
Cwmavon 92
Cwmbran 207
Cwmgwrach 165
Cwmparc 117, 209
Cynon Valley 30, 93–4, 127, 150, 279

dark figure of crime 6–11, 59, 108,
    138
Darvell brothers 41
Davies, Edmund 80
Davies, Graham 274
Davies, John 224
demonstrations 71, 114, 133–6, 170
Deri 247–8
Desborough Committee reports
    (1919–20) 206, 218
detectives *see* CID
Dinas Powys 50
direct action 136, 285
Director of Public Prosecutions 40
Dobash, Robert and Edward 137
dogs, regulation of 32, 38, 62, 165,
    166, 170
Dogs Act (1906) 170
domestic violence/incidents 7, 27, 32,
    71, 84, 92, 120–3, 137
Domestic Violence and Matrimonial
    Proceedings Act (1976) 27
Dowlais 88, 119, 131, 256
Downes, D. 81
drink-driving 38, 52, 162, 182
drug offences 71, 75, 82, 114, 163,
    182–3, 184, 272, 286, 289
    prosecutions 38
    reporting 11, 22, 23
drunkenness *see under* alcohol
Dyfed-Powys, crime rate 72, 73
Dyffryn House 207

Early Closing Association 37
East, David 70, 132, 133, 135
economic conditions, and crime 75–9,
    91, 123, 131, 287–8, 294
Edmund-Davies, Lord, report (1978)
    213, 222
Education Acts 163, 167
elderly 283

anxiety and fear of crime 2, 3–4, 6,
    112, 113, 157–8
embezzlement 146–8, 150, 226, 250
Employment of Children Acts 168
Emsley, Clive 187
ethnic conflict 127, 130–1, 268
Evans, Brinley 67
Evans, John, of Rhondda 166–7
Evening Express 177
explosions 41, 136

family, regulation of 166–8
Farrell, Arthur 30
Farrington, David 100, 288, 290
Fascism 134, 268
feminism 125, 214
Field, Simon 76, 148
financial crime 104, 146–8, 286, 289
    see also embezzlement; fraud
fines for offenders 48–9, 51, 53
firearms 117, 143, 144, 288
Food and Drugs Act 38, 165
football matches, violence at 129, 269
forgery 72, 146–8, 272
Forward Movement 177
Foucault, Michel 296
Francis, Hywel 58, 133
fraud 72, 106, 146–8, 150, 250, 272,
    289
Free Church Council 37, 172

gambling 176–7
gangs 101, 129, 145, 153, 156, 159
garrotting 142
Garth 117
Gatrell, Vic 284
Geary, Roger 131, 269
gender
    and criminals 95–7, 118–19, 290
    and drunkenness 96, 127–8, 175
General Strike 66, 132–3
Gethin, George 189
Gilfach Goch 10
Gill, Superintendent 127
Gill, Edward 267
Glamorgan
    courts 42, 50, 74, 143, 161
    crime rate 65–74 *passim*, 90, 91, 92,
        286, 287
    criminals 96, 98, 99, 100
    evidence for crime in 55
    non–reporting/reporting of crime 6,
        9, 12

property crime 144, 151
seasonality of crime 83, 84
sentencing 50, 52
victimless crime 164, 169, 182
violence 117, 129, 132
Glamorgan Gazette 71
Glamorgan police
  and causes of crime 79
  character and control 188–9, 190
  conditions of service 218–22 *passim*
  and crime/criminals 27, 182, 241,
    242, 245, 247, 248, 251, 252, 255,
    262, 263, 264, 270, 271, 276, 277,
    284; recording 24, 59; records 56,
    57
  deployment 13, 233, 234–5
  image, values and culture 224–5, 226
  numbers 13, 209–13
  profile 214, 215–16, 218
  prosecutions 38, 39, 40, 41, 42;
    alternatives to 33
  role and functions 228, 230, 231–2
  structure and organization 192, 196,
    197, 201, 202
  technical developments 202, 203,
    204, 205
  training and promotion 206–7, 208–9
  see also Lindsay
Glamorgan Police Mutual Benefit
  Association 220
Glamorgan Record Office 57
Glenn, Jeremy 217
Glynneath 92
Gorseinon 91, 92, 141, 225, 258
Gower 32, 157, 232
Gowerton 91, 92, 193
Gray, Jeremy 3, 237
Gwent 5, 61, 73, 116, 279
gypsies 169

Habitual Criminals and Prevention of
  Crimes Acts (1869–71) 241
handling stolen goods 72, 139, 150,
  151, 272, 289–90
Harris, Arthur 67
help lines 14
Herbert, David 89, 288
Highways Acts 165
Hobbs, Dick 289
Hocking, Samuel 220
Hodge, Constable 15, 16, 20, 22, 96,
  117, 120, 127, 246, 249, 250, 268,
  273

Holdaway, Simon 242
Home Office 31, 48, 78
  Departmental Committee on
    Criminal Statistics 60
  and police 70, 191, 192, 193, 205,
    209, 213, 220, 227, 228, 232, 257,
    259, 264, 265, 274, 280, 286, 293
  and recording of crime 24
  statistics and records 25, 55–60
    passim, 63
  and violence 124, 130, 132, 284
Home Secretary 69, 241
  and police 192, 202, 203, 212, 294
  and punishment 52, 142, 296
homicides 121–2, 232, 271
homosexuality 124, 126
hooliganism 71, 128–30, 184, 256, 269
Hopkinstown *see under* Pontypridd
Horner, Arthur 132, 133
hot lines 14, 277
Hough, Mike 265
Howard, Michael 52, 192, 296
Howell, Constable 232, 235
Humphries, Stephen 75
Hunt, Herbert, of Caerau 75

immigration 72, 130
incest 126
Incest Act (1908) 126
Incident Resource and System
  Computer *see* IRIS
indecent behaviour 176
industrial areas, crime in 90–4, 117,
  120, 127, 142–3, 154–5, 285, 287
  police and 189–90, 276
industrial unrest 65, 66, 71, 131–3,
  158, 190–1, 203, 210, 247, 262,
  268–9, 284, 292
  Cambrian strike (1910–11) 132
  coal strikes: (1911) 193, 220;
    (1919–21) 132, 268
  General Strike 66, 132–3
  miners' strike (1984–5) 10–11, 58,
    71, 133, 136, 192, 231, 269
  railway strike (1911) 132
  stay-down protests (1930s) 56, 66,
    133
inner cities 2, 11, 80, 105, 120, 277
insurance surveys 56, 71
IRIS 14, 84, 204–5

James, William, of Great Western and
  Tymawr collieries 9

Jenkins, J. Blandy 189
Jenkins, John D. 226
Jenkins, Roy 264
Jenkins, Sir William 68, 189
Jones, Joseph 66, 189, 197, 207
Jones, Lewis 6, 58
Jones, Oliver H. 189
Jones, William 208, 226
joy-riding 38, 71, 152
Judd, J. M. 208
juvenile delinquency 56, 99–101, 106,
    184, 258, 290
  arrests 31
  causes 74, 75, 77, 79–81
  crime statistics 66, 68–9, 70
  fear of 2, 295
  location of crime 87–8
  penal policy 52, 167
  property crime 143, 144, 150, 156,
    159
  prosecution 40; alternatives to 32–3,
    35
  recidivism 36, 50, 53, 101
  sentencing 48, 49–51, 53, 244
  under-age drinking 74, 173, 175–6
  violence 124, 128–30, 137
  see also young people

Kinsey, Richard 243
Kyffin, Colonel, of Radyr 278

Labour Party 71, 78, 80, 190, 264–5,
    296–7
larceny *see* theft
law, and crime 61–3
Lawrence, Judge 51
Lawrence, Robert 227, 244, 261, 286
Leary, John, of Swansea 174
Levi, Michael 104, 147, 290
Lewis, Thomas, of Trehafod 30
licensing regulations 62
  breaches of 32, 38, 39, 56, 57, 165,
    171–6
Lighting (Restrictions) Order 34
Lindsay, Henry 188–9
Lindsay, Lionel 12, 13, 38, 39, 42, 57,
    66, 132, 133, 134, 188–9, 190,
    197, 203, 206, 209, 210, 214,
    218–25 *passim*, 228, 241, 262,
    268, 269, 284, 285, 286
Little, Detective Sergeant Thomas 250
Llanbradach 93, 190
Llewellyn, Colonel W. H. C. 189

Llewelyn, Sir John T. D. 189
Lliw Valley 263
Lord's Day Observance Society 37
Lovell, William, of Cardiff 76–7

Maerdy 104, 133
Maesteg 91, 92, 213, 273, 287
magistrates/magistrates' courts 31, 39,
    40, 42–5, 46, 48, 49, 50, 185, 284
  and property crime 148
  records 57
  and victimless crimes 161, 164, 170,
    180
  and violence 120
Magistrates' Courts Act (1957) 43,
    161, 180, 230
Major, John 290, 296
Man, Constable 20
Mannheim, H. 78
Margam 150, 165, 189
Martin, J. P. 10, 237
Martin, Mary Jane 276
Mason, Joseph 241
Matthewstown 30, 275
Mawby, Rob 243
Mayne, Richard 265
Mays, J. B. 81
McCarthy, Patrick 118
McIntosh, Mary 289
McKenzie, Chief Constable 223
media, and crime 58, 66, 70, 71, 80
  anxiety and fear 3–4, 282
  and property crime 107, 138, 142,
    144, 157
  and prosecutions 41
  and reporting of crime 12–13
  and violence 114, 115, 124, 125, 268
Merseyside police 236, 238, 243
Merthyr Tydfil
  causes of crime 77, 78, 80, 82
  cost and victims of crime 108–9, 110
  courts 42, 45
  crime rate 65–6, 67, 70
  criminals 97, 98, 100, 103
  evidence for crime in 55
  Gurnos estate 95, 119, 120, 254,
    288
  location of crime 85, 88–90, 93
  property crime 138, 141, 144, 146,
    149, 150, 154, 156, 157
  reporting of crime 12, 13
  sexual offences 124
  timing and seasonality of crime 83

victimless crime 166, 167, 168, 169, 174, 175, 181
violence 116, 118–19, 121, 128, 134, 269, 285
Merthyr Tydfil police 188–92 *passim*, 196, 200, 209, 213, 215
and causes of crime 80, 82
and crime 24, 33, 34, 56, 231, 232, 252, 253, 255, 257, 261, 265–6, 269, 270–1, 273, 279
and prosecutions 37, 45
Metropolitan police force 27, 183, 187, 201, 223, 236
MI5 41
miners' strike (1984–5) 10–11, 58, 71, 133, 136, 192, 231, 269
mining communities 9, 10, 11, 77, 93–4, 131, 132, 133, 277
Miskin 93
Misuse of Drugs Act (1971) 62, 183
Mods 2, 129
Monmouthshire 205, 216, 217, 286
Mòr O'Brien, Anthony 132
morality, and victimless crime 163
Morgan, Colonel Ivor 148
Morgan, Jane 58, 132, 190
Morgan, Richard 166
Morgan, William, of Loughor 226
Morris, Minnie, of St Thomas 156
Morris, Thomas Gwilym 197, 222
Morriston 91, 93, 120, 141, 157
motor vehicles
influence on changes in crime 289
regulation 104, 161, 162, 163, 178–82, 223, 228, 230, 278
see also autocrime; traffic control
motoring offences 11, 22, 34, 56, 57, 62, 63, 73–4, 104, 178, 180–2, 184, 185
prosecutions for 37, 38, 39, 40, 43, 45, 165, 166, 181–2
Mountain Ash 90, 92, 93, 224, 267
Mumbles (Swansea) 4, 90, 181
Murray, Charles 81

Nantgarw 21, 22–3, 24, 104, 146
National Council for Civil Liberties 269
National Society for the Prevention of Cruelty to Children 37, 123, 167
Neath 16, 50, 55, 106, 131, 132, 168
crime rate 59, 66, 67, 90, 92
Neath police 188, 190, 192, 196, 227

and crime 25, 32, 132, 249, 252, 268, 270, 274
and prosecutions 32, 37, 38, 42
Nelson 129
Newport, fear of crime 5
Noaks, Lesley 5, 61, 279
North Wales 116
crime rate 72, 73
NSPCC 37, 123, 167

Oaksey Committee on police conditions of service (1948–9) 213, 222
Ogmore Vale 92
Onllwyn 157
Osmond, John 224

panics about crime 1, 66, 71, 142, 282
Parker, Chief Justice 52
Parliamentary Select Committee on violence in marriage (1975) 120
PBO (policing by objectives) 260
penal policy 51–4, 65
Penarth 91, 92, 158
Penlan (Swansea) project report (1987) 2
Penrhys 11, 77, 81, 93, 94–5, 104, 120, 136, 153, 184, 268, 286, 288, 297
Penygraig 90
Perks Committee 60
Peterson–super–Ely 16–17, 20, 23, 27, 28, 94, 104, 140
prosecutions 40
sentencing 48–9
Peterston–super–Ely police 232, 238, 245–6, 249, 250
poaching 150, 266
police 187–8, 280–1, 291–5
accountability 224, 292
archives 3, 57–8
camera surveillance 83, 153, 260, 281, 295
and causes of crime 80, 83, 120, 243–4
character and control 188–92
Charter target 262
civilianization and privatization 200, 212, 213, 230, 239, 264, 285, 295
community policing 13, 70, 232, 234, 253–4, 257, 275, 277, 280, 294
conditions of service 218–22
and crime 240, 293–5; (1900–38) 245–51; (1938–68) 231–2, 251–5;

(1969–89) 255–60; views on crime and criminals 240–5
and criminal damage 157
deployment 233–8
detectives *see* CID
efficiency and effectiveness 239, 260–2, 280; in crime detection 269–74, 280, 293; and crime prevention 265–7; police numbers and crime 262–5; public order 267–9
foot patrols 71, 160, 202, 233, 234, 237, 238, 245–51, 256, 266, 268, 277, 292
identity cards 295
image, values and culture 223–7, 281
numbers 209–13, 262–5
and penal policy 51–2
policing by objectives (PBO) 260
politicization 224, 245, 293
profile 213–18
and property crime 153, 156, 157
and the public 5, 12, 13, 204, 250, 274–9, 281, 292
recording of crime 8, 11, 23–7, 59–60, 283, 284
response to reports of crime 27–30, 252, 253, 260, 261, 262
reviews 56, 141, 147, 197
role and functions 6, 14, 187–8, 189–91, 227–32, 238–9, 240, 247, 248–50, 266, 280, 293; regulatory role 161, 162, 166–83, 186, 227–31 *passim*, 280, 293
and sexual offences 115, 124, 125
stop and search 249, 259
structure and organization 70, 192–202
summonses and arrests 30–2
technical developments 14, 202–6, 251, 252, 265
training and promotion 206–9
unit-beat policing 70, 194, 204, 234, 243, 253, 254, 255–6, 265, 271, 293
and violence 114–15, 120, 130, 132–3, 134, 136
and white-collar crime 147
Police Acts
(1896) 220
(1964) 191
Police and Criminal Evidence Act

(1984) 41, 259, 294
police boxes 14, 189, 204, 246, 248
police courts *see* magistrates' courts
political interest in crime 3, 4–5, 41, 52–3, 70, 71, 78, 80, 107, 114, 157, 264–5, 282, 284, 285, 286
Pontardawe 42, 92, 128, 159
Pontyclun 105, 165, 166, 250
Pontypridd
fear of crime 4
Hopkinstown 10, 11, 20, 30, 40, 48, 90–1, 158, 165, 209, 247, 249, 250, 267–8
location of crime 90, 92, 93
magistrates' court 36, 40, 42, 48
prosecutions 42, 90, 165
violence 128, 129
Pontypridd police 192, 200, 209, 258, 259, 267–8, 278
see also Welsby, Constable
Poor Law offences 165, 166, 168
Port Talbot 91, 92, 121, 157
Port Talbot police 32, 200, 235, 236
Porth 17–20, 24, 42, 77, 91, 92, 103–4
Porthcawl 92, 141, 287
press *see* media
Prevention of Terrorism Act (1976) 62
prisons 46–7, 53, 57, 99, 296
see also custodial sentencing
probation 46–53 *passim*, 124, 295
Probation Acts (1907, 1925) 47
Probert, Mary, of Cardiff 178
property crime 6, 69, 76–7, 137–60, 185, 266, 272, 283, 284, 287, 288–9, 295
cost 106–10, 159
recording 26
reporting 8, 138, 158
threat of 137–42
prosecutions 36–42, 100
alternatives to 32–6
burden of, on police and courts 42–5
prostitution 11, 33, 56, 86, 121, 154, 163, 177–8
protests *see* demonstrations
public
anxiety and fear of crime 1–6, 59, 71, 107, 108, 111, 112, 113, 115, 137, 185, 237, 282, 283
attitude to crime 12–13, 101, 291, 297
attitude to police 5, 12, 13, 204, 250, 274–9, 281, 292

response to property crime 160
see also reporting of crime
Public Health Acts 104, 278
public order
offences 22, 84, 126–30
police and 231, 267–9, 284–5
Public Order Acts (1936, 1963, 1986)
62, 134, 136, 269
Pugsley, Detective Sergeant John 250
punishment 46, 49, 51–4, 295–6
in the community 48
see also sentencing

Quetelet, Adolphe 12

racial conflict 127, 130–1, 268
railway strike (1911) 132
rape 25–6, 124–5, 272
Rawson, Thomas 189
Raynor, P. 48
recidivism 53–4, 77, 101–3, 284
Rees, P.C. John 249
reformers, social and moral 2, 37–8,
73, 80, 85, 282
Reiner, Robert 187, 209, 224, 245, 275
Reinke, Herbert 161
Reith, Charles 187, 274
religion 2, 66, 80, 130, 171, 172, 176
reporting of crime 116, 162, 204, 252,
253, 256, 262, 277, 283, 292
changes in 11–14
nature of 14–23, 59, 137, 138, 252
police response 27–30, 252, 253,
260, 261, 262
Reynoldston (Gower) 94, 140, 170,
245, 247
Rhondda
crime 6, 9, 68, 77, 103, 127, 151
fear of crime 5
penal policy 52
victimless crime 166–7
violence 132, 134
Rhondda police 243
Rhoose 210
Richard, Henry 72
Road Traffic and Safety Acts (1930,
1956, 1967) 11, 62, 161, 179, 180,
182, 291
robbery 56, 72, 86, 88, 92, 119, 138,
140, 142–3, 150, 154
Roberts, Constable William 176
Rockers 2, 129
Royal Commission on Criminal

Procedure (1981) 245
Royal Commission on Licensing
(1929–31) 174
Royal Commission on the Police
(1960–2) 191, 264, 274–5, 277,
279
rural areas, and crime 16–17, 23, 28,
72, 90, 117, 157, 232, 248

St Fagan's 210
St Nicholas 6, 22, 23, 94, 266
Scarman Report 207
Scourfield, D. 49
seaports, problems of 85, 117, 130,
142, 230
self-report surveys 56, 71, 113
sentencing 45–51, 54, 77, 295–6
alternative punishments 51, 53
custodial 46–7, 50–1, 52–3, 99, 114,
148, 296
police and 243–4
Seven Sisters 190
Sex Discrimination Act (1975) 215
sexual offences 69, 72, 84, 108, 115,
117, 119, 124–6
against children 7, 125–6, 176
recording 25–6
sentencing 48
Sexual Offences Act (1985) 177
Sheffield 61, 243
Shop Acts 104, 165, 171, 278
shoplifting 6, 56, 84, 88, 141, 150,
155–6, 167, 271
Showell, Albert 30
Sigadeli, George, of Margam café
165
Skewen 29, 92, 151, 235–6, 237, 273
Smith, David (Dai) 58, 132, 133
Smith, David J. 3, 237
Smithies, Edward 67, 104, 148
social conditions, and crime 75–83, 94,
123, 288, 296–7
social geography 81, 87, 92, 94, 288
social reformers *see* reformers
socialism 287, 296
society 284
control and regulation 160–86
and theft 137–60
violence in 113–37
Society of Retail Fruiterers and
Grocers 37
sociological studies 23, 26, 48, 61, 94
and fear of crime 4, 5

of police 202, 224, 225, 232, 237, 242–3, 255
soliciting *see* prostitution
South Wales Constabulary 29
  character and control 188, 189, 191–2
  conditions of service 219, 220–1, 222
  and crime 11, 56, 232, 242, 256–63, 269, 271–4, 277–8, 279, 280–1, 295
  crime rate 71, 72–4, 286
  and criminals 98, 100, 105
  deployment 234–6, 238
  image, values and culture 223, 224, 225
  location of crime 91–4
  numbers 210, 211, 213
  and property crimes 140–1, 147, 151, 153, 160
  prosecutions 40, 41, 45; alternatives to 33, 35, 36
  responding to reports 27, 29
  role and functions 231, 232
  structure and organization 60, 196, 197–202
  technical developments 204
  timing/seasonality of crime 83–4
  training and promotion 207, 209
  and victimless crime 169, 174
  and white–collar crime 147
South Wales Daily News 3
South Wales Echo 3, 71, 222
Special Branch 28, 41, 136, 285
Special Restriction (Coloured Alien Seamen) Order (1925) 230
stay-down protests (1930s) 58, 66, 133
Stephens, Mike 242, 243
Stewart, R. S. 74
Storch, Robert 187
street behaviour, regulating 176–8, 184, 292
Street Offences Act (1959) 33, 177, 178
street trading 163, 168, 171
Sullivan, Mary, of Swansea 178
Sully 20, 23, 27, 94, 238, 249, 271, 272
Sunday Closing Act (1881) 171
Sunday trading 11, 165, 171
supervision orders 48, 50, 51
Sutherland, E. H. 104
Swansea
  Bonymaen 105, 152

causes of crime 77
cost and victims of crime 106, 108, 110
courts 43, 45, 46
crime rate 65, 67, 68, 69, 70
criminals 96, 98–9, 100, 101, 102, 103, 105
evidence for crime in 55, 56
fear of crime 2, 4, 5
Greenhill 127
location of crime 85–7, 89–90, 91, 92, 93
Penlan 2, 81, 89, 95, 101, 111, 184, 267, 286, 297
prison 47, 53, 57, 95, 102, 103, 290
property crime 101, 141, 144, 145, 146, 148, 150–9 *passim*
reporting of crime 10, 12, 16, 17, 18
seasonality of crime 83, 84
sentencing 50, 51, 52
Strand 74, 85, 87
Townhill 87, 89, 90, 101, 153, 181, 254, 288
victimless crime 164, 167, 168, 169, 171, 174–81 *passim*
violence 113, 117, 118, 119, 121, 122, 127–33 *passim*
Swansea police
  and causes of crime 79
  character and control 188, 189
  conditions of service 220
  and crime 16, 17, 18, 23, 25, 32, 33, 34, 56, 86, 87, 106, 113, 232, 241, 246–55 *passim*, 257, 259, 261, 263, 268, 270, 271, 272, 273, 276
  and crime prevention 266–7
  deployment 233–4, 238
  numbers 13, 210, 213
  profile 217–18
  and prosecutions 38, 41, 43, 45
  role and functions 232, 238
  structure and organization 193, 196, 200, 202
  technical developments 14, 203, 204, 205
  training and promotion 196, 206
Swansea sex-shop murder 41
Swansea Valley 93

Taibach 105, 165, 170, 185, 250
Teddy Boys 2, 129, 268
temperance movement 37, 74, 172
terrorism 114, 136

Thatcher, Margaret 182, 209, 265, 269
theft 72, 84, 89, 104, 111, 139, 142,
    148–56, 267, 270, 271, 272
  dark figure 6–7
  kind 148–53; *see also* individual
    offences
  place 87, 153–6
Theft Act (1968) 63
Thomas, Captain Alfred 203
Thomas, D. A. 72
Thomas, Degwel 38, 52, 69, 80, 170
Thomas, Fred, of Caerau 241
Thomas, George 4
Thomas, Gwyn 58
Thomas, Lleufer 151, 174
Thomas, Melbourne 251, 271
Thomas, Percy 74
Thorp, John, of Pontypridd 10
Tongwynlais 24, 232, 235
Tonpentre 42, 91, 92, 124, 152, 193,
    210
Tonypandy 92
  riots (1910) 58, 132
Tonyrefail 21, 91, 110, 117
trade, regulation of 170–1, 184, 278
traffic control 178–82, 203, 230,
    254–5, 279
Trealaw 105, 176, 242
Trebanog 104
Treforest 22, 91
Treharris 103, 119, 193
Treherbert 92, 104
Trelewis 13, 133
Treorchy 90, 117, 133
Tylerstown 104

underclass 81, 136, 223, 243, 294
Underwood, Peter 3
unemployment, and crime 77–9, 104,
    287
urban environment, and crime 28–9,
    85–90, 96, 99, 117, 127, 140, 157,
    282

vagrancy 56, 86, 168–9
Vagrancy Acts (1824, 1898) 62, 163,
    165, 168, 177
Vale of Glamorgan 92, 157
vandalism *see* criminal damage
Vass, A. A. 48
Vaughan, Charles Clifford 224–5
Veysey, Arthur, of Taibach 165
victim support groups 108, 114, 291

victim surveys 5, 56, 71, 113
victimless offences 4, 23, 160–86, 289,
    291
victims of crime 106–10, 281, 291
  multiple victimization 90, 111, 141,
    291
Vigilance Association 37
Vigilance Society 177
violence 71, 72, 75, 76, 84, 86, 89, 92,
    94, 101, 113–37, 185, 283, 284,
    287, 288
  against police 71, 86, 117, 119, 221,
    275–6, 277–8
  in the community 69, 117–20
  costs and victims 108, 109
  fear of 6, 113, 115, 118–19, 127, 137
  opinions about 113–14
  reporting and recording 6, 7, 26–7,
    113, 114, 119–20, 137, 272
  statistics 114–17
  see also demonstrations; domestic
    violence; industrial unrest; public
    order; racial conflict; sexual
    offences

Walsh, D. P. 155
Walsh, Dermot 289
Ware, James, of Cardiff 118
wartime legislation 62, 230, 241
  see also World War I; World War II
watch schemes 70, 160, 257, 258, 267,
    295
Watkins, Cecil 208, 264
Watkins, Tasker, QC 191
Weekly Mail and Cardiff Times 66
Weinberger, Barbara 132, 161
Welford, Superintendent 265
Welsby, Constable 9, 20, 22, 30, 96,
    120, 219, 247, 249, 267
Welsh Campaign for Civil and Political
    Liberties 41
Welsh language activism 134, 136, 287
Welsh Socialist Republican Movement
    41
Welshness, and crime 287
West, D. J. 81, 99
West Cross (Swansea) 181
Western Criminal Record Office 205,
    242
Western Mail 3, 71, 75, 131, 163, 173,
    233, 237, 238
white-collar crime 104, 146–8, 185,
    291

Whittaker, Ben 187
Wilkie, David 133
Williams, Judge Gwilym 71
Williams, Llewellyn 53, 65
Williams, Reginald 166
Williams, Sir Rhys 189
Wills, Alfred, of Peterston–super–Ely
     28
Wilson, G. 237
Wilson, James 33, 34, 36, 38, 181, 189,
     203, 204, 207, 214, 223, 225, 230,
     241, 244, 251
women
  as criminals 96–7, 127, 290
  fear of crime 2, 3, 6, 113, 118–19,
     137, 185, 283
  in police force 213–15
  and property crimes 142
  victimization rate 5
Woodcock, John 3, 114, 197, 234, 257,
     280
Woodfield, Joseph 241
working class
  causes of crime 74, 75, 80, 81
  criminals 95, 103, 105, 118, 123,
     163, 185, 290
  in police force 215–17
  victims 118

workplace crime 9–10, 104, 154–5,
     291
World War I 2, 32, 47, 65, 104, 127,
     131, 132, 134, 146, 148, 150, 156,
     170, 178,182–3
  policing in 190, 191, 200, 203, 206,
     211, 221, 228, 230, 276
World War II 2, 10, 12, 50, 79, 83, 100,
     104, 115, 128, 131, 133, 138, 144,
     146–7, 148, 153, 156, 167, 170,
     180, 289, 295
  crime statistics 67–9
  policing in 191, 206–7, 212, 214,
     222, 226–7, 228, 263, 266, 276
Wrigley, Samuel, of Cardiff 101–2

Ynysyboeth 30, 275
Young, Constable George 182
young people
  and alcohol 74, 285
  criminals 95, 99–101
  and police 275, 277, 278
  and property crime 143, 157, 159
  violence 120, 124, 143, 285
  see also juvenile delinquency
youth culture 2, 114, 156
Ystrad Mynach 92
Ystradyfodwg 167